Charles R. Crane and Wilsonian Progressivism

Washington College

STUDIES IN RELIGION, POLITICS, AND CULTURE

Joseph Prud'homme
General Editor

Vol. 10

PETER LANG
New York • Bern • Frankfurt • Berlin
Brussels • Vienna • Oxford • Warsaw

Zacharie Leclair

Charles R. Crane and Wilsonian Progressivism

PETER LANG
New York • Bern • Frankfurt • Berlin
Brussels • Vienna • Oxford • Warsaw

Library of Congress Cataloging-in-Publication Data

Names: Leclair, Zacharie, author.
Title: Charles R. Crane and Wilsonian progressivism / Zacharie Leclair.
Description: New York: Peter Lang, 2017.
Series: Washington College studies in religion, politics,
and culture; vol. 10 | ISSN 2151-7010
Includes bibliographical references and index.
Identifiers: LCCN 2017002910 | ISBN 978-1-4331-3737-2 (hardcover: alk. paper)
ISBN 978-1-4331-3738-9 (ebook pdf) | ISBN 978-1-4331-4094-5 (epub)
ISBN 978-1-4331-4095-2 (mobi)
Subjects: LCSH: Crane, Charles Richard, 1858–1939.
Diplomats—United States—Biography.
Statesmen—United States—Biography.
United States—Foreign relations—1913–1921.
Wilson, Woodrow, 1856–1924—Friends and associates.
Classification: LCC E748.C926 L43 2017 | DDC 327.092 [B] —dc23
LC record available at https://lccn.loc.gov/2017002910
DOI 10.3726/b11001

Bibliographic information published by **Die Deutsche Nationalbibliothek.**
Die Deutsche Nationalbibliothek lists this publication in the "Deutsche Nationalbibliografie"; detailed bibliographic data are available on the Internet at http://dnb.d-nb.de/.

CONTENTS

FOREWORD

As is the case with many historians, the direction taken by my research and analysis at the start of my university career was shaped by one defining event. I had just started my B.A. in history at the Université de Montréal in 2001 when two planes collided with the World Trade Center's twin towers in New York and a third crashed into the Pentagon, destroying these prime symbols and instruments of America's economic and military supremacy. The American government quickly declared a "war on terrorism" and justified it with a renewed wave of puritanical rhetoric inherited from the "republican revolution" in the mid 1990s. Beyond feeling compassion for the shocking images of the September 11 attacks, however, the world also acknowledged how, with its arrogant hegemony, the American empire had certainly brought upon itself the condemnation of those who had been left behind among the nations.

The contrast between the unilateral conservatism ("neither isolationist nor arrogant") of President Bush's foreign policy during his presidential campaign in 2000 and his simultaneously religious and belligerent language after the event demonstrates the importance of the tragedy that took place on September 11. Yet the efficiency of his tone, confirmed by his dramatic increase in popularity since the invasion of Afghanistan, suggests that this moralistic approach to foreign policy, coupled with a clear desire for security, struck a chord in the American population. The success of this neo-Puritan rhetoric in the United States, for its part, can be explained by its strong historical roots.

As a French Canadian, my first studies in U.S. history were thus influenced by this new place moral fundamentalism had taken in American politics, and Woodrow Wilson emerged as a particularly interesting figure in his capacity as the founder of an internationalist diplomatic approach which was both messianic and policing in its tenor. It seemed to me, however, that Wilson's rigor and his sense of authority and moral responsibility set him apart from the contemporary heads of the world's greatest power and made them look rather deficient in comparison. In this regard, the discovery, during my master's degree research, of a philanthropist and international reformer like Charles R. Crane at Wilson's side helped nuance my understanding of this president who, in a spirit of reform typical of American progressivism, saw diplomacy as a way of building humanitarian relations between peoples.

During a speech given in the 2008 primary, Barack Obama expressed his desire to "end the mindset that got us into Iraq." Such a program would clearly be inherently difficult—if not impossible—to realize. Yet over the years, the deterioration of political language and the precedence of image over meaning have been directing the candidates and leaders toward simplistic diplomatic solutions that are politically rewarding in the short term but untenable and therefore irresponsible in the long term. One is forced to admit that even eight years later, this "mindset" still conditions the reflexes of American voters. They are ready, for instance, to watch their recently elected leader insult a powerful industrial giant who also happens to be the country's primary commercial partner or sabotage the delicate relations with a nuclear and sensitive regime which the previous administration spent eight years painstakingly rebuilding. They do not seem to object to this leader courting an old power nostalgic about its past hegemony and flattering the fringe radical groups of a fragile democratic country in the volatile context of the Middle-East. In an era when many Americans seem suspicious of moderate and nuanced ideas and one wonders whether they still adhere to the foundations of Republicanism which shaped Woodrow Wilson and Charles Crane's political thought, one cannot help but dread the diplomatic jolts of a White House inhabited by such an impulsive and short-tempered figure. Even George W. Bush's naive and erratic morality seems preferable to the spectacle—for that is indeed what it has become—of 2017. A hundred years after America's intervention in World War I, its responsibility in international events is greater than ever and the question to intervene or not to intervene now has even more substantial and terrifying consequences than it did back in 1917 when the United States still had a practically clean slate in international affairs. It goes without saying that the country's image is no longer immaculate and that America carries with it the weight of many geopolitical misdemeanors. Does it still have sufficient moral leeway to act in accordance with its own political weight? A new wave of isolationism is sweeping across the Western world, spurred on by the threat of radical Islam. Meanwhile, distrust toward the system is growing among the population and political outlooks are deteriorating along with the underlying principles of social life. How can we build a just, efficient, legitimate, and popular foreign policy amidst these issues when our own human arsenal has the morbid ability to destroy all life on earth? In such a context, the greatest stumbling block seems to be the inconsistency of diplomatic decisions and the general direction they are taking. Nothing discredits a country's foreign policy more than double standards and suspicious paradoxes that work in favor of commercial interests. Much like in 1917, our world today appears to be at a crossroads. What lessons can we learn from America's entry into World War I, from the Fourteen Points, from Wilsonian diplomacy, and from the system of postcolonial mandates? What is there to glean from Wilson and Crane's response to revolutionary Russia, a blatant case of diplomacy complacently based on illusion and ignorance? In an age when the UN Security Council is constantly hindered, how can we combine moral principles and collective participation with foreign policy? Is it possible to reconcile national interest with internationalism? This issue practically caused the failure of the Treaty of Versailles before the U.S. Senate in 1920 and continues to haunt debates on America's role in an increasingly complex world. I hope that, through the political journey of a man who was both exceptional and typical of his time, and while experiencing the joy of watching this figure participating, in his own way, in the great events of his time, this book will fuel informed, historically-based conversations on the past and on issues that were current then and are still just as current a hundred years later.

PREFACE

I have known Zacharie Leclair since the moment several years ago when he met with me to describe his idea for a doctoral thesis on Charles R. Crane, and asked me to serve as his adviser, to which I swiftly agreed. Only much later did Zacharie reveal to me how alternately impressed and disconcerted he was by the speed of my positive reply! With my friend Professor Bruno Ramirez serving as co-director, we proceeded to guide Zacharie along the research and writing of his thesis. Throughout the process, I enjoyed our interactions, and I was impressed by his development from a neophyte into a mature historical researcher. Now Zacharie has undertaken the transformation of his work into a book, and he has invited me to write the preface. It is a great privilege for me to serve as godfather at the christening, as it were, of this firstborn product of his historical talent.

Zacharie Leclair's book uncovers the unheralded career and contributions of Charles R. Crane. A philanthropist, reformer, and American diplomat, Crane was one of the few rich men of the day to throw himself into political reform, from promoting science and technology to laboring in favor of international democracy and freedom. Rescuing Crane from his existing near-total obscurity, the author reveals with brio the different ways in which

Crane operated as supporter and advisor to President Woodrow Wilson during the years from 1912 to 1921.

Although Crane refused service in an official capacity throughout most of the Wilson years, and possessed a certain amount of the "passion for anonymity" that a later President would demand of his advisers, it is fascinating (and fun) to discover the manifold nature of his activities inside the Wilson Administration as well as the remarkable set of international actors with whom he interacted. First, as fundraiser and idea man of sorts for Wilson as candidate and then as president, Crane worked behind the scenes to influence the selection of members of the administration, and served as a point of contact between the executive and outside reform forces. As a former supporter of Wisconsin progressive Republican senator Robert La Follette, he was able to help bridge the distance between the president and the Senator. As such, he played an important if unofficial part in solidifying the administration's legislative agenda, notably on antitrust laws and on the Seamen's law of 1916, and eventually helped clear the way for Wilson's appointment of Crane's ally Louis Brandeis to the Supreme Court.

After the outbreak of World War I, Crane became an increasingly close advisor to Wilson on international politics, and a bearer of the spirit of "Wilsonianism" throughout the world. Crane's diplomatic service extended in multiple directions: a longtime supporter of Russia and Russian folk culture, he pushed for recognition of the February Revolution and served as a member of the Root Commission, a special committee of inquiry. He championed Czech nationalist Tomáš Masaryk, to whom he furnished entrée to President Wilson, and played a major role in the creation of the Czechoslovak state. During the Versailles Peace Conference, he persuaded Wilson to engage with Chinese diplomat Wellington Koo, and to provide diplomatic support for China.

One highlight of the book is its discussion of Crane's involvement with the famous King-Crane Commission. At the time of the Versailles Peace Conference, Crane was named by Wilson to co-direct the commission, which was created to report to the President on the future of the Ottoman Empire, including Armenia, and the Middle East. In particular, the author describes Crane's complex (and anti-Semitic) attitude toward the question of Palestine and his opposition to the Balfour Declaration, which he convincingly links to Crane's opposition to Anglo-French secret treaties and his fear that the Zionists would represent a Trojan horse for French and British interests at the expense of the self-determination of Arab peoples.

The last chapter of the book covers Crane's official entry into the government and his service as American minister to China from 1920 to 1921. His appointment came at a time when the invalid Woodrow Wilson was subjected to the domination of his wife Edith, who remained jealous of the influence of Wilson's advisers. In that sense, the fact that the appointment was even made testifies to the reputation Crane enjoyed within the Wilson family for disinterested service. Moreover, it came at a decisive moment for the nation's Chinese policy, in the aftermath of World War I and of the movement of May 4, 1919. The author draws a complex and admirable portrait of Crane's work as American minister to China, exploring with finesse how Crane, in his first official position, was able to apply the principles he long supported informally by organizing humanitarian responses to the huge 1921 northwest famine.

Zacharie Leclair's study offers new approaches to several different areas of U.S. history: the historical literature on the progressive movement in the United States; the history of philanthropy and the relationship between the nonprofit sector and public policy; and most importantly, the history of the Wilson administration, its domestic policy and its various initiatives in international relations. The author opens up a wider understanding of the history of "Wilsonianism" and the complex relationship between Woodrow Wilson's principles and the implementing of policy by his supporters at the international level. In his study of Crane's service in China, he not only probes the intersection of Crane's philanthropic and political ideas, but reflects on this early use of what one might call "soft power" in the service of American diplomatic interests.

For all these reasons, I consider that Zacharie Leclair's book well deserves the title of "masterful," and I am very glad to welcome it into print.

Greg Robinson

Université du Québec à Montréal

ACKNOWLEDGMENTS

This work is the fruit of a long journey which involved many people and asked of them much more than I would have liked. Therefore, it is my responsibility to properly and sincerely thank those who supported this project until its culmination.

As this book was originally a doctoral dissertation, I first and foremost want to thank my thesis supervisors, Bruno Ramirez and Greg Robinson. Bruno, without knowing it, sparked my interest for American history and Wilsonianism and inspired me to start this project. Greg, for his part, became a patient mentor, an insightful editor, and an excellent intermediary who worked tirelessly to integrate me into this little circle of historians, while also proving to be an exceptionally generous friend. He has honored me today by writing the preface to my first book. Greg and Bruno, this book also belongs to you.

Furthermore, I wish to highlight the kindness and edifying feedback provided by my dissertation committee: Frédérick Gagnon, Bernard Lemelin, and François Furstenberg. I must also recognize Thomas Crane's warm generosity in allowing me to consult the Crane family archives.

I feel indebted to the historians, researchers, and writers who preceded me in the study of Wilsonianism. Any revision or contradiction of their work, new or old, should not be seen as an attempt to discredit their conclusions but rather as part of the perpetual dialogue between researchers for the purpose of better understanding of history and its actors.

Thank you to Elizaveta Vandalovsky for translating this document, a lengthy task with a deadline which turned out to be tighter than we had hoped for. Her questions about the text also helped me to clarify its meaning.

I am eternally grateful to my parents, Claude and Lucie, and to my sister Rachel, for their love and their interest in everything I do. More than anything, I can imagine what this book means to my father, who was forced by circumstance to study at the harsh "school of life." I also want to thank my parents-in-law, Anne and Manuel, for their support and particularly for giving life to the person I am about to mention.

Where would I be without my wife, Élisabeth, a true grace, a pillar of stability, love, and encouragement in my life as an "independent scholar"? Her keen intellect, her critical spirit, her shrewdness, and her insight have also made her an invaluable reader of my work whom I would not—and could not—have done without. Over the last few months, she has devoted a considerable amount of her free time—and there has not been much of it—to reading and rereading the text both before and during the translation process. I am not lending her to anyone.

Though I am indebted to all these people, I am naturally responsible for all of my ideas and for any mistake that may have inadvertently slipped into the text.

Charles R. Crane and schoolchildren in Damascus in 1919, during the King-Crane Commission. Used with permission from the Oberlin College Library Special Collections.

INTRODUCTION

Framework and Purpose

To historians, World War I generally appears, in a rather paradoxical manner, as both the height of the Progressive movement in the United States and the start of its decline. American Progressives of the time, particularly Wilsonian Progressives, generally construed the war as the beginning of a new era in human history. In that sense, the Paris Peace Conference of 1919, with Woodrow Wilson's preeminent figure at the head of an imposing American delegation, created a very particular setting for this transformation. From it emerged both traditional forces—like the decidedly active and aggressive imperial interests—and new forces, well illustrated by the presence of various diplomatic specialists from the countries that determined the outcome of World War I. In the midst of the main issues surrounding the German question and the planned dissolution of "blameworthy" empires, the United States presented themselves as the only disinterested[1] party in Paris. By its insistence on peoples' right to aspire to and achieve political and economic freedom (and liberalism), President Wilson's message bolstered various national movements, fuelled by the interempire conflicts of 1914–1918, and acted as a major inspiration in the victorious powers' efforts to mend international relations after the war. This political message rested on various moral and ideological considerations attributable not only to Wilson's own character and mind but especially to the specific context of American society in the Progressive Era and to the late nineteenth century intellectual sphere in which it originated.

In this context of foreign policy specialization in the dominant countries, one of the United States' diplomatic endeavors during the Versailles negotiations consisted in establishing a commission of inquiry called the King-Crane Commission. Its aim was to identify the potential challenges posed by the dismantling of the Ottoman Empire, accumulate data on the population and geography of the concerned regions and suggest solutions to territorial and political problems inherent to the imperial system and intensified by its collapse. As its name suggests, the King-Crane Commission was headed, along with a certain Henry Churchill King, by Charles Richard Crane, who will be the focus of this book.

Born in Chicago in 1858, Charles R. Crane was by then neither a novice to the American diplomatic services nor a stranger in President Wilson's entourage. In fact, without ever having been previously appointed to an official position, Crane had acquired extensive experience in American political circles and had a reputation that reached beyond the borders of his country. Trained in the industrial sector and heir to his father's fortune with the Crane Brass & Bell Foundry (which later became the Crane Plumbing Company), he devoted himself throughout his life to philanthropic activities and voyages. Crane consistently used his affluence to gain access to important circles and cultivate friendships wherever he went. He was on good terms with Russian and other European aristocrats as well as with the Chinese elite and could secure private meetings with any emir or Arab prince. Beyond his worldly occupations, Crane also harbored a great interest in the advance of science and technology and was a strong proponent of democracy and freedom in all areas, both locally and internationally. He belonged to a tradition of urban reform typical of American progressivism at the turn of the twentieth century, and his work can be situated more specifically in the very particular atmosphere that reigned in Chicago, which was then struggling with municipal corruption and purported moral decline.

Given that his career was based on a formidable network of relations, it comes as no surprise that a lasting friendship developed between Crane and Woodrow Wilson when the latter was chosen as the democratic candidate in the 1912 presidential election. While preferring to remain behind the scenes, Crane had long been a political player both locally in Chicago and in several Midwestern states. Though he was a Democrat by family tradition, he had indiscriminately supported Progressive leaders, be they Democrats or Republicans. Before turning to Woodrow Wilson of the Democratic Party in 1912 and becoming one of his main campaign contributors, Crane financially supported Wisconsin's Progressive-Republican senator Robert M. La Follette. In fact, he assisted many politicians over the years, both in the United States and elsewhere, and shared his assets liberally as long as a candidate embodied his progressive ideals. As he once explained to a young Canadian politician named William Lyon Mackenzie King while talking about Senator La Follette's importance in the Progressive movement, his priority was for democratic reform to prevail, even if this entailed rising above partisan divisions.[2] Here, Crane was referring to the 1913 Railway Valuation Bill, and he viewed La Follette's presence in the Senate as a powerful force in the Progressive movement capable of supporting Wilson's democratic program, the New Freedom.

Despite his multiple allegiances over the years, Crane's support for Wilson, once pledged, became unshakable and exclusive. After financing his presidential campaign, Charles Crane acted as a special advisor in an informal cabinet regularly called upon by Wilson which included other philanthropists as well as Colonel Edward M. House. This cabinet was, among other things, responsible for the Supreme Court nomination in 1916 of progressive lawyer Louis D. Brandeis, who had also supported Wilson during his campaign in 1912 and greatly contributed to the president's reform agenda, especially in regard to antitrust measures.

Charles Crane's role in Wilsonianism cannot be analyzed without considering Woodrow Wilson's other close collaborators like Louis D. Brandeis, Edward M. House, John R. Mott, and Cleveland H. Dodge. Crane and Brandeis' close relationship, for instance, attests to the "radical" nature of the progressivism endorsed by Crane and Wilson. Brandeis was at the time seen by both conservative Republicans and moderate progressive Democrats as difficult to control, incorruptible (like La Follette), and an advocate for unorthodox and potentially even dangerous ideas. Crane, on the other hand, operated primarily behind the scenes and appeared considerably less threatening to the opposition. When Theodore Roosevelt began competing against La Follette for the 1912 Republican nomination, Brandeis and Crane remained La Follette's two last major supporters. They only turned toward the Democratic convention and Wilson's candidacy after La Follette pulled out of the race to make way for Roosevelt, who had gained traction by rallying most of

La Follette's supporters like Amos Pinchot (who would later regret his change of heart) under his banner. Wilson's Secretary of the Navy Josephus Daniels mentioned in *The Wilson Era* that Brandeis and Crane were anticipated to become part of the new cabinet in 1912, but this idea was opposed by the Democratic establishment, namely by House, primarily out of geographic ("sectional") and ideological concerns. The Democratic Party needed more conservative southerners, and Wilson was consequently forced to rather reluctantly appoint James C. McReynolds, a notorious Kentucky traditionalist and racist, Attorney General instead of Brandeis, whom, incidentally, McReynolds despised as much for his Jewish heritage as for his radical views. On the subject of Crane, Josephus Daniels mentioned that he was an "unofficial tower of strength" for Wilson's cabinet. As for Brandeis and Wilson, Daniels said that "their minds ran together" and that his Supreme Court nomination in 1916 was "a blow full in the face for the forces of Privilege."[3] These two key figures of the Wilson administration thus attest to the relative radicalism of Wilsonian progressivism. Like Crane, House acted discretely—under cover—as the organizer of Wilson's campaigns. Crane primarily took care of the financial questions and of unifying the Progressives, whereas House was in charge of strategy and private persuasion. Both of them, with Brandeis at the forefront, participated in the drafting of the New Freedom and in forming Wilson's first cabinet. From the outset, House and Crane mutually appointed each other to ministerial posts, but both declined, preferring to operate more freely behind the scenes. Of note here is the fact that all three chose Wilson as the one who could best achieve their progressive ideals (in comparison with a fallen and controversial La Follette, an unreasonable, chatty and narcissistic Theodore Roosevelt or a William H. Taft associated with "Privilege"). Both Brandeis and Crane had no interest in an official position unless it could serve their desire for reform. They rallied around Wilson, seeing in him the talent and ambition to represent them in national politics at that particular point in time. Interestingly enough, however, both House and Brandeis lost practically all contact with Wilson in 1919, while Crane's role in Wilsonian diplomacy increased and he kept his privileged relationship with the president until the latter's death in 1924.

Since most of this book concerns Crane's involvement in international affairs at Wilson's side, we can note that he remained a devoted emissary and was relatively important at the time given the embryonic stage of American diplomatic services. After having first been appointed special commissioner in Russia during the Revolution of 1917, he was part of the American delegation at Versailles through the King-Crane Commission. In 1920, he embarked on his last political venture when Wilson offered him the crucial and highly coveted post of diplomatic minister to China, which he kept until June of 1921.

Crane's involvement reveals some crucial facts about Wilsonianism in an international context. He represented a very progressive and forward-thinking element in the American delegation that traveled to Versailles. More importantly, he was fairly critical of Western imperialism and had from the start suggested innovative and creative solutions to the colonial problem in Asia. He supported the complete emancipation of Arabs, Armenians, and Greeks in the Ottoman Empire and even supported India's emancipation from Great Britain. Conversely, most anti-imperialist Progressives had not yet dared to consistently apply Wilson's principle of self-determination to all nations. This principle was first created to redefine European borders based on "more or less" ethnic criteria at the whim of geopolitical concerns. Crane's decision to apply a concept derived from the West's presumed ability to govern itself to populations under imperial rule was thus a considerably avant-garde gesture at the time. In this sense, his discourse on human and political rights foreshadowed the coming of the United Nations era, despite the fact that large parts of his philosophy remained rooted in the intellectual context of the social gospel.

Crane had, like Wilson, been raised in the relatively rigid environment first of the Presbyterian and then of the Episcopal Church. After Wilson took office, Crane joined an informal circle made up of the president's friends who believed that the expansion of Christianity through missionary work, education, and philanthropy was the perfect agent of social and political progress. Particularly in league with Cleveland H. Dodge, who was perhaps the president's closest friend, John R. Mott of the Young Men's Christian Association (YMCA) and missionary James L. Barton, Crane did his part in promoting the views of the humanitarian and Christian community to Wilson. Wilson himself never concealed his complete sympathy for their vision and his confidence in its applicability to foreign relations. In this regard, they were undeniably aided by the war, which brought with it both misery and opportunity for change, allowing them to establish their philanthropic point of view and activities in the diplomatic practice of the United States.

Philanthropic and humanitarian concerns are thus, as we shall see, one of the most important aspects of Wilsonianism in American diplomatic tradition. They are especially salient in Crane's fundamental contribution to Woodrow Wilson's domestic and international agenda. In this book, we will focus on the political work and thought of Charles R. Crane primarily between 1912 and 1921 in order to better understand the relationship between Wilsonianism and humanitarian and reform movements, both in the United States and internationally. In other words, this book is a study of Crane's position and activities at the heart of the Wilsonian agenda. His portrait will help us look at Wilsonianism and, more broadly, progressivism, with fresh eyes, since his presence and importance in Wilson's entourage provide nuance to the manner in which Wilsonianism is generally understood.

Historiography and Debates on Wilsonianism

Charles R. Crane's political activities have already been mentioned more or less peripherally in works like Richard Hofstadter's *The Age of Reform* (1955); George F. Kennan's *The Soviet-American Relations, 1917–1920* (1956); Christopher Lasch's *American Liberals and the Russian Revolution* (1962); Harry Howard's *The King-Crane Commission* (1963); Jerry Israel's *Progressivism and the Open Door* (1971); Lloyd C. Gardner's *Safe for Democracy: the Anglo-American Response to Revolution* (1984); Betty M. Unterberger's *The United States, Revolutionary Russia, and the Rise of Czechoslovakia* (1989); and Orlando Figes' *A People's Tragedy. The Russian Revolution, 1891–1924* (1996). Two unpublished doctoral theses, however, directly touch upon Charles R. Crane's political activity: Leo J. Bocage's "The Public Career of Charles R. Crane" (1962), and more recently Jacob J. Sulzbach, Jr.'s "Charles R. Crane, Woodrow Wilson, and Progressive Reform 1909–1921" (1994). Both authors based their research on Crane's archives, but only Sulzbach, Jr. had access to the complete edition (1993) of the *Papers of Woodrow Wilson*, a body of archives representing a huge and relatively recent breakthrough in the study of Wilson's life and career.[4]

The above-mentioned works all examine Crane—like Wilson—through the political aspects of his public activities, yet somewhat at the expense of analyzing the impact of the thought process behind these activities. In some of the works, Crane's actions are exaggerated almost to the level of caricature. Most importantly, the authors have a tendency to put considerably less emphasis on his career's philanthropic motives than on other factors, thereby failing to identify the deeper meaning of both his political engagement and of Wilsonianism itself. This book therefore aims to reposition the messianic and humanitarian inclinations of these two figures at the centre of their historical analysis in an effort to compensate for the gaps and narrow outlook of previous studies.

Two other books are of some importance in the study of Crane's life. The most recent one is Norman E. Saul's *The Life and Times of Charles Richard Crane, 1858–1939* published in 2013. While it is the only academic book about Crane ever printed,[5] it does not focus much on Wilson's presidency. In fact, its perspective and approach greatly differ from the perspective adopted in this book. Instead of interpreting Crane's work as a manifestation of Wilsonian internationalism steeped in Christian and philanthropic considerations, Saul focuses primarily on Crane's promotion of Russian studies and generally overlooks the importance of his political influence. While he does present Crane as a forefather of globalism in the United States, the author does not discuss Crane's commitment to Wilsonian progressivism and only two out of seven chapters touch on his accomplishments during Wilson's presidency. The second book, written by professor and journalist David Hapgood and titled *Charles R. Crane: The Man Who Bet on People*, was published in 2010 by the Institute of Current World Affairs, an organization founded by Crane himself. The book is not academic in either form or methodology and does not use Crane's extensive yet essential correspondence or any other sources except his memoirs and those of his sons Richard and John Crane. It is in fact a very concise biography of Crane in which his time within Wilson's administration is only briefly touched upon. Two articles written during different time periods also discuss Crane's activities in specific contexts. First is Albert Parry's "Charles R. Crane, Friend of Russia" published in 1947, which depicts Crane as an American dandy more concerned with Russian culture than with political reformism ("it was cultural life much more than the country's politics that intrigued him"[6]). A more recent article by F. W. Brecher focuses on Crane's special contribution to Middle Eastern affairs between the wars. It is one of the few works that stresses his antipathy toward the Zionist cause, namely by exaggerating the importance of his friendship with Henry Ford and by failing to mention, among other things, Crane's role in the appointment of Zionist and progressive leader Louis Brandeis to the Supreme Court in 1916.[7] Crane's anti-Semitism is also exaggerated in Robert D. Kaplan's *The Arabists* (1993), where he features among several other protagonists. Without referring to any concrete sources, Kaplan depicts him as a rich and extravagant Orientalist who took pleasure in instigating revolts wherever he went. Overall, Crane's historical portrait reveals itself to be incomplete, inaccurate, and generally obstructive to a clear understanding of his political work. Above all, such a portrait goes a long way toward perpetuating a deformed view of Wilsonianism and of its significance in the Progressive Era.

Perspectives on progressivism in the United States generally align with the historiographical tendencies observed among American historians adopting a political and intellectual approach. Historians in Wilson's day began viewing the social change they witnessed during the Progressive Era as an "external" manifestation of a dichotomy in American society between the middle-class masses yearning for social reform and the "special interests" sphere responsible for urban political corruption and for the deterioration of democracy.[8] Soon after World War II, this progressive historiography gave way to a postprogressive interpretation, bolstered among other things by a pro-New Deal reaction to 1950s conservatism. This led to a more methodologically diverse analysis which was more critical toward Progressives and explained conflicts (even though consensus was still emphasized) through varied factors like the rise in immigration, urbanization, and industrialization as well as the decline of the old nineteenth century elite.[9] Around the 1960s, the intellectual history of progressivism adopted an increasingly "internalist" approach. Historians began considering progressivism from more and more complex angles. The Progressive movement was no longer seen as the work of one less and less influential group but rather as the product of multiple and often opposing sources gaining momentum through different (and not always coordinated) coalitions rather than through one monolithic impetus.[10] These pluralistic "internalist" interpretations were challenged by the New Left, which belonged to an "externalist" tradition and which viewed the Progressive movement as a platform for corporatist rather than reformist forces. According to this model, "Liberal Capitalism" used both the political system and the moderate components of reformism to its own ends.[11]

Most of the works dealing with Wilsonianism or with Woodrow Wilson himself focused on analyzing his "performance" as president. Where his foreign policy, his role in the war, and his involvement in the ensuing peacemaking process are concerned, we can highlight three general perspectives that focus on the evident failure in Versailles. The idealist approach, first of the three, appeared at the end of World War I and was used to explain the reasons behind the failure of the Treaty of Versailles both internationally and domestically through its rejection by the U.S. Senate. It also experienced a revival in the face of Nazism. Believing in the merit of Wilsonian principles, its adherents blamed Wilson's personal shortcomings (his romantic penchant, inflexible attitude, ignorance of the global situation, ethnic favoritism, health, etc.) for the Versailles failure. They also particularly deplored the way in which the project was sabotaged by the cynical and colonial dealings of the Allies and of the U.S. Congress.[12] A few positive contributions were later made by John Morton Blum, to whom Wilson's final "victory" consisted in his teachings to the nations rather than in his political work, and by Arthur S. Link, who praised Wilson's practical nature ever at the service of his "high ideals."[13]

Proponents of the realist perspective, for their part, posited that neutrality was impossible for Wilson given his ties to the Allies and called into question the president's sincerity. They concluded that self-determination was inherently flawed or impracticable. The realist trend was set into motion by Woodrow Wilson's first critics after his time as president, who laid heavy blame on the moralistic nature of Wilsonianism. For instance, one of the trend's initiators in the United States was Robert Lansing, a pragmatic politician who worked as Wilson's Secretary of State from 1915 to 1920. In *The Peace Negotiations: A Personal Narrative* (1921), Lansing expounds his own version of what happened at the Paris Peace Conference, writing that though he always obeyed Wilson, he often did so half-heartedly. His harsh attitude toward Wilson and especially toward the Allied governments was perhaps an attempt to protect his reputation and absolve himself of responsibility for Versailles' failure. In Europe, the realist critique was first launched by economist John M. Keynes and, strangely enough, by Freud.[14] Then, during World War II, it was carried on by Walter Lippmann and George F. Kennan,[15] who both participated in forging American foreign policy, guided by their realist perspective. Lippmann was part of Wilson's Fourteen Points team and supported the internationalist project but later reconsidered his position. Both Lippmann and Kennan promoted realist political thought and vehemently criticized Wilsonianism and the tendency toward idealism in American politics. From 1950 to 1970, realist thought persisted with the contribution of Robert E. Osgood, who strove to demonstrate how poorly the concept of collective security was articulated by Wilson in the Fourteen Points when it came to meeting the needs of a contemporary American state. He considered Wilsonianism to be at odds with American diplomatic tradition in the nineteenth and twentieth century.[16] Promoters of this perspective implicitly deplored Wilsonianism's tendency to prioritize internationalism, or international cooperation, over national interest, which was the guiding objective of "realist" foreign policy. In short, like idealists, they believed that a conflict existed between national interest (which was not necessarily immoral in nature) and the pursuit of a disinterested international mission. Unlike idealists, however, realists considered the principle of self-determination to be paradoxical.

Third on our list is the radical perspective, which emerged from the context of decolonization in the 1950s and 1960s and was fuelled by the disillusionment following the Cold War. Adherents of this perspective viewed the imperial dismantlement orchestrated by Wilson as a capitalistic push to implement the open door policy. Wilsonianism and the League of Nations project were thus construed as fitting into a fundamentally expansionist and hegemonic American political tradition. William Appleman Williams, Richard Van Alstyne, Arno Mayer, and Norman G. Levin[17] were notable supporters of this interpretation. According to the radical perspective, which can be associated with the New Left, Wilson's presidency was a triumph for the liberal-capitalist order and for the corporatist world. Wilson himself was seen as having been an instrument for the international expansion of liberal capitalism, particularly in light of his reaction to Bolshevism and of his insistence on commercial rights and open door policy in China. Radical historians viewed Wilson's principle of self-determination as a usurpation of Lenin's anti-imperialist critique and considered it to be incompatible with Wilsonian liberalism as the latter presupposed that a population could only qualify for political sovereignty by emulating the capitalist model. This current emerged from the context of the Cold War—of which Wilson was deemed the forefather—and from the growing criticism directed toward the war in Vietnam. It held Wilsonian diplomacy responsible for repressing revolutionary social movements and consolidating a distinctly American economic empire.

Starting in the 1980s, the historiography of Wilsonianism benefited from a psychohistorical shift in which Woodrow Wilson's mind in particular came under scrutiny, even though a nonmedical work dealing with the impact of Wilson's illness on his leadership in Versailles and on the Senate's rejection of the treaty had already been published in the early 1960s.[18] For instance, neurologist Edwin Weinstein adopted a psychomedical approach in his *Medical & Psychological Biography of Wilson* (1981) to explain Wilson's performance. Weinstein insisted that the president's political judgment had been affected by the repeated aneurisms he suffered over the years. The idea that Wilson's health problems had had an impact on his decisions tempered the severity of the New Left's interpretation, which had failed to take into account some more personal elements of Wilson's life. Another historiographical development in the 1980s was undeniably the emergence of the comparative approach. A comparative biographical profile appeared in John Milton Cooper's *The Warrior and the Priest* published in 1983. It consisted in a comparison of two progressive presidents, Woodrow Wilson and his great political rival,

Theodore Roosevelt. Cooper compared Wilson's religious background, his high principles, the coherence between his actions and these principles and their influence on his progressive policies with Roosevelt's belligerent attitude and more pragmatic style. This analysis resulted in a less rigid image of Wilson as a conservative politician and placed greater emphasis on the originality of his international program. Another such book, Thomas J. Knock's *To End All Wars. Woodrow Wilson and the Quest for a New World Order*, was published in 1992 as a response to the complaints voiced by realists and radicals. In this account of Wilson's performance in Versailles, Knock accentuated the creative and innovative dimensions of the president's program. Part of the historiography, however, reveals several less progressive aspects of his presidency such as racial segregation in the federal government and repression of dissent in the United States during and after the war. One of the most recent works that covers this topic is William H. Thomas, Jr.'s *Unsafe for Democracy: World War 1 and the U.S. Justice Department's Covert Campaign to Suppress Dissent* (2008), which shows the paradoxical relationship between the ideal pursued internationally and the suppression of civil liberties at home.

Additionally, the completion of a full sixty-seven volume edition of the *Papers of Woodrow Wilson* by Arthur S. Link in 1993 allowed many researchers to expand their understanding of Wilsonianism by finally giving them access to his immense public and private correspondence as well as to his other writings and speeches of lesser official importance. This improved and indexed access to his literary and epistolary life permitted a fuller glimpse into his intellectual evolution over the years and unveiled the diversity and complexity of his relationships. Later, as an addition to the *Woodrow Wilson Papers*, came an excellent study by Danish historian Niels A. Thorsen, *The Political Thought of Woodrow Wilson, 1875–1910* (1988). In it, Thorsen turned to Wilson's academic training and intellectual journey to retrace in those seminal moments the development of Wilsonian ideology. The years preceding his presidency thus became a crucial stepping stone to understanding his political work, and Thorsen even considered Wilson to be one of American history's greatest political thinkers. Another example of this new desire in historiography to dig deeper in order to explain better can be found in the realist but modern position of Lloyd E. Ambrosius in *Woodrow Wilson and the American Diplomatic Tradition: The Treaty Fight in Perspective* (1987) and *Wilsonian Statecraft: Theory and Practice of Liberal Internationalism During WWI* (1991). In these books, Ambrosius compares Wilson's earlier thinking with his evolving view of collective security. The goal was no longer to paint a rigid picture of Wilsonianism but to do justice to Wilson's adaptability while remaining critical in other regards. For instance, around the same time, Dutch historian Jan W. Schulte Nordholt published *Woodrow Wilson. A Life for World Peace* (1991). In this book, Wilson's faith and religious mindset were shown as central to the president's political career but presented as part of a very critical, typically European analysis of his religiously charged American rhetoric. Nevertheless, this work demonstrates, at least in some regards, a resurgence of the same critical European position that had emerged right after World War I. But the modern treatment of the realist position toward Wilson's foreign policy was not always so pessimistic. One may argue that Wilson's wariness of militaristic abuse and his faith in democratic political institutions should have steered him away from military solutions. Frederick S. Calhoun, however, remarked that though generally associated with pacifism, Woodrow Wilson was the president who most often resorted to military force to achieve his political goals. Wilson, though he embodied sound principles, is thus shown as a pragmatic politician capable of adaptation and able to justify his changing decisions. As a whole, Wilson knew that the use of force was not a permanent solution but that it still had a place among a set of economic, moral, and diplomatic provisions.[19] Calhoun thus managed in a way to reconcile the realist perspective (though his position dismisses Lippmann's in *Shield of the Republic*, 1943) and the idealist perspective by showing Wilson's ability to judge a situation pragmatically while also holding on to the superior principles that guided his thinking.

Another great advance among Wilsonian historians was probably the influence of postcolonial historiography, which reconsidered the very notion of self-determination and which examined the imperialistic and Eurocentric nature of the mandate system. This revival was based on a deconstruction of colonialist discourse and was marked by skepticism toward modernist political ideas. An article by George W. Egerton titled "Collective Security as Political Myth" (1983) serves as a striking example. Egerton saw in the League of Nations an attempt to control social chaos in foreign populations, and he shed light on Britain's general hostility toward collective security despite certain proleague convictions. Meanwhile, a book published in 1989 by historian and jurist David Fromkin, *A Peace to End All Peace*, explained the debacle in the Middle East by blaming Wilsonianism and its inherently unworkable and flawed principles. Fromkin reflects a new tendency to readjust the perspective toward non-European populations and emphasize the impact of Western politics on them. His assessment is quite harsh and his title mocks Wilson's motto "a war to end all wars." In the same vein, the recent publication of Erez Manela's *The Wilsonian Moment. Self-Determination and the International Origins of Anticolonial Nationalism* in 2007 made it possible to measure the international impact of Wilson's program. Through an analysis of four different nationalist movements, Erez Manela assessed the impact the Fourteen Points and the principle of self-determination of peoples had on the emergence of anticolonialist movements in Egypt, India, China, and Korea. The Wilsonian vision, expressed in universal terms, stimulated national awareness in regions dominated by Europeans. It turns out that, while demanding sovereignty over their homelands, the leaders of the nationalist movements examined by Manela used arguments based on Western criteria for evaluating their readiness for self-determination. The point of view adopted by Fromkin and Manela also illustrated a fairly recent tendency among historians and researchers to analyze American foreign policy from a non-Western perspective. Adopting a multinational approach meant no longer isolating events from their international contexts. It allowed researchers to stop seeing Wilsonian diplomacy as an answer to national demands in an American context and begin to understand it as a policy also forged by the wills and actions of nations. Thus, self-determination was not simply an anti-imperialist and liberal legacy left by a "disinterested" America but also a project launched in response to various European and Eastern national movements.

In the midst of all this, Crane stood out as a radical figure with a progressive, humanitarian and Christian understanding of social and diplomatic relationships. His portrait and his connection with Wilson fit into an ongoing historiographical debate about Wilson's domestic and international policy—traditionally depicted as conservative (Hofstadter, Williams, Sklar, Weinstein, etc.)—which often focused on the president's performance and particularly on his eventual failure. This book therefore aims in a more general manner to also mitigate this neo-liberal portrayal of Woodrow Wilson by emphasizing the religious and moral factors that shaped his version of progressivism as well as the preponderance of international factors, in which Crane was particularly involved. Finally, the generally binary vision most historians have had since the postwar era has prevented us from being able to fully appreciate the complexity of Wilsonianism in a progressive context. Analyzing Crane's contribution thus opens up new perspectives—both national and international—on how to interpret Wilson's era, all this in spite of considerable historiographical developments since the 1960s and of the New Left's criticism.

For its part, the scanty amount of literature that deals specifically with American foreign policy in the Middle East at the start of the twentieth century—a crucial aspect of Crane's diplomatic and philanthropic career—shows how late historians took an interest in this field of research. Of course, historians tend to react to the concerns of their era, which explains why this topic was the subject of so little study before World War II. Academics only began gravitating toward it after the United States expanded its power and influence worldwide—especially in the Middle East—during the Cold War. John DeNovo, a pioneer in this domain, rightfully deplored the complete lack of study on the history of the United States' relationship with the Middle East in the first half of the twentieth century. One of the few to have taken an interest in the subject, DeNovo described the American presence as a form of cultural and economic imperialism which was, however, practically devoid of direct political goals, and pointed out that the United States had indeed encouraged Middle-Eastern nationalism. Afterward, a book by Joseph L. Grabill covering a much greater span of time stood out by focusing on the importance of missionary influence on American politics in the area. The section relating to World War I in particular highlighted the way missionaries lobbied on behalf of the Ottoman Empire's Christian minorities, like the Armenians. In this regard, it is worth mentioning an earlier contribution by James B. Gidney on the subject of the Armenian independence movement and the American mandate project in Armenia.[20] At the same time, a major leap was achieved in regard to the humanitarian dimension of American relations with the Middle East through a very recent field of research, genocide studies. America's response to the Armenian massacre in 1915 was precisely what brought to light the immense recovery effort raised by philanthropists like Crane with the help of American missionary organizations and large-scale support from the American society. On the fringes of the Armenophile movement, it provided a clearer picture of the position held by philanthropic and missionary circles in American foreign policy.[21] In books that dealt with this subject, Crane is shown to take on a discrete but central role in the elaboration of an assistance plan for Armenians. This crucial aspect of his public contribution was, oddly enough, completely ignored in the two doctoral theses about Crane and in other works that mentioned or concerned him.

Overall, this historiographical overview of Wilsonianism shows that historians generally approached these connected fields of research from a purely political angle. This prevented them from making a more complete analysis of the "internal" factors and motives influencing America's decisions and attitudes. Hardly any emphasis was placed on the particular perspective and influence of Wilson's collaborators, and the significance of these relationships in regard to his identity as a progressive president went largely unnoticed. Firmly rooted within American, European, and Asian reform movements and at the forefront of American international relations, Charles Crane was a figure requiring further study. His work offers a fascinating outlook on the social realities in the United States and elsewhere and sheds light on his significance as an American progressive who acted as a crucial political and diplomatic liaison both in America and abroad, as well as between various social actors and President Wilson.

Related Topics and Questions

Several historical questions lie at the root of this research. To begin, how does the relationship between Crane and Wilson help characterize Wilsonianism, and, more generally, progressivism in the United States and worldwide? Then, how does Crane's involvement in Wilsonian diplomacy shape its execution and how does his presence in that context help us understand and interpret Wilsonianism and American progressivism? As we shall see, the presence of Crane among Wilson's close collaborators confirms a progressive and cosmopolitan understanding of the president's work and contradicts the notion entertained by postprogressive and radical historians that he was a conservative devoted to defending the interests of the old Anglo-Protestant elite.

Various specific topics intersect with this issue. First, and more generally, the studied context acts as a witness to the part played by Christian morality and proselytism in the expression of foreign policy in the Wilsonian era. This theme is often recognized in literature about Wilson but is rarely the subject of specific and detailed study; rather, it is tackled indirectly as a peripheral factor or simply added to facilitate understanding. As a major contributor, especially overseas, to the philanthropic and missionary domains, Charles Crane demonstrates the importance of evangelical and civilizing missions in Wilson's thought and political work.

Furthermore, some of the King-Crane Commission's provisions and the way in which legal and territorial issues were handled by Wilson and the American delegation illustrate the general attitude taken by Americans and Westerners toward Eastern populations. More specifically, the criteria for awarding the right to self-determination in the framework of the Treaty of

Versailles betray a baffling "double standard" given the egalitarian and universal principles at the core of Wilsonian rhetoric. The paradox between these principles and their implementation possibly stems from an imperialist understanding—at least to a certain degree—of international relations resulting from the positivist and nationalist intellectual atmosphere of the era. On the other hand, despite the aforementioned contradictions, the emerging discourse on human rights in Wilsonian diplomacy and the way in which Crane promoted it also fit into the set of themes discussed in this book. This "double standard" is perhaps most convincingly illustrated in the establishment of a system of mandates for "deimperialized" regions believed to be ill-suited to immediate self-determination. The criteria ruling the fate of these regions are certainly derived from an "orientalizing" ethnic bias coupled with a presumption, maybe even from a belief in the superiority of Western democracies. Crane's views on this subject remain ambiguous since he accepted the idea of mandates while still rejecting certain Orientalist assumptions. He did, however, entertain progressive ideas, such as a belief that progress could only be achieved by following the American model of historical development.

Similarly, Crane's views and activities were characterized by an obvious interest in supporting technological development around the world, particularly as a catalyst for the advancement of democratic institutions and of national sovereignty. This constant concern of Crane's stemmed from his vision of social progress as resulting from control of production methods, which he inherited from his industrial background, and through the pursuit of a modern, technocratic, efficient, and elitist state—in the Hamiltonian sense of the primacy of competence over social status. In short, for Crane, democracy and nationalism went hand in hand with technological development and state modernization in countries around the world, modeled, of course, after the United States during the Progressive Era.

This emphasis on efficiency and technology intersects with the previously mentioned presence in Versailles of "experts" in the United States' political-diplomatic contingent formed by Woodrow Wilson and which Charles Crane was a part of. Most of the experts participating in the American Commission to Negotiate Peace belonged to academic, military and, to a lesser extent, ecclesiastic professions.[22] Crane, on the other hand, was in a unique category among the other delegates. He had no diploma or formal recognition of any kind and had been selected purely because of his favorable reputation in the international and philanthropic domains. In this regard, his skills were substantial—particularly on the industrial, linguistic, and cultural levels—though they were also rather general and eclectic. His role at the head of the King-Crane Commission was not, however, to act as a specialist but to oversee a contingent of scholars in charge of gathering and studying all the documentation on the Ottoman territories affected by the Paris Peace Conference. His network of social relations, particularly in the Balkans and in the Middle East, was considered of crucial importance in order to move through those regions. The delegates, who had no actual decision-making power, were tasked with issuing recommendations for the use of Allied politicians in Versailles. Holding Crane in very high esteem, Wilson chose him precisely in order to make use of his well-informed judgment, especially since they both shared the same principles. Crane's subsequent appointment to a diplomatic post in China and the way in which he acquitted himself of his tasks there confirmed, in a sense, Wilson's faith in Crane's trustworthiness and in his ability to best represent the president's doctrine. Wilson had trust in the value of Crane's opinions, particularly in regard to the concept of self-determination which was one of the most sensitive issues in the president's international program. This trust in Crane, which manifested itself during the Versailles negotiations as well as throughout his other diplomatic appointments, is perhaps the thing that best expresses and illustrates Wilsonianism's distinctive trait: its humanitarian aspect. The humanitarian dimension of Crane's activities, specifically tied to his understanding of diplomacy, thus represents a major factor in his closeness with Wilson and attests to the true and often unrecognized nature of Wilsonian internationalism.

Sources

The fullest documentation on Crane can be found in the *Charles Richard Crane Papers 1869–1967* which are preserved at the Rare Books & Manuscript Library (Butler Library) of Columbia University in New York. There, one can also consult Crane's family archives, including all the documents belonging to his sons, who were greatly involved in his activities. The *Crane Papers* comprise nearly all of Crane's public and private correspondence throughout his life as well as his memoirs and contemporary commentaries about him (namely, an account written by Arnold Toynbee, a young historian and member of the British delegation in Versailles).

On the topic of the King-Crane Commission, the fullest documentation can be found in a digitized corpus, the *Oberlin College Archives*, which contains many pieces missing from the *Crane Papers*.

Two essential sources in the study of Wilsonianism are the *Papers of Woodrow Wilson* (*PWW*) as well as the *Public Papers of Woodrow Wilson* (*PPWW*). The former are Wilson's private and public archives in sixty-seven volumes, compiled and edited by Arthur S. Link, which include Wilson's immense correspondence and many of his published and unpublished academic texts. The *PPWW*, comprising six volumes edited by William E. Dodd and Ray Stannard Baker, are a compilation of public documents published by Wilson as well as most of his official speeches.

When it comes to America's diplomatic relations, particularly where Crane's mission in Russia in 1917 and his diplomatic ministry in China from 1920 to 1921 are concerned, the *Papers of the Foreign Relations of the United States* (*FRUS*)—composed of 375 digitized volumes—are an unavoidable, though incomplete source (they only include documents that passed through the Department of State).

Also useful, though to a lesser degree than Crane and Wilson's archives, are the archives of important figures like Edward M. House (*House Papers*, Charles Seymour ed.) and the accounts of contemporaries like Robert Lansing, Josephus Daniels, David F. Houston (Secretary of Agriculture and then of Treasury), and Joseph P. Tumulty (Wilson's personal secretary). Many of these accounts were edited and published in the 1920s and are still accessible today.

Structure and Content

In the first chapter of this book, we will paint a portrait of Charles R. Crane based on an analysis of his social background and of his intellectual and ideological foundations. We will chart his political rise and examine his first encounters with the world of politics and reformism. His views on social progress, democracy, religion, and education will all be identified and situated in the context of his later involvement in Wilsonian diplomacy.

In the second chapter, we will analyze the part he played in getting Wilson elected and in implementing the New Freedom. Still in line with the development of his personal approach to international relations, we will analyze his years of contribution to Wilsonian progressivism domestically and analyze the way in which they served as preparation for the extension of Wilson's program abroad. We will also observe the progressive strengthening of his relationship with Wilson during that period.

In the third chapter, we will focus on Crane's debut in Wilsonian internationalism through his selection in 1917 as a commissioner in a diplomatic delegation created to support the liberal phase of the Russian revolution embodied by the Provisional Government. His long-standing interest in Russia, his unique perspective on its future, his faith in this Provisional Government as a guardian of the democratic and nationalistic phase of the revolution as well as his interpretation and account of the facts contributed, through his position in the president's entourage, to shaping the response of Wilson's administration to the revolution. We will see that it was in this context, linked with the deterioration of neutrality up until the United States entered the war, that Crane would articulate his vision of diplomatic reform based on the Wilsonian model. We will also put particular emphasis on the spiritual dimension of his attitude toward the Russian issue in view of his own perception of his work as part of the Root Mission in 1917.

In the fourth chapter, we will observe that Crane's more general interest toward Slavic nations would lead him to also support their movements of national emancipation and democratization in central Europe. As a prime example of this tendency, his crucial and long-standing support for the Czechoslovakian cause will be described and analyzed based on its particularly strong humanitarian components. This will serve to show the impact and the application of Wilson's principle of self-determination. It will be examined in parallel with the faith Wilson had in the unity of the Christian world and his understanding of Christianity's philanthropic role in a Wilsonian reform of international relations.

In the fifth chapter, we will focus on Crane's presence in Paris from 1918 to 1919 as part of the American Commission to Negotiate Peace and his appointment to the King-Crane Commission. We will see how for Crane, the Ottoman question, Arab nationalism, Zionism, and the fate of Turkey's imperial minorities would represent the ultimate mission in Wilson's project of self-determination. This is also where he would more precisely articulate the messianic role he attributed to the United States as well as his ideal of a democratic, egalitarian, pacifistic world founded on Christian charity and fraternity between civilizations. We will observe how Crane was disillusioned with the politics of the powers in Versailles and with the persistence of traditional forces in diplomacy, but also satisfied with his "scientific and humanitarian" contribution to Wilsonian diplomacy. He demonstrated such strong faith in self-determination that he finally took on a position which was extremely unpopular in most political and diplomatic circles both in the United States and among the other Allied powers in Europe. This did not ruffle him, however: Crane had never viewed Wilsonian principles as an opportunity to win popularity contests, except perhaps when it came to winning the approval of Wilson himself.

In the sixth chapter, we will examine Crane's term as minister and chief of American diplomacy in China between 1920 and 1921, at the very end of Wilson's presidency. Far from being an insignificant extension of Crane's career in Wilsonianism after the debacle and disappointment of Versailles, the episode of his only official post in Wilson's administration will allow us to see the concretization of his singular view of humanitarian diplomacy, especially through his involvement and leadership in the international relief effort for the victims of the North China famine of 1920–1921.

Finally, this book will end with a reflection on Crane's role and significance both in Wilsonianism and as part of the Progressive movement in light of his political career and of his activities at the dawn of the 1920s.

Notes

1. This idea of "disinterestedness" stems from three views progressive America entertained about itself. Firstly, despite clear jingoist inclinations especially during the Spanish-American War and even among Progressives, classic colonialism, and a desire to conquer were still foreign to the American public. Secondly, the Progressive movement in the United States insisted on increased control of institutions by the public through rational and scientific management. The American delegation's experts thus believed themselves to differ from other national delegates. For the most part, they considered themselves to be acting with academic detachment and without being subject to the same type of weighty political accountability as their European counterparts. Finally, Wilson's own confidence that America would derive no material benefit from the war demonstrated an altruistic motivation which in turn influenced the American delegation's own perception of itself and of its role among the other nations. This idea was central to Wilson's *War Message* in 1917, in which he said: "We have no selfish ends to serve. We desire no conquest, no dominion. We seek no indemnities for ourselves, no material compensation for the sacrifices we shall freely make." Arthur S. Link, ed., *Papers of Woodrow Wilson (PWW)*, (Princeton: Princeton University Press, 1966–92), "War Message to Congress," Vol. 41, 2 April 1917, 525.
2. *Charles Richard Crane Papers, 1869–1967*, "Charles R. Crane to W.L. Mackenzie King," 26 February 1913, Columbia University, Rare Book & Manuscript Library, Butler Library. "His whole progressive program has the backing of the Republican party […] no doubt that the Progressives and the Progressive Democrats will get behind his measure."
3. Josephus Daniels, *The Wilson Era*. Vol. 1. *1910–1917*. (Chapel Hill: North Carolina University Press, 1946), 543.

4. Kendrick A. Clements indicates that the early influence of the *PWW* on historiography began being felt during the 1980s as available volumes multiplied. However, it is the completion of the 67 volumes in 1993 that marked a real shift in Wilsonian historiography. See Kendrick A. Clements, "The Papers of Woodrow Wilson and the Interpretation of the Wilson Era," *The History Teacher*, 27, 4 (1994): 475–89.
5. The publishing of Saul's book in 2013 coincided with the submission of the doctoral thesis this book is based on.
6. Albert Parry, "Charles R. Crane, Friend of Russia," *The Russian Review*, 6, (1947): 23–4. Parry primarily based his article on journalistic sources and testimonies of people from Crane's surrounding, namely, an unpublished interview with Crane's sister, as well as some of those who were present during the 1917 Root Commission in Russia. The *Crane Papers* were not taken into account.
7. F. W. Brecher, "Charles R. Crane's Crusade for the Arabs, 1919–1939," *Middle Eastern Studies*, 24, 1 (1988), 42–55. Brecher, on the other hand, made a moderate use of the *Crane Papers* as well as the *PWW*.
8. Beyond Charles A. Beard's seminal works, there are primarily the publications of Benjamin P. DeWitt, *The Progressive Movement* (1915) and Harold U. Faulkner, *The Quest for Social Justice* (1931).
9. The great figure of "postprogressive" interpretation is Richard Hofstadter, especially the book *The Age of Reform* (1955).
10. Of note are the works of Robert H. Wiebe, *Businessmen and Reform* (1962) and *The Search for Order* (1967) as well as John D. Buenker's *Urban Liberalism and Progressive Reform* (1973).
11. Three important works: G. Kolko, *The Triumph of Conservatism* (1963), J. Weinstein, *The Corporate Ideal in the Liberal State* (1968), and Martin J. Sklar, *The Corporate Reconstruction of American Capitalism* (1988).
12. Let us note the works of Ray S. Baker, *Woodrow Wilson and World Settlement* (1922), of Thomas A. Bailey, *Woodrow Wilson and the Lost Peace* (1944); *Woodrow Wilson and the Great Betrayal* (1945), and Alan Cranston's *The Killing of the Peace* (1945).
13. John Morton Blum, *Woodrow Wilson and the Politics of Morality*, Boston, Brown & Co., 1956, p. 199. Blum's summary: "Wilson's triumph was as a teacher." Then, Arthur Stanley Link, *Woodrow Wilson. Revolution, War, and Peace* (1979) and "The Higher Realism of Woodrow Wilson," *Journal of Presbyterian History*, 41, 1 (1963).
14. John M. Keynes, *Les Conséquences économiques de la paix* (1920); Sigmund Freud and William C. Bullitt, *Le président Thomas Woodrow Wilson* (1967).
15. Walter Lippmann, *U.S. Foreign Policy: Shield of the Republic* (1943) and George F. Kennan, *American Diplomacy, 1900–1950* (1951).
16. Robert E. Osgood, "Woodrow Wilson, Collective Security, and the Lessons of History." *Confluence*, 5 (1957), 341–54.
17. William A. Williams, *The Tragedy of American Diplomacy* (1959); Richard W. Van Alstyne, "Woodrow Wilson and the Idea of Nation-State," *International Affairs*, 37 (1967), 293–308; Arno Mayer, *Politics and Diplomacy of Peacemaking: Containment and Counterrevolution at Versailles, 1918–1919* (1967); N. Gordon Levin, Jr., *Woodrow Wilson and World Politics. America's Response to War and Revolution* (1968). As a recent and more moderate

expression of this perspective, see Donald E. Davis & Eugene P. Trani, *The First Cold War. The Legacy of Woodrow Wilson in U.S.-Soviet Relations* (2002).

18. Referring to Gene Smith's book, *When the Cheering Stopped: The Last Years of Woodrow Wilson* (1964).
19. F. S. Calhoun, *Uses of Force and Wilsonian Foreign Policy* (Kent: Kent State University Press, 1993), 53–4.
20. John DeNovo, *American Interests and Politics in the Middle East: 1900–1939*, Minneapolis: University of Minnesota Press, 1963; Joseph L. Grabill, *Protestant Diplomacy in the Near East. Missionary Influence on American Policy, 1810–1927* (1971); James B. Gidney, *A Mandate for Armenia* (1967). Also see Lawrence Evans, *United States Policy and the Partition of Turkey, 1914–1924* (1965).
21. See the thesis of Suzanne E. Moranian, "The American Missionary and the Armenian Question, 1915–1927" (1994); Peter Balakian, *The Burning Tigris: The Armenian Genocide and America's Response* (2003); Merrill D. Peterson, *Starving Armenians. America and the Armenian Genocide, 1915–1930 and After* (2004); Simon Payaslian, *United States Policy Toward the Armenian Question and the Armenian Genocide* (2005).
22. Dimitri Kitsikis, *Le rôle des experts à la Conférence de la Paix de 1919. Gestation d'une technocratie en politique internationale* (Ottawa: Éditions de l'Université d'Ottawa, 1972), 12.

Bibliography

Archives and Published Sources

Baker, Ray S. and William E. Dodd, ed. *The Public Papers of Woodrow Wilson*. New York: Harper, 1925–26.

Baker, Ray S. *Woodrow Wilson: Life and Letters*. Garden City, NY: Doubleday, 1927–39.

Charles Richard Crane Papers, 1869–1967. Rare Books & Manuscript Library, University of Columbia.

Daniels, Josephus. *The Wilson Era*. Chapel Hill: University of North Carolina Press, 1946.

House, Edward M. and Charles Seymour. *What Really Happened at Paris: The Story of the Peace Conference, 1918–1919, by American Delegates*. New York: Scribner's, 1921.

Houston, David F. *Eight Years with Wilson's Cabinet, 1913–1920*. Garden City, NY: Doubleday, 1926.

Lansing, Robert. *The Peace Negotiations: A Personal Narrative*. Boston, MA: Houghton Mifflin,1921.

Link, Arthur S., ed. *Papers of Woodrow Wilson*. Princeton, NJ: Princeton University Press, 1966–92.

Seymour, Charles, ed. *The Intimate Papers of Colonel House Arranged as a Narrative*. London: Ernest Benn, 1926–28.

Tumulty, Joseph P. *Woodrow Wilson as I Know Him*. Garden City: Double Day, 1921.

U.S. Department of State. *Papers Relating to the Foreign Relations of the United States*.

Monographs

Ambrosius, Lloyd E. *Woodrow Wilson and the American Diplomatic Tradition: The Treaty Fight in Perspective*. Cambridge: Cambridge University Press, 1987.

———. *Wilsonian Statecraft: Theory and Practice of Liberal Internationalism During World War I*. Lanham, MD: SR Books, 1991.

———. *Wilsonianism: Woodrow Wilson and His Legacy in American Foreign Relations*. New York: Palgrave Macmillan, 2002.

Balakian, Peter. *The Burning Tigris: The Armenian Genocide and America's Response*. New York: Harper Collins, 2003.

Bailey, Thomas A. *Woodrow Wilson and the Lost Peace*. New York: Macmillan, 1944.

———. *Woodrow Wilson and the Great Betrayal*. Chicago: Quadrangle Books, 1945.

Baker, Ray S. *Woodrow Wilson and World Settlement*. Garden City, NY: Doubleday, 1922.

Blum, John M. *Woodrow Wilson and the Politics of Morality*. Boston: Little, Brown & Co., 1956.

Buenker, John D. *Urban Liberalism and Progressive Reform*. New York: Scribner's Sons, 1973.

Calhoun, Frederick S. *Uses of Force and Wilsonian Foreign Policy*. Kent, OH: Kent State University Press, 1993.

Chamberlain, John. *Farewell to Reform. The Rise, Life and Decay of the Progressive Mind in America*. Chicago: Quadrangle, 1965 [c.1932].

Clements, Kendrick, A. *The Presidency of Woodrow Wilson*. Lawrence, KA: University Press of Kansas, 1992.

Cooper, John M. *The Warrior and the Priest*. Cambridge: HUP, 1983.

Cranston, Alan. *The Killing of the Peace*. New York: The Viking Press, 1945.

DeNovo, John. *American Interests and Politics in the Middle East: 1900–1939*. Minneapolis: The University of Minnesota Press, 1963.

Davis, Donald E., and Eugene P. Trani. *The First Cold War. The Legacy of Woodrow Wilson in U.S.-Soviet Relations*. Columbia: University of Missouri Press, 2002.

Evans, Lawrence. *United States Policy and the Partition of Turkey, 1914–1924*. Baltimore: The Johns Hopkins University Press, 1965.

Figes, Orlando. *A People's Tragedy. The Russian Revolution, 1891–1924*. New York, Penguin Books, 1996.

Freud, Sigmund and William C. Bullitt. *Le Président Thomas Woodrow Wilson*. Paris: Albin Michel, 1967 [c.1939].

Fromkin, David. *A Peace to End All Peace. Creating the Modern Middle East, 1914–1922*. New York: Holt, 1989.

Gardner, Lloyd C. *Safe for Democracy. The Anglo-American Response to Revolution, 1913–1923*. New York: Oxford University Press, 1984.

Gerson, Louis L. *Woodrow Wilson and the Rebirth of Poland 1914–1920. A Study in the Influence on American Policy of Minority Groups of Foreign Origin*. Hamden, CT: Archon Books, 1972 [c.1953].

Gidney, James. B. *A mandate for Armenia*. Kent, OH: Kent State University Press, 1967.

Grabill, Joseph L. *Protestant Diplomacy in the Near East. Missionary Influence on American Policy, 1810–1927*. Minneapolis: University of Minnesota Press, 1971.

Hapgood, David. *Charles R. Crane. The Man Who Bet on People*. New York: ICWA, 2000.
Hofstadter, R. *The Age of Reform. From Bryan to FDR*. New York: Vintage Books, 1955.
———. *The American Political Tradition and the Men Who Made It*. New York: Vintage Books, 1989 [c.1948].
Howard, Harry. *The King-Crane Commission. An American Inquiry in the Middle-East*. Beyrouth: Kayats, 1963.
Israel, Jerry. *Progressivism and the Open Door. America and China, 1905–1921*. Pittsburgh: University of Pittsburgh Press, 1971.
Kaplan, Robert D. *The Arabists. The Romance of an American Elite*. New York: The Free Press, 1993.
Kennan, George F. *American Diplomacy, 1900–1950*. New York: New American Library, 1954.
———. *The Soviet-American Relations, 1917–1920*. Princeton, NJ: Princeton University Press, 1956.
Keynes, John Maynard. *Les conséquences économiques de la Paix*. Paris: Nouvelle Revue Française, 1920.
Kitsikis, Dimitri. *Le rôle des experts à la Conférence de la Paix de 1919. Gestation d'une technocratie en politique internationale*. Ottawa: Éditions de l'Université d'Ottawa, 1972.
Knock, Thomas J. *To End all Wars. Woodrow Wilson and the Quest for a New World Order*. New York: Oxford University Press, 1992.
Kolko, Gabriel. *The Triumph of Conservatism: A Reinterpretation of American History, 1900–1916*. New York: Free Press, 1963.
Lasch, Christopher. *The American Liberals and the Russian Revolution*. New York: McGraw, 1962.
Levin, Norman G. *Woodrow Wilson and World Politics: America's Response to War and Revolution*. New York: Oxford University Press, 1968.
Link, Arthur S. *Wilson*. Princeton, NJ: Princeton University Press, 1947.
———. *Woodrow Wilson and the Progressive Era, 1910–1917*. New York: Harper & Brothers, 1954.
———. *Wilson the Diplomatist. A Look at His Major Foreign Policies*. Baltimore: Johns Hopkins Press, 1957.
———. *Woodrow Wilson. Revolution, War, and Peace*. Arlington Heights, IL: Harlan Davidson, 1979.
Lippmann, Walter. *U.S Foreign Policy, Shield of the Republic*. Boston: Little & Brown, 1943.
Mayer, Arno. *Politics and Diplomacy of Peacemaking: Containment and Counterrevolution at Versailles, 1918–1919*. New York: Knopf, 1967.
Manela, Erez. *The Wilsonian Moment: Self-Determination and the International Origins of Anticolonial Nationalism, 1917–1920*. New York: Oxford University Press, 2007.
Nordholdt, Jan W. S. *Woodrow Wilson: A Life for World Peace*. Berkeley: University of California Press, 1991.
Payaslian, Simon. *United States Policy toward the Armenian Question and the Armenian Genocide*. New York: Palgrave, 2005.
Peterson, Merrill D. *Starving Armenians. America and the Armenian Genocide, 1915–1930 and After*. Charlottesville: University of Virginia Press, 2004.

Saul, Norman E. *The Life and Times of Charles R. Crane, 1858–1939. American Businessmen, Philanthropist, and a Founder of Russian Studies in America.* Lanham, MD, Lexington Books, 2013.

Sklar, Martin J. *The Corporate Reconstruction of American Capitalism, 1890–1916: The Market, the Law, and Politics.* Cambridge: Cambridge University Press, 1988.

Smith, Gene. *When the Cheering Stopped: The Last Years of Woodrow Wilson.* New York: Morrow, 1964.

Thomas, William H., Jr. *Unsafe for Democracy. World War I and the U.S. Justice Department's Covert Campaign to Suppress Dissent.* Madison: University of Wisconsin Press, 2008.

Thorsen, Niels A. *The Political Thought of Woodrow Wilson, 1875–1910.* Princeton, NJ: Princeton University Press, 1988.

Unterberger, Betty M. *The United States, Revolutionary Russia, and the Rise of Czechoslovakia.* Texas: A&M University Press, 2000.

Weinstein, James. *The Corporate Ideal in the Liberal State, 1900–1918.* Boston: Beacon Press, 1969.

Weinstein, Edwin A. *Woodrow Wilson: A Medical and Psychological Biography.* Princeton, NJ: Princeton University Press, 1981.

Wiebe, Robert H. *Businessmen and Reform. A Study of the Progressive Movement.* Cambridge: CUP, 1989 [c.1962].

Wiebe, Robert H. *The Search for Order, 1877–1920.* London: Macmillan, 1967.

Williams, William A. *The Tragedy of American Diplomacy.* New York: Dell Publishing, 1972 [c.1959].

Theses

Bocage, Leo J. "The Public Career of Charles R. Crane." Ph.D. diss., Fordham University, 1962.

Sulzbach, Jacob John, Jr. "Charles R. Crane, Woodrow Wilson, and Progressive Reform: 1909–1921." Ph.D. diss., Texas A&M University, 1994.

Moranian, Suzanne E. "The American Missionary and the Armenian Question, 1915–1927." Ph.D. diss., University of Wisconsin, 1994.

Journal Articles

Brecher, F. W. "Charles R. Crane's Crusade for the Arabs, 1919–1939." *Middle Eastern Studies*, 24, 1, 1988, 42–55.

Clements, Kendrick A. "The Papers of Woodrow Wilson and the Interpretation of the Wilson Era." *The History Teacher*, 27, 4, 1994, 475–489.

Link, Arthur S. "The Higher Realism of Woodrow Wilson." *Journal of Presbyterian History*, 41, 1, 1963, 1–13.

Osgood, Robert E. "Woodrow Wilson, Collective Security, and the Lessons of History." *Confluence*, 5, 1957, 341–354.

Parry, Albert. "Charles R. Crane, Friend of Russia." *Russian Review*, 6, 2, 1947, 20–36.

Pomerance, Michla. "The United States and Self-determination: Perspectives on the Wilsonian Conception." *The American Journal of International Law*, 70, 1, 1976, 1–27.

Seltzer, Alan L. "Woodrow Wilson as *Corporate-Liberal*: Toward a Reconsideration of Left Revisionist Historiography." *The Western Political Quarterly*, 30, 2, 1977, 183–212.

Van Alstyne, Richard W. "Woodrow Wilson and the Idea of Nation-State." *International Affairs*, 37, 1961, 293–308.

· 1 ·

SOCIAL AND INTELLECTUAL FOUNDATIONS OF CHARLES R. CRANE: FROM THE CRANE COMPANY TO WOODROW WILSON'S ELECTION, 1858–1912

The Making of an Urban Progressive

Charles Richard Crane's proverbial discretion and his relatively late appearance on the public scene might give the impression that he rose up out of nowhere, *ex nihilo*. The spectacular rise of his political career is doubly shrouded in mystery due to the quasi-complete silence of his memoirs and those of his father about anything relating to the family's history and relationships. Nevertheless, despite the scarceness of information available on his family background, there are some aspects of his thought and previous life that proved to have a crucial bearing on his public career. Though Crane appears, in many respects, to be a singular and even exceptional figure in his surroundings, an analysis of his environment and formative years is essential and reveals conditions that shaped him and explain his progression and public work. The first step in defining Crane's personality, time, and accomplishments is thus an analytical narrative of his familial and intellectual foundations as well as his political evolution up until Woodrow Wilson's election.

Charles Crane was the eldest of nine children. His parents were both from Paterson, New Jersey, which, he later said, was known for producing a great number of famous entrepreneurs. His own family was itself full of adventurous entrepreneurs, whose spirit he clearly inherited. After working in the foundry and printing business in Brooklyn and learning many trades, his father, Richard Teller Crane (1832–1912), moved west in 1855 with his young family to join his uncle, Martin Ryerson, in Chicago. Inspired by his stories about the fur trade in Antebellum Michigan and tired of the miserly salaries and terrible work conditions back in New York, Richard also developed a taste for business. His uncle, by then owner of a lumberyard and a rich exporter, gave Richard his first business opportunity by allowing him to use part of his land so that he could build his own foundry. Ryerson also gave him a thousand dollars as well as the necessary wood to feed the furnace. In July of that year, everything was ready and the little factory began producing its first copper-fitting parts.[1]

His father's memoirs show two general principles that seem to have been passed on to Charles Crane. The first was a strong inclination to favor practical things and technical efficiency over intellectual labor. Richard Teller Crane explained that family tradition before the age of specialization rested on learning several trades. Thus, Charles' paternal grandfather from Massachusetts, Timothy B. Crane (1773–1846), was both a worker and an architect with great skill in mechanics, a field still in its infancy that would later become the work and passion of his son Richard Teller. With a modest but sufficient income, Timothy Crane's family did little to encourage formal education, and the children had to work from a very young age.

The second part of Richard Teller's legacy to Crane was a strong social and political conscience typical of New England's Anglo-Protestant middle class, as well as an interest in philanthropy as an expression of social and economic success. This inclination to use wealth for public and humanitarian reasons was, however, framed by two guiding principles: the rejection of vanity and all that was "ornamental," as well as the idea that aid was to be dispensed only to the most destitute and that charitable work should be primarily carried out locally. The first point, this concern with the necessary, manifested itself in Richard Teller's life through his efforts to help people become self-supporting by promoting the learning of trades in Chicago's public schools. Taking lessons from his own journey, Richard Teller believed that technical skill helped people to achieve professional and economic independence and that the entrepreneurial spirit which had guided him to fortune and prestige could do so for anyone. This faith in personal initiative did not, however, prevent a distinctly collective approach to his management of the Crane Company. Having himself experienced bad working conditions before becoming a company owner, Richard Teller understood the importance of keeping his employees satisfied.

When drawing up construction plans for his foundries, Richard made a point of setting up comfortable rest areas for his workers and elaborating safety measures that went beyond the norms of his time. By his own admission, he used his ingenuity to improve safety and comfort in his factories. What is more, he also implemented financial-aid programs for his employees and for their families.[2] Richard did all this in adherence to the principle that a happy worker is a productive worker. But this effort did not stem purely from utilitarian considerations. It was fueled by values linked to a much larger social vision. Having himself experienced upward social and industrial mobility thanks to, among other things, a very fortuitous lending hand from his uncle, Richard Teller believed that every employee, if given the right opportunity and support, had the potential to participate in technical progress and could achieve economic independence. He also had a rather paternalistic idea of business ownership and felt responsible for the well-being of his workers, deriving pleasure from their gratitude and affection: "For a person to be engaged in business as long as I have been and not to earn the good-will and esteem of his employees would be almost a calamity." On many occasions and to his great satisfaction, his employees did manifest admiration and loyalty toward him.[3] Besides showing his interest in volunteerism in the way he managed his company, Richard Teller also participated in the fight against corruption in Chicago, particularly by becoming an active member of the Citizens' Association and later of the Citizens' League.[4]

These two educational traits, namely, faith in technical progress and belief in the importance of humanitarian and public service, seem to have forged Charles Crane's social mentality. However, though Charles exhibited these traits in a general manner, some crucial differences can be noted between his vision and his father's, a testament to the social and cultural changes that had taken place over the span of a generation. First, about the practice of philanthropy, Charles Crane did not fully share his fathers' scruples about "ornamental" vanity and the primacy of the necessary. He was in love with Russian Orthodox culture as well as with the Chinese and Arab civilizations, and passionately promoted them his whole life. He also did not believe that charity work and public service had to be confined to one's immediate vicinity, as posited by his father, and instead felt a sort of messianic enthusiasm about the idea of changing the world outside his local scene. This change in vision about how to practice philanthropy came alongside a more general shift from Victorian to Progressive culture. On the one hand, Victorian reformism expressed itself in the "mugwump"[5] style of social activism to which Richard

Teller in many ways subscribed. In the unique context of 1860s Chicago—a period during which the Crane Company gained strength and expanded—the Midwest's economy and industrial sector experienced a significant diversification. This led, among other things, to the gradual replacement of Chicago's original elite, the Boosters, who were involved with land speculation and promoted free-soil ideology and a moralistic understanding of work similar to that of Jefferson and Lincoln, by new industrial leaders such as Richard Teller Crane. These new leaders, also of Anglo-American descent and hailing from New England or New York, but more urban and much richer than their predecessors, devoted themselves to a greater extent to the pursuit of efficiency in industry and its management.[6] Toward the 1890s, however, the situation changed even further, though there is no consensus on the causes of such a transformation.[7] Nevertheless, the crisis of the 1890s led to the coming of age of a generation[8] more conscious of social inequalities and intellectually capable of criticizing classic laissez-faire dogma. This generation forged an essentially urban movement of national scope. Combining their predecessors' work ethic and love of public service with a new vision of society and of the government's role, Charles R. Crane and other Progressives tackled what they considered to be the ills of American society with diligence, efficiency, and enthusiasm.

Chicago was a very unique location in the nineteenth century. It had gone from a population of 3,000 to 30,000 between 1830 and 1850. This demographic explosion continued throughout its industrialization after 1850. On the shores of Lake Michigan, Chicago was located right at the center of the corn, timber and meat markets, and sat on a giant cluster of important waterways.[9] It is in this frontier town that the Crane Company, which undeniably shaped Charles R. Crane's political career, rose to prominence as an important producer of metal products. At the time of Crane's birth in 1858, however, Chicago was not yet a great industrial city. Over the following decades and even after the great fire of 1871 had almost completely ravaged this wooden city, it grew to become an urban center on par with New York, Boston, and Philadelphia. In 1900, it had already become the second largest metropolis in the United States after New York. It already distinguished itself from other Midwestern cities, if only through its culture, one torn between emulating the East Coast's cultural norms and adapting to chaotic industrial development and immigration.[10] Yet with this growth came the kind of municipal corruption characteristic of this period, which, as Crane said, followed the "heroic" efforts that had been made after the fire of 1871. He described the period marked by Carter Harrison, Sr.'s term as mayor of Chicago as the time in which politics were at their (morally) lowest point, saying that "the attitude [in town] was frankly cynical." Crane was referring to the domination of public life by the gangster Michael C. McDonald, master of gambling and of Chicago's saloons and "boss" of the Irish immigrants and of the democratic political machine. "King Mike" was also a symbol of Chicago's dependence on vice and on the lifestyle of the immigrants—superstitious drunks and gamblers, according to the popular stereotype—and this earned him the hatred of the do-gooder Victorian elite. He was despised by many Republicans from the Northeastern states as well as by Protestant ministers and by the entire reformist press.[11] The forces bent on stopping urban corruption, nationally as much as locally, gave birth to various organizations striving to "clean up" municipal politics' unfair practices. The ensuing movement was baptized the "good government spirit." In Chicago, one of this movement's most prominent organizations was the Municipal Voters' League (MVL), founded in 1896 by George E. Cole. Its objective was to inject a bit of honesty and efficiency into public administration, particularly by advocating non-partisan criteria like merit and competitiveness in the allocation of public positions and competitive bidding for public works contracts (as opposed to the spoils system then in effect) and by publishing lists of party contributors.[12] Charles Crane was himself a member of the MVL and even served as its president for a few years until 1905. As pointed out by his assistant Walter Stowell Rogers (1877–1965), Crane was the MVL's most important financial contributor and proof that one had to have a certain appetite for risk to become head of an organization whose mission it was to attack corrupt and often criminal political and financial entities.[13]

Yet reform movements in Chicago preceded the MVL and municipal politics. They stemmed, rather, from social work and from the academic world. Historians of urban reform and progressivism in the United States generally consider Jane Addams's (1860–1935) humanitarian work as a turning point in the history of social sciences due to the way in which it combined a certain typically Christian style of "outraged" conscience with a completely prosaic approach to science for social purposes.[14] She was, along with journalist Lincoln Steffens, at the root of something Richard Hofstadter called an "ethos of responsibility" in the Victorian class.[15] By cofounding Chicago's Hull House with Ellen Gates Starr in 1889, Addams not only created a social and administrative center for the poor, but also played a major role in managing a set of social agencies developed particularly during the governorate of

John Peter Altgeld (1847–1902), whom she also supported during the 1892 election.[16] A pioneer in the fight against corruption and monopolistic power, democratic governor of Illinois John P. Altgeld, Prussian born and son of a farmer and worker, had studied law and made a small fortune as a lawyer and real-estate investor. Despite a career that was decidedly "bourgeois," Altgeld rose to wealth as a "self-made-man" and sympathized with various radicals, populists,[17] and labor activists. Because of this, his critics depicted him as a foreigner come to spread anarchy.[18] However, his term at the head of the State of Illinois remains a rare archetype of progressive democracy in the 1890s and one that inspired the "Midwestern" model of progressive governance. Like Addams's progressive spirit, it combined moral indignation with technical efficiency and a focus on social sciences, thereby foreshadowing the leadership style promoted by Robert M. La Follette in Wisconsin. Above all, Altgeld, through his alliance with Jane Addams, was an integral part of Chicago's very particular reformist climate.

The ties between Charles Crane's family and the type of humanitarian reformism embodied by Jane Addams go back to Hull House's creation in Chicago. It was more specifically through the Chicago Commons, created in 1894 by Graham Taylor, that Crane became involved in this social-work movement. His personal friendship with the professor of theology and first president of the University of Chicago, William Rainey Harper, fostered a lasting bond between the university and the social center run by Taylor. This led to the founding, in 1908, of the Chicago School of Civics and Philanthropy (which became the Graduate School of Social Service Administration in 1920), connected with the University of Chicago, of which Charles Crane was one of the administrators.[19] Such a partnership between the philanthropic and academic domains was not a mere coincidence. Since its founding via the financial provisions of oil magnate John D. Rockefeller[20] in 1892, the University of Chicago had promoted fundamental research and higher education from a social gospel perspective. Despite its nondenominational character, it fell under the authority of the American Baptist Education Society and, through the wills of Rockefeller and Harper, "would be a force for Christian moralism in the Midwest at the same time that it developed and promoted modern scientific research,"[21] thus spearheading philanthropic progressivism in the region. The university's social mandate was in fact well highlighted in its motto, "*Crescat, scientia, vita excolatur.*" In an American academic context, the direction taken by Harper constituted a sort of revolution in the philosophy of education, even though some of the larger universities of the East

Coast elite already had, at the turn of the twentieth century, presidents who were open to this new "social" approach to education and to the university's role in public affairs.[22] This approach was inspired by the German model in its scientific and organizational aspects but also enhanced by the moralistic impetus of the social gospel. Spurred on by Harper's efforts, the University of Chicago focused on the expansion of higher learning, on empirical research, social work, and improvement of the human condition in the city. It brought together a renowned teaching body including, most notably, the famed philosopher of pragmatism John Dewey. Dewey had been a creator of various schools and institutions throughout his career and was responsible for the University of Chicago's Laboratory Schools, where he set up a department of philosophy.[23] In fact, the University of Chicago's particular propensity for creating different schools stemmed from its close connection with urban reality. After all, it had been built on the site of the World's Columbian Exposition of 1893, which had then been left to crumble after the fair's end. Beyond Harper's deep-rooted view of the university as a public-service institution, one could find that "the concerns of more liberal teachers at the university matched those of liberal reformers among the urban elite."[24] Indeed, in the midst of urban squalor, the staff at the University of Chicago developed considerations similar to those of social reformers like Jane Addams. In this sense, new social knowledge served as the scientific basis of the social gospel.

From a religious perspective, Charles Crane's faith constitutes a complex aspect of his personality which deserves a contextual analysis. Crane, without a doubt, fit into this era of cultural renewal and evangelical resurgence sometimes called the "Third Great Awakening,"[25] which had led to an Anglo-Protestant social reform movement. Over the course of his active life, Crane seemed to endorse both the Christian and humanistic premises of the social gospel and collaborated with its leading figures, challenging the traditional alliance between Protestantism and economic laissez-faire policies. Still, throughout his life, Crane's personal religious practices were dissipated to say the least. Whereas his family had denominational roots in the Presbyterian Church before adhering to the Episcopal Church, the young Charles harbored a deep disappointment in institutionalized religion, whose insipidity and distance from original Christianity he deplored. Like so many upholders of the social gospel, Crane rebelled against the capitalistic and individualistic American Protestant church and against the hypocrisy of a social religion which he deemed dogmatic and self-righteous. "My mind is repulsed by their [orthodox creeds] narrow views," he confessed to his wife

Cornelia at the beginning of their relationship.[26] He did not diligently attend services at his own church, the Trinity Episcopalian Church of Chicago, but instead took pleasure in visiting the places of worship of different Christian denominations and even those of other religions. Nevertheless, his view of social progress rested on a belief in Christianity's moral superiority, a classic assumption entertained by other Progressives and particularly by Woodrow Wilson himself.

Furthermore, this growing awareness in the mostly Protestant and liberal social gospel elite occurred parallel to the advent of a novel type of urban journalism. Indeed, various journalists compiling first-hand information on political corruption in the cities were at the basis of this recent tendency to give empirical accounts of urban living condition. In *The Shame of the Cities*, the muckraker Lincoln Steffens (1866–1936) dedicated an entire chapter to describing a Chicago ruled by corruption but partially redeemed by the municipal reform movement to which belonged Crane's MVL. Steffens's way of depicting the corruption in Chicago aligned with Crane's. In his book, he emphasized Chicago's unscrupulous political practices, which he said went all the way back to the city's beginnings and reflected the overall development model of the Midwest, which was "a settlement of individuals and groups and interests with no common city sense and no political conscience. Everybody was for himself, none was for Chicago."[27] Steffens's stated aim in writing his investigative articles on municipal politics, which were initially published in McClure's Magazine, was to rouse public indignation (and guilt) about the current state of affairs while encouraging civic pride in the few reforms already underway especially in Chicago.[28] Lincoln Steffens, though deliberately sanctimonious in his writings, still paid proper tribute to the MVL and particularly to Charles Crane for his role in the league's management. After the municipal council elections in 1900, Crane was elected president of the MVL's executive committee while Walter Lowrie Fisher (1862–1935) became its secretary (he would then succeed Crane as president in 1906). Acknowledging Crane's discreet but effective contribution, Steffens expands further on each man's role by explaining that "He (Crane) leaves the game to Mr. Fisher, and says Fisher is the man, but Crane is a backer of great force and of persistent though quiet activity."[29] Even when serving as president, Crane preferred to leave the stage to others and focused instead on the action behind the scenes, though he certainly always kept his grip on the reins. Despite his "remarkable" discretion, it is under his leadership that, according to Steffens, the MVL was perfected and reached its peak in terms of efficiency. Moreover, it is precisely during

Crane's term at the head of the MVL that Steffens conducted his municipal inquiries and complimented Chicago for its fight against corruption and the boss system, a rare success case among the cities examined by the famous Californian muckraker.

Lincoln Steffens's importance in regard to Crane's developing political career, however, transcends the publication of *The Shame of the Cities* and his words of praise toward the MVL. According to his autobiography, Steffens had a particular knack for gaining the confidence of people from different circles, which proved very useful in the field of investigative journalism. He was close to individuals as varied—and sometimes as antagonistic—as Theodore Roosevelt (with whom he maintained a lasting friendship), Woodrow Wilson and the communist journalist John Reed (who was friends with the young Walter Lippmann[30]). Despite his iconoclastic tendency to attack the do-gooder elite, Steffens, it would appear, was full of humane and friendly curiosity which evidently drew people to him.[31] This gift allowed him to repeatedly act as a public intermediary between various figures, and he was in fact responsible for arranging the first meeting between Crane and Robert Marion La Follette in March of 1905. While Steffens had discovered and admired Charles Crane's progressive potential, the homage he paid La Follette in *Shame of the Cities* left no doubt as to the latter's influence and growing popularity within the Progressive movement.

Thus, Charles Crane's participation and leadership in the MVL demonstrates this climate of reform stemming from what Richard L. McCormick called "the discovery that business corrupts politics."[32] The MVL was a non-partisan, socially diverse organization which adopted a rhetoric of equality.[33] This independence, according to R. Schneirov, was the league's distinctive characteristic, as "the MVL abjured mugwump moralism" and "Chicago labor's support for reform was part of a new tide of cross-class urban progressivism that began to restir the political waters of Chicago during the late nineteenth century." And contrary to the Gilded Age's moral reformism which was centered on the individual, this version of progressivism went beyond simply attempting to fight corruption. It also promoted greater public control over the business community and addressed the social problems linked to labor.[34]

In this sense, the historic shift from "mugwump" reformism to an era of progressive thinking can be seen in the evolution from Richard T. Crane's civic engagement to the work carried out by his son Charles. One can thus say that some Progressives were literally the sons of mugwumps.

La Follette and the Wisconsin Idea

Robert Marion La Follette of Wisconsin was a specific component of this growing Progressive movement. Not as close to the business and industrial world as Charles Crane, he was an icon of the intellectualism inherent to progressivism. La Follette was not a career intellectual like Woodrow Wilson, for instance, but he epitomized the use of modern academic and scientific knowledge for the purpose of social and political reform.[35] Though "Fighting Bob" owed his political talent and determination solely to his own character and disposition, his progressive understanding of the role of experts in society was forged in the intellectual atmosphere of the University of Wisconsin. Through the influence of economist and Christian social gospeler Richard T. Ely and a few other young intellectuals, among them the famous historian Frederick J. Turner, the University of Wisconsin's new social science department founded in 1892 strove to promote the use of social sciences, which were considered impartial, in the State's political administration. The University of Wisconsin was more involved in politics than the University of Chicago and featured more of the academic world's headliners. It became established as a reference on efficient governance in the American Midwest and later on a national scale.[36] La Follette, himself a graduate of this university, was particularly prone to using its studies and methods, and his 1912 platform reflected the university's ideals.[37] In addition to increasing their public role, Ely, Turner and their colleagues openly waged an intellectual battle against social-Darwinism and laissez-faire economics as taught in particular by Herbert Baxter Adams at Johns Hopkins and by William Graham Sumner at Yale. Robert M. Crunden explains that, much like the spirit reigning at the University of Chicago, the University of Wisconsin's greater openness toward "dissenting" social theories could possibly be attributed to the Midwest's culturally unique atmosphere given that the region was geographically and intellectually less subject to New England's social and religious formalism.[38] It was in this environment that was both more relaxed but also driven by a spirit of insurgence against "special interests" and government corruption inherited from the populists that the figure of La Follette emerged, embodying this "crusading belligerence" symbolic of Midwestern progressivism.[39]

However, by constantly stirring up the masses against them, La Follette had earned himself a terrible reputation in conventional economic and political circles. On this topic, Steffens's account of their first meetings is of particular interest. Steffens, to whom La Follette had been described by Illinois and Wisconsin businessmen as a demagogue and an anarchist, was expected to write an unflattering report of the then governor of Wisconsin's political activities. Yet despite all of the preconceived notions instilled in him by La Follette's enemies, Steffens, upon meeting this man who some called "the Little Giant," found himself having to quite drastically alter his opinion. "The only hitch," Steffens wrote, "was that Bob La Follette's measures seemed fair to me, his methods democratic, his purposes right but moderate, and his fighting strength and spirit hopeful and heroic." Faithful to his own political mission, Steffens decided to make himself "Fighting Bob's" editorial voice, especially considering the latter's lack of support from the press. Steffens admired La Follette's incorruptible fighting spirit, which had helped him to defy and beat his own party's system to become governor. He also had faith in the leader's intellectual and administrative ability to carry out his political and legislative work. The journalist, in short, saw La Follette as more than some rabble-rouser, recognizing instead that his technical abilities did not fall short of his political charisma. He knew how to prepare himself for his tasks in a professional and well thought-out manner, and Steffens wrote of him that though "Impatient, he was slow and thorough. He prepared for a speech like a man writing a book."[40]

Ironically enough, La Follette was an unruly student; his primary interest lay in public speaking and theatre, not social studies. His speeches sounded more like sermons—agreeable to a do-gooder public—than like a progressive reformist program, and he derived pleasure from the fame he gained by winning rhetorical contests. If he was rigid and moralistic on stage—though he quickly shrugged off his parents' evangelical fervor[41]—La Follette would always go back to being warm and friendly when he got off the podium. He cultivated his popularity and gorged on it. Having obtained his law degree with difficulty, La Follette was admitted to the bar in 1880. He presented himself primarily as a sworn opponent of societal vices like homelessness and alcoholism during his beginnings as a district attorney, and his first political associations followed the mugwump trend. But political opportunism forced him to tone down his campaigns in favor of temperance since the Republican Party was counting on the support of "intemperate" ethnic groups like Norwegian and German immigrants, who made up a good part of Wisconsin's population.

Under the Republican banner, he was successively Wisconsin representative in the U.S. Congress, governor of Wisconsin, and U.S. senator before becoming a candidate for the Republican investiture in 1912 and then Progressive candidate in 1924. Though he had always adhered to the Protestant ethic (which promoted frugality, temperance, and labor) and to its corresponding social and economic laissez-faire ideals, La Follette became gradually aware of the nefarious impact interest groups had on democratic life and realized that monopolies threatened the Jeffersonian ideals which he, as a Midwesterner, endorsed. Though he did not subscribe to William Jennings Bryan's Protestant agrarian populism, La Follette already had a provincial and populist image which would work against him in his face off with Theodore Roosevelt.[42]

Crane, La Follette, and Louis D. Brandeis: The National Progressive Republican League

La Follette's complete conversion to progressivism and to the antitrust movement was also a product of his becoming acquainted, in 1910, with radical lawyer Louis Dembitz Brandeis. Like Charles R. Crane, Brandeis was determined to support the best candidate from a progressive perspective regardless of the party he belonged to. This non-partisan approach reflected many aspects of the era's political culture. Firstly, both parties had come to endorse very similar programs after the Reconstruction. Aside from protectionism and trusts, their political and economic philosophy was generally comparable. In fact, even in 1912, the platform proposed by Roosevelt (who, despite being a Progressive candidate, endorsed a more Progressive-Republican agenda) and the one proposed by Wilson were barely distinguishable from one another. Secondly, neither party had strong ideological affiliations, meaning that no permanent division existed between them. When it came to voting for progressive purposes rather than by tradition, the identity of the candidates ended up mattering more than the party they belonged to. Thus, after having supported Roosevelt and Taft in 1904 and 1908, Brandeis chose to back the Democrat Wilson in 1912. Already as of 1910, Taft had ceased to represent the hope in reform cherished by Brandeis due to his association with the most conservative circles. Meanwhile, Roosevelt, though useful for a time in his efforts to "raise America's awareness" of abuse and inequality, could not, according to Brandeis, think clearly when it came to monopolies. The trust problem had become a central issue for many reformers, and La Follette embodied the fight against global interests that Brandeis aspired to.[43]

La Follette and Brandeis had thus found common ground starting in 1910. They began working together to formulate a coherent reform program which the Wisconsin senator would then be able to champion by becoming the next Republican presidential candidate. Brandeis and Charles Crane lay at the heart of the movement to elect La Follette, along with other renowned progressives like the editor William Allen White and the environmentalist Gifford Pinchot. These proreform activities were structured around the National Progressive Republican League (NPRL), created in December of 1910 and of which Crane was elected treasurer and executive committee member. The NPRL ultimately served as a means to propel La Follette toward nomination and help progressives to gain control over the Republican Party.[44]

According to its January 1911 policy statement, the NPRL aimed to promote a people's government along with progressive legislation. These general goals were based on the idea that the "special interests" were constantly working against good governance by controlling the machinery of government and by deciding nominations and election results, and on the belief that monopolies were sabotaging legislative reform efforts to build a healthy and modern economic model. Crane, La Follette, and their colleagues in the NPRL thus advocated reforms of both the federal and state systems. They demanded direct election of U.S. Senators by the people and direct primaries for the nomination of elective officials. They also believed in the need for direct election of delegates to national conventions with opportunity for the voter to express his choice for President and Vice-President. Lastly, the NPRL promoted "a thorough going corrupt practices act."[45]

But beyond the problem of corruption and popular representation, there remained the crucial debate on monopolies, particularly relevant in 1911 and 1912 when Senator La Follette was drafting his antitrust law. Brandeis's position, which La Follette now availed himself to, encompassed some legislation to reinforce the 1890 Sherman Act and which would eventually lead to so-called "trust-busting" measures. This radical attitude was, however, not shared by some La Follette supporters, who preferred a regulatory approach. Among them were some of those same people who had once helped La Follette during his governorship, the members of the "Wisconsin Idea." Charles McCarthy, Charles Van Hise, and John R. Commons, of the University of Wisconsin clique, believed that measures aiming to destroy monopolies went too far and instead argued for the establishment of an interstate commission (much like the one that had previously been created in Wisconsin) capable of regulating business practices without destroying conglomerates. The premise of this perspective was that monopolies were still agents of significant technical and industrial progress which was essential to American society. In the eyes of Brandeis, La Follette, and Crane, however, the government's role was to encourage cooperation rather than combination.[46] The Wisconsin group's opposition in this debate foreshadowed the coming rift among Progressive Republicans and the position taken by Theodore Roosevelt during his 1912 campaign. According to some students of the antimonopoly movement, this divergence reflected the existence of two different geographical and social factions in the United States. The first was the more extreme Midwestern group led by La Follette and driven by populist tradition, while the second one was headed by Roosevelt and fuelled by the East Coast's moderate patrician class.[47] Yet the crucial presence and support of Brandeis, an (admittedly Jewish) professional from Massachusetts and of Crane, a well-to-do urban industrialist, showed that this division was not necessarily fuelled by the two above-mentioned criteria. Despite these tensions, it appears that Crane succeeded, for a time, in easing the dissent by acting as a mediator between the more radical Brandeis, a La Follette torn between two different philosophies of intervention, and the Wisconsin experts led by McCarthy.

Furthermore, Roosevelt's position among Progressive Republicans seemed ambiguous. The NPRL had invited him into the league to take advantage of his prestige and with the overt goal of generating an open opposition between him and Taft in the Republican Party. However, Roosevelt declined despite the relatively moderate measures proposed by the league, not yet being, as explained by La Follette, "sufficiently progressive" to lend his fame to such an organization. His public statements, on the other hand, showed him to be increasingly supportive of reform after having read Herbert Croly's *The Promise of American Life* in 1909, hoping to effect changes both by means of government regulation and through a moral crusade to "rebuild" America's citizens.[48] Particularly bitter after retrospectively observing his relationship with Roosevelt and the Progressive Republicans, La Follette added that in any case, Roosevelt had been in the habit of cultivating ambiguity about his political orientation in an effort to gain the most diverse support possible at the National Convention.[49]

Still, despite the legislative and political precision of La Follette's campaign and its temporary cohesiveness on a purely strategic level, the idea of his nomination was still cause for surprise. "Fighting Bob" was not the type of politician to peddle compromise as was expected from the leader of a national party as far-reaching and diverse as the Grand Old Party. Like the democratic populist William J. Bryan, La Follette preferred to face defeat rather than to betray his convictions. Brandeis was acutely aware of this fact but still viewed La Follette, with his remarkable fighting spirit, as "the best statesman we have for the accomplishment of the reforms that are needed at this time."[50]

The Roosevelt Intrusion

It was thus as treasurer of the NPRL, to which he also generously contributed, that Charles Crane first appeared on the national scene. His association with La Follette was consistent with his previous anticorruption efforts in Chicago. It was also a natural extension, at the federal level, of his ideals of efficiency, good governance, public integrity, and accountability which he had previously applied at the municipal and state levels via, for instance, his involvement in Chicago's MVL.

So long as Roosevelt, recently returned from an African safari, a Brazilian jungle expedition, and a triumphal tour of European aristocratic circles, did not reenter the world of national politics, La Follette stood a good chance of securing the Republican nomination in 1912 against Taft. But despite La Follette's considerable public magnetism, Roosevelt appeared to be the logical strategic and political choice for a progressive nomination, and his likelihood of winning the primary elections against Taft seemed greater than La Follette's. Increasingly aware of this reality and finding La Follette to be unfit after a disastrous speech during a banquet in Philadelphia on February 2, 1912,[51] Amos and Gifford Pinchot, William Kent, Joseph McCormick, and a few other well-known Progressive Republicans asked La Follette to abdicate so that Theodore Roosevelt could take his place in the presidential race. This mass desertion did not, however, convince Crane or Brandeis to abandon La Follette. Even before the fiasco in Philadelphia, La Follette had started to sense the dissent brewing in his party and, having started to distrust his lieutenants, he soon called on the mutineers to show their hand. The Pinchot brothers[52] therefore organized a conference in Washington on January 18, 1912 to develop a new election strategy and, if necessary, to determine La Follette's status. The latter refused their invitation but counted on the loyal presence of Crane's secretary, Walter S. Rogers, to report back on the proceedings.[53] Nothing was decided given that no clear declaration had been made by Roosevelt about his intentions. Despite this, all suspected that Roosevelt would soon enter the presidential race and Amos Pinchot called a second meeting on January 29. This time, Crane himself made an appearance and his presence and allegiance were now a crucial issue due to his status as the league's financial contributor—he had pledged to give $5,000 each month until the National Convention in Chicago. Brandeis, in his capacity as representative of the La Follette Eastern supporters and the brain behind the progressive program, was also in attendance. Roosevelt's supporters finally presented him with two alternatives: withdrawing in favor of Roosevelt or withdrawing with no clear successor. La Follette, however, refused this false choice and turned to the remainder of his loyal followers to reaffirm his status. He was pleased to find among them the coveted Crane, whose righteousness he knew and whose loyalty he had never doubted:

> "I had never for one moment believed that he would abandon me. He is a man of few words, but with great consistancy [*sic*] of purpose. He had been in the conference with the Pinchots for hours, and subject to as strong an appeal as it was possible for them to make, and I watched his face with keen interest as he read the statement. There was no change of expression [...] So I knew that I would at least have one strong supporter to the end."[54]

This statement demonstrates the key role of Crane's support in the Republican nomination. Others like Charles E. Merriam and Louis Brandeis also remained at La Follette's side, but no one had as much weight as Crane, primarily due to his part in financing the progressive league. Nevertheless, despite the devotion of La Follette's supporters, Roosevelt's popularity and connections within the party were too strong in the context of a divided NPRL.

After a first successful round of primaries for Roosevelt, however, the Republican Party's conservative wing won the nomination at the National Convention after Taft gained the support of TR's great ally and former Secretary of State Elihu Root. The rift between the Progressives—themselves split into La Follette and Roosevelt supporters—and the Conservatives in the Republican Party gave birth to a third major party of which TR became the standard-bearer. This marked the end of Fighting Bob's national campaign and the start of what would become a pivotal election in American history and in Crane's career.

Crane and the Presidential Election of 1912: Toward a Progressive Democrat Candidate

Abandoned by most of his followers in favor of Roosevelt, La Follette did not pledge his support to the new "Bull Moose" party.[55] In fact, after his expulsion from the race for the Republican nomination, his position in the 1912 presidential campaign became rather incongruous. While fighting Roosevelt's candidacy—which, to him, constituted nothing less than a transgression against the Progressive movement[56]—and while urging the population to reject Taft's conservative candidacy, La Follette still advocated loyalty to the Republican Party, which had after all fostered the development of these "Progressive powers" in Congress. He did, however, rather discreetly support Wilson, though he still doubted the reformist potential of a too conservative Democratic Party which had not yet freed itself from the control of the "bosses."[57]

Crane and Brandeis were two of the last major figures to stay at La Follette's side until Taft's nomination, which was followed by TR's transfer to the Progressive Party. Only then did Brandeis and Crane finally turn toward the new Democratic candidate. Woodrow Wilson, over the course of a few years, had gone from quasi-total anonymity to national renown as the head of a state reform movement during his time as Governor of New Jersey from 1910 to 1912. Crane, and especially Brandeis as a Bostonian, took on the challenge of bridging the gap between Wilson's speeches and position and New England's voters. These voters were more hostile toward the Democratic candidate from Virginia, especially where protectionism and antitrust measures were concerned. Brandeis, along with the Texan Edward M. House, then became the main creator of Wilson's election platform. The New Freedom was unique in that it tried to reconcile two great American philosophies about public life and the role of the State. Indeed, Wilson's program was inspired by the Jeffersonian entrepreneurial ideal while also advocating the methods of Hamiltonian federalism.

For Charles Crane, Governor Wilson represented hope in a political revival. The two men first met during Wilson's ceremony of inauguration as president of the University of Princeton in 1902. Crane discovered his skill as statesman when Wilson was appointed governor of New Jersey, as it was then that "his political methods and his genius for constructive statesmanship were both clearly in view." His nomination in Baltimore as Democratic presidential candidate in 1912 stimulated Crane's enthusiasm for politics like nothing had since the years of Grover Cleveland. He became one of the biggest financial contributors and organizers of Wilson's presidential campaign and "took an active interest in the campaign, having an official status at the western headquarters in Chicago but also [spending] much time in New York where the larger movements were planned." In fact, while he was still supporting La Follette for the Republican nomination, Crane had already started contributing to Wilson's Democratic candidacy to increase the likelihood of a progressive election across the board. Right before the Democratic Convention, after having donated $10,000 to Wilson for his campaign, Crane became the vice-president of Wilson's finance committee and established his position as top donor with a $40,000 contribution.[58]

He played such a large part in financing the campaign primarily because Wilson's team was rather modest compared to that of Taft or Roosevelt, who both had the support of very rich backers. It was thus a campaign of limited means, and Crane wrote that "The machinery was simple and our resources small. The comparatively few large contributions that came to us were from old Princeton friends of Mr. Wilson—Cleveland Dodge, Cyrus (Hall) McCormick, Jr., and the Jones brothers of Chicago." In addition, Wilson received public support from a few renowned university presidents like Harvard's Charles W. Eliot—with whom Crane fostered a deep and lasting friendship—and Edwin A. Alderman from the University of Virginia.

Crane explained that despite the frugality of his campaign, Wilson knew how to earn peoples' sympathy and appeal to their common sense. Crane believed that Wilson could get by without the usual advertising machines because, like Gandhi and other great prophets of this world, he had succeeded in establishing himself as one of the figures who would have a lasting impact on their epoch and would change the course of history.[59] Though usually quiet and level-headed, Crane seemed to light up whenever it came to discussing Wilson's political talent and oratory skill.

Paradoxically enough, even though his traditional position in favor of free trade and thus against protectionism made Charles R. Crane a "natural" Democrat,[60] he had the social and intellectual profile of a Republican. He was a Progressive and had inherited from his father a certain kind of "mugwump" tradition but had partially rejected his "self-made" family's anti-intellectualism and come to hover somewhere between a Victorian formalism tinged with social gospel humanitarianism and an affinity for the more radical ideas of his time. From the particular context of the Midwest and of Chicago, Crane ended up borrowing a Republican bias proper to his social status while simultaneously rejecting the Democratic Party's shameful affiliations with the immigrant community's political machine. Yet the rejection of La Follette by Progressive Republicans and the ensuing rift in the Republican Party caused a shift in Crane's political allegiance, which had already been fluid to begin with.

Due to his experience with his father's businesses, Charles Crane was also predisposed to idealize efficiency as a work value and a social philosophy. This aspect fit partially into his family's tradition of practicality but also went hand in hand, in a more pronounced manner, with the start of the age of specialization represented by the Wisconsin Idea and by La Follette's political career. Forged during the 1912 presidential campaign by this little group of men who had supported Wilson's nomination and to which belonged Crane and Brandeis, the Wilsonian program was a decisive step toward a type of progressive governance which combined elements of technocracy and of social science.

Louis D. Brandeis's involvement alongside Charles Crane and Edward M. House in Wilson's presidential campaign was perhaps the most crucial element in shaping the evolution and characteristics of Wilson's first term as president. It was in fact Brandeis, a Jewish lawyer of Czech descent, who ended up articulating the New Freedom program, particularly by clarifying and adapting Wilson's vision in regard to trusts and then familiarizing him with the idea of government regulation and increased public control.

Many historians have pointed out the rudimentary nature of Wilson's program at the start of his presidential campaign and his insistence, almost to the exclusion of everything else, on tariffs as the primary topic of debate.[61] In addition to being a traditional spearhead, along with the gold standard issue, for the Democratic Party and its primarily rural electorate, the debate over protectionism reflected the influence of classic liberal thinkers on Woodrow Wilson, which would also play a significant role several years later in his Fourteen Points. But tariff policies did not sufficiently rouse peoples' passions to supplant the Progressive Party. Instead, it was the impact of monopolies on American society and America's corporatist tendencies[62] that had been causing the greatest dismay among voters since the turn of the century. The subjugation of competitiveness for the profit of large conglomerates and to the detriment of consumers and taxpayers dampened a public opinion already fed by the alarmist reports made by the sensationalist press.

One can certainly say that in election debates of the time, topics like tariffs, the regulation of monopolies, the problems of the working class, and the banking system constituted complex issues that required precisely the touch of an expert.

Notes

1. Richard Teller Crane, *The Autobiography of Richard Teller Crane, 1832–1912* (Chicago, Crane Co., 1927), 10–32, 235.
2. For a detailed technical description of the safety measures taken by Richard T. Crane, one can refer to *The Autobiography of Richard Teller Crane*, 210–11. To sum it up, filtration and air purification devices were installed, the oil containers were kept in a separate building and the oil was routed through insulated pipes; there was even an air-conditioning system, and Richard Teller made sure to set up his factories inside spacious, well-lit buildings with high ceilings, changing rooms, and warm showers for employees. In fact, heating and ventilation of buildings became one of the Crane Co.'s strengths from the 1860s onward. See p. 107–20.
3. *Autobiography*, 176–95. Still, Richard T. Crane does not seem to have developed truly close ties with his employees. His memoirs do not show any specific information on the origins or condition of the workers in his factory. Furthermore, there is no mention of the trade unions or strikes that affected the working class and Crane's factories. On the topic of the union struggle in Chicago and at the Crane Co., one must read Richard Schneirov, *Labor and Urban Politics. Class Conflict and the Origins of Modern Liberalism in Chicago, 1864–97* (Chicago: University of Illinois Press, 1998), 22–35. It appears that Crane's factories were one of the main areas of labor disputes in Chicago between 1864 and 1872.
4. *Autobiography*, 216–7.
5. The term comes from a derogatory epithet used in the 1880s to describe representatives of the well-off Protestant middle class who revolted against political corruption and the political machine controlled by immigrants. Richard Hofstadter traced the origins of progressivism back to mugwump reformism bent on the purification of social and civil mores and the implementation of antivice measures. Hofstadter points out a fundamental nuance between mugwump and progressive thinking: the abandonment of laissez-faire and a charitable view of humanitarian aid in favor of a more social, and eventually political, approach to reformism. R. Hofstadter, *The Age of Reform. From Bryan to FDR* (New York: Vintage Books, 1955), 166–8.
6. R. Schneirov, *Labor and Urban Politics*, 22–3.
7. Some historians explain that progressive thinking appeared as a result of dissatisfaction related to the idea of "upheaval in status" (Hofstadter, *The Age of Reform*, 135) and general discontent channeled by a culturally Anglo-Protestant elite (M. McGerr, *A Fierce Discontent. The Rise and Fall of the Progressive Movement in America, 1870–1920* (Oxford: Oxford University Press, 2003). Others, like R. Schneirov (*Labor and Urban Politics*, 260, 289), put greater emphasis on the pressure exerted by the labor movement on local urban politics and reject the interpretation of a specific classes' uprising when faced with its decline and in reaction to a civil and economic crisis starting in 1893. For the epistemological implications of this perspective, also see Samuel P. Hays, *American Political History as Social Analysis* (Knoxville: University of Tennessee Press, 1980), 203–32.
8. Richard Hofstadter remarks that contrary to the "grey-haired" populists and mugwumps in the postwar period, the Progressives were those just entering the prime of their life at the start of the 1890s. Thus, Roosevelt became the youngest president in American history,

Walter Lippmann achieved public renown before the age of thirty and Bryan was only thirty-six years old when he made his famous Cross of Gold speech (*The Age of Reform*, 166–7).

9. Hélène Trocmé, *Chicago, 1890–1930. Audaces et débordements* (Paris: Éditions Autrement, 2000), 14–30.
10. Henry F. May, *The End of American Innocence. The First Years of Our Own Time, 1912–1917* (Oxford: Oxford University Press, 1959), 101–2.
11. Richard C. Lindberg, *The Gambler King of Clark Street: Michael C. McDonald and the Rise of Chicago's Democratic Machine* (Southern Illinois University Press, 2009), 1–7.
12. Jon C. Teaford, "Good Government Movement," in *The Encyclopedia of Chicago*, 2004.
13. *Charles Richard Crane Papers*, "Memoirs," 122.
14. Robert M. Crunden, *Ministers of Reform. The Progressives' Achievement in American Civilization, 1889–1920* (Chicago: University of Illinois Press, 1982), 68.
15. R. Hofstadter, *The Age of Reform*, 203–8.
16. Harvey Wish, "Altgeld and the Progressive Tradition," *The American Historical Review*, 46, 4 (1941): 814. See also Hofstadter, *The Age of Reform*, 145.
17. Here, one should note that the term "populism" necessarily refers to the historical farmers' movement of the South and the Midwest in the second half of the nineteenth century, a current associated with the figures of Ignatius Donnelly, Tom Watson, James Weaver, and William J. Bryan. It thus does not have the contemporary and slightly derogatory meaning that has been attached to the word populism.
18. After taking office, Altgeld pardoned the accused anarchists arrested at Haymarket Square in 1886. Conservative criticism against him was merciless. See John Chamberlain, *Farewell to Reform. The Rise, Life and Decay of the Progressive Mind in America* (New York, John Day Co., 1932; Chicago: Quadrangle, 1965), 67–74. Altgeld, often seen as an extremist, even scared some of the more "timid" Progressives, according to Hofstadter in *The Age of Reform*, p. 165. Theodore Roosevelt, whom Daniel Aaron called a "pseudo-progressive", was no stranger to the popularization of Altgeld's image as an anarchist. D. Aaron, *Men of Good Hope. A Story of American Progressives* (New York: Oxford University Press, 1961), 250.
19. Graham Taylor, *Chicago Commons through Forty Years* (Chicago: Chicago Commons Association, 1936).
20. John D. Rockefeller's controversial image lies equally in the monopolistic nature of his businesses and in his embodiment of the "robber baron" stereotype (according to an expression used by Matthew Josephson, "The Robber Barons," *John D. Rockefeller. Robber Baron or Industrial Statesman?* (Ed. Amherst College, Heath & Co., 1949), 34–48). Rockefeller was tremendously criticized by the muckrakers (Ida Tarbell, in *The History of the Standard Oil Company* (1904), presents him as a cold and calculating boss "victim of a money-passion which blinds him to every other consideration in life"), and explains his social generosity as a tendency to "atone" for his greed through excessive philanthropy. His humanism can perhaps better be explained by the influence of his Baptist faith on his understanding of charity and his career as a founder of humanitarian organizations, as suggests the passing on to later generations of his social ethic. As a self-made-man, Rockefeller's social climb from a modest childhood might also have pushed him to redistribute

his riches. See Allan Nevins, *John D. Rockefeller*; John E. Harr, and Peter J. Johnson, *The Rockefeller Conscience* (NY: Macmillan, 1991), 4–6; Ferdinand Lundberg, *The Rockefeller Syndrome* (Secaucus (NJ): Lyle Stuart Inc., 1975), 95–115; Ron Chernow, *Titan: the Life and Time of John D. Rockefeller, Sr.* (NY: Random House, 1998), 299–329.

21. Quoted from Bachin, Robin F. "University of Chicago." *Encyclopedia of Chicago*. Two books serve as reference on the University of Chicago's first years of existence: Richard J. Storr, *Harper's University: The Beginnings* (1966); and Steven Diner, *A City and Its Universities: Public Policies in Chicago, 1892–1919* (1980).
22. Charles Weneger, *Liberal Education and the Modern University* (Chicago: University of Chicago Press, 1978), 1–61. Also see Martin Balmer, *The Chicago School of Sociology. Institutionalization, Diversity, and the Rise of Sociological Research* (Chicago: University of Chicago Press, 1984), 14–5.
23. Many works mention Dewey and either partially or extensively discuss his role in the creation of a social pedagogy at the University of Chicago and the implications of pragmatism when facing the emergence of social sciences and empiricism. See, mainly, Christopher Lasch, Henry May, Robert Crunden, Ronald Steel, John Patrick Diggins, and Jonathan Hansen.
24. Martin Balmer, *The Chicago School of Sociology*, 22–3.
25. William G. McLoughlin, *Revivals, Awakenings, and Reform. An Essay on Religion and Social Change in America, 1607–1977* (Chicago: The University of Chicago Press, 1978), 150–78. Yet this designation is controversial and criticized as being complacent, with some deeming that it is an uncritical vehicle for the evangelical point of view. McLoughlin identifies two groups within the social gospel: those who were avowedly Christians and focused on Christ's example, and those who were avowedly humanists, including various socialists, atheists, and positivists. Despite being somewhat influenced by the social sciences, Crane seemed to have been attached to the figure of Christ his whole life. He was also, however, open to any manifestation of sincere spirituality. His attachment to missionary efforts worldwide and to Christ's example classifies him more as a Christian social gospeller rather than a humanitarian, even though the boundary between the two groups was fluid rather than rigid. One can also observe that Crane's commitment to missionary goals increased after he began collaborating with John R. Mott of the YMCA during the 1917 Revolution in Russia.
26. *Crane Papers*, "Charles R. Crane to Cornelia W. Smith," December 16, 1878.
27. Lincoln Steffens, *The Shame of the Cities* (NY: Sagamore Press, 1957 [c. 1904]), 164–5.
28. Steffens, *The Shame of the Cities*, 1. However, Steffens's praise went out primarily to the few strong men like Crane who were "bosses" of reformism rather than to the passive and alienated population. This paradoxical aspect of Steffens's radicalism was pointed out by Christopher Lasch, *The New Radicalism in America. The Intellectual as a Social Type* (NY: Knopf, 1965), 251–85.
29. Steffens, p. 181.
30. On the topic of Walter Lippmann's left-wing period and his friendship with John Reed, one can refer to the exhaustive biography by Ronald Steel, *Walter Lippmann and the American Century* (Boston: Atlantic-Little, Brown, 1980), especially chapters 3, 4, and 5.

31. Lincoln Steffens, *The Autobiography of Lincoln Steffens* (NY: Harcourt, Brace & Co., 1931), vii.
32. Richard L. McCormick, *The Party Period and Public Policy. American Politics from the Age of Jackson to the Progressive Era* (NY: Oxford University Press, 1986), 311–56. Though he brings nuance to this idea, McCormick admits that it was at the basis of a local urban movement toward progressivism. However, its impact on the national scene of the Progressive movement as a rebellious antibusiness wake-up call was limited. In fact, the divide between the business world and reformers of all sorts was never so large, and on the contrary, progressivism and business mutually influenced each other, as demonstrated, namely, by Robert H. Wiebe in *Businessmen and Reform. A Study of the Progressive Movement* (1962). For a criticism of these interpretations, one can refer to David P. Thelen, *The New Citizenship. Origins of Progressivism in Wisconsin, 1885–1900* (1973) and to Samuel P. Hays, *American Political History as Social Analysis* (1980), especially Chapter 6, "The Politics of Reform in Municipal Government," 205–32.
33. On this topic, one can note that revisionist historians emphasized—and perhaps exaggerated—the league's elitist, antiunion, and nativist nature (see Joan S. Miller, "The Politics of Municipal Reform in Chicago during the Progressive Era" (Master's thesis, Roosevelt University, 1966). Nevertheless, in Chicago itself, where Crane was active, the MVL was led by reformers who, unlike mugwumps, agreed to associate their program with the labor movement. In fact, many members of the MVL were left-wing liberals, like the evangelical socialist Raymond Robins.
34. R. Schneirov, *Labor and Urban Politics. Class Conflict and the Origins of Modern Liberalism in Chicago, 1864–97*, 350–6.
35. R. Hofstadter, *Anti-Intellectualism in American Life* (New York: Vintage Book, 1963), 198–9. See in particular Chapter 8, "The Rise of the Expert," where Hofstadter underscores the importance of La Follette's contribution to the Progressive movement and his ability to convert his generation's ideas into political action.
36. Stuart Morris, "The Wisconsin Idea and Business Progressivism," *Journal of American Studies* 4, 1 (1970): 39–60.
37. Hofstadter, *Anti-Intellectualism*, 199–201; Henry F. May, *The End of American Innocence. The First Years of Our Own Time, 1912–1917* (New York: Oxford University Press, 1959), 99–106; Robert M. Crunden, *Ministers of Reform*, 65–89.
38. Robert M. Crunden, *Ministers of Reform*, 64. See also David P. Thelen, *Robert M. La Follette and the Insurgent Spirit* (Boston: Little Brown and Co., 1976), 17.
39. Allan Nevins, "Foreword," in *La Follette's Autobiography* (Madison: University of Wisconsin Press, 1912), v.
40. Lincoln Steffens, *The Autobiography of Lincoln Steffens*, 320–3.
41. That is to say that La Follette was neither pious nor a churchgoer, probably in reaction to his stepfather's excessive zeal and rigid moralism. This did not, however, mean that he rejected or intellectually questioned the philosophical and theological basis of Protestant faith. A clearer and more-detailed portrait is painted by David P. Thelen (*Robert M. La Follette and the Insurgent Spirit*, 1–15). Simply put, spiritual devotion was not one of La Follette's defining traits like it was for Woodrow Wilson and, in a different way, for Charles Crane.

42. History's view of La Follette remains paradoxical because his political style and affinities intersected with the populist tradition while also marking the start of a distinctly progressive movement, something which the populists lacked. See Charles Noble, "Wilson's Choice: The Political Origins of the Modern American State," *Comparative Politics*, 17, 3 (1985): 320; David P. Thelen, *The New Citizenship. Origins of Progressivism in Wisconsin, 1885–1900*, (Columbia: University of Missouri Press, 1972), 309–12; Robert S. Maxwell, *La Follette and the Rise of the Progressives in Wisconsin* (New York: Russell & Russell, 1973 [c. 1956]), 12–3.
43. Alpheus T. Mason, *Brandeis: A Free Man's Life*, (NY: Viking Press, 1946), 365–8.
44. *Crane Papers*, "R. M. La Follette to CRC," December 28, 1910.
45. Robert M. La Follette, *La Follette's Autobiography*, 212.
46. *Crane Papers*, "Brandeis to Crane," November 11, 1911.
47. William L. Neuman, "Why Reform Fails: the Rise and Fall of Antimonopoly Reform in the United States: 1875–1975." (Ph. D. diss., University of Wisconsin, 1982), 753–4.
48. About this aspect of the Progressive movement, one can read Chapter 3, "Transforming Americans," in Michael McGerr's *A Fierce Discontent. The Rise and Fall of the Progressive Movement in America, 1870–1920*, 77–117. Even though he came from the American elite, the "upper-ten," Roosevelt endorsed the values of the upper middle class. Unlike other representatives of the elite, TR abhorred the upper-ten's luxury and ostentation at the turn of the twentieth century.
49. Robert M. La Follette, *La Follette's Autobiography*, 213.
50. Alpheus T. Mason, *Brandeis*, 369. Quoted from *Boston American*, October 19, 1911.
51. La Follette was tired, already irritated by the defection of some of his supporters, and worried about his daughter's hospitalization when he stepped up in front of an association of editors and journalists to make a speech. Unable to captivate his audience's attention as he usually did, the ever combative La Follette pressed the matter until he antagonized his audience. The press treated this event as a "collapse," which further quickened his demise by offering those who doubted him an ideal pretext to turn their back on his candidacy. See his own account in Robert M. La Follette, *La Follette's Autobiography*, 256–9. The incident was also discussed in Alpheus T. Mason, *Brandeis*; David Thelen, *Robert M. La Follette and the Insurgent Spirit*; and many other works.
52. Though they were Theodore Roosevelt's close friends, the Pinchot brothers were not the traitors depicted by La Follette in his autobiography. In fact, they tried at first to reconcile the two men. They were then forced to make a decision after failing to guide them to a compromise. In reality, La Follette had no faith in the progressivism of TR, whom he viewed as an opportunist. For another perspective on this issue, one can refer to Amos Pinchot's personal account in *The History of the Progressive Party, 1912–1916* (NY: New York University Press, 1958). Also see Robert M. Crunden, *Ministers of Reform*, 208.
53. Robert M. La Follette, *La Follette's Autobiography*, 252.
54. La Follette, *Autobiography*, 254–6.
55. From one of Roosevelt's statements where he asserted his confidence at the start of the fateful campaign, "Bull Moose" refers to the Progressive Party made up of Progressive Republicans in reaction to Taft's last minute victory at the primaries.

56. La Follette, *Autobiography*, 316. "Roosevelt forced his way into the campaign, divided and demoralized the Progressive forces [...]" For an interpretative description of the antagonistic relationship between Roosevelt and La Follette and its impact and significance in the Progressive movement, one can refer to Thelen, David P. *Robert M. La Follette and the Insurgent Spirit*, 96–8.
57. On this topic, see the explanation given by Arthur S. Link in *The Road to the White House* (Princeton: Princeton University Press, 1947), 468.
58. Arthur S. Link, *Wilson. The Road to the White House*, 403–4, 471, 484–5. One can note how ironic it was for a Progressive like Crane, who abhorred the power money had over politics, to be involved in politics primarily through considerable monetary donations.
59. *Crane Papers*, "Memoirs," 152–3.
60. *Crane Papers*, "Memoirs," 130. During the 1884 and 1892 elections, Crane had voted for the Democrat Cleveland, whom he admired: "As a natural Democrat I had ardently followed the growing personality and career of Grover Cleveland [...]."
61. Arthur S. Link, *Woodrow Wilson and the Progressive Era, 1910–1917*, 20–1.
62. In this regard, Alan Trachtenberg speaks of America's "incorporation," a process by which the United States, following the Civil War, underwent a reorganization of industrial and political structures along with a large-scale shift in underlying assumptions about economy and government. See A. Trachtenberg, *The Incorporation of America. Culture & Society in the Gilded Age* (NY: Hill & Wang, 1982), 3–5.

Bibliography

Archives and Published Sources

Charles Richard Crane Papers, 1869–1967. Rare Books & Manuscript Library, University of Columbia.

James Ford Rhodes Papers. Massachusetts Historical Society.

Baker, Ray S. and William E. Dodd, ed. *The Public Papers of Woodrow Wilson*. New York: Harper, 1925–26.

Baker, Ray S. *Woodrow Wilson: Life and Letters*. Garden City, NY: Doubleday, 1927–39.

Baruch, Bernard M. *Baruch*. New York: H. Holt, 1957–1960.

Crane, Richard T. *The Autobiography of Richard Teller Crane*. Chicago, 1927.

Croly, Herbert. *The Promise of American Life*. New York: Capricorn Books, 1964 [c.1909].

Daniels, Josephus. *The Wilson Era*. Chapel Hill: University of North Carolina Press, 1946.

Houston, David F. *Eight Years with Wilson's Cabinet, 1913–1920*. Garden City, NY: Doubleday, 1926.

La Follette, Robert Marion. *La Follette's Autobiography*. Madison: University of Wisconsin Press, 1968 [c.1912].

Link, Arthur S., ed. *Papers of Woodrow Wilson*. Princeton, NJ: Princeton University Press, 1966–92.

Pinchot, Amos. *The History of the Progressive Party, 1912–1916*. New York: New York University Press, 1958.
Seymour, Charles, ed. *The Intimate Papers of Colonel House Arranged as a Narrative*. London: Ernest Benn, 1926–28.
Steffens, Lincoln. *The Shame of the Cities*. New York: Sagamore Press, 1957 [c.1904].
———. *The Autobiography of Lincoln Steffens*. New York: Harcourt, Brace & Co., 1931.
Tarbell, Ida M. *The History of the Standard Oil Company*. New York: Harper & Row, 1966 [c.1904].
Taylor, Graham. *Chicago Commons through Forty Years*. Chicago: Chicago Commons Association, 1936.
Tumulty, Joseph P. *Woodrow Wilson as I Know Him*. Garden City: Doubleday, 1921.

Bibliographic Guides

Buckingham, Peter H. *Woodrow Wilson: A Bibliography of His Times and Presidency*. Wilmington, DE: Scholarly Resources, 1990.
Bellot, Hugh Hale. *American History and American Historians: A Review of Recent Contributions to the Interpretation of the History of the United States*. Norman: University of Oklahoma Press, 1952.
Parish, Peter J., ed. *Reader's Guide to American History*. Chicago: Fitzroy Publishers, 1997.

Encyclopedias

Balmer, Randall Herbert. *Encyclopedia of Evangelicalism*. Louisville, KY: John Knox Press, 2002.
Encyclopedia of Chicago, 2004.
Shelton, Dinah L., ed. *Encyclopedia of Genocide and Crimes against Humanity*. Detroit: Macmillan Reference USA, 2004.

Monographies

Aaron, Daniel. *Men of Good Hope. A Story of American Progressives*. New York: Oxford University Press, 1961.
Allerfeldt, Kristofer, ed. *The Progressive Era in the USA: 1890–1921*. Burlington, VT: Ashgate, 2007.
Balmer, Martin. *The Chicago School of Sociology. Institutionalization, Diversity, and the Rise of Sociological Research*. Chicago: University of Chicago Press, 1984.
Blum, John M. *The Republican Roosevelt*. Cambridge: Harvard University Press, 1954.
Buenker, John D. *Urban Liberalism and Progressive Reform*. New York: Scribner's Sons, 1973.
———. *The Income Tax and the Progressive Era*. New York: Garland, 1985.
Burns, James M. *The Workshop of Democracy. From the Emancipation Proclamation to the Era of the New Deal*. New York: Vintage Book, 1985.

Chamberlain, John. *Farewell to Reform. The Rise, Life and Decay of the Progressive Mind in America*. Chicago: Quadrangle, 1965 [c.1932].

Chambers II, John W. *The Tyranny of Change. America in the Progressive Era, 1900–1917*. New York: St-Martin's Press, 1980.

Chernow, Ron. *Titan: The Life and Time of John D. Rockefeller, Sr*. New York: Random House, 1998.

Chessman, G. W. *Theodore Roosevelt and the Politics of Power*. Boston: Little, Brown & Co., 1969.

Childs, Marquis and James Reston, ed. *Walter Lippmann and His Times*. Freeport, NY: Books For Libraries Press, 1968 [c.1959].

Clements, Kendrick A. *William Jennings Bryan, Missionary Isolationist*. Knoxville, TE: University of Tennessee Press, 1982.

———. *The Presidency of Woodrow Wilson*. Lawrence, KA: University Press of Kansas, 1992.

Cooper, John M. *The Warrior and the Priest*. Cambridge: HUP, 1983.

Crunden, Robert M. *Ministers of Reform. The Progressives' Achievement in American Civilization, 1889–1920*. Chicago: University of Illinois Press, 1982.

Diggins, John Patrick. *The Promise of Pragmatism: Modernism and the Crisis of Knowledge and Authority*. Chicago: University of Chicago Press, 1994.

Diner, Steven J. *A City and Its Universities: Public Policies in Chicago, 1892–1919*. 1980.

Dorreboom, Iris. *The challenge of Our Time: Woodrow Wilson, Herbert Croly, Randolph Bourne and the Making of Modern America*. Atlanta, GA: Rodopi, 1991.

Ekirch, Arthur A. *Progressivism in America: A Study of the Era from Theodore Roosevelt to Woodrow Wilson*. New York: New Viewpoints, 1974.

Forcey, Charles. *The Crossroads of Liberalism. Croly, Weyl, Lippmann and the Progressive Era, 1900–1925*. Oxford: Oxford University Press, 1961.

Gould, Lewis L. *The Progressive Era*. Syracuse, NY: Syracuse University Press, 1974.

———. *Four Hats in the Ring. The 1912 Election and the Birth of Modern American Politics*. Lawrence, KA: University Press of Kansas, 2008.

Hansen, Jonathan M. *The Lost Promise of Patriotism. Debating American Identity, 1890–1920*. Chicago: University of Chicago Press, 2003.

Hapgood, David. *Charles R. Crane. The Man Who Bet on People*. New York: ICWA, 2000.

Harbaugh, William H. *The Life and Times of Theodore Roosevelt*. London: Oxford University Press, 1975 [c.1961].

Harr, John E and Peter J. Johnson. *The Rockefeller Conscience. An American Family in Public and in Private*. New York: Macmillan, 1991.

Hays, Samuel P. *American Political History as Social Analysis*. Knoxville: University of Tennessee Press, 1980.

Hofstadter, Richard. *Social Darwinism in American Thought*. Boston: Beacon Press, 1992 [c.1944].

———. *The American Political Tradition and the Men Who Made It*. New York: Vintage Books, 1989 [c.1948].

———. *The Age of Reform. From Bryan to FDR*. New York: Vintage Books, 1955.

———. *Anti-Intellectualism in American Life*. New York: Vintage Books, 1963.

———. *The Paranoid Style in American Politics*. New York: Alfred A. Knopf, 1965.

Kloppenberg, James T. *Uncertain Victory. Social Democracy and Progressivism in European and American Thought, 1870–1920*. Oxford: Oxford University Press, 1986.

Kolko, Gabriel. *The Triumph of Conservatism: A Reinterpretation of American History, 1900–1916*. New York: Free Press, 1963.

Lasch, Christopher. *The New Radicalism in America. The Intellectual as a Social Type*. New York: Knopf, 1965.

Latham, Earl. *John D. Rockefeller. Robber Baron or Industrial Statesman?* Boston: Heath & Co., 1949.

Leuchtenburg, William E. *The Perils of Prosperity, 1914–1932*. Chicago: University of Chicago Press, 1993 [c.1958].

Lindberg, Richard C. *The Gambler King of Clark Street: Michael C. McDonald and the Rise of Chicago's Democratic Machine*. Carbondale: Southern Illinois University Press, 2009.

Link, Arthur S. *Wilson*. Princeton, NJ: Princeton University Press, 1947.

———. *Woodrow Wilson and the Progressive Era, 1910–1917*. New York: Harper & Brothers, 1954.

Lundberg, Ferdinand. *The Rockefeller Syndrome*. Secaucus, NJ: Lyle Stuart Inc., 1975.

Mason, Alpheus T. *Brandeis: A Free Man's Life*. New York: Viking Press, 1946.

Maxwell, Robert S. *La Follette and the Rise of the Progressives in Wisconsin*. New York: Russell & Russell, 1973 [c.1956].

May, Henry F. *The End of American Innocence. The First Years of Our Own Times, 1912–1917*. New York: Oxford University Press, 1959.

McCormick, Richard L. *The Party Period and Public Policy. American Politics from the Age of Jackson to the Progressive Era*. New York: Oxford University Press, 1986.

McGerr, Michael. *A Fierce Discontent. The Rise and Fall of the Progressive Movement in America, 1870–1920*. Oxford: Oxford University Press, 2003.

McLoughlin, William G. *Revivals, Awakenings, and Reform. An Essay on Religion and Social Change in America, 1607–1977*. Chicago: The Chicago University Press, 1978.

Mowry, George E. *The Era of Theodore Roosevelt, 1900–1912*. New York: Harper, 1958.

Nevins, Allan. *John D. Rockefeller: The Heroic Age of American Enterprise*. New York: C. Scribner's Sons, 1941.

Noble, David W. *The Paradox of Progressive Thought*. Minneapolis: University of Minnesota Press, 1958.

———. *The Progressive Mind, 1890–1917*. Minneapolis: Burgess, 1981.

O'Neill, William L. *The Progressive Years. America Comes of Age*. New York: Dodd, Mead and Company, 1975.

Saul, Norman E. *The Life and Times of Charles R. Crane, 1858–1939. American Businessman, Philanthropist, and a Founder of Russian Studies in America*. Lexington Books, 2013.

Schneirov, Richard. *Labor and Urban Politics. Class Conflict and the Origins of Modern Liberalism in Chicago, 1864–1897*. Chicago: University of Illinois Press, 1998.

Sklar, Martin J. *The Corporate Reconstruction of American Capitalism, 1890–1916: The Market, the Law, and Politics*. Cambridge: Cambridge University Press, 1988.

Steel, Ronald. *Walter Lippmann and the American Century*. Boston: Little, Brown & Co. 1980.

Stettner, Edward A. *Shaping Modern Liberalism. Herbert Croly and Progressive Thought*. Lawrence, KA: University Press of Kansas, 1993.

Storr, Richard J. *Harper's University: The Beginnings*. Chicago: University of Chicago Press, 1966.

Thelen, David P. *The New Citizenship. Origins of Progressivism in Wisconsin, 1885–1900*. Columbia: University of Missouri Press, 1972.

———. *Robert M. La Follette and the Insurgent Spirit*. Boston: Little Brown & Co., 1976.

Thorsen, Niels A. *The Political Thought of Woodrow Wilson, 1875–1910*. Princeton, NJ: Princeton University Press, 1988.

Trachtenberg, Alan. *The Incorporation of America. Culture & Society in the Gilded Age*. New York: Hill & Wang, 1982.

Trocmé, Hélène. *Chicago, 1890–1930. Audaces et débordements*. Paris: Éditions Autrement, 2001.

Urofksy, Melvin I. *Louis D. Brandeis and the Progressive Tradition*. Boston: Little, Brown & Co., 1981.

Wegener, Charles. *Liberal Education and the Modern University*. Chicago: University of Chicago Press, 1978.

Weinstein, James. *The Corporate Ideal in the Liberal State, 1900–1918*. Boston: Beacon Press, 1969.

White, Morton G. *Social Thought in America. The Revolt Against Formalism*. Boston: Beacon Press, 1976 [c.1949].

Wiebe, Robert H. *Businessmen and Reform. A Study of the Progressive Movement*. Cambridge: CUP, 1989 [c.1962].

———. *The Search for Order, 1877–1920*. London: Macmillan, 1967.

Theses and Memoirs

Bocage, Leo J. "The Public Career of Charles R. Crane." Ph.D. diss., Fordham University, 1962.

Miller, Joan S. "The Politics of Municipal Reform in Chicago during the Progressive Era." M.A. diss., Roosevelt University, 1966.

Neuman, William L. "Why Reform Fails: The Rise and Fall of Antimonopoly Reform in the United States, 1875–1975." Ph.D. diss., University of Wisconsin, 1982.

Sulzbach, Jacob John, Jr. "Charles R. Crane, Woodrow Wilson, and Progressive Reform: 1909–1921." Ph.D. diss., Texas A&M University, 1994.

Journal Articles

Blumenthal, Henry. "Woodrow Wilson and the Race Question." *The Journal of Negro History*, 48, 1, 1963, 1–21.

Clements, Kendrick A. "The Papers of Woodrow Wilson and the Interpretation of the Wilson Era." *The History Teacher*, 27, 4, 1994, 475–489.

Diggins, John P. "Republicanism and Progressivism." *American Quarterly*, 37, 4, 1985, 572–598.

———. "From Pragmatism to Natural Law: Walter Lippmann's Quest for the Foundations of Legitimacy." *Political Theory*, 19, 4, 1991, 519–538.

Hollinger, David A. "Science and Anarchy: Walter Lippmann's Drift and Mastery." *American Quarterly*, 29, 5, 1977, 463–475.

McCormick, Richard L. "The Discovery That Business Corrupts Politics: A Reappraisal of the Origins of Progressivism." *The American Historical Review*, 86, 2, 1981, 247–274.

Morris, Stuart. "The Wisconsin Idea and Business Progressivism." *Journal of American Studies*, 4, 1, 1970, 39–60.

Nichols, David K. "The Promise of Progressivism: Herbert Croly and the Progressive Rejection of Individual Rights." *Publius*, 17, 2, 1987, 27–39.

Noble, Charles. "Wilson's Choice: The Political Origins of the Modern American State." *Comparative Politics*, 17, 3, 1985, 313–336.

Noble, David W. "The *New Republic* and the Idea of Progress, 1914–1920." *The Mississippi Valley Historical Review*, 38, 3, 1951, 387–402.

O'Leary, Kevin C. "Herbert Croly and Progressive Democracy," *Polity*, 24, 6, 1994, 533–552.

Rodgers, Daniel T. "In search of Progressivism." *Reviews in American History*, 10, 4, 1982, 113–132.

Seltzer, Alan L. "Woodrow Wilson as Corporate-Liberal: Toward a Reconsideration of Left Revisionist Historiography." *The Western Political Quarterly*, 30, 2, 1977, 183–212.

Walker, Larry. "Woodrow Wilson, Progressive Reform and Public Administration." *Political Science Quarterly*, 104, 3, 1989, 509–525.

Wish, Harvey. "Altgeld and the Progressive Tradition." *The American Historical Review*, 46, 4, 1941, 813–831.

Wolgemuth, Kathleen L. "Woodrow Wilson and Federal Segregation." *The Journal of Negro History*, 44, 2, 1959, 158–173.

· 2 ·

CHARLES R. CRANE AND THE WILSON ADMINISTRATION: A TIME OF DOMESTIC REFORMS, 1912–1916

"Democracy and Efficiency": Expertization, Reform, and Wilsonian Thought

Charles R. Crane proved to be a critical player in Woodrow Wilson's political rise toward presidency. Along with Louis Brandeis and Edward House, he supported Wilson in the formulation and the implementation of the future president's progressive program, the New Freedom. Given that Crane and especially Brandeis seem to be "expert" advisors in Wilson's entourage, the program they contributed to should be analyzed by emphasizing the typically progressive traits of Wilson's administration. These traits allow us to measure and uncover the full scope of Crane's presence in the highest presidential circles and help situate both him and Wilson in the Progressive movement in general. Indeed, the progressive outlook on power and efficiency in politics shared by Crane, Brandeis, and Wilson has to be viewed in light of Crane and Brandeis's prior involvement with La Follette as shown in the previous chapter.

Wilson's style and program at the start of his presidential career can first be characterized by the federal government's increased involvement in social and political affairs and, especially, by the expansion of the president's power in the governmental structure as a whole. For instance, Wilson reinstated certain habits lost since the time of Thomas Jefferson, such as speaking before Congress when presenting his tariff reform program and disciplining certain members of his own party.[1] As president, Wilson followed the tenets he had first proposed in his 1885 doctoral thesis at Johns Hopkins University, *Congressional Government*, namely, making the president the *de facto* head of the government.[2] Though his thesis was dominated by a heroic vision of the government's head and a critical outlook on the shortcomings of America's departmental and electoral system, Wilson also used it to develop, in a more general way, his organizational view of state power. He wrote that "The highest type of statesmanship is the *constructive*, that which is exhibited in the conception and execution of policies, in the building up of uniform systems of law and the establishment of great principles of legislation."[3]

Yet the piece of writing most aptly heralding Wilson's presidential style was undoubtedly an article titled "Democracy and Efficiency" published in the *Atlantic Monthly* on October 1, 1900 at the start of his term as President of Princeton. The article was a reflection of the Progressive Era's aforementioned ideological assumptions and was written in reaction to the preoccupations of the time. Issued in the wake of the Spanish-American War and the ensuing debates on imperialism in the United States, the article expressed a public and government philosophy concerning the role of the executive branch in American democracy as well as American democracy's place in international relations. Though Wilson's presidency is generally seen as an example of expertise's growing place in the government, there remains among historians a tendency to minimize, perhaps rightly, the president's openness to using technology in his administration. In *Anti-Intellectualism in American Life*, Richard Hofstadter even depicts Wilson as an enemy of experts, whose rhetoric he mistrusted:

> Wilson was not disposed, before the war, to make the extensive use of intellectual advisers in politics [...] he had a persistent distrust of what he called "expert" [...] he did not conceive of experts as likely agents or administrators of reform, but rather as hirelings available only to big business and special interests.[4]

It is true that Wilson had, at times, opposed a government of experts under the influence of Big Business, preferring instead a true people's government. "What I fear is a government of experts," he explained, and added: "God forbid that in a democratic country we should resign the task and give the government over to the experts." His fear that technocratic power might discourage popular participation did not, however, mean that Wilson shunned the contribution of specialized advisors in the implementation of his program, as was believed by Hofstadter. He was concerned, rather, with preventing administrative expertization from leading to the public's disengagement in regard to issues now become too complex. Candidly, he advocated a thorough knowledge of public affairs for all, saying that "if we don't understand the job, then we are not a free people." To Wilson, a worker's down to earth understanding was worth more than the dull rhetoric of an intellectual, as "the man who is down against the daily problem of life doesn't talk about it in rhetoric; he talks about it in facts. And the only thing I am interested in is facts."[5] Beyond the positivist influences of such a declaration, and beyond the ironic fact that it was Wilson—known for his disembodied approach to real things[6]—who had authored it, the excerpt suggests that he had faith in science and had not adopted an anti-intellectual attitude. To this effect, his article "Democracy and Efficiency" helped to clarify his view on the position science and technology should have in representative democracy. He wrote that "Representative government has had its long life and excellent development, not in order that common opinion, the opinion of the street, might prevail, but in order that the best opinion, the opinion generated by the best possible methods of general counsel, might rule in affairs."

However, in the eyes of Wilson (and Crane, for that matter), achieving efficiency was not democracy's ultimate goal. On the contrary, he recognized that "Other forms of government may be equally efficient" and that "many forms of government are more efficient."[7] Without ever clearly defining efficiency, he posited that it should help to preserve representative democracy, which was the objective he strove toward.

Wilson's historical reputation as a sentimental and backward-looking leader, which had been popularized by Hofstadter[8] but was in fact established earlier by Wilson's contemporaries who were "disillusioned" with his policies, seems questionable. Despite a formalistic education led by a rigid Presbyterian father with a provincial background, Wilson's numerous and varied writings show an evolution which, at the turn of the twentieth century, places him at the center of a movement toward efficiency and progressivism. Relatively recent access to the full extent of his academic writings (both as a student and as an intellectual) reveals among other things that he read the works of Richard T. Ely, a "dissident" economist from the University of Wisconsin and a "Christian" social gospeler who had inspired La Follette's reformism by integrating social sciences in government management.[9] Hofstadter's assessment that Wilson had missed the turn of the century and its flow of crucial ideas does not stand up to an analysis of this body of work. It shows that, despite some old-fashioned views, Wilson had easily grasped the wave of change that had washed over his time as suggested in "Democracy and Efficiency." Of course, Wilson was relatively conservative like many Progressives, but he was also quite harsh in his judgments on some of the twentieth century's developments.

His presidential career shows that Ely's theses also had a repercussion on Wilson's presidency. The reports that Wilson had a backward-looking disposition, though true and verifiable in some ways, can be partly attributed to the New Freedom's Jeffersonian bent. He underwent, however, a gradual and sometimes hesitant progression, charted by historians, toward a more Hamiltonian belief in the need for increased federal control over the country. This occurred particularly during the 1912 presidential campaign when he was forced to formulate a clearer program to compete with Roosevelt and his New Nationalism, a program inspired by New Hamiltonianism and promoted by Herbert Croly in progressive circles.[10] Wilson, much like Croly (with whom he had more in common than was originally believed), pursued Jeffersonian ends through Hamiltonian means.[11] But while it is acknowledged that Croly influenced TR in the creation of his New Nationalism,[12] Wilson's inspiration for the New Freedom can be traced back to his exchanges with Louis D. Brandeis. Previously involved, as we have seen, in La Follette's Progressive Republican movement with Crane, Brandeis had also refused to join the ranks of Roosevelt and later of the Progressive Party. As explained by William Diamond, Wilson had done little to develop his economic thought and his ideas on the topic were informed by his sense of morality and his political convictions rather than by any kind of in-depth or scholarly analysis.[13]

Wilson, Brandeis, and the Origins of the New Freedom

Before meeting Brandeis in Sea Girt, New Jersey on August 28, 1912, and despite having won the democratic nomination, Wilson had no concrete plan for handling his party's economic platform besides maintaining its traditionally antitariff stance (which will be further explained in this chapter).[14] However, Wilson's views did seem to align with those of the muckrakers in regard to industrial monopolization as a threat to the individual freedoms of small businesses and consumers. Though he praised the corporate world's potential for efficiency (ironically much like Theodore Roosevelt himself), Wilson remained attached to a moralistic view of the economy stemming from what Melvin Urofsky called "Wilson's stern Protestantism"[15] which prized hard labor, frugality, honesty, efficiency and their result, material success. In this sense, Wilson's view of the economy was, on a general level, compatible with that of Brandeis, La Follette, and many of their contemporaries. Yet neither of them endorsed a strict Darwinian concept of economy as they believed that reason, like morality, could serve to draw a line where the "fight for survival" ended in business. Having become Brandeis's loyal student, Wilson quickly adopted his antitrust arguments and waged war on Roosevelt's New Nationalism during his presidential campaign.[16] Moreover, Wilson slowly abandoned the Gilded Age's characteristic standpoint on gigantism and industrial integration (through natural elimination of inadequate businesses) as a way to increase efficiency. Instead, he began favoring Brandeis's point of view according to which expansion would eventually upset the harmony and lead to less fluid management in the conglomerate sector.[17] In the past, he had only condemned illicit mergers (that went against the 1890 Sherman Act), but he now began also denouncing "largeness" achieved by means of destruction of the competition and market control. His preference for the "small entrepreneur" and the influence Brandeis had over him were making him increasingly Jeffersonian. But paradoxically enough, these same fruitful meetings with Brandeis (arranged by Crane) also led him to elaborate a distinctly Hamiltonian plan which responded in a radical manner to the national problem of trusts.

Brandeis's influence on the perspective adopted by Wilson in regard to trusts and national economy in general can be seen most clearly during this meeting in Sea Girt on August 28. A *New York Times* press report released the following day made public the content of their conversation about potential "industrial reforms" to achieve greater "industrial freedom." A *New York Times* journalist reported Brandeis's overall impression of Wilson after this meeting. Brandeis, it would seem, commented: "I found Gov. Wilson a man capable of broad, constructive statesmanship, and I found him to be entirely in accord with my own views of what we need to do to accomplish industrial reform." Pressed by journalists to justify the changes in his political allegiance from the times of Taft to Wilson, Brandeis explained that he chose his party based on its candidate's ability to best pave the path toward industrial freedom.[18] Under

Wilson's possible leadership (and despite his reputation as a "rural Tory" which Roosevelt encouraged[19]), the Democratic Party was finally becoming a beacon of social progress. This had much to do with the man destined to lead it: "I am for Wilson because I found him in complete sympathy with my fundamental convictions, which are opposed to the convictions of Mr. Perkins and others of the new party [the Progressive Party, whose executive secretary was the progressive businessman George W. Perkins]." According to Brandeis and Wilson, the flaw in Roosevelt's program lay in his treatment of trusts, which rested "upon a fundamental basis of regulated monopoly." More importantly, if Brandeis and Wilson were planning on using the 1890 Sherman Act[20] to extend its reach through other bills, the New Nationalism's idea of regulating existing trusts would, according to Brandeis, make legal *de facto* that which was not legal *de jure*. With some biblical moralism, Brandeis and Wilson both denounced the propensity New Nationalists had for "trying to make evil good." Meanwhile, they themselves were trying to destroy this evil and reintroduce good "as a substitute." Brandeis explained this in more concrete terms: "We must undertake to regulate competition instead of monopoly." Moreover, he accused the New Nationalists of being at odds with their own ideal of progress by favoring what he called "industrial absolutism," claiming that "there can be no progress for the workingman under an absolutism." To Brandeis, industrial monopolization was a form of absolutism because it destroyed the opportunities of entrepreneurs and instead favored large, already established conglomerates. This idea was echoed in one of Wilson's campaign slogans in which he claimed that the New Freedom protected men "on the make" rather than those who were "already made." By pointing to trusts as the greatest cause of socioeconomic inequality, Wilson also heralded a new era of federal control over competition to serve as a bulwark against Roosevelt's belief in the (limited) regulation of trusts: "Monopoly is created by unregulated competition, by competition that overwhelms all other competitions, and the only way to enjoy industrial freedom is to destroy that condition." In short, Wilson wanted to get to the root of the problem by destroying the monopolies while Roosevelt, who believed that trusts were efficient and fostered progress, thought that regulating them would suffice. Wilson also represented a unique opportunity in Brandeis's eyes because, as a presidential candidate, he "[had] no obligations and [had] made no promises" and was thus free to make his own decisions without being swayed by any economic interests or lobbies.[21] Roosevelt and his program, on the other hand, seemed like slaves to the trusts, whose existence they implicitly allowed. Right from that first meeting in Sea

Girt, the Democratic Party's program distanced itself from the Progressive Party's. From a social and economic standpoint, the program took on a more interventionist approach due to Brandeis's contribution and his good relationship with Wilson.

The program's outline was still vague, however, since Brandeis had yet to clarify this idea of "regulated competition" which he and Wilson endorsed. About a month after Sea Girt, on September 27, 1912, right after winning the democratic nomination, Wilson asked Brandeis for an official and explicit report on the best way to regulate competition. It was then published by the progressive journalist Norman Hapgood (also friends with La Follette, Steffens, Brandeis, and Crane, all of whom had turned away from Roosevelt's New Nationalist leadership to support Wilson's campaign) in *Collier's Weekly*. A copy of the report was also sent to Wilson to help him prepare for the campaign which was now moving west. Its aim was to help the people clearly distinguish Wilson's campaign from Roosevelt's while suggesting tangible alternatives to the flaws in Roosevelt's program. Remarkably, Brandeis based his antitrust plan on the legislation he had largely written for La Follette in 1911,[22] and he did not hesitate to tailor it to the needs of Wilson's program. Brandeis's new plan was composed of three sections. The first section set out to rid the 1890 Sherman Act of its ambiguities by defining the parameters of an "unreasonable" monopolization based on the experience gathered in twenty-two years of antitrust legislation. The second section suggested a strengthening of the act's implementation by the courts in order to force the dissolution of illegal trusts. The third section recommended the creation of a commission to support public and legal agents in the administrative aspects of the Sherman Act. The similarities between this plan and the one put forward by the University of Wisconsin clique are striking. They demonstrate that though the divide between Wilson and Roosevelt's treatment of trusts seemed vast during the 1912 campaign, both plans were not so different when it came down to the details. Though their campaigns might have been similar enough that the journalist and biographer William Allen White called it a case of "tweedle-dum and tweedle-dee," Roosevelt and Wilson did differ from one another, and they perhaps owed this difference in part to their respective philosophies, styles, and temperaments. Regardless of these differences extensively discussed by historians, the importance of Brandeis's (and indirectly Crane's) role in the formulation of Wilson's economic program is indisputable. Brandeis was even aptly described by Melvin Urofsky as no less than the "architect of the New Freedom."[23]

Crane, Brandeis, and the Making of the Wilson Cabinet

While Brandeis was the "architect of the New Freedom" on an intellectual level, Crane was its financial and strategic architect through his work as an organizer, treasurer, and intermediary in the campaign. Surprisingly, despite Brandeis's increasingly close ties with the future president and his prominent role in putting together Wilson's economic platform, his influence in Wilson's circle waned soon after the creation of the presidential cabinet. It was in fact the establishment of the presidential administration—a perilous endeavor within a party with such strong geographical and ideological divisions—that decreased Brandeis's influence on Wilson. It did not, however, have any negative effect on Crane. At first, Wilson and his main unofficial advisor Edward M. House had considered both Charles Crane and Louis Brandeis as potential cabinet members. A preliminary list published in the *New York Herald* on February 22, 1913[24] shows that Brandeis was considered for the post of Secretary of Labor and Trade (which would eventually be split into two separate departments and given to William B. Wilson and William C. Redfield, respectively) before being suggested for the post of Attorney General. Crane, for his part, would have taken on the duties of Postmaster General or Secretary of War, though nothing suggests that he was formally offered either position. In fact, Crane himself made no mention of this in his memoirs, though to Wilson's great exasperation, newspapers at the time were rife with rumors concerning the cabinet's composition.[25] House's memoirs reveal that he was planning on backing Crane's nomination as Postmaster General[26] but suddenly decided against it. Pro-Wilson journalists, with Norman Hapgood at their head, generally supported the nomination of Brandeis and Crane to an official post. House, however, feared a cabinet that would include both of them and decided that "If I put in Crane I would leave out Brandeis, or vice-versa." The reasoning behind this decision is very telling about the public profile of both men. Crane, according to him and many others, belonged to the same radical Progressive movement as the rebellious La Follette. Including Crane would therefore mean "too much La Follette." The cabinet needed to be reorganized around the party's more conservative center, and Crane and Brandeis had both spent too much time in Republican circles—fairly progressive circles, but Republican circles nonetheless. House in fact revealed in his personal diary that he was becoming more and more concerned with not including too many ex-Republicans in Wilson's cabinet, deeming it "positively necessary to put in some rock-ribbed democrats." Yet even at this stage, it seems that Crane was being considered by House as he still included him in lists of prospective candidates. House wrote, for instance, that "it would not do to name more than McAdoo, Houston and Crane and perhaps Walter [Hines] Page." It is thus not his old political affiliations so much as his profile as a "radical" that undoubtedly explains Crane's absence from the final cabinet lineup.

As for Brandeis, though he was greeted with some disgruntlement by the public, many hoped that he would be chosen. Hapgood informed Wilson of this in a letter written on January 30, 1913, in which he refuted attacks against Brandeis in an attempt to convince the president-elect to ignore them. Ever since the legal battles he had waged against trusts on a state level, Brandeis had gained a reputation as an "inflexible, unreasonable, and discourteous" man, but Hapgood asserted that many of his past and present collaborators (La Follette, William Kent, Gifford and Amos Pinchot, Lincoln Steffens, etc.) still held him in high esteem. In any case, argued Hapgood, Brandeis was held in contempt precisely by those whose interests were pitted firmly against his, that is to say, Big Business. Still, Brandeis's chances were probably dashed by Cleveland Hoadley Dodge, one of Wilson's closest friends and an old classmate from Princeton (both men graduated in 1879), who also happened, like Crane, to be an important contributor during the 1912 and 1916 campaigns. Dodge convinced Wilson that there was never smoke without fire and that no truly honest man could flaunt such a polarizing public image without some justification,[27] essentially implying that Brandeis at least partially deserved this backlash against him. On the other hand, Dodge never stood against Crane's potential nomination, and this position was surprisingly taken up by House. As the main organizer of Wilson's cabinet, House, for his part, viewed Brandeis's nomination in a favorable light, as demonstrated by the preliminary lists he put together. In a letter to Wilson dated November 22, 1912, House mentioned having dined with Brandeis the previous night and reported being pleased with the encounter, writing that "His mind and mine are in accord concerning most of the questions that are now to the fore. He is more than a lawyer; he is a publicist and he has an unusual facility for lucid expression." House also recounted that Hapgood was present at this meeting and that they all later met at the thermal baths in Hot Springs, Arkansas at Charles Crane's invitation. There are no accounts of this meeting, though one can assume that it was held to discuss the cabinet and the lists of candidates that concerned them directly. Though he knew that it was impossible to build a cabinet that would please everyone, House ended up yielding to the argument that the controversial Brandeis would do more harm than good in Wilson's administration and the idea of his nomination was abandoned.[28] By January 17, 1913, the cabinet was almost fully formed according to House. Crane featured on the tentative list along with Bryan, McAdoo and perhaps Daniels, while Brandeis had already been ruled out.[29] In truth, Brandeis's greatest critics, like his friends, admired his numerous talents. In order to discredit him, they were forced to attack his personality as well as his supposedly insufficient "professional ethic." A true smear campaign, revealed in Wilson's correspondence, was led against his nomination.[30] This wave of panic coming primarily from Boston's business circles was based more on rumor than on fact as House's lists had remained private and Wilson was extremely quiet on the subject of the cabinet nominations. In fact, only Bryan's nomination for Secretary of State had been confirmed.

As for Charles Crane, he did all that was in his power to defend Brandeis and convince Wilson that Brandeis's circle of admirers went beyond the Democratic Party and that La Follette, a great Progressive Republican force in Congress, counted among them:

> La Follette has worked with Brandeis for several years and greatly prizes Brandeis's wisdom, patience, and sympathy. He also believes that Brandeis, more than anyone else in Washington and in authority, can pull together the Progressives—whether La Follette, Democratic or Bull Moose—and harmonize progressive legislation.[31]

In this sense, Crane also defended Brandeis because his presence could potentially serve to rally the stray Progressives who had been dispersed by the Roosevelt-La Follette affair. This unity remained a constant concern for him throughout his whole political career.

So many people from different backgrounds and with different allegiances defended Brandeis on the basis of his personal integrity that it was hard, retrospectively, not to doubt the legitimacy of his opponents' motivations.[32] Yet for Wilson and House, who under severe time constraints and with insufficient information had to quickly form an executive team made up of men who were both capable and "adequate," caution in choosing the cabinet members became paramount. Among those who might have feared Brandeis's appointment to the cabinet, namely, for his anti-segregationist views and his support of civil liberties, was the Secretary of the Navy and a notorious racist from North Carolina, Josephus Daniels. Before his nomination to Wilson's cabinet, he had supported the disfranchisement of black citizens in his home state.[33] Yet Daniels was still a Progressive in many ways and he viewed Brandeis's candidacy in a favorable light, calling him (not without prejudice to all the others) the "ablest Jew in America."[34] Daniels, who had also fought against the railroad trusts in the southern states, appreciated Brandeis's presumed antibusiness bias. He declared that Brandeis represented the primary reference on industrial matters for the whole Progressive movement and considered him a threat to the "exploiters." In fact, despite the divide between them, Daniels admitted to being "under his personal charm" and hoped, to no avail, that House and Wilson would name Brandeis to a cabinet post. Daniels even reported a comment, which he attributed to Wilson, hinting at the president's personal disappointment after realizing that he would have to abandon the idea of nominating Brandeis as Secretary of Commerce or Attorney General. In response to a letter from the Bostonian historian James Ford Rhodes, who wrote that "The best men here, men of affairs as well as lawyers, all of whom voted for you or President Taft, will regard the appointment of Mr. Brandeis as a member of your cabinet, should it be made, with profound regret,"[35] Wilson bitterly admonished Brandeis's detractors, the Massachusetts Democrats. Referring to Brandeis as the "greatest man" among the "best men" mentioned by Rhodes, Wilson declared: "They deny me the right to name their greatest man in the Cabinet, but they likewise deny New England a seat in the Cabinet."[36] And the president did not fail to carry out his "vengeance," promptly denying all departmental representation to New England. Yet Wilson was not truly satisfied until he appointed Brandeis as judge of the Federal Supreme Court, where the latter enjoyed a long career between 1916 and 1939.

Rumors about Charles Crane's possible nomination to a cabinet post, on the other hand, had not been met with as much concern among New England's business establishment. Few people took issue with the idea, besides perhaps a few republican journalists who viewed Crane's influence in Wilson's team as proof that it was under the control of a "bathtub trust."[37] However absurd this insinuation might be, Crane was, in 1912, getting ready to succeed his recently deceased father at the head of the Crane Company and taking on such a demanding position did not seem feasible.[38] Crane's independence of fortune, his new familial responsibilities at the Crane Company and his preference for discreet influence undoubtedly led him not to press Wilson for an official nomination. Though he was still included in House and Wilson's last cabinet lists (the president attempted as a last resort to name him Secretary of Finance), House, for unknown reasons, finally advised Wilson against including Crane in the final roster. As only justification, House commented tersely that "I did not believe Crane could fill the place satisfactorily." Instead, House suggested that Wilson offer him an external post, a piece of advice which Wilson later followed.[39]

We have thus far carefully considered the roles played by Charles Crane and Louis Brandeis, as well as their relationships with Wilson, in the elaboration of an original democratic and progressive program. The goal of this analysis was not only to explain Wilson's victory in the election but also to show a more "radical" side of Wilsonianism. At the very least, it aims to demonstrate the way in which Wilsonianism deviated from standard conservatism despite its usual depiction in most commentaries on Wilson. Crane and Brandeis, as the only two "surviving" La Follette supporters to have crossed directly over to Wilson's side in 1912, represented cards up the president's sleeve which contrasted with the Democratic Party's conservative and Bryanite elements. They had the potential to gradually unite the progressive forces, particularly progressive Republicans like Jane Addams and the Pinchot brothers who would come to support Wilson in 1916. As La Follette had once expressed to Crane, his strategy as a strong figure in the Senate was "to preserve and possibly strengthen our little band of Progressives in the Senate and House for the next Congress." La Follete wrote that "If Wilson is elected and proves Progressive they will be of real service to him in the event that the democrats fail him on progressive measures."[40] In truth, Crane and Wilson had more faith in the groups of Progressives dispersed among the three other parties than they did in the Democratic establishment.

While highlighting Wilsonianism's lesser known aspects, this analysis of the creation of Wilson's 1912 political platform and of its protagonists' Progressive Republican antecedents will help to situate Crane in the world of progressive reformism, particularly in light of his ties with La Follette and Brandeis. It will also serve to characterize him more clearly in relation to many crucial issues of his time, which will soon be carefully examined in the context of the implementation of Wilson's New Freedom program.

Wilson's New Freedom in Action and Crane's Progressivism: 1913–1916

Crane's crucial contribution during the campaign, and even during the cabinet's creation, had brought him closer to the president-elect and led him to become a first-rate confidant and advisor to Wilson. One event in particular provides striking evidence of his new place in national politics. Charles Crane was the first to be granted an audience with Wilson at the White House on March 5, 1913, the day following the new president's inauguration. Having been unable to attend the reception, Crane wished to personally congratulate the president and telephoned Wilson's personal secretary Joseph P. Tumulty in the early morning to enquire about the president's immediate availability. Tumulty replied that Wilson had just entered his office and had an hour to spare before his cabinet meeting. Strangely enough, Crane's conversation with a purportedly smiling and cordial Wilson concerned the importance of avoiding office seekers. A leader's greatest duty, according to a piece of Muslim wisdom Crane shared with Wilson that very morning, was to avoid wasting time on profiteers. Toward the end of the meeting, Wilson made Tumulty deliver a message aimed at these very profiteers discouraging them from coming to claim their "due" at the White House. According to Crane, this was the president's first official act. When he mentioned it in his memoirs, Crane seemed to look back on the event with great pride.[41]

Crane's later involvement in Woodrow Wilson's administration may not have been as direct as this first episode, but its results were much more significant in regard to the establishment of the New Freedom and the progressive reforms that ensued. Besides having become the president's close confidant, Crane also cultivated friendships with many other members of Wilson's entourage and even of the cabinet. His work behind the scenes became an important cog in the machinery of small politics in the Wilson Administration. Josephus Daniels described Crane as an "Unofficial tower of strength [...] a remarkable man to whom I became attached" and wrote that "He was a genuine progressive and had been a Progressive republican, but he was not of the Teddy type [...] his first interest was in supporting a real progressive for president."[42] It is thus as a pillar, a rallying point and an intermediary that Crane distinguished himself in Wilson's administration, working tirelessly for the benefit of the Progressive movement.

Our first example concerns the organization of the Department of Agriculture led by David Franklin Houston. In accordance with his resolution taken the day after his conversation with Crane about wasted time, Wilson began delegating executive initiatives to his secretaries. Houston was one of the first to seize this opportunity to assume full responsibility over his department. Hailing from North Carolina, Houston had been introduced to Wilson in 1911 by House. Like Wilson, Houston pursued an academic career before becoming president of the University of Texas from 1905 to 1908, then of the Washington University in St. Louis from 1908 to 1912, and then entering the world of politics. He had studied political science and economy rather than agriculture, and he was in fact transferred to the Treasury Department (much closer to his area of expertise) in 1920 to replace Wilson's son-in-law William G. McAdoo, who had resigned. However, the challenges of the rural world at the time were necessarily of an economic and political nature, and Houston led the Department of Agriculture accordingly.

The connection between Houston and Crane in light of the latter's memoirs is quite unclear. Why he dedicated such a large part of his story to the organization of the Department of Agriculture remains to be explained, especially when considering that he did not mention any of the departmental negotiations following Wilson's election. It is apparent, however, that Crane's disapproval of high protective tariffs had led him to adopt Houston's "agrarian" point of view, and his faith in a "Jeffersonian" model for society had already been confirmed by his support for Brandeis and Wilson. In his memoirs, Crane had nothing but praise for Houston's expert contribution to the Wilson Administration. He even mentioned a comment made by Wilson that, in order to avoid dealing with administrative details, he often asked Houston to summarize the issues discussed during cabinet meetings. Crane also added that Wilson was always on the best of terms with Houston. As was his habit, Crane had observed Houston's university career and professional occupations during his own philanthropic involvement in academic circles, but had only truly gotten to know Houston when he became part of Wilson's cabinet. Crane noted that Houston's values closely coincided with the president's and that both men shared, according to him, an "uncompromising" approach to public service. Such was Houston's administrative skill that he could take on any cabinet post, according to Crane.[43]

The first measures undertaken by the new Wilson Administration undeniably bore the stamp of both David F. Houston and, to a lesser extent, of Charles Crane. In their mind, the anticipated economic reforms had to involve projects directly relating to agriculture and concerning protective tariff reform and banking reform. Ever since the Civil War and the large scale industrialization that followed, high customs duties had had an extremely negative impact on Southern and Midwestern farmers. Without necessarily putting the foundations of protectionism into question from an intellectual perspective,[44] the Democrats had been demanding, since the end of Cleveland's time, the reduction of tariff barriers on the vast majority of products, both manufactured and agricultural. Wilson's tariff policy in the 1913 Underwood-Simmons Act, however, was developed from a much more authentic free-trade perspective than the preceding antitariff attempts in the times of Cleveland.[45] Having read the works of nineteenth century British economists and philosophers, Wilson, despite his "frontier" style patriotism[46] and contrary to most Americans of his time, had adopted a classic view of global trade. This was due to the fact that his ideas stemmed from the academic world rather than the political one.[47] Historians of the "corporate-liberal school" viewed the Underwood Act, along with the Revenue Act and the Sixteenth Amendment, as a step toward the corporatization of the federal government and evidence of its subjugation to Big Business interests. One must note, however, that the cut in protectionist taxes and the newly implemented income tax were supported primarily by rural politicians and constituents.[48] Like most rural Democrats, Wilson and Houston considered the trust issue to have arisen as a consequence of protectionist policies. The Underwood Act was therefore part of a larger program intended to restore competition as defined by Brandeis, House, Houston, and Crane. The latter, in light of his "self-made" family and business experience detailed in previous chapters, understood the monopolistic consequences of protectionism. His views aligned with theirs, and he wrote that he "had been an ardent devotee of the doctrine of the tariff for purpose of revenue only and had no sympathy whatever for protection in any form," this "despite [his] connection with [a] manufacturing house that had had to struggle up from a very small beginning."[49]

In their minds, customs duties were thus inevitably linked with the notion of economic competition and therefore with social possibilities and freedoms. As Wilson had explained to journalists a few days after his historic appearance before Congress on April 8 to promote the tariff reform: "I don't expect the tariff to effect an immediate reduction of the cost of living [...] [but] it will bring about a competitive situation which will make it impossible by arrangements of price to keep up the present artificial levels of cost."[50]

Even during his campaign for the democratic nomination, Wilson was advised by House to place more emphasis on the problem of tariffs in his speeches, noting that the candidate's rivals Oscar W. Underwood and Champ Clark were using it as a central issue in their race for the nomination, and House "was sure Wilson could do it better than they." House thus decided to introduce Wilson to his good friend Houston, who had a significant amount of knowledge to share on the subject. During a New York supper on December 7, 1911 involving a few democratic activists and organizers, House sat Houston next to Wilson so the latter could model his future speeches after the plan elaborated by Houston and overseen by House. For House, this planned meeting served the double purpose of shaping Wilson's opinion on tariffs while also ensuring Houston's enthusiastic support for Wilson's candidacy.[51] From this point onward, Wilson emerged on the national scale as the main opponent to republican protectionism and as an icon for rural Democrats who had, until then, been less inclined to support him.

Elected representatives from the South and the Midwest also proved to be crucial in the formulation and adoption of the Underwood Act, illustrating the agrarian features of the tariff reform. The lower customs taxes were intended not only to restore balance between Big Business and entrepreneurs and consumers but also, in a more general manner, to help the rural world get back on equal footing (in regard to economic competition) with powerful conglomerates, primarily in the northeastern states. In fact, Wilson insisted that farmers should from then on be considered businessmen in their own right and that they deserved to once again benefit from favorable economic conditions:

> Are not the farmers business men? [...] These smaller men, who constitute the body of the nation, so far as business is concerned, do not want to be left alone. They want to be set free of artificial trammels, of high prices, and of the restricted opportunities that have been created by our tariff-walled system of privilege.[52]

This system of privilege which tariff reform was meant to help destroy would become one of Wilson's greatest concerns in the coming electoral campaign. In his view, industrialization, urbanization, and mass immigration had disadvantaged the countryside. Politicians (especially Republicans) led by big industrial interests had constantly encouraged the development of cities and of their factories, to the detriment of the agricultural sector. "All the life blood of the country is being drained from the farms into the factories," he declared, and judged that "A great many of the morbid conditions of our society are due to this same excessive fostering of one side of national life at the expense of the other."[53] The key factor in this process was, according to Wilson, that protectionist measures had made agricultural surplus superfluous by artificially blocking exportation through customs taxes. This had in turn made farming and rural life less appealing to many Americans, thus draining the sector of its vitality and of its future prospects.

The 1913 Underwood-Simmons Act was therefore a decisive political decision reflecting the new legislative and executive Democratic order as well as the climate of reform which was prevalent in American society as a whole. The rehabilitation of the rural world did not end there, however, and tariffs would be reduced within a second set of reforms once again paradoxically situated between the Jeffersonian ideal to restore competition and the Hamiltonian ideal to increase federal intervention. The Department of Agriculture's reorganization within the Wilson Administration is another element rarely mentioned in Wilsonian historiography. It was in this context that David Franklin Houston, chosen as head of the Department of Agriculture, emerged as a beacon of Wilsonian reformism. However, his agricultural reform went largely unnoticed because his department hardly required any intervention on the president's part, as opposed to tariff, banking, and antitrust reforms, which had received greater attention from Wilson and therefore from the public. Wilson also appreciated Houston's pragmatic personality, his rigor, his discretion, and his knack for synthesis.[54] Breaking away from past federal policies that were limited to investing in technical and scientific research on agriculture, Houston focused on measures that offered direct federal help to farmers. This decision was shaped by his Jeffersonian perspective and by his Southern background which made him favor small entrepreneurs, as well as by his progressive and humanitarian understanding of federal power which led him away from "state rights" rhetoric.

In this regard, the 1914 Smith-Lever Act represented a major accomplishment in Houston's career. It served as an example of the manner in which progressive principles could be applied in the agricultural sector through the implementation of social measures formulated by experts working for the State. Like Wilson, Houston believed that rural life should "not only be profitable: it must also be comfortable, healthful, and attractive." To this end, Houston wanted better financing for farmers, a more efficient distribution of products, and agricultural education in rural areas. For instance, while reorganizing the federal Department of Agriculture, Houston based his reforms on the work of experts like those of the Land Grant colleges and on the legal assistance provided by Francis Gordon Caffey (Solicitor of the U.S. Department of Agriculture from 1913 to 1917). On a legislative level, Houston's reforms were promoted by the democratic representative of North Carolina, Asbury Francis Lever. He endorsed the same expertise and direct intervention-based methods as Houston, and Houston called him "one of the ablest and most satisfactory legislators it has been my fortune to know." Houston also called upon Walter Hines Page, who was friends with Wilson and Crane, to translate the plethora of scientific documents produced by academics and by the Department into a simpler and clearer language accessible to farmers. Houston understood, however, that handing out literature—no matter how cleverly worded—in the countryside would not suffice to adequately inform the farmers. He drew up a direct training program which led to the Agricultural Educational Extension Act, also called the Smith-Lever Act, signed on May 8, 1914. Made to resemble cooperatives, the program was implemented by the Land Grant colleges, which organized meetings in rural districts to converse with farmers about the agricultural modernization and rationalization initiatives carried out by Houston and his Department. The Department of Agriculture introduced many other measures aiming to ease the tensions caused by the dual federal and state jurisdiction, to minimize wasted resources, and to increase production and distribution efficiency. For instance, it became easier for farmers to obtain credit and they were offered better terms (on a seasonal rather than on a three-month basis). Roads were repaired after it was calculated that their poor condition was increasing the cost of transport.[55] No other secretary in Wilson's cabinet did a better job of embodying expertise, a characteristic trait of the president's administration, than Houston. Though he could have headed off any department due to his reputation as an experienced administrator, Houston accepted his post in the Department of Agriculture because, as Crane explained, "he had some great constructive measures in mind for the economic advancement of the farmer."[56]

The reforms concerning agriculture, the rural world, and other peripheral areas which Crane praised so highly could not, however, have reached such a magnitude if not for the fact that they intersected with the monetary and banking domains. If the president had already envisioned moderately lowering customs duties to encourage agricultural export before his 1912 electoral campaign, the idea of a banking reform had not crossed his mind even after his election.[57] When Wilson took office, America itself seemed to have already understood the necessity of banking and monetary reforms. Serious concerns were raised by the population after the 1912–1913 hearings and the publication of the Pujo Committee's report.[58] The report vehemently and rigorously denounced the hidden schemes linking J. P. Morgan, Wall Street, and a plethora of financial institutions, which together formed the "Money Trust." These events followed the creation of the Aldrich Plan, led by the Senator of Rhode Island (also author of the Payne-Aldrich Tariff Act in 1909) and father-in-law to John D. Rockefeller, Jr. The plan was proposed in 1912 by the National Monetary Commission, whose affiliation with the "Money Trust" made it seem even more like an all-powerful financial empire. In fact, the Aldrich Plan had largely been written by Paul M. Warburg, a prominent Jewish German-born banker who worked for Kuhn, Loeb & Co. This, in the eyes of the public and of most Democrats and Progressives, constituted definitive proof that a handful of manipulative bankers had control over the country's financial resources. In view of the Wilsonian program's demands, which were "to destroy monopoly and unleash the potential economic energies of the American People," and of the public's attitude toward trusts and toward the financial establishment, Wilson had to formulate a sound banking and monetary reform project which would not become a "Bryanistic cheap money scheme."[59] Countless complex steps and twists preceded the adoption of the Glass-Owen Bill in 1913, showing just how many different factions were clashing over its terms. But the adoption of the bill also demonstrates that people generally agreed on the necessity of establishing a central bank. Opinions diverged primarily concerning the government's precise role in banking matters. For the most part, representatives of Big Business, who had incidentally launched the debate about banking reform a few years prior,[60] deplored the idea of federal control over banking policies. "Bryanite" Progressives and Radicals, for their part, feared that this project could increase the power of the "Money Trust." Unlike the Aldrich Plan, the Federal Reserve System was designed in such a way as to remain under the cabinet's jurisdiction through the Treasury Department. It proposed a decentralized structure achieved by the creation of twelve regional banks which were selected by David F. Houston and William McAdoo (Secretary of the Treasury). These two men led an intense national campaign to both conscientiously pick the cities which would host one of the Reserve's banks and to explain and "sell" the bill in particularly hostile regions.[61] The Secretary of Agriculture had such an important role in passing a bill that primarily involved the Departments of Treasury and Trade because of his knowledge of economy as well as the faith Wilson had in the soundness of his judgment. But above all, Houston's involvement shows the importance of the agricultural issue in the financial and banking domains as well as its place in the Wilson Administration's economic policies. It was Houston who, during the endless negotiations and amendments to the project prepared by Virginia's representative Carter Glass and Oklahoma Senator Robert L. Owen, convinced Wilson to adopt a "decentralized" plan,[62] to the great displeasure of most of the Big Business's leading figures.[63] This version was most popular among Progressives and small Southern and especially Midwestern entrepreneurs. At the same time, a small amount of Midwestern bankers also supported this bill, either as it was written or with some minor amendments. Charles Crane himself, through his close ties with Wilson's cabinet, his position as a successful businessman, and his renown as a Progressive in Illinois and Wisconsin (La Follette's state), took charge of promoting the bill in this region:

> In Chicago, where I was held largely accountable for interpreting the Wilson administration, I was always sought out, when I came to town, to listen to an attack on the iniquity of the proposed Federal Reserve Act. The president of the largest bank in Chicago, at that time the First National Bank [it is question here of James Berwick Forgan, not to be confused with David R. Forgan who was the president of the National City Bank of Chicago and favorably disposed toward Wilson's Reserve plan], was particularly bitter. He predicted all kinds of disaster if the Act passed the Congress.[64]

Crane also tried to enhance the plan with the help of a few Chicago bankers like his friend Edmund D. Hulbert, president of the Chicago Merchants Loan and Trust Company (mistakenly called Merchants Bank and Trust Company in his memoirs). Crane even reported having suggested to Wilson that he consult Hulbert ("one of the few bankers in the country who was in sympathy with Wilson's purpose"[65]), which the president had then done at his request. Hulbert's main contribution, according to Crane, was to include the state banks in the Federal Reserve System through a subscription to the Reserve's supply of money and administrative eligibility for the Federal Reserve Board.[66] Crane himself presented Hulbert's proposal to Senator Owen who, after hearing the suggestions and Crane's account of his interactions with Chicago's bankers, expressed his desire to meet Hulbert in the following terms, recounted by Crane:

> As President Hulbert really understands the Act and as he is one of the few bankers in the United States who has made any constructive suggestion, I should be very glad to see what he has in mind [...]. Certainly these are most valuable suggestions and I think they should be included in the Act.

Though modest and discreet, Crane's influence on the adoption of the Federal Reserve Act was significant. He contributed to elaborating the most widely accepted plan by integrating the "constructive" criticism of those who, like Hulbert, supported Wilson's perspective. Crane's role in the Federal Reserve case was also delicate because he was tasked with "selling" the plan in an economically and politically crucial region that, however, tended to oppose any government attempts to implement a centralized banking system. There is no doubt that his renown in industry and commerce and his many connections in the Midwestern business community made him indispensable to banking reform at a national level. Previously in favor of the Aldrich Plan, at least where institutional centralization and monetary stabilization were concerned, Crane nevertheless criticized the plan's damaging ties with Wall Street: "Aldrich could never get the measure through because of Wall Street influence which had become a great public scandal during the Taft administration […] Wall Street really directed the affairs of the Government." Crane noted that Wilson had become president because he opposed this type of governance and it was now more than ever his duty to scrupulously preserve his independence from Big Business.[67]

The New Freedom's most unfriendly measure toward Big Business was not, however, the Federal Reserve Act but rather the new antitrust legislation with the establishment of the Federal Trade Commission and the passing of the Clayton Act in 1914. Yet Crane's memoirs and correspondence seem to show that he played no part in the New Freedom's most antimonopolistic policy (which also happened to most closely concern the business sector that had shaped him). This does not mean, however, that Crane was indifferent to Wilson's antitrust legislation or to industrial and labor issues as his writings would suggest. For one, this matter required specific technical skills which he did not possess. But further still, Crane was consistently sympathetic to the conditions of industrial workers, having himself, through the family business, taken part in their tasks and their fates.[68]

It therefore comes as no surprise that Crane's most direct contribution to the New Freedom concerned working conditions in the maritime sector, which was particularly outdated in this respect. Crane had had the opportunity of observing sailors' daily lives over the course of his numerous overseas voyages. This sympathy for their plight along with his political influence resulted in the drafting of the Seamen's Act, sponsored by La Follette and adopted on March 5, 1915. The act regulated the sailors' working and living conditions on American merchant vessels and was strongly promoted by Andrew Furuseth, president of the International Seamen's Union, who had been campaigning for this type of trade union reform for almost twenty years. Furuseth's great breakthrough came during a chance meeting with Charles Crane while the latter was visiting San Francisco in 1906. Crane, who enjoyed visiting the ports of the various places he travelled to, spotted an "old seadog" and came over to converse with him as was his habit. The conversation greatly impressed Crane, who from the character, intelligence and sincerity of the man he had just met "realized that [he] had got hold of a real personality."

Just as Wilson had sought to improve the quality of life of farmers in order to make their lifestyle more appealing and help preserve the country's agricultural wealth, Furuseth strove to give American sailors—and eventually foreign sailors—conditions at least equal to those of other American workers. Yet seamen were also subject to marine and commercial trusts and legal action had to be undertaken to establish their rights, otherwise sailors would desert their posts for more appealing ones on land. This, according to Furuseth, would inevitably lead to the decline of the American and Western navy. Feeling sympathy for Furuseth's reformist vision and admiration for the man himself, Crane promised to help him and introduced him to Senator La Follette, best placed among his friends to promote the signing of this prounion sailor's bill in Congress:

> It seemed to me that the best opportunity for advancing the Furuseth plan was for him to present it to Senator La Follette (at that time my relations with him were very close). I felt that it was the sort of thing that would interest him and if it did, he would push it with all his great energy and understanding of senatorial proceedings. I wrote to Senator La Follette and Andrew Furuseth went to see him.[69]

Though Crane did not record a precise date for this meeting, the comment in which he mentioned his closeness with La Follette helps us pinpoint the date of the event to somewhere around 1911 or 1912.

The bill had first been presented in 1912 under the presidency of Taft, who had vetoed it. Wilson's arrival to power represented a second chance for the bill which Crane was happy to seize. He set up a meeting between La Follette and Wilson on March 14, 1913 during which Wilson pledged his support and his "genuine interest in the Seaman's bill [*sic*]," which he considered "of capital consequence," though he was not familiar with its details before the meeting on March 14.[70] On June 26 of the same year, Andrew Furuseth himself wrote to Wilson to plead his case, to which the president replied: "I think I appreciate fully the deep significance of the seamen's cause, and you may be sure that I will espouse it in every way possible." Now ready to ratify the bill, Wilson approached William Hughes, Senator of New Jersey and in charge of the naval committee, to get his help in expediting the process. Wilson was most likely prompted to make haste by the sinking of a steamship, the *State of California*, off the coast of Alaska on August 17, 1913. Furuseth claimed that the deaths could have been prevented if the number of experienced sailors and lifeboats on board had been consistent with the parameters proposed in the Seamen's Bill.[71]

The bill elaborated by Furuseth and La Follette proposed among other things to decrease the severity of sailors' punishments and prison sentences, to improve the quality of their food rations, to reduce their weekly work hours, to regulate the payment of their wages, and to introduce standards for a safe minimum number of experienced sailors and lifeboats on board. These measures applied to America's merchant navy worldwide and also to ships docked in American ports regardless of their provenance or the origin of their crew. As such, it intersected with other countries' jurisdictions and even clashed with international trade treaties. On top of this, the United States had already taken part in an international conference on maritime safety in London. Early adoption of measures independently from other participants could have been negatively perceived by the international community. As a result, John Bassett Moore, an American lawyer and member of the Tribunal (Permanent Court of Arbitration) at The Hague, warned Wilson of the bill's international ramifications. Though it had already been ratified by the Senate on October 23, 1913, Wilson reluctantly agreed, writing that "much as I would like to see the bill passed and thoroughly as I believe in its principles and main provisions [...] it would not be wise to have it made law before we know the results of the conference which we, ourselves, called."[72]

The project was consequently dismantled by the House of Representatives and Wilson graciously sent Furuseth as a delegate to the conference in London in November of 1913. The latter resigned, however, and rejected the Convention for the safety of life at sea as it did not measure up to the standard of his own bill. Even though the forces favoring the La Follette Bill remained powerful in Congress, the Senate ratified the London Convention provided that the United States keep a right of abrogation. At the same time, based on advice given by Robert Lansing, assistant to the Secretary of State, and by William C. Redfield from the Department of Commerce, the Secretary of State William Jennings Bryan pressed Wilson to veto the Seamen's Bill. In response to this upsetting news, Furuseth wrote Wilson an eloquent plea on March 2 reminding him of his message to Congress in December of 1913 where he had insisted on the importance of adopting the bill after the Conference in London. Furuseth also reminded him of his often displayed sympathy toward the bill, namely, before the members of the American Federation of Labor. Furuseth then vigorously rejected the argument that the bill went against international treaties: "It is very difficult for us seamen, Mr. President, to understand how any nation can justly make any complaint because the

United States chooses to make the seaman a freeman [...] I therefore most earnestly urge you to approve this bill."

Wilson replied the next day that his interest in the Seamen's Bill was just as great as before, but that repudiating international treaties was out of the question. Wilson agreed with the State Department and with Bryan, who, though not opposed to the plan's underlying principles, demanded a veto and proposed to review the project after the war once international conditions became more clement.[73] La Follette skillfully suggested to Wilson that Congress grant the president a deferment giving him time to adjust to the stipulations of the foreign treaties.[74] Then, at Furuseth's request, Crane quickly telephoned Tumulty to ask that Wilson grant Furuseth and La Follette an audience. Tumulty allowed it immediately and even asked Crane: "Can't I just tell the President that you are for the bill?"[75] Tumulty evidently understood the power of Crane's opinions and trusted in his influence over the president. This desperate effort from all sides to obtain the president's signature was crowned with success as, with Crane's help, Furuseth and La Follette secured a private audience with Wilson the very next day, on March 4, 1915. A major reversal followed suit: the two men succeeded in reassuring the president regarding the bill's international effects and Wilson finally signed the Seamen's Act.

The meeting set up by Crane, along with La Follette's suggestion, allowed Wilson to keep his conscience clear while limiting the bill's potentially negative consequences as much as possible. He told his Secretary of War: "I debated the matter of signing the bill very earnestly indeed, weighing the arguments on both sides with a good deal of anxiety." As for his reasoning, Wilson explained that he "finally determined to sign it because it seemed the only chance to get something like justice done to a class of workmen who have been too much neglected by our laws."[76] Samuel Gompers of the American Federation of Labor quickly rejoiced in the signing of the Seamen's Act and Furuseth, thankful for what he called an "Emancipation Proclamation of the Seamen," sent Wilson this emphatic note:

> In signing the Seamen's bill you gave back to the seamen, so far as the United States can do it, the ownership of their own bodies, and thus wiped out the last bondage existing under the American flag [...] The moral greatness of this act will silence opposition in foreign countries and compel them to follow your lead.

Furuseth also recognized Crane's merit in supporting the bill since their first meeting in 1906 and using all of his influence to help it get passed. He in fact continued to seek Crane's support in regard to the newly ratified bill.[77] Despite this promising success, the bill was not implemented without several hurdles. As explained by Crane a few years later, an essentially republican bureaucracy disloyal to Wilson had caused difficulties in putting the bill into effect.[78]

Another example of Crane's exceptional sway over Wilson during his first presidential term was the event of Louis Brandeis's nomination to the Supreme Court in 1916. Brandeis and Crane were unique among Wilson's special advisors as they both bore the mark of their affiliation with La Follette and with the NPRL. They had actively participated in the creation of antitrust policies both at the state and municipal levels. With *Harper's* editor Norman Hapgood, they formed a sort of trio destined to extol the virtues of Wilson's program, which they had helped set apart from the Bull Moose platform in 1912. Not belonging to the Democratic machine, their main achievement was to help Wilsonianism converge with their progressive aspirations rather than with the Democratic traditions embodied by Bryan and the East Coast's political machine. Though neither was part of the cabinet, they both succeeded in pursuing their political and militant activities. The outrage caused by rumors of Brandeis's cabinet nomination in 1912, however, had alerted Crane to the amount of work required to secure a place for Brandeis in the Supreme Court, where a position had opened following the death of Justice Joseph R. Lamar. Well ahead of the action, Crane wrote Wilson a letter to ensure that the latter would consider Brandeis's candidacy despite the lobby effort that had risen up against him:

> Outside of a small and hopelessly irreconcilable group in Boston—to which Dr Eliot does not belong—I believe the appointment of Mr Brandeis would be a most popular one throughout the United States and give the best possible encouragement to the progressives both inside and outside of the party.[79]

In Crane's mind, the presence of a Progressive figure like Brandeis in the Supreme Court represented a considerable asset for the Progressive movement and for the coalition of Progressives around the country even if it meant alienating a few Bostonian reactionaries, Democrats and Republicans. Wilson's reelection campaign, which would soon be starting, also called for the revival of the country's progressive forces, severely shaken by the schism between La Follette and Roosevelt. Emboldened by the success of his first term, Wilson could now rightly stand before the country as a progressive champion. Nominating Brandeis to a Supreme Court position was another step toward affirming the progressive character of Wilson's administration while correcting his "failure" to give Brandeis an official position in 1912. Charles Eliot, for his part, had always been a valuable supporter given his good reputation both in conservative and progressive circles. Crane himself kept Eliot up to date on attacks against Brandeis, writing to him even while Eliot was vacationing in Bermuda (February 16, 1916), doubtless to encourage him to publicly join the debate.

Another member of the NPRL, William Kent, also implored Wilson to appoint Brandeis to such an important post. "The Supreme Court of the United States is the real living Constitution," he argued, "and therefore [I] see clearly the necessity of having on the bench men with a vision of improving average human conditions, which is the end and the aim of democracy."

As if to give more weight to his claims, Kent added that La Follette and Charles Crane shared his good opinion of Brandeis.[80] Amos Pinchot, who had previously abandoned La Follette in favor of TR, also joined the wave of support for Brandeis, describing his possible nomination as "extremely valuable" to Wilson's progressive program, "this fight of education and constructive statesmanship." That same day, Wilson sent the Senate a message indicating that he had chosen Louis Brandeis for Supreme Court judge.[81] Norman Hapgood and Amos Pinchot, among others, applauded this decision and hoped for the Senate's approval. When it came, Pinchot, who had been bombarded with all manner of criticism for supporting Brandeis, humorously exclaimed that "the appointment proves the existence of a personal God."[82] Despite these utterances of joy, controversy was unavoidable in conservative circles and Crane was forced to defend the nomination. On the other hand, Cleveland H. Dodge, who had opposed Brandeis in 1912, became one of his supporters. Crane gave Wilson the good news, writing in a letter that "Your friend Cleveland Dodge is demonstrating his loyalty and devotion to you and your Administration by defending in his usual vigorous way the nomination of Brandeis."[83] In a letter to his daughter Josephine, Crane's remarks seem to indicate that he rather enjoyed the turmoil caused by Brandeis's nomination and rejoiced in the defeat of the dark forces wielded by Big Business.[84] The wave of opposition to Brandeis, in his mind, constituted clear proof that the Republican Party was still under "the firm grip [of] the invisible government," the special interests. As in 1912, discontent came largely from conservative circles in Boston where, according to Crane, Brandeis was criticized both on the basis of his social thought and of is Jewish background: "Boston made a racial and social matter of it and the feeling was very bitter."[85]

Aside from Wilson's two successful presidential campaigns, Brandeis's nomination represented for Crane the epitome of his work for the benefit of the New Freedom. Brandeis served twenty-two years in the Supreme Court but also distinguished himself as a prominent Zionist activist and organizer, which would eventually put some distance between him and Crane.

The 1916 presidential campaign kept Crane particularly busy. The president's reelection was a crucial step for the Progressive movement in the United States and Crane made good use of his role and influence as an intermediary and rallying force to consolidate his position as Wilson's esteemed special advisor. Personally involved in the president's reelection and viewing the Progressive movement's destiny as a millenarian imperative especially in the context of a world war that seemed to be taking on increasingly apocalyptic proportions, Crane constantly prayed for Wilson to be granted a second term by the American people.[86] He also naturally followed the course toward greater involvement in international affairs taken by Wilson since the start of World War I. He had in fact acted on his interest in foreign policy well before Wilson had begun to do so and before Brandeis became involved in the Zionist movement. Though the New Freedom had initially been conceived for the purpose of implementing a specific set of domestic reforms, Wilson's second term, paradoxically earned through his "neutrality" stance, gave Crane the opportunity to put his skills and passion for international affairs to good use as part of Wilsonian internationalism. Wilson had good reason to be grateful for these services: no envoy had ever been more lastingly loyal, more enthusiastic or closer to embodying and promoting Wilson's ideals than Charles Crane.

Notes

1. A good description of Wilson's party discipline (especially in Congress) can be found in James M. Burns, *The Workshop of Democracy* (NY: Vintage Books, 1985), 385–9. See also Kendrick Clements's point of view: *The Presidency of Woodrow Wilson* (Lawrence (KA): University Press of Kansas, 1992), 7–14, 31–52.
2. For a detailed analysis of Wilson's academic work, refer to Niels Aage Thorsen, *The Political Thought of Woodrow Wilson, 1875–1910* (Princeton (NJ): Princeton University Press, 1988). Chapter 3 directly touches on *Congressional Government*, 41–67.
3. Woodrow Wilson, "Congressional Government" in the *Papers of Woodrow Wilson (PWW)*, Vol. 1, 572.
4. R. Hofstadter, *Anti-Intellectualism in American Life*, 209. Hofstadter adds that "Wilson thought of big business, vested interests, and experts as a solid combine that could be beaten only by returning government to 'the people.'"
5. Quoted from Hofstadter, *Anti-Intellectualism in American Life*, 209–10.

6. The journalist Herbert Croly once said that with Wilson, "even the most concrete things seem like abstractions." See H. Croly, "Presidential Complacency," *New Republic*, Vol. 2, March 27, 1915.
7. Woodrow Wilson, "Democracy and Efficiency," *PWW*, Vol. 12, 8–12.
8. See Hofstadter, *Anti-Intellectualism*, 208: "In his tastes, his ideas, and his reading he was a somewhat parochial Southern version of a Victorian gentleman, his mind pleasantly fixed in the era just before the United States became a complex and modern society [...] he had just missed exposure to the remarkable *fin de siècle* sunburst of critical thought whose impact carried over into the Progressive Era." One can also read, in *The American Political Tradition*: "At heart he was a sentimental traditionalist [...] he was essentially a spokesman of the past," 313.
9. For more information on the influence of Ely and more generally of the German school on Wilson's thought, see Niels Aage Thorsen, *The Political Thought of Woodrow Wilson*, 68–88. Ely, though at the forefront of progressive theory and expertization, remained—like Wilson—a promoter of nineteenth century Protestant civic morality. His style, as demonstrated by David W. Noble, was more often reminiscent of a social gospeller than a "modern" technocrat. See D. W. Noble, *The Paradox of Progressive Thought* (University of Minnesota Press, 1958), 171–3.
10. There is a vast amount of literature on this subject but we owe all of it to Arthur S. Link's classic *Woodrow Wilson and the Progressive Era, 1910–1917*, 18–24. In *The Age of Reform*, Hofstadter points out Wilson's hesitation in regard to the means necessary to "restore competition" and links his antitrust mindset with a populist mistrust of industrial corporatism, like that which was displayed by Bryan (246–7). Many historians besides Hofstadter compared Roosevelt and Wilson in terms of personality as well as political philosophy. For a comparative biography of the two rivals, see John Milton Cooper, *The Warrior and the Priest. Woodrow Wilson and Theodore Roosevelt* (Cambridge: Harvard University Press, 1983).
11. James M. Burns, *The Workshop of Democracy From the Emancipation Proclamation to the New Deal*. See Chapter 11 "The New Freedom," 393. Burns remarks that Croly, though he deplored Hamilton's elitist "bias," still endorsed his centralizing nationalism and demanded the advent of a strong presidential leadership, which, in 1912, could just as well have been provided by Roosevelt as Wilson. In this regard, it is significant that his view of democratic leadership, this elitist "bias," harbors, besides a strong scientistic presumption, a hint of mysticism that David W. Noble called the "religion of democracy" ("The New Republic and the Idea of Progress, 1914–1920," *The Mississippi Valley Historical Review*, 38, 3, (1951): 390–1). In *Crossroads of Liberalism. Croly, Weyl, Lippmann and the Progressive Era, 1900–1925* (Oxford: Oxford University Press, 1961, 15–25) Charles Forcey underscores the positivist influences (particularly Auguste Comte) of Croly to explain his "utopian" understanding of republicanism. For diverging views of Croly's progressivism, see David K. Nichols, "The Promise of Progressivism: Herbert Croly and the Progressive Rejection of Individual Rights," *Publius*, 17, 2 (1987): 27–39; and Kevin C. O'Leary, "Herbert Croly and Progressive Democracy," *Polity*, 26, 4 (1994): 533–52.
12. Edward A. Stettner, *Shaping Modern Liberalism. Herbert Croly and Progressive Thought* (Lawrence: University Press of Kansas, 1993), 74–6. Also see Forcey, *Crossroads of Liberalism*,

127–30, which qualifies this influence and describes it, at most, as an interaction rather than a direct causality.

13. William Diamond, *The Economic Thought of Woodrow Wilson* (Baltimore: Johns Hopkins University Press, 1966 [c. 1943]), 50–1. An analysis of Wilson's studies and career shows his aversion to mathematics and "exact" sciences, which would explain why he never wrote anything on economy. His readings sometimes covered economic topics and some comments seem to show a faith in the basic principles as long as they were founded on philosophical considerations. Wilson seemed to despise the mathematics of economy, where gain and private interest came above everything according to the theories of Mill and Ricardo, for example, but admired the more distinguished theses of Smith, Bagehot, and Burke. Also see Arthur S. Link, *Wilson: The Road to the White House*, 23–6.
14. In fact, the first correspondence between Wilson and Brandeis did not concern trusts, though they would quickly become a central aspect of their exchanges, but rather the issue of lowering customs duties previously suggested by Wilson, to which Brandeis was favorable. *PWW*, Vol. 24, 1 August 1912, 580.
15. Melvin Urofsky, *Louis Brandeis and the Progressive Tradition* (Boston: Little Brown & Co., 1981), 69.
16. *PWW*, Vol. 25, September 2, 1912, 69–79. During a speech made in Buffalo a few days after his meeting with Brandeis at Sea Girt, Wilson publicly expressed for the first time a recurring argument in the presidential campaign to the effect that Roosevelt's presidency had fostered the current monopolistic conditions and that his Bull Moose platform was inadequate because it implicitly allowed the existence of trusts.
17. Ironically, only a few weeks before the meeting of August 28, Wilson declared in his democratic nomination speech in Sea Girt on August 7, 1912 that "Big business is not dangerous because it is big, but because its bigness is an unwholesome inflation created by privileges and exemptions [...]" Ray S. Baker and William E. Dodd, ed., *Public Papers of Woodrow Wilson*, Vol. 2, *College and State* (New York, Harper, 1925–26), 464. But though he still made a distinction between large businesses and trusts, under Brandeis's influence, Wilson began considering the size of trusts as a factor of inefficiency: "the trusts are not efficient [...] They passed the point of efficiency. Their object is not efficiency [...] Their object is monopoly, is the control of the market, is the shutting out by any means, fair or foul, of competition in order that they may control the product," *PWW*, Vol. 25, September 17, 1912, 152–3.
18. *PWW*, Vol. 25, August 28, 1912, 57.
19. William Harbaugh, *The Life and Times of Theodore Roosevelt* (NY: Oxford University Press, 1975 [c.1961]), 419. Also see John M. Cooper, *The Warrior and the Priest. Woodrow Wilson and Theodore Roosevelt*, 191, 208, 212.
20. In regard to the Sherman Act, Wilson corrected the journalists' question when they asked how he was planning on strengthening the 1890 Act and he answered: "Not so much to strengthen it as to supplement it. We want a law that will assist people in their business instead of tying them up." *PWW*, Vol. 25, August 28, 1912, 58.
21. This seemingly tendentious point was nevertheless corroborated by Arthur S. Link in *Woodrow Wilson and the Progressive Era, 1910–1917*, 24, who considers it as one of the main historic significances of Woodrow Wilson's election in 1912.

22. *PWW*, Vol. 25, September 30, 1912, 286–304. Brandeis was referring to the La Follette-Stanley Anti-Trust bill, presented on August 19, 1911. The other project sponsored by La Follette, the Federal Commission bill, received contributions from the professors at the University of Wisconsin, among them Charles McCarthy, author of *The Wisconsin Idea*, who were at the root of the Progressive Republican position on the matter of trusts.
23. Melvin I. Urofsky, *Louis D. Brandeis and the Progressive Tradition*, 68–86.
24. Article reproduced in Charles Seymour, ed., *Intimate Papers of Colonel House*, Vol. 1 (London: Ernest Benn, 1928), 113.
25. *PWW*, vol. 27, 31 January, 3 February 1913, 93–6.
26. *PWW*, Vol. 27, January 8, 1913, 23. Taken from his memoirs, this statement shows House's interest in Crane's candidacy for a cabinet post: "[Crane] was discussed and it is my purpose to suggest him for Postmaster General."
27. *PWW*, Vol. 27, January 10, 17, 30, 1913, 27, 61, 92–93.
28. Charles Seymour, ed., *House Papers*, Vol. 1, 91–2. Also see Kendrick Clements, *The Presidency of Woodrow Wilson*, 33. For a list of cabinet members and the specific reasons for their nominations, see Arthur. S. Link, *Woodrow Wilson and the Progressive Era, 1910–1917*, 25–33. The first major reform started by Wilson in 1913 related to customs duties, and getting the support of as many Democrats as possible was crucial. However, it was necessary to strike a balance between support from the Democrats and a wider support from Republicans and from the business community. William J. Bryan, appointed Secretary of State, already irritated a lot of people because of his weight inside the party and his role in Wilson's nomination in 1912. Adding Brandeis to the mix would certainly have been too much.
29. *PWW*, Vol. 27, January 17, 1913, 62.
30. Alpheus T. Mason, *Brandeis: A Free Man's Life*, 386–97.
31. *PWW*, "CRC to WW," Vol. 27, February 10, 13, 1913, 107–8.
32. It appears, further, that Wilson was conscious of the "interested" nature of Brandeis's opponents, as shown by his request to a certain Arthur W. Tedcastle, one of his Boston acquaintances, to gather some "disinterested" opinions on the controversial lawyer by looking "outside of that circle" (the circle being that of his enemies in Massachusetts). *PWW*, Vol. 27, January 3, 1913, 7–8.
33. Arthur S. Link, *Wilson. The Road to the White House*, 501. Organizer of Wilson's campaign in North Carolina and editor of the Raleigh *News and Observer*, Daniels wrote in a column on October 1, 1912: "We abhor a northern policy of catering to Negroes politically just as we abhor a northern policy of racial equality [...] The South is solidly Democratic because of the realization that the subjection of the negro, politically, and the separation of the negro, socially, are paramount to all other considerations in the South." This clearly racist statement had an equally clear racist purpose: to ensure the Southern vote. See Henry. Blumenthal, "Woodrow Wilson and the Race Question," *The Journal of Negro History*, 48, 1 (1963): 5. Once the campaign finished and his Department obtained, Daniels was at the forefront of segregation practiced in the federal government. See Kathleen L. Wolgemuth, "Woodrow Wilson and Federal Segregation," *The Journal of Negro History*, 44, 2 (1959): 158–73.

34. There remain very few documented traces of the impact anti-Semitic feelings had in the smear campaign led against Brandeis based on his Jewish background. Though one can imagine that this fact upset many people at the time, including a fair amount of democrats, arguments against Brandeis did not openly call out his Jewish heritage but rather his radical opposition to Big Business. What is more, he himself seemed to have been very discreet on the matter, making very little mention, at least at the time, of his ethnic background. As a nonpracticing Jew, Brandeis only discovered an interest in the Jewish cause and began experiencing Zionist patriotism around 1913–1914, after Wilson's cabinet was formed. In fact, the turmoil roused by the rumors and then by the reality of his Supreme Court nomination led to a much greater resistance based on his new position in the Zionist movement and his Jewish background than his previous attempt at obtaining a cabinet post had. See Melvin Urofsky, *Louis D. Brandeis and the Progressive Tradition*, 75; and Alpheus T. Mason, *Brandeis: A Free Man's Life*, 387–8.
35. *James Ford Rhodes Papers*, "Correspondence, 1908–1917," Card 2, SH 1551 E, Massachusetts Historical Society, 218. (Incomplete letter, not included in the *Wilson Papers*).
36. Josephus Daniels, *The Wilson Era*, Vol. 1, *The Years of Peace, 1910–1917*, 542–3.
37. David Hapgood, *Charles R. Crane. The Man Who Bet on People*, 42. "Bathtub trust" as a reference to the Crane Plumbing Company was meant to be a rude label to undermine members of Wilson's entourage, who were accusing Roosevelt and Taft of being the businessmen's pawns.
38. *Crane Papers*, "Memoirs," 120–1.
39. *PWW*, Vol. 27, January 24, 1913, 70–1.
40. *Crane Papers*, "La Follette to CRC," August 21, 1912.
41. *Crane Papers*, "Memoirs," 153–4. See also *PWW*, Vol. 27, March 5, 1913, 153. The issue of job seekers was also discussed during the cabinet's first meeting. According to the Secretary of Agriculture Houston, Wilson had from the very beginning been firm in his view that positions should be granted based on merit, much to the chagrin of those used to the system of partisan appointments like Bryan. Wilson also tasked his cabinet members with hiring and organizing the posts, thus giving them greater power in front of Congress and of the public. See David F. Houston, *Eight Years with Wilson's Cabinet, 1913 to 1920*, Vol. 1 (Garden City: Doubleday, 1926), 40–1.
42. Josephus Daniels, *The Wilson Era*, 87.
43. *Crane Papers*, "Memoirs," 130, 155.
44. In this regard, though a large part of the historiography continues to view American protectionists and "liberals" as ideological opposites, it is worthwhile to note the interpretation of Judith Goldstein, *Ideas, Interests, and American Trade Policy* (Ithaca: Cornell University Press, 1993), 92, 128–9. She considers, rather, the existence of two traditions based on latent attitudes of hostility toward the outside world, a type of isolation and mercantilist self-sufficiency belonging to another age: "Although tariff differences were central to each party's identity, 19s parties still argued within one general economic paradigm [...] free trade was a manifestation of British Imperialism." More often than not, therefore, members of Congress defended one opinion or the other based on the interests of the groups they represented. The debate, so to speak, followed geographical demarcations and

their corresponding economies without necessarily considering the liberal option in and of itself.

45. David A. Lake, *Power, Protection and Free Trade* (Ithaca: Cornell University Press, 1988), 148–9. Lake, unlike Judith Goldstein, saw the Underwood Act as a clear break in an era ruled by protectionism. This interpretation is quite classic, but its premise is interesting because it explains America's tariff situation through its reaction to British trade policy. The relative trade decline in Great Britain and its transition from a hegemonic free trade position to a more prudent "opportunistic" stance at the turn of the twentieth century might have led the United States to liberalize their market in order to avoid the retaliatory tariffs of other European countries.
46. Two of Wilson's academic texts particularly illustrate his patriotic thought: *Division and Reunion, 1829–1889* (New York: Longmans-Green, 1893, 3–4); and "The Course of American History," *PWW*, Vol. 9, 262–7. See the analysis of N. A. Thorsen, *The Political Thought of Woodrow Wilson, 1875–1910*.
47. Goldstein also explains that the free trade theses popular at the end of the nineteenth century had not managed to spread beyond academic circles. This explained why most of the epoch's politicians, as well as the general public, were not familiar with classical economic theory (86–8).
48. Incidentally, Wilson's Democratic Party line was followed almost to the letter since only five democratic representatives and two senators (whose loss was made up for by two Republicans, including La Follette) dared to oppose the bill. Wilson's skill in obtaining bipartisan support while also controlling his party's uncooperative members was decisive in this regard. See J. Goldstein, 119.
49. *Crane Papers*, "Memoirs," 130. Crane implicitly understood that lowering customs duties would lower government revenue, and Wilson had come to the same realization when he proposed and managed to pass the bill on tariffs. Still, one must not lose sight of the fact that debates on this topic went back to 1909, that it had already garnered a certain consensus at the national scale and that the Sixteenth Amendment in 1913 allowing the implementation of such a bill had already been adopted before Wilson's inauguration. See John D. Buenker, *The Income Tax and the Progressive Era* (New York: Garland, 1985), 57–8.
50. *PWW*, Vol. 27, April 14, 1913, 302.
51. Seymour, ed., *House Papers*, Vol. 1, 47.
52. *PWW*, Vol. 23, December 24, 1911, 610. This excerpt is taken from a conversation between Wilson and a journalist for the New York *World*. Wilson was still Governor of New Jersey at the time and would soon be competing for the democratic nomination.
53. *PWW*, Vol. 23, January 3, 1912, 641–2. The excerpt comes from a speech specifically on the topic of tariffs to the National Democratic Club in New York given by Wilson in order to help standardize urban Democrats' opinions on the subject and to ensure cooperation in his party.
54. *PWW*, Vol. 29, February 18, 1914, 270.
55. For a description of reforms made during the Wilson Era by the Department of Agriculture, see David F. Houston, *Eight Years with Wilson's Cabinet, 1913 to 1920*. Houston's work in the Department of Agriculture remains a rather neglected aspect of Wilsonianism's historiography, often seeming less significant than other major themes like the reform of

protectionism, the banking reform or Wilsonian diplomacy. Link's work was long seen as a definitive authority on Wilson given that he had "inherited" and edited the massive amount of documentation which would become the *Wilson Papers*. The second (*The New Freedom*) of the three *Wilson* volumes (1956) concerns Wilson's first mandate until the start of his neutrality and describes the most reform-oriented part of his presidency. Little mention is made of Houston's role or of the importance of agricultural reforms. Yet Kendrick A. Clements, taking advantage of the completion of the *Wilson Papers* in 1993, published a new study of Wilson's presidency (*The Presidency of Woodrow Wilson*) and showed that Houston was more important than previously thought in the administration's reform work. Let us briefly note the interpretation provided by Hofstadter, who viewed Wilsonianism as a current turned toward the old Southern order and thus open in principle to paying attention to rural demands, though still in a more or less progressive capacity. Let us also note the New Left's interpretation (from G. Kolko and J. Weinstein to Martin J. Sklar), which considers tariff reform as part of the corporatization of the economy and of the federal government. Nevertheless, neither interpretation paid much attention to the contributions made by Houston and by the Department of Agriculture to Wilson's reformism. Let us, however, mention the analysis made by Elizabeth Sanders in "Farmers and the State in the Progressive Era" in *The Progressive Era in the USA: 1890–1921*, ed. Kristopher Allerfeldt (Burlington: Ashgate, 2007), 41–65. Sanders emphasizes the importance of the agrarian movement in the process of nationalization and in the implementation of measures benefiting farmers. She qualifies most interpretations that limit progressivism to the urban sphere and insists on the role played by "peripheral" regions and by rural demands, which were addressed by the Wilson Administration.

56. *Crane Papers*, "Memoirs," 156.
57. Arthur S. Link, *Wilson: The New Freedom*, 201–2. As a matter of fact, it seems that on the eve of the campaign for the democratic nomination, around December of 1911, Wilson's stance toward the Aldrich Plan was as hostile as Bryan's. House believed both men to be wrong and promised to convert them. See Seymour, *House Papers*, Vol. 1, 50.
58. Led by Louisiana's Representative Arsène Pujo, the committee was formed during Taft's presidency in 1912 and gave a detailed account, including a public and direct interrogation of J.P. Morgan himself, about how the "Money trust" artificially restricted credit in order to limit economic competition. For the Pujo Committee's full report, see Herman E. Krooss, ed., *A Documentary History of Banking and Currency in the United States*, Vol. 3 (New York: Chelsea House, 1969), 2107–95.
59. Link, Arthur S. *Wilson: The New Freedom*, 202. Houston, in his memoirs, deplored Bryan's incompetence in regard to economic and banking issues. Though he did not understand much about the Federal Reserve Act (even after Houston's patient explanation about the rural credit linked with the Reserve's policies), he continued to oppose what he considered to be a suspicious idea! (*Eight Years with Wilson's Cabinet*, 81–5). Bryan's antibanking attitude was also described by Crane in his memoirs (p. 159) and by Joseph P. Tumulty, who insisted on the importance of avoiding another division in the Democratic Party like the one in 1896 caused by differing opinions on the gold standard issue, and warned that Bryan should be treated with "watchful and careful prevision." Despite being opposed to certain aspects of the Reserve Act, Bryan "moved forward with the President in the

most generous fashion and remained with him [...]" Joseph P. Tumulty, *Woodrow Wilson as I Know Him* (New York: Doubleday, 1921), 175–6. This does, however, seem like a watered-down version of the events, especially when compared to an account by Samuel Untermyer, the democratic delegate to New York and a member of the Pujo Committee, who described Bryan's radical attitude and his readiness to defiantly break away from the administration. See Link, *Wilson: The New Freedom*, 207.

60. James Livingston, *Origins of the Federal Reserve System. Money, Class, and Corporate Capitalism, 1890–1913* (Ithaca: Cornell University Press, 1986), 188–212.
61. David F. Houston, *Eight Years with Wilson's Cabinet*, 101–3. The trip began on January 18, 1913 and lasted one month. The distribution of Reserve bank branches was based on complex criteria like the lines of communication, commercial relations, banking habits, and economic conditions of the cities and regions under consideration. Houston affirmed that this "competition" to host a Reserve bank helped raise people's enthusiasm for the bill because it allowed regions that were generally neglected in the economic processes to participate.
62. *Crane Papers*, "Memoirs," 156.
63. Arthur S. Link, *Wilson: The New Freedom*, 218, 229.
64. *Crane Papers*, "Memoirs," 157. In regard to David R. Forgan's support, see Link, *Wilson: The New Freedom*, 205, 224.
65. *Crane Papers*, "Memoirs," 157. This statement made by Crane seems to have proven true later on. See Link, *Wilson: The New Freedom*, 224.
66. No other source allows us to corroborate Crane's statement. However, by comparing the May 1913 Owen Bill and the Glass Bill from June 5, 1913 one can note that the addition mentioned by Crane matches the chronology described in his memoirs. See Herman E. Krooss, ed. *A Documentary History of Banking and Currency in the United States*, Vol. 3, 2196–229. Hulbert's provision was added to the final bill on December 23, 1913 (Vol. 4, 2447).
67. *Crane Papers*, "Memoirs," 156–8.
68. *Crane Papers*, "Memoirs," 4–5. Such were Crane's memories of his years at the Crane Company: "The years among the workmen, when I myself was a workman, were a real education. In the later conduct of the business I could understand and sympathize with the workman's point of view and could talk with him in his own language."
69. *Crane Papers*, "Memoirs," 138–40.
70. *PWW*, "Wilson to Rudolph Spreckels," Vol. 27, March 15, 1913, 188.
71. *PWW*, Vol. 28, June 26, June 30, and August 22, 1913, 15–16, 204. Hughes responded favorably, telling Wilson that he would mark it down in his calendar and attend to the task as soon as possible. See p. 245.
72. *PWW*, Vol. 28, October 16 and 20, 1913, 412–3, 420.
73. *PWW*, "Bryan to Wilson" and "Furuseth to Wilson," Vol. 32, March 1, 1915, 302–5.
74. *PWW*, "La Follette to Wilson," Vol. 32, March 3, 1915, 312.
75. *Crane Papers*, "Memoirs," 160. Crane's memoirs might be slightly inaccurate where the date of this conference is concerned. Crane recollected having organized the meeting shortly after the start of Wilson's presidency, whereas the Wilson papers indicate that it took place between March 1 and 4, 1915, that is to say between Bryan's letter and the

signing of the Seamen's Act. We can make an allowance for the fact that Crane's memoirs might not have been completely accurate when it came to factual information, particularly as they were written many years after the described events. Still, Crane's account remains highly plausible given his overall role in the implementation of the Seamen's Act.

76. *PWW*, "Wilson to Newton D. Baker," Vol. 32, March 5, 1915, 324.
77. *Crane Papers*, "Andrew Furuseth to Charles Crane," January 27, 1916.
78. *Crane Papers*, "CRC to Norman Hapgood," December 23, 1920.
79. *PWW*, "Crane to Wilson," Vol. 35, January 27, 1916, 535.
80. *PWW*, "William Kent to Wilson," Vol. 36, January 27, 1916, 19–20. However, Wilson only received this letter after Brandeis's nomination, and it therefore had no impact on his decision. *Ibid.*, 136.
81. *PWW*, "Tumulty to Amos Pinchot," Vol. 36, January 27, 1916, 22–3. On June 1, 1916, the Senate's vote ratified Brandeis's selection by a margin of fourty-seven (out of which three were Republicans: La Follette, Norris and Poindexter) to twenty-two.
82. *PWW*, "Amos Pinchot to Norman Hapgood," Vol. 36, February 2, 1916, 86–7.
83. *Crane Papers*, "CRC to Wilson," February 17, 1916.
84. *Crane Papers*, "CRC to Josephine Crane Bradley," February 7, 1916.
85. *Crane Papers*, "Memoirs," 166.
86. *Crane Papers*, "Crane to House," June 2, 1916; "Crane to Wilson," May 29, 1916.

Bibliography

Archives

Charles Richard Crane Papers, 1869–1967. Rare Books & Manuscript Library, University of Columbia.

James Ford Rhodes Papers. Massachusetts Historical Society.

Published Primary Sources

Baker, Ray S. and William E. Dodd, ed. *The Public Papers of Woodrow Wilson*. New York: Harper, 1925–26.

Baker, Ray S. *Woodrow Wilson: Life and Letters*. Garden City, NY: Doubleday, 1927–39.

Baruch, Bernard M. *Baruch*. New York: H. Holt, 1957–1960.

Crane, Richard T. *The Autobiography of Richard Teller Crane*. Chicago, 1927.

Daniels, Josephus. *The Wilson Era*. Chapel Hill: University of North Carolina Press, 1946.

Houston, David F. *Eight Years with Wilson's Cabinet, 1913–1920*. Garden City, NY: Doubleday, 1926.

Krooss, Herman E., ed. *A Documentary History of Banking and Currency in the United States*. New York: Chelsea Pub., 1969.

La Follette, Robert Marion. *La Follette's Autobiography*. Madison: University of Wisconsin Press, 1968 [c.1912].

Link, Arthur S., ed. *Papers of Woodrow Wilson*. Princeton, NJ: Princeton University Press, 1966–92.

Seymour, Charles, ed. *The Intimate Papers of Colonel House Arranged as a Narrative*. London: Ernest Benn, 1926–28.

Tumulty, Joseph P. *Woodrow Wilson as I Know Him*. Garden City: Doubleday, 1921.

Bibliographic Guides

Buckingham, Peter H. *Woodrow Wilson: A Bibliography of His Times and Presidency*. Wilmington, DE: Scholarly Resources, 1990.

Bellot, Hugh Hale. *American History and American Historians: A Review of Recent Contributions to the Interpretation of the History of the United States*. Norman: University of Oklahoma Press, 1952.

Parish, Peter J., ed. *Reader's Guide to American History*. Chicago: Fitzroy Publishers, 1997.

Monographies

Aaron, Daniel. *Men of Good Hope. A Story of American Progressives*. New York: Oxford University Press, 1961.

Allerfeldt, Kristofer, ed. *The Progressive Era in the USA: 1890–1921*. Burlington, VT: Ashgate, 2007.

Buenker, John D. *Urban Liberalism and Progressive Reform*. New York: Scribner's Sons, 1973.

———. *The Income Tax and the Progressive Era*. New York: Garland, 1985.

Burns, James M. *The Workshop of Democracy. From the Emancipation Proclamation to the Era of the New Deal*. New York: Vintage Book, 1985.

Chamberlain, John. *Farewell to Reform. The Rise, Life and Decay of the Progressive Mind in America*. Chicago: Quadrangle, 1965 [c.1932].

Chambers II, John W. *The Tyranny of Change. America in the Progressive Era, 1900–1917*. New York: St-Martin's Press, 1980.

Chessman, G. W. *Theodore Roosevelt and the Politics of Power*. Boston: Little, Brown & Co., 1969.

Childs, Marquis and James Reston, ed. *Walter Lippmann and His Times*. Freeport, NY: Books For Libraries Press, 1968 [c.1959].

Clements, Kendrick A. *William Jennings Bryan, Missionary Isolationist*. Knoxville, TE: University of Tennessee Press, 1982.

———. *The Presidency of Woodrow Wilson*. Lawrence, KA: University Press of Kansas, 1992.

Clifford, A. J. *The Independence of the Federal Reserve System*. Philadelphia: University of Pennsylvania Press, 1965.

Cooper, John M. *The Warrior and the Priest*. Cambridge: HUP, 1983.

———. *Woodrow Wilson*. New York: Alfred A. Knopf, 2009.

Crunden, Robert M. *Ministers of Reform. The Progressives' Achievement in American Civilization, 1889–1920*. Chicago: University of Illinois Press, 1982.

Diamond, William. *The Economic Thought of Woodrow Wilson*. Baltimore: The Johns Hopkins Press, 1943.

Eckes, Alfred E. *Opening America's Market. U.S. Foreign Trade Policy Since 1776*. Chapel Hill: University of North Carolina Press, 1995.

Ekirch, Arthur A. *Progressivism in America: A Study of the Era from Theodore Roosevelt to Woodrow Wilson*. New York: New Viewpoints, 1974.

Goldstein, Judith. *Ideas, Interests, and American Trade Policy*. Ithaca, NY: Cornell University Press, 1993.

Gould, Lewis L. *The Progressive Era*. Syracuse, NY: Syracuse University Press, 1974.

———. *Four Hats in the Ring. The 1912 Election and the Birth of Modern American Politics*. Lawrence, KA: University Press of Kansas, 2008.

Hansen, Jonathan M. *The Lost Promise of Patriotism. Debating American Identity, 1890–1920*. Chicago: University of Chicago Press, 2003.

Hapgood, David. *Charles R. Crane. The Man Who Bet on People*. New York: ICWA, 2000.

Harbaugh, William H. *The Life and Times of Theodore Roosevelt*. London: Oxford University Press, 1975 [c.1961].

———. *The American Political Tradition and the Men Who Made It*. New York: Vintage Books, 1989 [c.1948].

———. *The Age of Reform. From Bryan to FDR*. New York: Vintage Books, 1955.

———. *Anti-Intellectualism in American Life*. New York: Vintage Books, 1963.

———. *The Paranoid Style in American Politics*. New York: Alfred A. Knopf, 1965.

Kloppenberg, James T. *Uncertain Victory. Social Democracy and Progressivism in European and American Thought, 1870–1920*. Oxford: Oxford University Press, 1986.

Kolko, Gabriel. *The triumph of Conservatism: A Reinterpretation of American History, 1900–1916*. New York: Free Press, 1963.

Lake, David A. *Power, Protection, and Free Trade. International Sources of U.S. Commercial Strategy, 1887–1939*. Ithaca, NY: Cornell University Press, 1988.

Lasch, Christopher. *The New Radicalism in America. The Intellectual as a Social Type*. New York: Knopf, 1965.

Link, Arthur S. *Wilson*. Princeton, NJ: Princeton University Press, 1947.

———. *Woodrow Wilson and the Progressive Era, 1910–1917*. New York: Harper & Brothers, 1954.

Livingstone, James. *Origins of the Federal Reserve System. Money, Class, and Corporate Capitalism, 1890–1913*. Cornell University Press, 1986.

Mason, Alpheus T. *Brandeis: A Free Man's Life*. New York: Viking Press, 1946.

Maxwell, Robert S. *La Follette and the Rise of the Progressives in Wisconsin*. New York: Russell & Russell, 1973 [c.1956].

May, Ernest. *The World War and American Isolation, 1914–1917*. Cambridge: Harvard University Press, 1966 [c.1959].

———. *Imperial Democracy. The Emergence of America as a Great Power*. New York: Harper & Row, 1973.

May, Henry F. *The End of American Innocence. The First Years of Our Own Times, 1912–1917.* New York: Oxford University Press, 1959.

Mayer, Arno. *Politics and Diplomacy of Peacemaking: Containment and Counterrevolution at Versailles, 1918–1919.* New York: Knopf, 1967.

McCormick, Richard L. *The Party Period and Public Policy. American Politics from the Age of Jackson to the Progressive Era.* New York: Oxford University Press, 1986.

McCartney, Paul T. *Power & Progress: American National Identity, the War of 1898, and the Rise of American Imperialism.* Baton Rouge: Louisiana University Press, 2006.

McGerr, Michael. *A Fierce Discontent. The Rise and Fall of the Progressive Movement in America, 1870–1920.* Oxford: Oxford University Press, 2003.

McLoughlin, William G. *Revivals, Awakenings, and Reform. An Essay on Religion and Social Change in America, 1607–1977.* Chicago: The Chicago University Press, 1978.

Mowry, George E. *The Era of Theodore Roosevelt, 1900–1912.* New York: Harper, 1958.

Noble, David W. *The Paradox of Progressive Thought.* Minneapolis: University of Minnesota Press, 1958.

———. *The Progressive Mind, 1890–1917.* Minneapolis: Burgess, 1981.

O'Neill, William L. *The Progressive Years. America Comes of Age.* New York: Dodd, Mead and Company, 1975.

Ratner, Sidney. *The Tariff in American History.* New York: Nostrand Co., 1972.

Saul, Norman E. *The Life and Times of Charles R. Crane, 1858–1939. American Businessman, Philanthropist, and a Founder of Russian Studies in America.* Lexington Books, 2013.

Schneirov, Richard. *Labor and Urban Politics. Class Conflict and the Origins of Modern Liberalism in Chicago, 1864–97.* Chicago: University of Illinois Press, 1998.

Sklar, Martin J. *The Corporate Reconstruction of American Capitalism, 1890–1916: The Market, the Law, and Politics.* Cambridge: Cambridge University Press, 1988.

Steel, Ronald. *Walter Lippmann and the American Century.* Boston: Little, Brown & Co. 1980.

Stettner, Edward A. *Shaping Modern Liberalism. Herbert Croly and Progressive Thought.* Lawrence, KA: University Press of Kansas, 1993.

Thelen, David P. *The New Citizenship. Origins of Progressivism in Wisconsin, 1885–1900.* Columbia: University of Missouri Press, 1972.

———. *Robert M. La Follette and the Insurgent Spirit.* Boston: Little Brown & Co., 1976.

Thorsen, Niels A. *The Political Thought of Woodrow Wilson, 1875–1910.* Princeton, NJ: Princeton University Press, 1988.

Trachtenberg, Alan. *The Incorporation of America. Culture & Society in the Gilded Age.* New York: Hill & Wang, 1982.

Urofksy, Melvin I. *Louis D. Brandeis and the Progressive Tradition.* Boston: Little, Brown & Co., 1981.

Weinstein, James. *The Corporate Ideal in the Liberal State, 1900–1918.* Boston: Beacon Press, 1969.

Well, Donald R. *The Federal Reserve System. A History.* Jefferson, NC: McFarland & Co., 2004.

White, Morton G. *Social Thought in America. The Revolt Against Formalism.* Boston: Beacon Press, 1976 [c.1949].

Wiebe, Robert H. *Businessmen and Reform. A Study of the Progressive Movement*. Cambridge: CUP, 1989 [c.1962].

———. *The Search for Order, 1877–1920*. London: Macmillan, 1967.

Theses

Bocage, Leo J. "The Public Career of Charles R. Crane." Ph.D. diss., Fordham University, 1962.

Moranian, Suzanne E. "The American Missionary and the Armenian Question, 1915–1927." Ph.D. diss., University of Wisconsin, 1994.

Neuman, William L. "Why Reform Fails: The Rise and Fall of Antimonopoly Reform in the United States, 1875–1975." Ph.D. diss., University of Wisconsin, 1982.

Sulzbach, Jacob John, Jr. "Charles R. Crane, Woodrow Wilson, and Progressive Reform: 1909–1921." Ph.D. diss., Texas A&M University, 1994.

Journal Articles

Blumenthal, Henry. "Woodrow Wilson and the Race Question." *The Journal of Negro History*, 48, 1, 1963, 1–21.

Diggins, John P. "Republicanism and Progressivism." *American Quarterly*, 37, 4, 1985, 572–598.

———. "From Pragmatism to Natural Law: Walter Lippmann's Quest for the Foundations of Legitimacy." *Political Theory*, 19, 4, 1991, 519–538.

Hollinger, David A. "Science and Anarchy: Walter Lippmann's Drift and Mastery." *American Quarterly*, 29, 5, 1977, 463–475.

McCormick, Richard L. "The Discovery That Business Corrupts Politics: A Reappraisal of the Origins of Progressivism." *The American Historical Review*, 86, 2, 1981, 247–274.

Morris, Stuart. "The Wisconsin Idea and Business Progressivism." *Journal of American Studies*, 4, 1, 1970, 39–60.

Nichols, David K. "The Promise of Progressivism: Herbert Croly and the Progressive Rejection of Individual Rights." *Publius*, 17, 2, 1987, 27–39.

Noble, Charles. "Wilson's Choice: the Political Origins of the Modern American State." *Comparative Politics*, 17, 3, 1985, 313–336.

Noble, David W. "The *New Republic* and the Idea of Progress, 1914–1920." *The Mississippi Valley Historical Review*, 38, 3, 1951, 387–402.

O'Leary, Kevin C. "Herbert Croly and Progressive Democracy," *Polity*, 24, 6, 1994, 533–552.

Rodgers, Daniel T. "In search of Progressivism." *Reviews in American History*, 10, 4, 1982, 113–132.

Taussig, F. W. "The Tariff Act of 1913." *The Quarterly Journal of Economics*, 28, 1, 1913, 1–30.

Walker, Larry. "Woodrow Wilson, Progressive Reform and Public Administration." *Political Science Quarterly*, 104, 3, 1989, 509–525.

Wolgemuth, Kathleen L. "Woodrow Wilson and Federal Segregation." *The Journal of Negro History*, 44, 2, 1959, 158–173.

· 3 ·

CHARLES R. CRANE AND REVOLUTIONARY RUSSIA, 1917

Despite Charles Crane's constant involvement in the world of academia and his faith in the social benefits of knowledge, he cannot be considered an intellectual, either in his career or in his proclivities. Yet his interest in art and science (especially technical sciences) and his acquaintanceship with various leaders of the academic community in the United States and abroad situated him within a certain cultural elite of his era. Few men at the time could, like Crane, converse about distant cultural practices or even school the president on various Arab parables he had learned during his voyages in the Middle East.[1] His cultural tastes, though they did revolve around certain specific infatuations, had been shaped in his youth by successive travels to Russia, China, the Balkans, and the Middle East. Rebuffed by formal education and literally sick with boredom,[2] Charles obtained his father's permission to go on a first expedition abroad, on the condition that it be conducted in a "serious" and educational manner. Thus, between 1877 and his father's death in 1912, Crane divided his time between constructive wanderings, political reform, and his work at the Crane Co.

A Fascination with Russia

Russia was undeniably his earliest and most enduring "exotic" interest. A great admirer of the Russian language, Crane devoted himself to learning the rudiments so that he could converse with the friends he had met during his travels in Russia since his first expedition in 1887. At his return from another trip to Russia in 1889, he was already taking language lessons and promising the Russian geographer, Count Semenov Tyan Shansky, that he would improve his knowledge of Russian and of the Cyrillic alphabet in order to continue their correspondence in that language rather than in French, which was then spoken by many of the aristocrats Crane had befriended.[3] He later participated in the creation of a department of Russian studies at the University of Chicago through his longtime partnership with its president, William R. Harper. In 1914, he also financed the training and supported the hiring of William Harper's son, Samuel Harper, as teacher and director of this new program.[4] Crane became the chief organizer of colloquiums and conferences on Russian studies at the University of Chicago, inviting and conveying—often at his own expense—many renowned Russian and Slavic speakers whom he counted among his friends. His aim in these endeavors was not strictly academic, as Crane also simultaneously strove to broaden America's understanding of Russia's population and of other Slavic peoples while improving their reputation in the United States. Crane was rather dissatisfied with what he called the media's excessively harsh treatment of Russian news. He regularly complained that American newspapers, which he claimed were ruled by Jewish-Republican interests (particularly by the New York banker Jacob Schiff), denounced the pogroms and anti-Semitic measures carried out by the Russian government without any nuance. This made Russian society look barbaric to Americans and effectively stymied commercial and cultural relations between the two countries. Unlike Samuel Harper,[5] Crane did not deny the facts relayed to him by his own informants, but he argued that the press's own "Jewish bigotry" indirectly caused harm to the Jews in Russia while also negatively impacting public opinion in the United States. Crane was not the only observer to adopt this position, and his views aligned with those of other Russophiles (William R. Harper, his son Samuel, and Lincoln Steffens counted among the most well-known) in Europe and North America. More than once, his friends called upon him to engage with the press and refute or correct its "Russophobic" arguments.[6]

The political significance of his pro-Russian bias became more concrete during the Russo-Japanese war in 1905 and related to the geopolitical and diplomatic situations in the Far East. Crane had always favored Russia, a Christian country where resided several of his personal friends. He consequently denounced Japan's militarism and expansionism in the Pacific and disputed its claims upon the Siberian archipelago of Sakhalin. Simultaneously, Japan's activities in the Pacific threatened another of Crane's "protégées," China, which was on the one hand prey to the colonial ambitions of Britain, Japan, and Germany but had on the other hand been declared "open door" by the United States under the doctrine of John Hay, President McKinley's secretary of state from 1898 to 1905.[7]

The media's deplorable treatment of Russian affairs did not have an impact only on cultural and political matters. It also directly affected Charles Crane's business objectives. Indeed, a greater sympathy for Russian culture in the United States could in turn stimulate American industrial opportunities in Russia. Crane was therefore at the forefront of American economic forays into Russia and was particularly involved in an important railroad contract between the Crane Company, Westinghouse, and the Russian government. Also conducting business in Russia was his good friend Cyrus H. McCormick Jr., who had traveled there on behalf of the International Harvester Company.[8]

Developing friendships primarily with members of Russia's enlightened aristocratic community, Crane had adopted their nationalistic, liberal, and moderate point of view as well as their cultural tastes. He developed a passion for Russian Orthodox music and architecture, Russian romantic literature, and artifacts typical of Russian folklore. He was fascinated by the Cyrillic alphabet, by Old Slavonic liturgical hymns, by the majestic domes crowning Russian monasteries and basilicas, by Russia's iconographic art. Enchanted, also, by the visible discipline and fervor of the working classes, by the Old Believer's raw spirituality and by Russia's vast landscapes and intense climate, he became unconditionally attached to this image of a prerevolutionary and liberal Russia projected by Russia's reformist nobility.

Crane's infatuation with Russia, Europe's least industrialized country, also fit into a paradoxically progressive current of reaction to modernity. Skeptical, at times, about the true benefits of industrial and capitalist progress, some liberals had developed a tendency to idealize the "primitive" state. Russia was to them, as described by Christopher Lasch, "a museum of preindustrial antiquities."[9] Though Crane himself never explained or analyzed his cultural tastes, he may also have owed his fascination with Russia to a certain romantic penchant stemming from a growing disappointment with modernity. Crane, in his own way, had the same ambiguous relationship with this idealized medieval (or feudal, as it was often called) past—associated in turn with Germany or Russia—as many of his compatriots. Though he admired some of its cultural relics, Crane, like his liberal Russian friends, hoped to ultimately see this "feudal" Russia break out of its Tsarist obscurantism, pushed forward by the forces of progress.

Revolutionary Sympathies

Most illustrious among Crane's Russian friends was undeniably the historian and politician Pavel Milyukov. Having invited Milyukov to teach Russian history at the University of Chicago in 1901 and 1903, Crane describes the ensuing events both in his memoirs and in a letter written on March 17, 1917 to Gilson Gardner, a journalist and an old friend from the NPRL days in Chicago. Shortly after receiving Crane's invitation to teach, Milyukov was arrested for having organized a dissident student meeting against the Tsarist regime. In prison, he learned English in preparation for his future conferences in Chicago. During the 1905 Revolution, he created the Constitutional Democratic Party (known as K-D or Kadet party) and led the Duma's Progressive Bloc until the Tsar's abdication in February of 1917. He helped found Prince Georgy Lvov's Provisional Government and became its minister of Foreign Affairs.[10]

Lvov and Milyukov were favorites of those whom Christopher Lasch called the "war liberals."[11] According to Lasch, "war liberals" believed in the use of force, but contrary to conservatives like Roosevelt (at least where foreign policy was concerned) and Henry Cabot Lodge, they strove to reconcile armed intervention with liberal and democratic principles. However, according to Lasch, the "war liberals" differed from "anti-imperialists" like William J. Bryan, Walter Lippmann (only during that period), and Lincoln Steffens, who had formed a much more precise judgment on the diplomatic and international policy of the European—and sometimes even of the American—powers. Lasch classified Crane as one of these "war liberals" along with Wilson, in what was perhaps an incomplete analysis of Crane's position as it appears in the *Crane Papers*. Crane's reservations about the war were evidence that he had formulated a strong and fairly precise critique of the war's "imperialist" stakes. Though he did not directly use the word "imperialism,"

Crane often spoke of the peoples' exploitation by the aristocratic leaders, both among the Entente and the Central Powers. He correspondingly condemned the war's negative consequences on the populations it affected, particularly the ones dominated by the Ottoman and Austro-Hungarian regimes. As a discerning reader of the Harvard historian Albert Bushnell Hart, Crane sent Wilson Hart's interpretation of the causes of the war in an article where the historian criticized the conflict's imperialistic undercurrent.[12] After reading it, Wilson proclaimed his increasing dismay at the immoral relations between the European countries and asserted his "utter condemnation" of such a context.[13] One must note, however, that Hart was somewhat pro-Allied in his point of view. He placed the blame primarily on Austro-Hungarian and German intrigues and endorsed a rather militaristic and Rooseveltian perspective, advocating greater investment in military defense and compulsory military service in the United States even before the start of the preparedness debate in 1915 and 1916. Neither Crane nor Wilson supported this type of perspective, which was only good for warmongers like Roosevelt. At the time of the article's publication in the fall of 1914, Crane was still very much engaged in distinctly pacifistic ventures.

It does nevertheless appear that Crane appreciated and supported Russia's war efforts against the Central Powers during the first months of the war, and this, in some way, implicitly undermined the neutrality of his position. His view on the matter, however, extended beyond the war's military perspective and its immediate goals. He had already begun contemplating the idea of a postimperial world where the Slavic peoples, freed from German militarism (and from impiety!), emerged in Europe as a regenerative cultural force. As of 1914, he began expressing this intuition to his friend Charles Eliot, the president of Harvard University:

> I believe we are seeing Russia at her best [...] Russia is fighting to become emancipated from Prussian domination and her whole heart is in this war. Whatever else Russia at her worst threatens, she does not threaten Europe, and certainly does not begin to be the menace to the Peace of Europe that Germany has been these last forty years. And the Russian spirit is not a military one. Tolstoy represents it much more than von Treitschske. I believe the next century is going to see the Slavs make great contributions to the culture of the world and that these contributions are not going to be wanting in a strong spiritual quality.[14]

According to Christopher Lasch, America's position on the Russian Revolution was a facet of the country's overall positions and sympathies on the war in Europe and evolved parallel to them.[15] Given their constant concern with order, the "war liberals," among whom Lasch counted Crane, generally saw the Revolution as a threat to civilization. "Anti-imperialists," on the other hand, stood against colonial exploitation and expansionism and thus viewed the Revolution in a more favorable light. Lasch's characterization of Crane as a "war liberal" with reference to the Russian Revolution does not, therefore, hold up to scrutiny in light of his correspondence throughout the war and of his influence on Wilsonian policy in regard to revolutionary Russia.

Over the course of the years and of his voyages and philanthropic activities, Charles Crane earned a reputation, certainly exaggerated by contemporary standards, as an "expert" in international relations, particularly where Russia was concerned. It is in light of this and of his achievements during the victorious 1912 presidential campaign that Wilson decided to name him ambassador to Russia (a major strategic location both in terms of European and Asian affairs). Conscious of the importance of his times for the United States and for its place in the world, Crane himself exhibited great interest in the Wilson Administration's diplomatic appointments. Along with Wilson's private advisor Edward M. House, Crane participated in the discussions concerning diplomatic appointments and even recommended a few candidates, among them his first cousin Martin A. Ryerson whom he proposed for the post of ambassador to France. Ryerson was a member of the University of Chicago's Board of Trustees since its inception and the son of that very wood contractor who had helped Crane's father set up the Crane Foundry.[16] His was one of several names Crane had slipped to Wilson to help build the president's diplomatic corps abroad, yet none of the men recommended by Crane were nominated except for the one he suggested as an alternative for the post Wilson had offered him.[17] The idea of appointing Crane as ambassador to Russia first emerged during a discussion between House and Wilson on March 25, 1913. Crane refused, but it is interesting to note with what unusual insistence Wilson pressed his friend to take on the mission. In his memoirs, House even described a telling exchange with Wilson during which the president asked House to enlist Norman Hapgood's help in convincing Crane to accept the post in Russia. This ploy was conceived and carried out despite Crane's explanation that the death of his father and his new familial and business responsibilities prevented him from being able to grant their request. House also called Hapgood and advised him to urge Crane to use the utmost discretion regarding the post he had been offered. House later explained that discretion was not Crane's forte,[18] a clear reference to the reputation Crane had earned after his forced resignation as minister to China. Tapped for the Chinese post by Taft in 1909, Crane was forced to backtrack—literally—because he had publically expressed some rather unfriendly opinions about Japanese politics. Secretary of State Philander Knox, who detested Crane, relieved him of his duties before Crane even had a chance to assume them. Outrage at Knox's infamy filled the newspapers and saturated Crane's personal correspondence, and a petition showing that he was supported by a diverse group of reputable people was published shortly after his expulsion from the post.[19]

Yet time was short, and while House and Wilson persisted fruitlessly in trying to secure a positive response from Crane, Secretary of State William Jennings Bryan grew impatient about the delay. In a message dated June 25, 1913, Bryan even suggested to Wilson that someone be appointed interim ambassador until Crane became available, exclaiming about the urgency of the situation that "We need someone in Russia now!"[20] Indeed, Saint Petersburg had been putting pressure on the United States to renew various trade agreements, and an American ambassador was sorely needed there. At the beginning of August, the impasse still remained unresolved and Bryan once again suggested sending an interim ambassador until Crane could (hopefully) take on the duties himself. He even proposed a candidate, the editor Henry Means Pindell from Illinois, as a temporary replacement.[21] Though Crane approved this candidate,[22] he did not succeed in making himself available for the post in Russia, and regretfully explained to Wilson:

> I have tried hard to arrange my affairs so as to do myself the honor [*sic*] of serving you and taking part in the administration I am so happy about [...] All efforts, however, in that direction have been vain and I now feel obliged to renounce for an indefinite period any ambition I have had to aid you. I am most unhappy about it, but will be most willing to help anyone you select to take my place.[23]

The president's disappointment could not be concealed and, in a burst of affection, he once again renewed his request:

> May I not beg that we may at least leave this thing for consideration when you can free yourself a little from the obligations now pressing upon you? I cannot get my own mind to assent to a permanent disappointment [...] I appreciate the feeling you show in the matter, especially the feeling toward myself. I am deeply grateful to have such friends."[24]

Crane's response, though it did not fulfill Wilson's wishes, still served to raise him in the president's esteem. It was followed by a lull in Wilson's determination, possibly due to a belief that he had found in Pindell a suitable interim candidate. Since the latter appears never to have taken up the post, however, Wilson renewed his efforts in May of the following year. Yet the message sent on May 15, 1914 suggests that he had delayed in making this decision not because Pindell would temporarily be performing the ambassadorial duties in Russia but rather because he still hoped that Crane would eventually give in. Crane once again had to reiterate his regret and offered once again to help whoever would replace him.[25] The time had now come—barring an indication from Crane to the contrary—for Wilson to take "the second best course if [he could not] take the best."[26] Wilson's answer, sent on May 21 and labeled "private and personal," seems to indicate that the president had finally resigned himself to the worst: having to look elsewhere for an American representative to the Russian government:

> My dear Friend, It is cheering to be associated with anybody as disinterested as you are. I value your letter of the eighteenth very highly. It fills me with admiration at the same time that it brings me a great disappointment. I cannot find a real substitute but I will look around and see what the field affords.[27]

Though the letter contains no new information, one can note the warmth of its tone and the fact that Crane's refusal of a prestigious post which many more ambitious men would have gladly accepted had made a good impression on Wilson. This type of position, which offered only very modest wages, was at the time generally given as a "reward" to wealthy friends of the government. Wilson's insistence on appointing Crane, however, stemmed from his belief in the importance of diplomatic service, and he rejected the idea of nepotism and whims as factors in the selection of a candidate. Crane's presence at the embassy in Russia seemed to him desirable and even essential. Such a concern with picking the "best" agent—who in this case, ironically, also happened to be a "wealthy friend of the regime"—was part of Wilson's overhaul of the government and of its services through the "expertization" of public affairs as described at the beginning of the previous chapter. Though Crane was in no way an "expert" in the conventional sense as he had no formal education in the domain, he was, in his era, an authority on international matters. He was also a reputed political reformer and organizer in progressive circles and had some panache as a successful business leader. Above all, he had proven his loyalty during the 1912 campaign and firmly adhered to the principles of Wilsonianism.

In fact, it remains astonishing that Crane's business relationship with Russia via the Crane Co., an obvious conflict of interest, did not pose an obstacle to his selection as ambassador. Wilson was in fact not the only one eager to see Crane accept the ambassadorship; American businessmen with interests in Russia also hoped for his appointment. When Crane asked one of his business partners, Thomas Meyer of the Westinghouse Electric Company in Saint Petersburg, what he could do to help with the business in Russia, Meyer unambiguously replied: "you can help us by becoming U.S.A. ambassador [...] as you are on friendly terms with the President." Meyer was well aware of Crane's frequently publicized opinion on the Russian issue and knew he could benefit from a man with such valuable assets, one who "knows the country well and is favourably disposed toward the Slavonic race." Meyer also viewed Crane's charitable involvement in Russia as another advantage in regard to the diplomatic post, pointing out that Crane was already known to the Tsar and the Tsarina as he had worked with them to coordinate several philanthropic endeavors in Russia. Much like Wilson, House, and Bryan before him, Meyer had to once again accept Crane's refusal as the latter was now struggling with health problems on top of his professional and familial obligations.[28]

Ultimately, after over two years of delay, it was David R. Francis[29] who, with Crane's approval and his promise to help with the task, was appointed at the head of the American embassy in Russia. Crane began by imparting to him his perspective on Russian-American relations, which he believed should be founded on cooperation based on their Christian kinship. It was in this sense that Crane constantly complained that relations with Russia were determined by Jews rather than by real Christians. "The Jews [more explicitly, the New York banker Jacob Schiff] have for a long time controlled the bridge between Russia and America," he affirmed, and so "the 98 000 000 Christians here have had no relation with the 170 000 000 Christians over there—although they are the strongest base for both political and social sympathy." In order to decrease the influence of certain "Russophobic" Jews on the embassy, he then contributed to dispatching his protégé, Samuel Harper of the University of Chicago, as special advisor to the new ambassador. In a letter to his daughter Josephine, Crane explained the understanding he had with Wilson on this matter: "The President was entirely sympathetic and agreed with me that we should [...] allow Samuel Harper to go to Russia now in an unofficial way so as [...] to help the new Ambassador [...]" Harper, to them, presented many advantages: he was "well informed about Russia [...] trusted [...] by the government, by the revolutionists and by the Jews."[30] Given the aforementioned facts, that Harper was trusted by the Jews may come as a surprise, but Crane constantly explained that the Jewish lobby which he believed to be so harmful to American diplomacy in Russia consisted only of a handful of "hot-headed" individuals. On many other occasions, he expressed his admiration for other American Jews. Some of them, like the Zionist Richard Gottheil, who was Crane's good friend and whom Crane called "the finest Jew I know," even helped him to refute what was seen as the Jewish-German propaganda.[31]

Thus, though he himself had refused the post, Crane succeeded in placing one of "his men," and now hoped to see Samuel Harper also act behind the scenes to carry out the kind of diplomatic policy Crane had always wished for. And indeed, it was these ideal and impeccably timed diplomatic conditions that allowed Crane's Russian friends to hasten the Tsar's abdication and to form the new Provisional Government.

Moreover, Crane's schedule cleared up considerably following the sale of his shares in the Crane Company to his brother in 1914 for a staggering sum of 14 million dollars.[32] It was also during this time that for tax reasons, Crane left Chicago and moved to Woods Hole, Massachusetts, which happened to be one of the centers of decision-making and influence on the East Coast. Finally free from the family business and from other worries in Chicago, with a large sum of money at his disposal, Crane was able to serve wherever he wished and make the kind of political, cultural, and humanitarian contributions he desired. The outbreak of the war in Europe had also made many Progressives, including Wilson and Crane (who had always had a strong interest in foreign policy), turn their attention abroad.

In May of 1915, Crane was once more asked to serve in the American diplomatic corps. He was again needed in Russia, but this time, the position he was offered involved considerably lesser power and visibility than a post at the embassy. To understand this appointment better, one must look at the context in which it was made. Though Wilson was often perceived, quite rightly in fact, as a president who acted as his own secretary of state,[33] it turns out that William J. Bryan, who was given the official post as a "reward" for his crucial support during the 1912 campaign and because of his standing in the Democratic party,[34] distinguished himself oddly enough both by his fierce antiwar rhetoric and by the ineffectiveness of his work at the State Department. Even though Bryan abandoned the post halfway through his term in protest against infringements on the policy of neutrality, the few international treaties he managed to negotiate foreshadowed Wilson's messianic and moral approach as well as his position as a peaceful mediator among belligerent countries. One of the first measures taken by Bryan as Secretary of State pertained to maintaining world peace and establishing the United States' position as a leader in the peace movement. Bryan's plan was to defuse conflict situations by negotiating, through multilateral treaties between countries, one-year period of "investigation" under the promise of cessation of hostility. Called "cooling off" periods, these treaties reflected Bryan's idealism but also served as reminder of the obstacles standing in the way of world peace, as their endorsement coincided with the start of World War I. Whatever the case may have been, the "investigations" involved the establishment of national commissions designed to develop strategies to help de-escalate the growing tensions.[35] It was in this particular context and owing to his status both as *éminence grise* in regard to Russia and as a staunch promoter of world peace that Crane was appointed by Bryan, on May 8, 1915, as commissioner for the "cooling off" treaty between Russia and the United States. This nomination followed a treaty signed by the two countries on October 1, 1914 and demanded no specific action on Crane's part (though it also offered no compensation) except in the case of a formal disagreement between the two countries, which did not occur until the October Revolution and the ensuing disintegration of diplomatic relations.[36] Though this episode once again led nowhere, its interest resides in the fact that Crane had once more been considered for a position involving relations with Russia. Incidentally, in a letter to his youngest son John Oliver Crane, with whom he would later travel and who would also pursue a diplomatic career, Crane described a visit he paid to Bryan at the State Department to congratulate him on these peace treaties.[37]

Crane was thus on the leading edge of American knowledge and discussion of the Russian issue. Since his very first trips to Russia in the 1880s, Crane had entered the public and media debate by pitting himself against the journalist and explorer George Kennan (1845–1924, not to be confused with his cousin twice removed George F. Kennan, a diplomat and historian), whose harsh criticism against Russia's exile system in Siberia he deplored. It is hard to understand how a friend of democracy like Crane could strive to defend or qualify this type of repressive punitive system, but a letter written to his friend Count Semenov Tyan Shansky seems to indicate that above all, Crane feared the way a Russophobic reaction in the United States could lead to inimical commercial policies toward Russia.[38]

When the 1917 Revolution broke out, Crane asserted that he personally knew most of the Provisional Government's members and attested to their quality. He urged Wilson to recognize this new government formed during the February Revolution (March in the western calendar)[39] and the president obliged on March 22, 1917, one week after Tsar Nicholas II's abdication.

The liberal nature of the first phase of the Revolution meant that Wilson, receiving most of his intelligence from Charles and Richard Crane and often through the State Department, naturally adopted an optimistic attitude toward it. The early comments about the Revolution made by Wilson and the men in his inner circle documented by Secretary of the Navy Josephus Daniels in his journal betray a wave of barely contained jubilation: "[Wilson] spoke of a 'glorious act' of the Russians." The president doubted, however, whether these events constituted reason enough to join the war.[40] Daniels, for his part, recognized Crane's importance as Wilson's primary supplier of information about the February Revolution and understood how this information had shaped Wilson's first impressions: "Crane knew well the leading spirit and said they were men of ability and had the confidence of Russia." Daniels was undoubtedly referring to comments Crane had made directly to Wilson and his entourage as he had spent part of March in Washington. In his memoirs, Edward House also recognized Crane's superior understanding of the Russian issue, writing that "[Crane] knows more about it than most."[41] Furthermore, Wilson's timetable indicates that he and his wife were having supper with Charles and Cornelia Crane on March 23.[42] No transcript of their conversation exists, but it is easy to deduce that they were discussing the situation in Russia and the following day during a cabinet meeting, Wilson expressed his hope that the Revolution remain permanent, declaring (smilingly, according to Daniels) that "It ought to be good!" One of the reasons Wilson could so easily rejoice at the turn of events was that (with the help of Crane's explanations) he was able to identify with the individuals involved in the February Revolution and with the Provisional Government "because it has a professor at the head." Indeed, Crane told Wilson the story of Professor Milyukov, who was head of the Constitutional Democratic Party and would soon be in charge of foreign affairs in the Provisional Government. During a second cabinet meeting on the same day, Wilson himself decided to share Milyukov's story as had been recounted to him previously by Crane.[43] Several days later, on March 28, Crane reiterated his confidence in the Provisional Government's members in a letter which will be the subject of further discussion in this chapter. In it, he wrote that "the men in the provisional government of Russia are the best group running any one of the great powers," confirming his previously mentioned suspicions about the leaders of the other great powers.[44]

Moreover, it was Crane who gave Wilson a memorandum written by Samuel N. Harper between July and September, 1916. Robert Lansing, the new secretary of state,[45] had through Crane and his son Richard asked Harper for an account of his impressions of the situation in Russia. The memo Harper produced was part fact and part fantasy. On the one hand, Harper, like Crane, knew most of the people involved in the Provisional Government and could confirm that they were in support of pursuing the war and its goals at the side of the Allies. On the other hand, Harper conjectured that Russia might have pulled out of the conflict and given its support to Germany if it had not been for the Revolution, concluding that the Provisional Government stood as the only rampart against Germany's eastward expansion. Professor Harper also based this idea on a theory concerning the Tsarina, who some believed to be under the influence of a German "agent" (Rasputin). She was said to have exhibited pro-German tendencies and to have succeeded in also influencing the Tsar.[46]

This recent interpretation adopted by Wilson dovetailed very well with his own view (which became increasingly firm as diplomatic relations with Germany soured) of the war as a struggle between democracies and autocracies. Historians did not all agree with Wilson's Manichean view of the conflict. The concept of a combat between the forces of freedom and the forces of tyranny for the purpose of establishing a new liberal world order was at the heart of Wilsonian neutrality since 1914. Yet Wilson fostered no illusions about the tyrannical nature of Allied diplomacy and understood that European politicians, even Allies, were part of a condemnable colonial framework. This separation of the actors into opposing camps only made sense if the United States was added into the Allied equation as a moral leader and arbiter of democratic nations.[47] By joining the side of democracy, Russia, which had until then remained the only autocratic Allied country, simplified the new configuration which would be used to analyze the stakes of the war.

As early as March 17, only a few days after the fall of the Tsarist regime, House wrote to Wilson with advice on how to proceed: "I think this country should aid in every way the advancement of democracy in Russia for it will end the peril which a possible alliance between Germany, Russia and Japan might hold for us."[48] House also expressed his view of Wilson as the only true democratic world leader and predicted that the latter would emerge from the conflict as a "central figure" and a "great liberal." House even suggested, not without a touch of extravagance, that the recent developments in Russia had resulted from Wilson's teachings.[49] While America's understanding of the February Revolution was based on idealistic ideas and attitudes, it was also undoubtedly shaped by urgent strategic considerations pertaining to the country's safety and to the justification of a departure from its policy of neutrality. Since Russia's retreat from the war could pose a significant threat to Allied military objectives, Wilson endeavored to make Russians aware of their decisive role in the conflict's resolution and encouraged them to persevere in the war effort.

Crane, for his part, received "on the ground" information from Samuel Harper and from Thomas Whittemore, who worked for the Red Cross in Russia, as well as from members of the Synod of the Russian Orthodox Church for whom he organized choral concerts in the United States. During the first month of the Revolution, the reports that reached Crane through Whittemore bore witness to the chaotic but peaceful and popular character of the Provisional Government's first steps. His source also reported the existence of an anti-Jewish sentiment that could degenerate into a full-blown massacre if American Jews did not watch their tongues, which suggested that the revolutionaries in Petrograd diligently read American newspapers. Though he seemed to rejoice in the mass movement that had led to the February Revolution, Whittemore did not harbor indulgent feelings toward the state of affairs. And while he commented with some generalization about "the mildness which characterizes all Russian anarchy," he recognized the gravity of the situation, already evident in the emerging reactionary forces which exhibited even more radical attitudes than the February liberals (soviets and monarchists alike). "It is the beginning of revolution and counter-revolution," he wrote, and added that "It must not be supposed that monarchy is dead in Russia. Many are wearing the red under duress."[50] This last comment, which perhaps foretells the Bolshevik coup in October of 1917, did not seem to put Crane off in the slightest. Impatient to get his own taste of the peaceful yet revolutionary atmosphere in the field and to see with his own eyes the parading soldiers playing "La Marseillaise,"[51] Crane immediately started planning another trip to Russia to ascertain the testimonies relayed by his informants.

In mid-March, Crane had already decided to leave for Russia to the great joy of many of his collaborators, especially in philanthropic circles. For instance, John R. Mott (1865–1955), a Christian philanthropist, activist and Secretary General of the YMCA's international committee, declared that "No errand he has ever made could have been more timely or significant. The almost unbelievable events of the last few days make possible some very far-reaching work on his part."[52] This comment, made to the editor of the *Christian Herald*[53] Roger H. Williams, referred not only to Crane's political eminence in Russia but also to his long-standing involvement in charitable activities. On the eve of his departure for Halifax where he was to get on a ship to Petrograd, Crane wrote Wilson a letter on March 28, 1917 expounding his view of the relations that should be established with Russia and their importance for maintaining international equilibrium:

> It now looks as though your hope for a "League to Enforce Peace" [an allusion to the budding idea of a League of Nations, already incorporated in the 1916 Democratic platform and articulated by Wilson on May 27, 1915 before the League to Enforce Peace] was coming into being quite naturally by the rapid extension of democratic governments. With Russia and China directed by their people we shall not have to concern ourselves so much about the military autocracies of Germany and Japan. I feel that there is going to be a great and rapid diminution of these twin menaces. We ought to do everything in our power to develop and to establish on firm foundations these two peoples and hold strongly to the principles of direct relations with them [...] the men in the provisional government of Russia are the best men running any of the great powers.[54]

This internationalist declaration, one of the clearest put forward by Crane, undeniably shows that he was a true Wilsonian. His letter touched on typically progressive themes like the idea of an unavoidable process of worldwide democratization. It also confirmed that he, like other Progressives, had also come to see the war as having become a confrontation between democracies and tyrannical regimes, a premise strengthened by the outbreak of the February Revolution. Starting in March 1917, this contention became one of the president's main arguments to justify America's belligerent stance.[55] Crane also began alluding to a new factor in Wilson's international program. In expressing that "we ought to do everything in our power," he accepted the use of America's military-diplomatic might in European affairs even at the risk of direct confrontation with other powers. Of greater importance yet was the fact that Crane, in the name of national independence and international security, encouraged Wilson to continue supporting a type of democratic revolution in Russia and China similar to the one that would soon be developed in his Fourteen Points. Crane believed that with time and with sufficient promotion, the democratic self-determination of peoples could serve as a bulwark against "autocratic" militaristic and imperialist powers like Germany, Japan, and the Ottoman Empire. Crane also advocated the establishment of "direct relations," thereby breaking with the traditional diplomatic system dominated by spheres of interest.

Lastly, Crane's words were imbibed with a good deal of optimism in regard to the outcome of the Russian Revolution and of the European conflict overall. A few days later, on April 2, 1917, Woodrow Wilson delivered his message asking for Congress' authorization to declare war on Germany in view of upholding the principle according to which the world had to be made "safe for democracy."[56]

Crane in Russia: "A Peaceful Anarchy"

On March 29, 1917, Crane boarded the last ship leaving for Europe before America entered the war. On a Norwegian vessel leaving from Halifax, the Kristianafjord, Crane undertook a rather perilous journey at a time when boats crossing the ocean were at risk of being attacked by German submarines. Yet complications had arisen even before the vessel set sail in the form of British authorities, who delayed the departure in order to inquire into a group of revolutionaries, one of them Leon Trotsky, aboard the ship. According to Crane, these men were aided by certain New York Jews and by Zionist bankers established in Palestine, an assumption he made based on a classic anti-Semitic presupposition about the allegiance between revolutionaries and Jewish financiers. When Trotsky was apprehended, Lincoln Steffens, who was also part of the voyage, called upon Milyukov (then still Minister of Foreign Affairs for the Provisional Government) for help and secured Trotsky's release. Ironically and to Crane's great chagrin, Trotsky was later responsible for overthrowing the Provisional Government.[57] In Crane's mind, the Jewish schemes against the Provisional Government, and therefore against American interests, were consistent with a "steady anti-American note" in certain Jews. Crane used this expression several times when describing the part he believed had been played by East Coast Jews in the Russian Revolution. He did not explain what purpose their support of such a faction of socialists abroad might serve, but many incoming and outgoing epistolary comments seem to indicate that New York Jews of German descent might have acted this way to prompt Russia to cease hostilities against Germany, it being understood that Lenin and Trotsky's anti-war intentions had already been established in light of their anti-imperialist stance on European politics. Crane's exasperation with Jews who were critical of Russia, however, visibly preceded the start of World War I.[58]

Despite this supposed Jewish control over the media which he regularly decried,[59] Crane felt so satisfied with the American media's overall treatment of the first days of the Revolution before his departure that he had nothing to add to it. What is more, despite the return to Russia of the radical exiles, Crane did not lose faith in the Revolution's democratic character, seeing it, rather misguidedly, as the fruit of a grassroots movement in Russian society. He believed that "the Russian people are fundamentally very democratic, as 80% of the people are small landed proprietors [...] they have a genius for cooperative movements."[60] Yet in Crane's opinion, the Russian peoples' democratic character predated the February Revolution since, as early as February 1916, he expressed to Wilson his view of the Russians as having a predisposition for self-government, describing them as "simple in their modes of thought and the most democratic I know of."[61] This sentiment naturally brings to mind the Jeffersonian bias which was discussed in the previous chapter and which Crane displayed by supporting Wilson and Brandeis's version of progressivism. As seen previously, Crane's family history had also endowed him with a clear entrepreneurial perspective, helping to bring him closer to Wilson and his other collaborators like House, Brandeis, La Follette, and Houston and shaping his interpretation of the Russian Revolution's meaning. Simultaneously, Crane's belief in the power of cooperative movement as an engine of social change reflected another progressive value typical of the Midwest and embodied most notably by La Follette.[62] His family had not suffered excessively from the crisis in the 1890s, and he was decidedly more urban than rural, but Crane was still partly heir to a tradition of concerted—and in some ways even popular and entrepreneurial—involvement in political reformism. He had thus learned to value popular initiatives to take charge of the political machinery as demonstrated by his participation in citizen's organizations like Chicago's Municipal Voter's League.

Crane's comments following the Revolution showed another bias inherent to a tradition of progressive "gentility," this time in regard to alcohol consumption in Russia. He asserted that the success of democracy in Russia depended among other things on the peoples' willingness to stop consuming vodka, a widespread vice among the Russian population. This bias can be explained by the "dry" social current found both in American progressivism and in Victorianism. Generally promoted by mugwumps and other moral reformers since the second half of the nineteenth century and still strong during the advent of progressivism, the fight against alcoholism enjoyed a revival after World War I.[63] Even Wilson's cabinet did not escape the influence of William

J. Bryan and his famous "grape juice diplomacy."[64] Though he did not propose any prohibition measures domestically, there were at least two instances in which Crane described alcoholism as an obstacle to efficient self-determination in Russia.[65]

Despite an Atlantic crossing in the company of Bolsheviks, Crane's first days in Petrograd reinforced his enthusiasm about the success of the Revolution, which he described as "purely Russian and very characteristic." On May 4, 1917, Crane shared his first and favorable impressions with his son Richard. Contrary to the assertions of his friend James Bryce, Crane claimed that the revolutionary movement was supported and propelled by the entire population, which he said had abandoned the old Tsarist symbols like the emperor, the flag and the St. Sophia cross. Crane also refuted all rumors of civil unrest during this first stage of the Russian Revolution, writing that "there is absolutely no class feeling and no bitterness or resentment." Though acknowledging the existence of more radical ideologies, Crane, in a staggering display of optimism, described a climate of overall innocence and joy: "Notwithstanding a great deal of flammatory oratory and speakers all through the streets, there was not a particle of brutality. The crowds were entirely orderly and good natured." He attributed this friendly atmosphere to the light and easy yoke imposed by the Provisional Government and admired its components. "The actual government is practically a peaceful anarchy," Crane wrote, "but nevertheless it is a very orderly government, and without the use of force through soldiers or policemen, and the jail doors wide open, it is perfectly safe [...] It is the most impressive picture."

According to him, the Russian population thus demonstrated that they were able to adopt American-style democracy based on the principle of "self-government," in that "the people generally recognize their individual responsibilities and carry out in a simple way work formerly done by officials."[66] This point of view foreshadowed one that he would articulate more clearly as of 1919, the year of his appointment to the Commission of Inquiry in the Middle East. His experiences in revolutionary Russia served as preparation for his future role in the implementation of the Fourteen Points and allowed him to imagine democracy's norms and possibilities based on a population's "aptitude."

Crane's commentary broadened over the course of his stay. A little over a week after his first telegram to his son, he sent Richard Crane a second one to explain the Revolution's impact on the Russian Church. These details were meant for his close, longtime collaborator, John R. Mott of the YMCA.

Crane wanted to let him know that the Russian Church had not taken part in the revolutionary movement which, he said, was not only secular but also "entirely materialistic and socialistic in aims." This comment on the "socialistic" nature of the Revolution was not meant in a pejorative way since Crane concurrently boasted that the Church seemed to be following the example set by society and by the Provisional Government in instituting a populist and democratic internal organizational reform. "[The] New church will probably be socialistic, certainly democratic and free and bishops will have to come down to the people for support and inspiration." Much in the same way Crane saw the February Revolution as having followed American democracy's example, he viewed these clerical changes as a result of "protestant leanings" on the part of American Churches, particularly in regard to the adoption of elements belonging to the Congregational model of governance.[67] His enthusiasm toward this ecclesial regeneration was not based purely on his imagination. The democratic reforms carried out by the Provisional Government did indeed prompt similar reforms in the Church, and many prelates had ties to members of the Provisional Government.[68]

The Root Mission and the Vision of Evangelical Diplomacy

The connection between the United States' entry into the war and the launch of the Root Mission appears to be essential when looking at the evidence and at the chain of events. For instance, Wilson's War Message to Congress on April 2, 1917 included a very telling section about Russia's place within the intertwined stakes of the war and of the ensuing peace negotiations:

> Russia was known by those who knew it best [undoubtedly Crane] to have been always in fact democratic at heart [...] generous Russian people have been added in all their naive majesty and might to the forces that are fighting for freedom in the world, for justice, and for peace. Here is a fit partner for a league of honour.[69]

This excerpt, which repeats almost word for word Crane's comments about Russia's democratic disposition, demonstrates not only Crane's influence on Wilson's attitude toward the Russian Revolution but also his impact on the decision to abandon neutrality in favor of intervention. It also unmasks the motives behind the strategy as of then employed by the American government to ensure Russia's continuing contribution to the war. Concerned with maintaining the integrity of the Eastern front, Wilson became increasingly interested in the Russian issue and realized that Crane's ties with the Provisional Government and his presence in the field constituted important assets in regard to achieving his diplomatic and military aims.

Crane's presence in Russia, for its part, was fuelled by rather ambiguous motives since he became involved in two different but interconnected initiatives.[70] John Mott quickly joined Crane in Petrograd, accompanied by the Czech professor Tomáš Masaryk[71] and by Samuel Harper, to lead a mission on behalf of the YMCA whose aim it was to collaborate with the Russian Church and to help with its reform. Between 1900 and 1914, the YMCA's intensive work in Russia, particularly in the domain of education, represented an extension of the social gospel (sometimes called "applied Christianity" by the YMCA youth) and of the great step taken overseas by America's Christian missions at the turn of the twentieth century. Shaken by the start of the war, the YMCA then focused its energies on the matter of war prisoners, in which Mott proved to be a key player. The February Revolution and the United States' entry into the war forced the YMCA to restructure its efforts once again as it could no longer operate from a position of neutrality.[72] The organization led by Mott then became involved in the diplomatic relations between Russia and the United States. Not much documentation remains about this informal mission led, in a way, by Crane and Mott's personal initiative. Even books about the YMCA and about Mott's work seem to misunderstand this discreet and almost secret venture, and historians tended to view it as part of another venture then underway in Russia, a special diplomatic mission headed by Theodore Roosevelt's former secretary of state, 1912 Nobel Prize winner Elihu Root. In fact, Crane himself worried at first that the Root Mission would get in the way of the private plans he shared with Mott, Harper, and Masaryk. He was even somewhat surprised at his appointment to the commission by Wilson, remarking that he felt "more or less disturbed by the approach of the [Root] Commission, of which I seem to be a member."

The idea for this mission, first proposed by House, was presented to Secretary of State Lansing by Wilson himself, who seems to also have personally pushed for Crane's nomination on the grounds that he was already conveniently in Russia at the time. It is even possible that Crane may have been initially chosen to lead this mission. This is hinted at by records of backlash against such a choice, without any concrete justification, by British dignitaries then visiting the White House. Though each selected member was in favor of the Provisional Government and "genuinely enthusiastic for the success of the Russian revolution,"[73] Wilson did attempt to form a diverse and non-partisan team. In the end, however, the delegation could easily be mistaken for a gathering of Crane's friends. Cyrus H. McCormick Jr., Samuel Harper (though he accompanied the delegation in an unofficial capacity), and John Mott, whose nomination Crane had personally requested, were all part of the expedition. Yet Crane saw the appointment of Elihu Root, "the most orthodox of republicans," to the head of the mission in 1917 as proof of Wilson's ability to raise himself above base partisanship.[74] Wilson in fact proposed a varied roster of candidates like Samuel Gompers, a representative of the working class (Lansing agreed with this choice, viewing it as a guarantee against any designs entertained by Russian socialists of establishing a separate peace with Germany, but House ultimately opposed the selection) and Oscar Strauss, a Jew (Lansing opposed this nomination on the basis that it would be dangerous to emphasize the "Jewish element"). Ultimately, the Root Mission counted three other members besides Root, Crane, Mott, and McCormick.[75]

Mott's presence in the diplomatic mission and Crane's determination to secure a place for him there are highly significant factors that expose the deeper motive behind Crane's presence in Russia. Crane explained in his memoirs that the Tsar's abdication had in turn annihilated the head of the Orthodox Church, especially the ministers involved in the Tsarist government, giving the Russian people an opportunity for reform. After driving away preachers like Rasputin, the old synod was abolished to permit the construction of a new one which would now have to be accountable to parishioners. In short, Crane envisioned a sort of representative democracy at work within the Russian Church, with men and women voting openly in their dioceses. In consultation with the Provisional Government, the new synod began studying the current religious situation in order to create a new Ecumenical Orthodox Church. Convinced that Wilson would encourage a reconstruction of the Russian Church and believing that "the most important thing going on in Russia then was the revolution in the Russian Church," Crane insisted that the Root Mission ought to include more than just businessmen and politicians. There had to be at least one person who represented the religious dimension in the diplomatic relations between Russia and the United States and who displayed the corresponding values, "the greatest spiritual wisdom and authority." Crane naturally recommended that Wilson invite John R. Mott, one of the most internationally influential religious leaders of his time,[76] to speak to the Russians on behalf of America and of the President. He also pressed his friend to accept this nomination,[77] and Mott obliged.

In keeping with his aforementioned views on the "spiritual" relations between Russia and the United States, however, Crane feared the addition to the party of a "bad Jew" while knowing that the mission had to include at least one member with a Jewish background. One such "bad Jew," Herman Bernstein, strove to join the mission. According to a letter written by Samuel Harper, it was Crane who thwarted the attempt with the help of his son Richard at the State Department.[78]

The commissioners appointed by Wilson joined Crane in Petrograd on June 13, 1917, having crossed through Siberia to avoid German submarines. Their aim was to help the Provisional Government fight against the radical forces and encourage it to continue siding with the Allies during the war.[79] Yet Crane and Mott also had an underlying mission which was implicitly backed by Wilson. They hoped to help the Orthodox Church with its ecclesial reform and to give it a greater role in the Russian Revolution, which it did not yet have according to one of Crane's reports to Mott.

Even before Mott's arrival, Crane had sent him a telegram with an outline of the speech he had asked the renowned evangelist to deliver before the assembly of the new synod in Moscow. The assembly was, according to Crane, moved at the thought of hearing a message from America and impatient for Mott's visit. Crane himself travelled to Petrograd to greet the delegation and ask for Elihu Root's permission to lead this project, which Root granted. Back in Moscow, Crane, and Mott were received by the synod's newly elected archbishop, Platon, who knew Crane personally and Mott by reputation. Seeking advice, Mott read him the speech he had prepared for the assembly, which the archbishop showered with praise. He only advised Mott to put more emphasis on the importance of keeping Russia involved in the war effort, which, following the Provisional Government's example, the Russian Church also supported.[80] In his memoirs, Crane reported that Mott's speech on June 19, 1917 thrilled the assembly, describing that "When Mr. Mott had finished the whole assembly arose as one man and without any announcement immediately began to sing a most beautiful church hymn." He even compared this spontaneous reaction, in a rather excessive manner, to the Biblical episode of the Pentecost, and declared that the "Holy Spirit had descended on the assembly through that address."[81] Afterward, the whole assembly jumped up to applaud Mott and thank him for his contribution. As he had rarely done during his career, Crane displayed a high degree of enthusiasm and exuberance, and in a letter to an American missionary, he designated Mott's speech as the Root Mission's most significant achievement: "With all of the political, military and the other talents of the commission the really great, inspiring and permanent achievements of the commission will be left by Dr. Mott." He sent a similar account to his son Richard: "Mr. Mott's visit has made a profound impression on the minds and hearts of the Russian people and will be remembered for a century." Crane also personally gave Wilson an account of Mott's mission in the new Russian Church and thoroughly explained the components of the internal reform it had initiated. Crane stressed that Mott had been welcomed and accepted as Wilson's representative speaking on the president's behalf about essential topics like "the church itself, its relationships to the Christian World, and the importance of its position, not only in the [Russian] empire but in America, and its relation to the winning of the war." In this sense, Crane believed he was building a diplomatic alliance between the United States and Russia based on religious unity between the two countries. He saw religion as a more durable and promising basis for cooperation than the ever changing political conditions. This belief was fuelled by an assumption that a peoples' religious fervor was inherently stable, permanent, and impervious to cultural and demographic changes. Not only had the Church pledged support to the war effort, but the reformist spirit seemed to Crane undoubtedly better represented and protected there than in secular society, which had to contend with the rapid expansion of anarchist forces. As Crane expressed to Wilson, the Church, "the most truly representative assembly of the new Russia," carried within it the germs of representative democracy and needed protection from the forces that increasingly threatened the Provisional Government.[82] He also explained to his son that the Church formed a bulwark against social chaos, as "In the general anarchy prevailing in Russian affairs the Church gives the note of perfect order not only in its church service, but also in its very extensive organization. It is a comfort to follow the orderly processes of its evolution." In early July of 1917, while the social climate was becoming more and more radical after the failed offensive in June,[83] Crane added:

> I am beginning to believe that we have a real mission here in Russia. For many of the members of the Commission, and for some of the Americans here it has become a kind of religion, as well as a patriotic duty to America, to help Russia by moral support, by faith in her future.[84]

In retrospect, one will find it hard to contradict Crane's belief in the importance of Mott's speeches—not because they truly made their mark on history, but because the Root Mission was ineffectual and may in fact have been counterproductive where political repercussions were concerned.[85] Fuelled by a missionary spirit and a sense of *noblesse oblige* as much as by strategic considerations, this diplomatic commission succeeded neither in supporting the Provisional Government's fight against the radicals nor in preventing Kerensky's downfall and the signing of a separate peace with Germany. Furthermore, Root made an excessively optimistic report of his findings to Lansing which was quickly disproved by the later events.[86]

After the Root Mission ended on July 9, 1917, Crane was the only member to remain in Russia and witness the deterioration of the political climate. Thanks to his contacts and the freedom of movement his fortune allowed him, he was able to observe the return of the exiled radicals that same year and the changes this brought. A wave of radicalism in Russia followed the Root Mission, and Crane, alerting Wilson immediately, explained that "The enthusiasm of the revolution is being followed by dismay over the magnitude of the new problems and the difficulties of firmly establishing a new state on the wreckage." Crane naturally campaigned to keep Russia on the side of the Allies while recognizing that the Provisional Government's issues stemmed from its involvement with the war: "She must at one and the same time consolidate the Revolution and wage a war." The situation was not aided by the fact that Germany took advantage of this conundrum by supporting the extremists. As a result, Crane began advocating a degree of political repression to control the extremists, which represented a turn toward the right for a Provisional Government that had previously been excessively liberal. When the Bolshevik socialists, including Lenin and Trotsky, were arrested by the Provisional Government, Crane applauded this "new psychology" which had emerged around the third week of June. The new, more repressive policies led Crane to briefly believe that Russia was once again dedicated to the Allied plan, and he stated that "the spirit of the country is one of wealthy enthusiasm for the war."[87]

His hope was short lived, however, and Crane once again devoted himself to ecclesiastical reform in Russia, aided by Prince Lvov who had left his post at the head of the Provisional Government to make way for Kerensky. Though Kerensky was a powerful orator, Crane believed that he lacked organizational skills. The country no longer seemed to be preoccupied with continuing the war effort and Kerensky was forced to arm the Bolsheviks in order to suppress Kornilov's revolt. Crane, on the other hand, viewed Kornilov in quite a favorable light and thought Kerensky had been wrong to cease associating with this illustrious military commander whom Crane called "a courageous, high-minded and devoted patriot." Imprisoned by Kerensky for his attempted coup, Kornilov fled when the Bolsheviks took power and enlisted as commander in the White armies. It was the failure of his coup that finally alerted Crane to the situation's complete hopelessness, and he ended his stay in Russia right around the fall of the Provisional Government, feeling that "there was no help for Russia for a long time to come."[88] Before leaving, Crane also convinced Milyukov, whose arrest had been ordered by the Bolsheviks, to flee to Crimea.[89]

Crane, for whom Russia's fate was a constant concern, thought that the unfolding events had led to the worst possible outcome for his beloved country. The liberals had been chased from the Revolutionary movement, the Russians had broken ranks with the Allies by signing a separate peace with the Central Powers and those in whom Crane had personally believed were now being hunted by the Bolsheviks and threatened with death. Only the Church still offered some potential for reform before the arrival of the Bolsheviks, which led Crane to conclude that "If political Russia could have paralleled religious Russia, what a happy state she might have been!"[90] Things worsened with the Allied intervention against the Bolsheviks, which had in fact been demanded by those same exiled friends of Crane's. Lvov, fallen leader of the Provisional Government, wrote to Crane as the Bolsheviks were spreading their power to all the soviets outside Petrograd to tell him that America must continue playing a role in the creation of a new liberal Russia, even by force of arms:

> Bolshevism has found a fertile soil in the base and anarchistic instincts of the people. It is in this sense a Russian sickness, and can only thus be cured by foreign intervention. The re-establishment of order and of the healthy forces in Russia can only be achieved under the protection of an organized army.

Similarly to many of his progressive colleagues like Milyukov and Rodzianko, Prince Lvov endorsed Wilson's vision of the reconstruction of a world order based on the precepts of liberal democracy, and was "convinced that the World War is giving birth to a new world order led by the United States." These flattering predictions may have been pronounced solely in an attempt to obtain America's military aid or they may have truly reflected the opinion of liberal Russia, but they ultimately had little impact on Wilson's hesitant and half-hearted decision to intervene in Russia's civil war.[91]

In short, Crane's presence in Russia in the midst of the February Revolution and his role as liaison between his contacts in the Provisional Government and the Wilson Administration, especially through the Root Mission, demonstrate a typically Wilsonian sympathy for popular government and moderate liberalism. In turn, his enthusiastic involvement in the reconstruction of the Orthodox Church in the wake of the revolution, particularly noticeable through his recommendation of John R. Mott's nomination, acts as a reflection of Wilson and some of his collaborators' marked tendency to consider spiritual progress as a driving force of social progress. Indeed, it was Wilson's belief that the Bible stood at the root of modern democracy and that human progress was inexorably tied to the Gospel. As he once expressed in a speech in 1911, "The Bible, with its individual value on the human soul, is undoubtedly the book that has made democracy and been the source of all progress," and in his mind, all the moral dignity achievable to man through the exercise of democracy stemmed from the word of God, who "reveals every man to himself as a distinct moral agent, responsible not to men, not even to those men whom he has put over him in authority, but responsible through his own conscience to his Lord and Maker."[92]

Crane, formerly a member of the Presbyterian Church like Wilson and then a member of the Episcopal Church, did not express his religious motivations as fervently as the president. Yet his actions and comments during the time he spent in Revolutionary Russia demonstrate a like-minded approach to the ideas of progress, democracy, and man's place in society, and a similar evaluation of Christianity's importance in social reform. Crane's religious understanding of the relationship between peoples did not have much ground for expression in regard to domestic affairs and was instead most clearly articulated once he invested himself in foreign policy and diplomacy, starting with the Russian Revolution.

An analysis of Charles Crane's later involvement in Wilsonian internationalism will shed more light on this missionary perspective at the basis of the new diplomacy endorsed by Wilson and Crane. Particularly important in this regard was the issue of self-determination, to which the events in Russia were a sort of introduction for Crane.

Notes

1. *Crane Papers*, "Memoirs," 153–4.
2. The *Crane Papers* do not give a precise diagnosis of Crane's health, but letters written by his doctor, especially around the 1880s, show that he suffered from various troubles like dizziness, nausea, nosebleeds, and an inconsistent appetite. Doctor Jewell classified these symptoms under "general neuraesthenia." Crane also fell ill with malaria

shortly after enrolling in the Stevens Institute in Hoboken, where he was going to study mechanical engineering in 1876. The doctor assessed that Crane's lungs may have been weakened, potentially because of the manufacturing environment in which he had grown up from the age of ten. As Crane once told his wife-to-be, his doctor even prescribed, as a method of recovery, to travel often while eating lightly in order not to upset his stomach. See *Crane Papers*, "Memoirs," 4–7; "CRC to Cornelia W. Smith," February 14, 1879; "Dr. J. S, Jewell to CRC," March 16, April 13, and November 30, 1881.

3. *Crane Papers*, "CRC to Count Semenov," January, 1889. It nevertheless seems that Crane remained in the habit of using French with his Russian friends, particularly with Georgy Lvov. See "Memoirs," 190.
4. *Crane Papers*, "Harry Pratt Judson (U. Chicago) to CRC," November 4, 1914. For a more detailed description of Crane's contacts with Russian professors and his involvement in the propagation of Russian and Slavic culture in the United States, see Norman E. Saul, *The Life and Times of Charles R. Crane* (2013), 56–61.
5. Christopher Lasch, *The American Liberals and the Russian Revolution* (New York: Columbia University Press, 1962), 10, 28.
6. *Crane Papers*, "CRC to Charles W. Eliot," December 30, 1914; "Christobel Pankhurst to CRC," January 10, 1915. Activist and suffragette C. Pankhurst asked of Crane that Russia's "friends" intervene to prevent Germans and western Russophobes, particularly the Jews, from spreading their propaganda. Pankhurst was referring to some articles written by the Fabian socialist Henry Noel Brailsford that were up for publication. It would seem that the latter was also severely blamed by Great Britain for his (alleged) antiwar and Russophobic position. See Lasch, *The American Liberals*, 11–12.
7. See Jerry Israel, *Progressivism and the Open Door. America and China, 1905–1921* (Pittsburgh: University of Pittsburgh Press, 1971), 56–9.
8. Norman E. Saul, *The Life and Times of Charles R. Crane*, 50–2.
9. Christopher Lasch, *The American Liberals and the Russian Revolution*, 25–26. The Progressives' relationship with modernity was sometimes complex and even contradictory. In *The Progressive Mind, 1890–1917*, David W. Noble explains that many Progressives viewed (democratic) industrial progress and efficiency as a remedy for corrupt, coercive, and aristocratic traditions inherited from the Middle Ages—an idea shared among others by Henry Ford, Frederick J. Turner, and Frederic W. Taylor. Noble does, however, notice a parallel tendency to glorify a utopian return to ancestral simplicity out of distaste for the complex nature of European civilization (37–80, 191–3).
10. *Crane Papers*, "CRC to Gilson Gardner," March 17, 1917.
11. Christopher Lasch, *The American Liberals and the Russian Revolution*, viii–xix.
12. *Crane Papers*, "CRC to WW," August 4, 1914. Hart's article does not appear in the *Wilson Papers* nor in the *Crane Papers*, but his ideas feature in one of his books from the American Nation Series called *The War in Europe* (Vol. 26), and a review of this work was published in the October 25, 1914 edition of the *New York Times*.
13. *Crane Papers*, "WW to CRC," August 4, 1914. Wilson expressed this "utter condemnation" of the conflict on the very same day that he received Crane's letter and read Hart's article, which suggests a very strong and spontaneous reaction to these documents.

14. *Crane Papers*, "CRC to Eliot," December 15, 1914. Despite his support of Wilsonian neutrality at this stage of the war, Crane displays, perhaps unconsciously, a certain pro-Allied penchant in this passage.
15. Lasch, *The American Liberals and the Russian Revolution*, xi–xii.
16. *Crane Papers*, "CRC to WW," March 27, 1913. However, a subsequent message from Crane suggests that Ryerson had indeed been nominated at his request but had apparently refused. See *Crane Papers*, "CRC to WW," October 1, 1913.
17. The suggestion of Paul S. Reinsch, a professor at the University of Wisconsin, as ambassador to South America was kept, but he was instead given the position of minister to China. *PWW*, "CRC to WW," Vol. 27, March 21, 1913, 203.
18. *PWW*, "House Diary," Vol. 27, March 25, April 3, April 4, 1913, 228, 259, 262. "That is Crane's trouble—loquacity."
19. *Crane Papers*, October 29, 1909. A detailed account of this revoked nomination can be found in Leo Bocage's "The Public Career of Charles R. Crane" (Ph. D. diss., Fordham, 1962). Some other factors were Crane's isolation as a supporter of the Russian position as well as Taft's personal worries about Crane's criticism of the Wall Street Jews. See Jacob Sulzbach's "Charles R. Crane, Woodrow Wilson and Progressive Reforms: 1909–1921" (Ph. D. diss., Texas A&M University, 1994), 92–4. In *Progressivism and the Open Door*, Jerry Israel particularly emphasizes Crane's anti-Japanese position to explain his sudden dismissal.
20. *PWW*, "William Jennings Bryan to Wilson," Vol. 28, June 25, 1913, p. 4.
21. *PWW*, "WJB to WW," Vol. 28, August 4, 1913, 111–2. We know of Pindell that he never reached his post at the Russian embassy, but an editorial note in the *Crane Papers* mentions his refusal while a later letter from Wilson to Crane indicates that he had actually accepted an interim post. *PWW*, "WW to CRC," Vol. 28, October 3, 1913, 353. See also *Crane Papers*, "H. Kohlsaat to CRC," September 27, 1913.
22. *Crane Papers*, "CRC to WW," October 1, 1913.
23. The message was not present in the *Wilson Papers*, but appeared in Crane's correspondence. *Crane Papers*, "CRC to WW," September 30, 1913.
24. *PWW*, "WW to CRC," Vol. 28, October 3, 1913, 353. An editorial note mentions that this letter, dated October 3, is the first trace of an exchange between them about Crane's nomination to the post in Russia. Crane's correspondence, however, reveals, as shown here, that the subject was discussed prior to this.
25. *PWW*, "CRC to WW," Vol. 30, May 18, 1914, 46.
26. *Crane Papers*, "CRC to WW," October 15, 1913; "WW to CRC," May 15, 1914.
27. *Crane Papers*, "WW to CRC," May 21, 1914. Two letters written by Wilson to Crane on June 16 and 17, 1914, describe their conversations about potential substitutes. Wilson sought Crane's approval in regard to the nomination of a "substitute" ambassador to Russia.
28. *Crane Papers*, "Thomas Meyer to CRC," September 17, 1914. Meyer's letter referred to these two elements that had previously prevented Crane from giving in to the requests Wilson had been making for over a year.
29. In *The Soviet-American Relations, 1917–1920*, Vol. 1, *Russia Leaves the War* (3–41), George F. Kennan paints a surprising portrait of David R. Francis, former governor of Missouri, as

ambassador to Russia. Without mentioning Wilson's efforts to recruit Crane for the post, Kennan presents Francis as a petty provincial politician, a "dry" who had trouble adapting to the diplomatic environment in Saint Petersburg and who even became the laughing stock of his European colleagues due to his Protestant abstinence and frugality. One can't help thinking that Wilson's first choice would have been much more presentable in Russian diplomatic high society, even though Crane was never quite the "*bon vivant*."

30. *Crane Papers*, "CRC to Josephine Crane Bradley," March 19, April 5, 1916.
31. *Idem*. A few years prior, Gottheil had shared with Crane his impressions on the "bad Jews," whom he called "a small clique of snobs," and added that "The great mass of the Jewish population in the United States does not, I am sure, take so low an estimate of diplomatic positions." He was referring to those Jews who sought diplomatic posts simply out of self-interest. Gottheil and Henry Morgenthau, another Jew appointed by Wilson as ambassador to the Ottoman Empire, both agreed with Crane about these "bad Jews." See *Crane Papers*, "R. Gottheil to CRC," July 5, 1913. To show how much Crane esteemed Richard Gottheil, one can note that he personally recommended Gottheil to Wilson for the embassy in Constantinople (Ottoman Empire) in 1913 following Mrs. Gottheil's entreaties. See *Crane Papers*, "Emma Gottheil to CRC," January 26, 1913; and "CRC to WW," March 24, 1913.
32. The *Crane Papers* contain no information on this subject, but the works of Hapgood (p. 25) and Bocage (p. 97) report contradictory amounts drawn from the press.
33. Arthur S. Link, *Woodrow Wilson. Revolution, War and Peace* (Arlington Heights: Harlan Davidson, 1979), 14. This book, Link's most recent among his monographs on Wilson, is a more favorable revision of his previous work *Wilson the Diplomatist. A Look at His Major Foreign Policies* (1957). Crane himself once made a comment about Wilson acting as his own Secretary of State. As early as June, 1915, shortly after Wilson famously responded to Germany's scuttling with the phrase "too proud to fight," Crane told Wilson that his people as well as the whole world had turned him into their Secretary of State. *Crane Papers*, "CRC to WW," June 26, 1915.
34. Arthur S. Link, *Woodrow Wilson and the Progressive Era, 1910–1917*, 26–7. Let us also note that Wilson did not see appointing a novice like Bryan to the State Department as a great risk because he initially believed that "It would be the irony of fate if my administration had to deal chiefly with foreign affairs," which is in fact what ended up happening. R. S. Baker, *Woodrow Wilson: Life and Letters*, Vol. 4, 55. See Kendrick A. Clements, *William Jennings Bryan, Missionary Isolationist* (Knoxville: University of Tennessee Press, 1982), 59.
35. Clements, *William Jennings Bryan, Missionary Isolationist*, 65–6. See also Link, Arthur S. *Woodrow Wilson and the Progressive Era, 1910–1917*, 82.
36. *Crane Papers*, "W. J. Bryan to CRC," May 8 and 10, 1915; and "Robert Lansing and Woodrow Wilson to CRC," June 14, 1915. Crane accepted the post offered by Wilson and Bryan. *Crane Papers*, "CRC to WJB," May 15, 1915.
37. *Crane Papers*, "CRC to JOC," September 30, 1914.
38. *Crane Papers*, "CRC to Count Semenov," January, 1889.
39. *Crane Papers*, "Memoirs," 174.
40. *PWW*, "Josephus Daniels Diary," Vol. 41, March 20, 1917, 444–5.On the other hand, Arthur Link explains that for many pro-Allied Americans, the end of the Tsarist autocracy

and the establishment of a liberal and patriotic government confirmed Russia's loyalty toward the Allies in this conflict. It constituted a crucial step toward American intervention. See *Woodrow Wilson and the Progressive Era, 1910–1917*, 274–5.

41. *PWW*, "House Diary," Vol. 41, March 25, 1917, 468.
42. *PWW*, "CRC to WW," Vol. 41, March 28, 1917, 494. A letter from Crane written to Wilson mentions this supper without however providing any further details.
43. *PWW*, "Josephus Daniels Diary," Vol. 41, March 24, 1917, 461–6.
44. *PWW*, "CRC to WW," Vol. 41, March 28, 1917, 494. Crane had also declared a few days after the Tsar's abdication that "the new Russia is in the best possible hands." *Crane Papers*, "CRC to Gilson Gardner," March 17, 1917.
45. Lansing was nominated in 1915 to replace Bryan who had abdicated in protest to Wilson's reaction to the Germans sinking the *Lusitania*. Shortly after entering the State Department, Lansing hired Richard T. Crane III, Charles Crane's eldest son, as his personal secretary.
46. *PWW*, "Samuel Northrup Harper to Richard Crane," Vol. 41, March 16, 1917, 415–7. Crane also heard echoes about the Rasputin episode in a memo sent by Thomas Whittemore, a Byzantinist and Egyptologist from Harvard in the employ of the Red Cross in Petrograd. *Crane Papers*, "Thomas Whittemore to CRC," March 14 (27), 1917.
47. For several perspectives on the matter, see Lasch, *The American Liberals and the Russian Revolution*, 41; Norman G. Levin, *Woodrow Wilson and World Politics. America's Response to War and Revolution* (NY: Oxford University Press, 1968), 42–9; Arthur S. Link, *Woodrow Wilson. Revolution, War, and Peace*; Lloyd E. Ambrosius, *The Wilsonian Statecraft. Theory and Practice of Liberal Internationalism during WWI* (Lanham: SR Books, 1991), 100–2; Frederick S. Calhoun, *Uses of Force and Wilsonian Foreign Policy* (Kent: Kent State University Press, 1993), 109, 117.
48. *PWW*, "House to WW," Vol. 41, March 17, 1917, 422–3.
49. *Idem*. At the time of his discharge, it is true that some liberals and friends of Crane, like Maksim Kovalevsky, were readers of Wilson's works, particularly *The State*. See Max M. Laserson, *The American Impact on Russia, 1784–1917* (New York: Collier, 1950), 466–8. It is also true that a number of Russian and Ukrainian constitutionalists at the turn of the twentieth century had been considerably influenced by American—and British—political thought. Laserson even underscores that liberal Russians had welcomed Wilson's 1912 election with relief because it was a break from the previous "imperialist" presidencies of Roosevelt and Taft, and the liberal press repeatedly printed the president-elect's inaugural speech (487–488).
50. *Crane Papers*, "Thomas Whittemore to CRC," March 14 (27), 1917. This reference to people wearing the red under duress applied to those who posed as communists under the coercion of soviets in Petrograd despite remaining attached to the idea of reforming the monarchy or subscribing to the Provisional Government's liberal principles. Less than a week later, Whittemore sent Crane another missive informing him of "constant threatening" and of the anticipated return (decreed by the Provisional Government) of the exiled political radicals. According to Whittemore, the majority of the population wanted the same thing as the Provisional Government: liberal reforms and carrying out the war until the end. He explained that there was only "a small, very important and very

violent minority that does not want this." *Crane Papers*, "Thomas Whittemore to CRC," March 20 (April 2), 1917.

51. *Crane Papers*, "Thomas Whittemore to CRC," March 20 (April 2), 1917.
52. *Crane Papers*, "John R. Mott to Roger H. Williams," March 22, 1917.
53. The *Christian Herald* was a monthly publication of Scottish origin founded by Michael P. Baxter. Its American branch was set up in 1878 in New York. This interdenominational journal dealt with religious subjects and supported philanthropic causes. Its tone was of the "inspirational" type and it received acclaim for its very artistic cover pages. The *Christian Herald*, which hosted a column by Billy Graham in the 1950s, printed up to one million copies by the end of the 1920s. It went out of print in 1992. See Theodore Peterson, *Magazines in the Twentieth Century* (Chicago: University of Illinois Press, 1972 [1964]), 390, 396; Randall Herbert Balmer, *Encyclopedia of Evangelicalism* (Louisville: John Knox Press, 2002), 135–6.
54. *Crane Papers*, "CRC to WW," March 28, 1917.
55. This justification was based on an inaccurate assumption that the whole Provisional Government of Russia adhered to a Wilsonian definition of anti-imperialist war. In reality, only some of its members subscribed to this view.
56. *PWW*, "War Message to Congress," Vol. 41, April 2, 1917, 519–27.
57. *Crane Papers*, "Memoirs," 177. On this topic, Crane wrote with particular bitterness: "The Trotsky legion began to arrive from New York and Lenin was piloted across Germany [...] fully provided with German money [...] to wreck the struggling new government."
58. The *Crane Papers* contain many comments reflecting Crane's interpretation of this Jewish "propaganda" against Russia. They can be spotted as early as 1889, especially in regard to rumors about the pogroms, and escalate around 1913, when Crane became an actor in the Wilson Administration and saw his political, philanthropic and diplomatic possibilities expanding. Some of his comments will be discussed later on.
59. *Crane Papers*, "Memoirs," 177. "They [the Jews] controlled the press and other organs of public expressions."
60. *Crane Papers*, "CRC to Gilson Gardner," March 17, 1917. Crane's friends doubted his optimism toward the peasant democracy in Russia. Though he rejoiced in the fall of the Tsarist regime, the former British ambassador to the United States and Crane's good friend James Bryce believed that the Russian people would resist self-determination and modernization since "the vast mass of the peasantry [is] worshipping the Tsar as a sort of God," aptly adding that the movement came from the elite rather than from the masses, for "one doubts what fruits universal suffrage will bear in such a population. The Revolution has been the work of a small section."*Crane Papers*, "James Bryce to CRC," April 3, 1917.
61. *Crane Papers*, "CRC to WW," February 17, 1916.
62. The historian David Thelen describes this theme as a new civic awareness emerging first in Wisconsin from the economic crisis of the 1890s and represented by the so-called "voluntary associations," before these issues were taken up in a political way by the Progressives: "The early Wisconsin Progressives put more faith in developing new voluntary associations and the techniques of mass, popular, grass-roots pressure than they put in their leaders." See David P. Thelen, *The New Citizenship. Origins of Progressivism in Wisconsin, 1885–1900*, 3, 55, 71–80.

63. Michael McGerr, *A Fierce Discontent. The Rise and Fall of the Progressive Movement in America*, 81–89, 294. McGerr explains that the movement in favor of prohibition had long been a facet of the Progressive struggle against vice, especially in the rural Victorian middle class. The war mobilization served as context and justification (grain rationing, anti-German repression, etc.) for this project aiming to improve the moral climate of the time, which was seen as a factor of social decline.
64. Clements, Kendrick A. *William Jennings Bryan, Missionary Isolationist*, 59–60. Bryan's refusal to serve wine at receptions given by the State Department, which was approved by Wilson before he even entered the cabinet, was seen by European dignitaries as a manifestation of "rural barbarism."
65. Crane on the other hand, drank wine and particularly enjoyed the vineyards of Mount Carmel in Palestine. *Crane Papers*, "CRC to CSC," June 15, 1919. Nevertheless, he was also quite frugal in certain ways, if only for health reasons. The historian Arnold Toynbee, who spent time with him during the Paris Conference in 1919, mentioned that Crane, while dining at some of the best restaurants in Paris, invariably ordered boiled chicken and rice pudding. "Mr. Crane's tastes happened to be plain," Toynbee stated several decades later. *Crane Papers*, "Charles R. Crane, by Arnold J. Toynbee."
66. *Crane Papers*, "CRC to Richard Crane," May 4, 1917. This description of a childish and joyful revolution was in part truthful, as some harmless and carnivalesque episodes did occur alongside other chaotic and incredibly cruel ones. Orlando Figes, *A People's Tragedy. The Russian Revolution, 1891–1924* (New York, Penguin Books, 1996), 318–21.
67. *Crane Papers*, "CRC to Richard Crane," May 14, 1917.
68. Orlando Figes, *A People's Tragedy*, 348–51.
69. *PWW*, "War Message to Congress," Vol. 41, April 2, 1917, 519–27.
70. This double activity on Crane's part fit into what the historian George F. Kennan called a "number of private or semi-private American organizations [who] likewise sent representatives or missions to Russia." See *Soviet-American Relations, 1917–1920*, Vol. 1, *Russia Leaves the War* (Princeton: Princeton University Press, 1956), 21. This collection of "diplomatic" initiatives reflected the great sympathy liberal Americans had toward the Provisional Government, which had a lot of well-wishers back in America.
71. Right before the Russian Revolution, Masaryk, a collaborator in the Slavic Studies department at the University of Chicago and future first president of Czechoslovakia, was exiled to London and had received a death sentence from the Austro-Hungarian government. See *PWW*, "Norman Hapgood to WW," Vol. 41, January 29, 1917, 56–7. Hapgood asked Wilson to intervene and to meet Masaryk, who was campaigning for an independent Bohemia. As will be shown later, Crane himself secured an audience for Masaryk with the American president.
72. Donald E. Davis and Eugene P. Trani, "The American YMCA and the Russian Revolution," *Slavic Review*, 33, 3 (1974): 471–2. On Mott's involvement in work concerning the prisoners of war (POW), see Charles Howard Hopkins, *John R. Mott, 1865–1955: A Biography* (Grand Rapids, Eerdmans, 1979), 450–2.
73. *PWW*, "Thomas W. Brahany Diary," Vol. 42, April 24, 1917, 126; "WW to Robert Lansing," Vol. 42, April 12, 1917, 43–4.

74. *Crane Papers*, "Memoirs," 168. Crane wrote that Wilson stood up to the democratic spoilsmen (he did not name them, however) who wanted to take part in the mission in Russia. The *Papers of Woodrow Wilson* show that House insisted from the beginning on having a Republican representative in the mission. Vol. 42, April 10, 1917, 29–30.
75. Samuel R. Bertron, James Duncan, and Charles E. Russell were the other three men appointed to the Root Mission. Russell, born in Iowa to an abolitionist evangelical family, was a muckraker, a prowar socialist, and an activist, most notably a cofounder of the NAACP. Duncan was a Scottish American union leader from the American Federation of Labor and friends with Samuel Gompers. Bertron was a New York banker, one of the few representatives of the business community within the delegation. *PWW*, Vol. 42, May 10, 1917, 262. In *The American Liberals and the Russian Revolution*, Lasch suggests that it was the explorer George Kennan who first proposed the creation of a commission in Russia. Yet a careful look at the *PWW* reveals that it was actually French diplomats in the United States who asked House to suggest it to Wilson. See Lasch, 41–2 and *PWW*, Vol. 42, starting from April 7.
76. Wilson, during an interview for *Harper's Weekly* in 1914, praised Mott in the following manner: "One of the most notably useful men in the world." Quoted from C. H. Hopkins, *John R. Mott, 1865–1955: A Biography*, 435. See also Martti Muukkonen, *Ecumenism of the Laity. Continuity and Change in the Mission View of the World's Alliance of YMCA, 1855–1955*, 257–61; and Risto Ahonen, "John R. Mott as an Ecumenical Leader" in *The Finnish Evangelical Lutheran Mission* (on-line).
77. *Crane Papers*, "Memoirs," 184–5. Crane specified that his messages to Wilson and Mott were sent by telegram but no trace of this correspondence on this specific topic can be found in either the *Crane Papers* or in the *PWW*.
78. *Crane Papers*, "Samuel Harper to Roger Williams," April 22, 1917.
79. For an official statement of the Root Mission's goals, see *Papers Relating to Foreign Relations of the United States (FRUS)*, Vol. 1, *Russia, 1918* (U.S. State Department), 144–6.
80. *Crane Papers*, "Memoirs", 185–7. For Mott's full speech, see *Crane Papers*, "Address of John R. Mott […] Moscow, 19 June 1917," 11.
81. *Crane Papers*, "Memoirs," 187. Crane not only saw Mott's work as an "act of the apostles" but he also compared him to Paul the Apostle, "CRC to Mildred Nelson Page," June 27, 1917.
82. *Crane Papers*, "CRC to Mildred Nelson Page," June 27, 1917; "CRC to Richard Crane," July 6, 1917; "CRC to WW," June 21, 1917.
83. For more on the June, 1917 offensive and its impact on the Provisional Government's collapse: Orlando Figes, *A People's Tragedy*, 407–12.
84. *Crane Papers*, "CRC to Richard Crane," July 6, 1917; "CRC to X," July 8, 1917.
85. In fact, the explorer George Kennan, who had initially supported the creation of this mission, later scoffed at it in a comment conveyed to the State Department. *PWW*, "G. Kennan to Robert Lansing," Vol. 49, August 22, 1918, 320.
86. Christopher Lasch, in *The American Liberals and the Russian Revolution*, 43–5, stressed this excessive optimism. In fact, though it expressed faith in the success of self-government in a liberal Russia remaining firmly on the side of the Allies, this success depended, according to Root's report, on the aid given to Russia. The commission proposed to aid Russia

both materially (this was coordinated primarily by the YMCA) and morally, through, for instance, propaganda to counteract that which was supposedly being disseminated by Germany. The magnitude of the aid proposed by the commissioners was considered essential to the survival of a liberal and Allied Russia and reflected the already precarious state of the Provisional Government when this report was completed in 1917. For the full version: *FRUS*, Vol. 1, *1918, Russia* (U.S. State Department), 131–46.

87. *Crane Papers*, "CRC to WW," June 21, 1917; "CRC to unknown recipient," July 8, 1917.
88. *Crane Papers*, "Memoirs," 202. Let us note that Crane's preference for Kornilov over Kerensky is further indication that he was not a "war liberal" despite Lasch's description. Lasch himself pointed out that the "war liberals" had massively supported Kerensky in fear that a civil war would weaken Russia in its battle against Germany. Crane, on the other hand, was more concerned about a Bolshevik takeover than a German invasion and he did not trust in Kerensky's ability to control the communists. See Lasch, 45–6.
89. Donald E. Davis and Eugene P. Trani, *The First Cold War. The Legacy of Woodrow Wilson in U.S.-Soviet Relations* (Columbia, University of Missouri Press, 2002), 42. The authors explain that Milyukov's resignation, which signified the Provisional Government's almost inevitable fall, also struck a fatal blow to the Root Mission, which suddenly saw all of its objectives fall into obsolescence.
90. *Crane Papers*, "Memoirs," 189.
91. Not included in the *Crane Papers*, this message from Lvov to Crane between October and November, 1918 can be found in the State Archive of the Russian Federation in Moscow. Quoted from Orlando Figes, *A People's Tragedy*, 650–2.
92. *PWW*, "An Address in Denver on the Bible," Vol. 23, May 7, 1911, 11–3.

Bibliography

Archives

Charles Richard Crane Papers, 1869–1967. Rare Books & Manuscript Library, University of Columbia.

Published Primary Sources

Baker, Ray S. and William E. Dodd, ed. *The Public Papers of Woodrow Wilson*. New York: Harper, 1925–26.

Baker, Ray S. *Woodrow Wilson: Life and Letters*. Garden City, NY: Doubleday, 1927–39.

Baruch, Bernard M. *Baruch*. New York: H. Holt, 1957–1960.

Daniels, Josephus. *The Wilson Era*. Chapel Hill: University of North Carolina Press, 1946.

Harper, Samuel N. *The Russia I Believe In: The Memoirs of Samuel N. Harper*. Chicago: University of Chicago Press, 1945.

Link, Arthur S., ed. *Papers of Woodrow Wilson*. Princeton, NJ: Princeton University Press, 1966–92.

Seymour, Charles, ed. *The Intimate Papers of Colonel House Arranged as a Narrative*. London: Ernest Benn, 1926–28.

Tumulty, Joseph P. *Woodrow Wilson as I Know Him*. Garden City: Doubleday, 1921.

U.S. State Department. *Papers Relating to the Foreign Relations of the United States*.

Bibliographic Guides

Buckingham, Peter H. *Woodrow Wilson: A Bibliography of His Times and Presidency*. Wilmington, DE: Scholarly Resources, 1990.

Beisner, Robert L. and Hanson Kurt W., ed. *American Foreign Relations since 1600. A Guide to the Literature*. Santa Barbara, CA: ABC-CLIO, 2003.

Bellot, Hugh Hale. *American History and American Historians: A Review of Recent Contributions to the Interpretation of the History of the United States*. Norman: University of Oklahoma Press, 1952.

Haines, G. K. and J. S. Walker, ed. *American Foreign Relations. A Historiographical Review*. Westport, CT: Greenwood Press, 1981.

Parish, Peter J., ed. *Reader's Guide to American History*. Chicago: Fitzroy Publishers, 1997.

Encyclopedias

Balmer, Randall Herbert. *Encyclopedia of Evangelicalism*. Louisville, KY: John Knox Press, 2002.

Monographies

Ambrosius, Lloyd E. *Woodrow Wilson and the American Diplomatic Tradition: the Treaty Fight in Perspective*. Cambridge: Cambridge University Press, 1987.

———. *Wilsonian Statecraft: Theory and Practice of Liberal Internationalism during World War I*. Lanham, MD: SR Books, 1991.

———. *Wilsonianism: Woodrow Wilson & His Legacy in American Foreign Relations*. New York: Palgrave Macmillan, 2002.

Berlin, William S. *On the Edge of Politics. The Roots of Jewish Political Thought in America*. Westport, CT: Greenwood Press, 1978.

Burns, James M. *The Workshop of Democracy. From the Emancipation Proclamation to the Era of the New Deal*. New York: Vintage Book, 1985.

Calhoun, Frederick S. *Uses of Force and Wilsonian Foreign Policy*. Kent, OH: Kent State University Press, 1993.

Clements, Kendrick A. *William Jennings Bryan, Missionary Isolationist*. Knoxville, TE: University of Tennessee Press, 1982.

———. *The Presidency of Woodrow Wilson*. Lawrence, KA: University Press of Kansas, 1992.

Cooper, John M. *The Vanity of Power. American Isolationism and the First World War, 1914–1917*. Westport, CT: Greenwood Publishing Corp., 1969.

———. *The Warrior and the Priest*. Cambridge: HUP, 1983.

———. *Woodrow Wilson*. New York: Alfred A. Knopf, 2009.

Curti, Merle E. *American Philanthropy Abroad*. New Brunswick, NJ: Rutgers University Press, 1963.

Davis, Donald E. and Eugene P. Trani. *The First Cold War. The Legacy of Woodrow Wilson in U.S.-Soviet Relations*. Columbia: University of Missouri Press, 2002.

Feingold, Henry L. *Zion in America*. New York: Twayne Publishers Inc., 1974.

Ferrell, Robert H. *Woodrow Wilson and World War I, 1917–1921*. New York: Harper & Row, 1985.

Figes, Orlando *A People's Tragedy. The Russian Revolution, 1891–1924*. New York, Penguin Books, 1996.

Hapgood, David. *Charles R. Crane. The Man Who Bet on People*. New York: ICWA, 2000.

Holmes, James R. *Theodore Roosevelt and World Order. Police Power in International Relations*. Washington: Potomac Books, 2006.

Hopkins, Charles H. *John R. Mott, 1865–1955: A Biography*. Grand Rapids: Eerdmans, 1979.

Iriye, Akira. *From Nationalism to Internationalism. U.S. Foreign Policy to 1914*. London: Routledge, 2002.

Israel, Jerry. *Progressivism and the Open Door. America and China, 1905–1921*. Pittsburgh: University of Pittsburgh Press, 1971.

Keegan, John. *The First World War*. New York: Random House, 1998.

Kennan, George F. *American Diplomacy, 1900–1950*. New York: New American Library, 1954.

———. *The Soviet-American Relations, 1917–1920*. Princeton, NJ: Princeton University Press, 1956.

Kennedy, David M. *Over Here. The First World War and American Society*. New York: Oxford University Press, 1980.

Lasch, Christopher. *The American Liberals and the Russian Revolution*. New York: McGraw, 1962.

———. *The New Radicalism in America. The Intellectual as a Social Type*. New York: Knopf, 1965.

Laserson, Max M. *The American Impact in Russia, 1784–1917*. New York: Collier, 1950.

Leuchtenburg, William E. *The Perils of Prosperity, 1914–1932*. Chicago: University of Chicago Press, 1993 [c.1958].

Levin, Norman G. *Woodrow Wilson and World Politics: America's Response to War and Revolution*. New York: Oxford University Press, 1968.

Link, Arthur S. *Wilson*. Princeton, NJ: Princeton University Press, 1947.

———. *Woodrow Wilson and the Progressive Era, 1910–1917*. New York: Harper & Brothers, 1954.

———. *Wilson the Diplomatist. A Look at His Major Foreign Policies*. Baltimore, Johns Hopkins Press, 1957.

———. *Woodrow Wilson. Revolution, War, and Peace.* Arlington Heights, IL: Harlan Davidson, 1979.

Livermore, Seward W. *Woodrow Wilson and the War Congress 1916–1918.* New York: Octagon Books, 1968 [c. 1957].

Mamatey, Victor S. *The United States and East Central Europe, 1914–1918. A Study in Wilsonian Diplomacy and Propaganda.* Princeton, NJ: Princeton University Press, 1957.

Manela, Erez. *The Wilsonian Moment: Self-Determination and the International Origins of Anticolonial Nationalism, 1917–1920.* New York: Oxford University Press, 2007.

May, Ernest. *The World War and American Isolation, 1914–1917.* Cambridge: Harvard University Press, 1966 [c.1959].

———. *Imperial Democracy. The Emergence of America as a Great Power.* New York: Harper & Row, 1973.

Mayer, Arno. *Politics and Diplomacy of Peacemaking: Containment and Counterrevolution at Versailles, 1918–1919.* New York: Knopf, 1967.

McCartney, Paul T. *Power & Progress: American National Identity, the War of 1898, and the Rise of American Imperialism.* Baton Rouge: Louisiana University Press, 2006.

McLoughlin, William G. *Revivals, Awakenings, and Reform. An Essay on Religion and Social Change in America, 1607–1977.* Chicago: The Chicago University Press, 1978.

Muukkonen, Martti. *Ecumenism of the Laity. Continuity and Change in the Mission View of the World's Alliance of YMCA, 1855–1955.* Joensuu: University of Joensuu Publications in Theology, 2002.

Noble, David W. *The Paradox of Progressive Thought.* Minneapolis: University of Minnesota Press, 1958.

———. *The Progressive Mind, 1890–1917.* Minneapolis: Burgess, 1981.

Notter, Harley. *The Origins of the Foreign Policy of Woodrow Wilson.* New York: Russell & Russell, 1965.

Saul, Norman E. *The Life and Times of Charles R. Crane, 1858–1939. American Businessman, Philanthropist, and a Founder of Russian Studies in America.* Lanham, MD: Lexington Books, 2013.

Steel, Ronald. *Walter Lippmann and the American Century.* Boston: Little, Brown & Co. 1980.

Thelen, David P. *The New Citizenship. Origins of Progressivism in Wisconsin, 1885–1900.* Columbia: University of Missouri Press, 1972.

———. *Robert M. La Follette and the Insurgent Spirit.* Boston: Little Brown & Co., 1976.

Thorsen, Niels A. *The Political Thought of Woodrow Wilson, 1875–1910.* Princeton, NJ: Princeton University Press, 1988.

Trask, David F. *Victory without Peace. American Foreign Relations in the Twentieth Century.* Huntington, New York: Robert E. Krieger Publishing Company, 1975.

Unterberger, Betty M. *The United States, Revolutionary Russia, and the Rise of Czechoslovakia.* Texas A&M University Press, 2000.

Urofksy, Melvin I. *Louis D. Brandeis and the Progressive Tradition.* Boston: Little, Brown & Co., 1981.

Van Alstyne, Richard W. *The Rising American Empire.* Oxford: Oxford University Press, 1960.

Walworth, Arthur. *Wilson and His Peacemakers. American Diplomacy at the Paris Peace Conference, 1919*. New York: Norton, 1986.

Williams, William A. *The Tragedy of American Diplomacy*. New York: Dell Publishing, 1972 [c.1959].

Theses

Bocage, Leo J. "The Public Career of Charles R. Crane." Ph.D. diss., Fordham University, 1962.

Sulzbach, Jacob John, Jr. "Charles R. Crane, Woodrow Wilson, and Progressive Reform: 1909–1921." Ph.D. diss., Texas A&M University, 1994.

Journal Articles

Ahonen, Risto. "John R. Mott as an Ecumenical Leader. What Was Mott's Vision?" *The Finnish Evangelical Lutheran Mission*, 2010, 1–5.

Parry, Albert. "Charles R. Crane, Friend of Russia." *Russian Review*, 6, 2, 1947, 20–36.

Pomerance, Michla. "The United States and Self-determination: Perspectives on the Wilsonian Conception." *The American Journal of International Law*, 70, 1, 1976, 1–27.

Smith, Daniel M. "National Interest and American Intervention, 1917: A Historiographical Appraisal." *The Journal of American History*, 52, 1, 1965, 5–24.

Van Alstyne, Richard W. "Woodrow Wilson and the Idea of Nation-State." *International Affairs*, 37, 1961, 293–308.

· 4 ·

"GODFATHER OF CZECHOSLOVAKIA": CHARLES R. CRANE AND THE "NEW CENTRAL EUROPE," 1917–1918

Crane, a Friend of Small (Slavic) Nations

Charles Crane was, in his time, rightly considered a friend of Russia, especially starting in 1917. His fascination with Russia also extended to the Slavic world in general and he lamented its subjugation by the Central Powers. The Slavic peoples of Central Europe and of the Balkans, particularly the Czechs, Slovaks, Serbs, and Bulgarians, had awakened in Crane a sense of urgency in regard to forming autonomous homelands in the wake of the collapse of the German, Austro-Hungarian, and Ottoman imperial systems. At the beginning of World War I in 1914, Crane who had long supported Bohemian, Bulgarian, and Serbian nationalist groups, increased his contribution by publishing anti-imperialist journals and supporting patriotic and Slavophile artists and intellectuals.

With a clique of Slavophile friends among whom featured many former Root Mission members and followers like Samuel Harper, Cyrus H. McCormick, Jr., and John R. Mott, Crane led what he informally called the "American Friends of a New Middle Europe."[1] Together, they relayed information to American government officials and to Wilson himself (owing to the president's friendship with Crane), organized fundraisers, wrote newspaper commentaries, and acted as efficient intermediaries between Slavic nationalist leaders and various political circles. They even became involved with official diplomacy and made themselves informal advisors to American decision-makers.

Crane believed that Europe's greatest tragedy was the massive amount of peoples still under the yoke of the imperial system and unable to achieve a level of civilization similar to the one brought about by American democracy, which he, Wilson and many others viewed as the ideal social and political system. Before the start of the war, however, he took greatest issue with the Ottoman Empire's heinous encroachment upon the Balkans and upon part of Central Europe and with the idea of Muslim dominion over Christian Europe. As early as 1905, the Bulgarian diplomat and organizer for the Red Cross P. M. Matthieff had begun warning his correspondent Charles Crane of the dangers Bulgaria faced if Bulgarian Christians were allowed to be mistreated by the Turks.[2] Taking advantage of the disruptions in the Ottoman Empire and of the Young Turk Revolution,[3] the Kingdom of Bulgaria made its independence official in 1908. Though it had an alliance with the Balkan League, which included Greece and Serbia, Bulgaria came into conflict with these two countries in 1911 over the partitioning of Macedonia, a clash which then led to the Balkan Wars of 1912–1913, a prelude to World War I. When the Central Powers went to war against the Triple Entente countries, neutral Bulgaria found itself surrounded by four warring entities: the Ottoman Empire, Austria-Hungary, Russia, and the small but very agitated Kingdom of Serbia (belonging to Austria-Hungary but supported by the Entente) which had set the war into motion on June 28, 1914. While the Austro-Hungarian and Ottoman Empires sought to make Bulgaria their ally due to its strategic position right next to Serbia (where the assassination of Archduke Franz Ferdinand of Austria had taken place), Russia and its allies were pressing Bulgaria to remain neutral. Bulgaria, meanwhile, was torn between nationalist, pan-Slavic, and pro-German sentiments.[4]

Crane, in light of this ambiguity, strove to support the nationalist sentiment in favor of neutrality and peace in the midst of the Russian and German forces struggling for control. His steadiest Bulgarian collaborator in this endeavor was Andrea S. Tsanoff, a professor and editor who had studied at Amherst College (class of 1871) in Massachusetts. Crane, who called Tsanoff a "missionary for peace," offered him as well as other American missionaries working in Sofia his financial support. Through a journal called "Zornitsa" (which he later abandoned), Tsanoff undertook to spread his pacifistic and neutralist perspective across Bulgaria. For a glimpse into Crane's contribution to this peace mission, one need look no further than his correspondence with James Levi Barton, an American missionary and director of the American Board of Commissioners for Foreign Mission (ABCFM). Barton greatly admired Bulgaria's resolve to remain neutral despite the explosive war context on the Eastern Front and particularly in regard to the inextricable Balkan issue. Barton, informed of Crane's activities by way of a report written by Andrea Tsanoff on the methods employed to promote neutrality (methods he believed to be responsible for Bulgaria's success in "keeping down the war spirit"), wrote a letter of praise to Crane on January 8, 1915: "I want to express my appreciation of what you are doing to help on the cause of peace in Bulgaria." Simultaneously, Barton hoped to see Crane increase his contribution to Tsanoff's pacifistic journal and proposed an injection of fresh funds to ensure as broad a distribution as possible.[5] Indeed, the matter was becoming more pressing due to the fragile situation in the Balkans considering the multilateral pressures exerted on Bulgaria. For Serbia and for Greece (itself split between both camps) as well as for the strength of the Allied position on the Eastern Front, it was crucial that Bulgaria not be swept up by the Central Powers, thus forming a gigantic pro-German mass from Berlin to Constantinople and completely isolating Serbia. Keeping Bulgaria out of the conflict was therefore the most direct way to ensure that its army would not be co-opted by the Central Powers in order to quash the Kingdom of Serbia. With the help of another long-time friend and American collaborator, the editor of the *Christian Herald* Roger H. Williams, Crane sent Tsanoff, among other things, a $500 check and a promise to provide more financial support in the future.[6]

Tsanoff was not only active in trying to keep the peace in his country but also strove to convince international authorities and neutral nations like the United States to act as peaceful mediators in the warring countries. In a letter published in Boston's *Sunday Globe* on February 28, 1915, Tsanoff demanded that the United States "do their utmost for the cessation of this war." He insisted that the survival of Europe's Christian civilization depended on active intervention and that it was now time for passive spectators to mobilize. If the war were to continue, however, Tsanoff admitted half-heartedly that despite their general desire for peace, Bulgarians would take up arms to defend their country.[7]

Crane, for his part, was not successful in reducing the pressures exerted on Bulgaria despite the antiwar propaganda he had sponsored. In a letter dated June 29, 1915, Tsanoff explained to Crane that "The Dual Alliance is urging Bulgaria to keep her neutrality, while the Entente is trying its best to have us go into the war against Turkey. Both parties, as you know, are promising compensations [territories]."[8] To Crane, the carrying out of such illegitimate negotiation over rights to whole regions constituted one of European diplomacy's shortcomings and emphasized the need for a reconstruction of international relations based on the Wilsonian model. And despite his efforts, Tsanoff could feel his country slipping further and further into the clutches of the Germans, especially since its king, Ferdinand I, was of German descent and personally sympathized with the Central Powers' cause despite his officially neutral position. Finally, the Central Powers and the Young Turk government offered to restore Bulgaria's pre-1878 borders (taken by the Ottomans) in exchange for its neutrality, which effectively circumvented both Crane's pacifistic strategy and the Allied forces' less pacifistic one. Though in principle, both Crane and Tsanoff deemed it important for Bulgaria to remain neutral, this official neutrality was worth nothing to Tsanoff when it could be "bought" by the Central Powers in exchange for territorial concessions. It became futile, from that point onward, for Crane to continue supporting the peace effort in a Bulgaria which now had to be swayed in favor of the Allies. Yet in order to make Bulgaria lean in its direction, each warring alliance ended up threatening it by breaking-off diplomatic relations. When Bulgaria allied itself with the Central Powers, Tsanoff blamed the Entente's weakness on the Eastern Front and Serbia's provocations concerning the Macedonian territories claimed by Bulgaria. He compared his country's situation to that of Belgium, which had been invaded by Germany, and lamented the fact that without the Entente's help, Bulgaria had no choice but to turn toward the Triple Alliance to protect itself from Serbia and the advances of Austria-Hungary and Germany. Tsanoff simply hoped that Bulgaria, which had been forced despite its wishes to declare war on England, France, and even Russia (its historical ally), would at least be spared a war with the United States. In this at least his wish was granted. Diplomacy between the United States and Bulgaria did not suffer despite the latter's allegiance with the Central Powers.[9]

Paradoxically enough, Crane's reputation as a philanthropist and a friend of Bulgaria led to a call for assistance from none other than queen Eleonore of Bulgaria just as her country had finally sided with the Triple Alliance. She was working as a nurse in the Bulgarian army and asked Crane to invest in a school for war nurses that would be up to American standards,[10] despite the already confirmed involvement of the American Red Cross (a fundamentally neutral organization), Columbia University, and the Carnegie Foundation in this project. This put Crane in a rather peculiar position. He was a private citizen from a neutral country and had been asked for help by the supreme ruler of a warring country, one allied with the Central Powers, no less. More specifically, Queen Eleonore, who had already been turned down by the United States, was now asking Crane to help push other philanthropists into making donations to her medical school, which was staffed partly with people who had trained at Bulgaria's American College of Samokov (nowadays located in Sofia). Crane is unlikely to have given her his support and in fact appears never to have responded to her letter, yet it is not his reaction that concerns us but rather the arguments with which Queen Eleonore justified her demand. Emphasizing that nurses had been recruited from American missionary institutions, Eleonore argued that "It would really be an American concern […] in that way again representing a means of influence of culture, as for many years, in so many instances, Bulgaria has enjoyed through American generosity." Of course, she understood that the timing was wrong, but hoped that her insistence on the idea of an America at the service of the world and capable of powerful cultural influence would convince Crane to lend her the necessary funds.

Bulgaria was now seen as an enemy by the Allies and by some Americans incapable of remaining "impartial in thought as well as in action," to quote Wilson's famous entreaty for neutrality. Yet various liberal figures and even a few British observers sympathized with Bulgaria's plight, understanding that it had been propelled into the war against its will by the merciless Balkan context. In a letter to Crane penned on August 18, 1915, Alfred Mitchell-Innes, a British diplomat stationed in Uruguay, wrote in an informal and mischievous tone of his wish that Great Britain would succeed in reconciling Serbia, Greece, and Bulgaria to rebuild the Balkan League of 1912 as their interests and destinies were aligned, thus implying the destruction of Austria-Hungary and of the Ottoman Empire. He argued that Greece and Serbia could well afford some leniency toward Bulgaria; after all, Bulgaria's military force had helped them win their independence from the Turks. The diplomat then gently mocked Crane's philanthropic activities ("you say you are working hard. What are you doing? Politics or helping the poor sorely tried Belgians and Servians?") all the while chiding him for his epistolary laxness ("Surely you are the scrappiest correspondent God ever made—if he did make you, of which I am not certain").[11] The sly humor of such a comment aside, it would seem that Crane's humanitarian pursuits were the subject of a recurrent humorous allusion of sorts while also being a source of diplomatic intelligence. Despite Mitchell-Innes's hopes, however, the Balkan League, with at its core a strong and autonomous Bulgaria, could no longer be revived because the Triple Alliance had already swallowed it up and sacrificed it for its own strategic purpose of isolating Serbia on the Eastern Front. In a letter to Crane, Tsanoff lamented that this, combined with the British and French stratagem to absorb Greece (a means of defending Macedonia, which Bulgaria was laying claim on), forced Bulgaria's hand in its decision to join the Central Powers.[12] In short, the geopolitical mess created by the imperial system had prevailed over the nationalistic and pacifistic efforts supported by Crane.

Though we have looked, thus far, at Crane's efforts in Bulgaria, Crane's strongest Slavophile sympathy (besides Russia) undeniably lay with the Czechs who, like the Serbians, were then under the power of the Austro-Hungarian Empire. He obtained most of his information on the Czech issue from Tomáš Masaryk (1850–1937). Born in a small Moravian town in the Austro-Hungarian Empire, Masaryk had become a highly sought-after specialist on Slavic matters in England and in the United States. In his memoirs, Masaryk described the characteristic manner in which he had become acquainted with Crane:

> Un matin, de bonne heure—c'était en 1902, probablement—arrive chez moi un Américain [...] Avant qu'il n'ait fini de m'expliquer le but de sa visite, j'ai supposé que c'était un journaliste [...] Or c'était Mr. Crane, industriel à Chicago [...] Mr. Crane était ami du professeur Wilson [...] Tous deux, ils nous ont beaucoup aidé, à ce moment.[13]
>
> [One early morning—it was probably in 1902—an American came to see me [...] Before he had finished explaining the purpose of his visit, I assumed he was a journalist [...] However, it was Mr. Crane, a businessman from Chicago [...] Mr. Crane was friends with Professor Wilson [...] Together, they greatly aided us at that moment.]

Masaryk did not specify why Crane had visited him that morning in 1902, but we know that from that time onward, he became one of Masaryk's most regular collaborators in the Slavic Studies project at the University of Chicago, in which Pavel Milyukov had also participated. Though Masaryk is generally considered the father of the Czechoslovak nation, the awakener of its national conscience, and even its president-liberator, he did not think true patriotism required grandiose pro-Slavic speeches and was critical of overly patriotic talk about love of the Slavic nation: "Si vous aimez votre pays, inutile d'en parler, mais faites quelque chose d'intelligent [...] Les gens peuvent se griser de ces grands mots, ce n'est pas de cette façon-là qu'ils apprendront à travailler."[14] ["If you love your country, there is less need for talk and more need for intelligent action [...] Grand words can be intoxicating, but they will not teach people how to work."] Indeed, though he later took on the image of the philosopher statesman, Masaryk valued concrete action over empty rhetoric, which perhaps contributed to his prompt acceptance of Crane's offer to help him in his quest for self-determination in Czechoslovakia.

Crane also expressed his admiration of Slavic peoples without exaggerated wordiness and instead devoted his energies to supporting projects of national promotion. Some of these projects did, however, adopt a romantic—even a messianic—perspective on Slavic nationalism. One of these "romantic" projects supported by Crane to promote Slavic unity was his patronage of the Czech artist Alphonse Mucha (1860–1939). After their first meeting in 1904 during a Russophile banquet also allegedly attended by Theodore Roosevelt (though in an informal capacity, as in the context of the Russian-Japanese war, the United States had sided with Japan), a lasting patronage began between Crane and Mucha which culminated, in terms of political success, in the adoption in 1931 of the new 100 korun banknote featuring one of Mucha's paintings. This illustration reflected not only the artist's nationalist and romantic vision but also Crane's role in both the artistic and political aspects of Mucha's work. In 1908, Crane asked Mucha to paint his daughter Josephine and when she got married to Harold Bradley, he hung the painting in the prairie style house which he had commissioned the architect Louis Sullivan (Frank Lloyd Wright's mentor) to build for them in Wisconsin. It was that very painting of Josephine Crane Bradley which was to become the personification of "Slavia," feminine symbol of the Slavic nation and of the unifying elements of pan-Slavism, and which would later feature on the above-mentioned 100 korun banknote.[15] According to art historian Anna Daley, the use of this "Slavia" on Czechoslovakian banknotes illustrates the extent to which Mucha was indebted to Charles Crane. She also explained that:

> Mucha's use of what was at least partly a representation of Crane's progeny on the country's currency was even more appropriate when, in 1924, Josephine's sister, Frances, became a member of Czechoslovakia's first family with her marriage to President Masaryk's son, Jan.[16]

Jiri Mucha, who often accompanied his father but who had not yet been born when the latter met Crane, reported that Alphonse Mucha had been greatly impressed with Crane's understanding of the Slavs. Crane, for his part, had seen in Mucha that which the pragmatic Masaryk could not offer: a Slavic messianism capable of forging a patriotic and unifying sentiment in Czechs and Slovaks. Mucha's recollections, penned by Jiri, offer in this regard a rare glimpse of Crane's personality and of his unique approach toward those he decided to encourage and employ. As a biographer, Jiri wrote about his father's patron that "Unassuming, calm, with an inscrutable face and a strangely introverted look, Crane observed everything but spoke only when absolutely necessary. He had the air of a chess-player tirelessly pondering the next move of his bishop, knight or rook." If one is to trust Jiri Mucha's account, which remains uncorroborated and even questionable, then his father's studio located in Massachusetts near Crane's home in Woods Hole might have been the forum in which was decided the destiny of Central Europe. He wrote that "Crane would drive over for long silent visits, listen to father's views on the tasks facing the Slavs" and "sometimes bring with him his friend Woodrow Wilson, then a professor at Princeton University." On these occasions, according to Jiri, "they would unwittingly prepare the future map of Europe."[17]

This perspective, combined with Masaryk's account of their first meeting in 1902, suggests that Crane had imagined a project of self-determination for the inhabitants of Central Europe years before the circumstances of the 1914–1918 war. Indeed, Mucha's undeniable masterpiece in regard to his nationalist goals was *The Slav Epic*, a series of twenty paintings also sponsored and funded by Crane which he started in 1910. The paintings depicted the (idealized) origins and historical development of Slavic peoples. A letter Mucha wrote to Crane, probably his last, shows, through the detailed updates he tried to give about the progress of his work, the extent to which the artist was dependent on his patron and submitted to his will. Referring to the start of the painting *The Hussite King* and the preliminary work pertaining to it, Mucha promised "As soon as I have the composition finished on canvas I will send you some photographs. I should be glad to know how you find my last canvasses, of which I sent you some photographs some time ago." He also mentioned the idea of including a painting of the war in Europe in the *Epic* but abandoned this plan after Crane failed to send a positive response.[18] Jiri also described his father's torturous wait for a confirmation that Crane would continue funding his project, which the artist apparently received in a Christmas stocking at the house of Crane's daughter Frances Leatherbee.[19] Yet according to Jiri Mucha, it would seem that Alphonse also had faith in Crane's taste and artistic sense. Both he and his wife saw Crane as more than simply a "parvenu" and instead thought him a man of "intelligence and culture" who was fully capable of appreciating and judging a work of art.[20]

Crane's rapport with Masaryk greatly differed from his relationship with Mucha, quite possibly because Masaryk did not depend on subsidies from his "old friend from America."[21] Their interaction had a much more direct international impact on Europe's reconstruction in a postwar context. As we shall later see, the Czech issue, closely connected with the Russian issue, was of particular interest to Crane. He saw it as one of the main challenges for the Slavophiles and considered it to be the primary issue pertaining to imperialism and self-determination. While Crane's attraction to Slavic nationalism preceded the war, it was the war that gave him the opportunity to take action.

Crane, from Charitable Neutrality to "The War to End All Wars"

For Crane, the war also represented another opportunity to absorb the atmosphere on the front, which he had already experienced as a tourist in 1878 toward the end of the Russo-Turkish War. The experience had moved him, and as he later wrote to A.G. Gardiner, editor of the London *Daily News*, "the events there [...] made a very deep impression upon me as a young man."[22] It was, in a way, a consciousness-raising experience that awakened in him the idea of addressing the issue of small imperial states in the Balkans and in Central Europe and constituted a pivotal moment in Crane's career.

Crane's interest in soldiers' conditions in the trenches increased after the start of World War I. He supported and financed John R. Mott's European mission on behalf of the YMCA which aimed to unite various Christian humanitarian and educational organizations to help with the relief and aid effort for European populations. Crane was of particular help to Mott in 1916, when the latter undertook a European tour of the trenches and prisoner-of-war camps and implemented an aid initiative for the improvement of soldiers' conditions, whether Allied or not. Mott told Crane in a letter that the "most inspiring and hopeful sight is that practical ministry on behalf of the millions of men and boys in the training camps, in the trenches, and in the prisoner-of-war camps, which you have done so much to make possible."

This expression of gratitude followed another $10,000 donation promised to Mott by Crane at New York's Century Club. For both men, attenuating the misery of soldiers and civilians in Europe served more generally "to lay foundations for better relations between nations and races after the struggle is over." They saw philanthropy as a means of building a peaceful world, and the extending reach of American philanthropy in Europe allowed them to start hoping for more empathic relations between countries after the war.

Never, according to Mott, had so many young people devoted themselves to a Christian and humanitarian cause. Their involvement, in part motivated by his work toward an ecumenical consolidation of charitable movements, could bring about Europe's regeneration:

> I question whether in the history of the human race there has ever been a time when so many people have forgotten themselves in the service of their own and of other peoples [...] the spirit [of philanthropy] everywhere manifested is beyond all praise, and is preparing the way for a new Europe.[23]

On April 6, 1917, just as the United States was entering the war, Mott offered President Wilson the YMCA's voluntary help and became secretary general of the National War Work Council, thus benefiting from government and military support in his initiatives. Crane, for his part, became financially involved with a $150,000 donation to a new fund connected to the War Work Council and with the YMCA.[24] As for Wilson, he had long supported Mott and the YMCA's international philanthropic peace-keeping initiatives. As early as 1914, Crane and Mott visited the State Department before attending a meeting with Wilson—secured by Crane—which Mott considered very satisfactory. According to Mott, the President had demonstrated a "sincere interest" in his European mission and had promised his cooperation, while Crane invested $5,000 dollars to help with Mott's European tour.[25] Crane also mentioned, in a letter to his son John, this visit first to the State Department, where he and Mott had gone to congratulate Bryan on the success of his "cooling off" treaties mentioned in the previous chapter, and then to the White House. He explained that "the president thinks [Mott] is doing the most important work in the world—organizing all of the students of the world for Christian and social service" and that "Mr. Mott is just going to Europe to try to hold together the missionary work of the various warring nations."[26]

After several trips to Europe in 1914 and 1915, Mott was encouraged by Crane to go on another "pilgrimage" to the trenches and prisoner-of-war camps. Regarding the mediation efforts of the United States, Crane compared Mott's mission in Europe to the political work with the warring countries undertaken at that time by Edward House. The State Department's archives refer to House as "Personal representative of President Wilson to the European Governments" and it was in this capacity that Wilson sent him to Europe in December of 1915 to facilitate negotiations between the warring countries. A message sent by Robert Lansing to the American ambassadors in Europe on December 22, 1915, however, specified that House was not there on a peace mission and had instead been charged with "taking information to our ambassadors" so that they could gain "a more intimate knowledge of this Government's attitude regarding certain phases of international questions" and give their own points of view in return.[27] House's role was thus to relay the president's political vision to American diplomacy's agents "in the field."

Crane saw Mott's work as evolving parallel to House's diplomatic endeavors, but in the different and equally—if not more—important domain of Christian philanthropy. Crane's comparison all too clearly demonstrates his view of philanthropy's crucial role in international relations. He deemed that despite its discretion, Mott's peace work completed and even supplanted House's:

> He can go with a very important mission and yet not attract the attention that even quiet Colonel House now attracts and supplement in a most valuable way, among the churches and the universities of all the warring countries, the work the Colonel has done and the information he has gathered in the political world.[28]

Between 1914 and 1917, both Crane and Mott supported Wilson's policy of neutrality and had even insisted, during an evening spent with the president on January 6, 1915, that he ought to strictly uphold it. Their conviction in the benefits of neutrality might have stemmed from their pacifistic outlook given that peace was essential to the improvement of relations between peoples whereas war was destructive to the human condition. Yet neutrality to them also represented a chance to increase the United States' moral leadership, and this not only without "getting their hands dirty" in the war but also by maintaining their status as a "disinterested" nation capable of arbitrating with a clear conscience among the warring countries. In their mind, it was important "not to limit America's rendering her great service by premature action or by departing from strict neutrality." From a more strategic perspective, Crane, like Lenin, believed that the European imperial system had slowly been eroded from within by the war and saw the present time as a unique opportunity, "because of the exhaustion of the belligerents," for the United States to extend its global diplomatic, economic, and humanitarian influence.[29]

Paradoxically, this meant that the conduct of the war toward an Allied victory could represent a true opportunity for peace by destroying the militaristic and imperialist basis for international relations. From this perspective, neutrality was imperative so long as the Allies, including Russia, remained ahead in the conflict. Yet despite this relative but implicit pro-Allied penchant, and despite Wilson's directives, Mott believed that America displayed true neutrality because all the countries involved seemed dissatisfied with the

United States' policy. Had the United States truly been biased, one side or the other would have had cause to rejoice. As it were, many Europeans were exasperated with America's neutrality and "peace without victory" rhetoric.[30] Among them was one of Charles Crane's British friends, Lady Elinor Grogan, who bemoaned that "the president and, I suppose the people of U.S.A., still don't understand what we are fighting for, and the sort of people we are." She affirmed that "If we were to make peace now, the untold sacrifices of these two and a half years would be in vain."

She also requested that Crane use his influence to sway the president, insisting that the Allied cause naturally aligned with Wilson's democratic principles and that "we are fighting for just the things America stands for." In an almost peremptory tone, Grogan pushed her argument further by challenging Crane to reconsider neutrality, which even the greatest generosity of service could not justify:

> while we admire beyond words the bondless charity you bestow on the suffering world here—why don't you go a little farther and understand us and give us your sympathy whole heartedly [...] as sure as fate, if the Allies don't win, *your* day of reckoning will come with the Germans.[31]

Grogan's desperate tone reflected the Allies' dire need for military support in the face of the Central Powers' increasing ascendancy over the Western Front and the Atlantic. Wilson, unsurprisingly, was being pressured from all sides to join the war. Though it remains unclear whether Grogan's letter convinced Crane to abandon his neutral position, the chronology of his correspondence reveals an evolution in his attitude toward increased support of the Allies and of American intervention. Little over two months after Grogan's letter, the Russian Revolution broke out in March of 1917 and threatened to compromise and even to obliterate the Eastern Front. From that point onward, Crane and Mott pledged their full support to Wilson and to his War Message of April 2, 1917, going so far as "carrying" that message to the Russians.

It was upon his departure from Russia a few weeks after the end of the Root Mission that Crane was given the opportunity to once again immerse himself in the trench atmosphere that had had such a powerful impact on him in his youth and that had motivated him to support Mott's humanitarian effort. He chose to travel through Scandinavia rather than through Siberia like his fellow commissioners in order to join the Allied troops in the trenches of the Western Front. After stopping in Stockholm and Oslo where he visited several Viking archaeological sites, he boarded the *Maud*, a ship captained by

Roald Amundsen, a Norwegian adventurer to whom Crane donated fifty tons of coal for an upcoming Arctic expedition.[32] After crossing the North Sea and stopping over in London, Crane arrived in France, where he visited a British trench set up near Boulogne. Equipped with a steel helmet and wearing a gas mask, he walked through the flooded trenches dug from Flanders clay over which poured a constant shower of both rain and bullets from the German artillery. He was then brought behind the lines and shown the training facilities for trench combat and snipers, even participating in the training exercises of the recruits. Despite the bleak portrait he painted of his stay there, Crane took pleasure in the British soldiers' morale and declared that he was proud of being an Anglo-Saxon. Afterward, he was taken to a French trench where he was greatly impressed with the military acumen of the French, writing that "It was an interesting and characteristic experience with French psychical and military spirit. One felt the clarity of the French mind [...] One also felt that every Frenchman had a touch of real military genius."[33] After returning to Paris to visit the French military staff, Crane was received by John J. Pershing's Expeditionary Force,[34] and upon his return to Washington, he relayed a message from Pershing to Wilson stating that things were going for the better and that relations with the Allies remained excellent.

Crane, Masaryk, and Wilson's "New Europe"

As a Slavophile, Charles Crane saw the Russian and Czechoslovakian issues as inevitably linked since they were expressions of the Slavic peoples' progression toward democracy and self-determination, a concept also developed in his protégé Alphonse Mucha's *Slav Epic*. Moreover, from a strategic perspective, both nations could play key roles in Central and Eastern Europe by forming a barrier against the influence of Germany and of its allies. Masaryk in fact also joined Crane in Russia during the 1917 Root Mission, but for military rather than diplomatic purposes. His task there was to mobilize support in an Allied country and to journey through the prison camps to find, among Austro-Hungarian prisoners, Czech and Slovak volunteers in order to form a national Czechoslovakian army, the *Česká Družina*. This, for Masaryk, constituted the first real piece of his future state which could then begin devoting itself to beating back the German and Austro-Hungarian forces. Despite being on good terms with the Provisional Government—he and Milyukov had been colleagues in the Russian Studies department at the University of Chicago and Masaryk had previously paid a visit to Milyukov in Russia—the father of Czechoslovakia was forced to renegotiate, not without some delay, his army's passage into Siberia after the Bolshevik coup. In exchange, he promised complete neutrality (a promise he did not keep) in the Russian civil war, and agreed to certain conditions specifically formulated by Stalin, the Commissar for Nationalities' Affairs.[35]

Even before the Russian Revolution, Masaryk had already become involved in Czechoslovakia's self-determination efforts and had in fact incurred the displeasure of the Austro-Hungarian authorities. He was vacationing in Germany at the time of the Archduke Franz Ferdinand's assassination and declared himself utterly surprised by the turn of events. Though he feared Germany's military power, he put little stock in the abilities of Austria-Hungary and imperial Russia, which he considered to be two decadent regimes weakened by internal dissent. Of his Czech compatriots gone to fight in the Austro-Hungarian army he said that they went with the revulsion of men condemned to the slaughterhouse and that a movement of resistance had even sprung up, with all of the ensuing persecution. His diplomatic tour, which followed the start of the war, was also a four-year exile which he used to further Czechoslovakia's national cause. Visiting Holland, France, Great Britain, Italy, Russia, he worked to shine light on the general issue at the heart of Slavic nationalism: the importance of destroying Austria-Hungary and of transforming Central Europe.

Masaryk's national mission had very high personal stakes, however, for as he saw it, if his side did not win, he could never return to Austria.[36] Political repression was also merciless toward his family, and Austrian authorities even imprisoned his daughter Alice, who was incidentally good friends with Crane's eldest daughter Josephine. In his memoirs, Masaryk described a petition urging Alice Masaryková's release which had been launched by a group of American women from the University of Chicago's settlement houses, where Alice herself had worked and formed connections with, among others, Josephine Crane and Mary McDowell (known for her involvement with the Hull House). It was Mary who, after receiving a letter from Alice, alerted Crane of her friend's imprisonment in Vienna and beseeched him to intervene.[37] A few months later, Masaryk himself implored Crane not once but thrice to ask for the U.S. Embassy's aid in demanding his daughter's release, most likely with the help of Richard Crane, then Lansing's assistant at the Department of State.[38] A curt telegram, "Alice imprisoned fifth november please intervene as asked last letter" sent on November 29 from the embassy in London, shows Masaryk's insistence despite consisting of only ten words. Though it is difficult to determine Crane's exact involvement and influence in the Alice Masaryková affair, a letter he wrote to Josephine seems to show that he invested a considerable amount of time in trying to aid his friend. He even managed to mobilize a large group of Slavophiles to help him with the task. Crane's chosen method was to spark a reaction from the American public, namely, through articles he published in the *New York Times* and the *Christian Science Monitor*. He hoped to muster the same kind of support as had been given to Edith Cavell,[39] a nurse and spy executed by the Germans in 1915 to the great consternation of Allied sympathizers. Simultaneously, Crane's newspaper publications helped to raise awareness and gain support for an independent Bohemia.[40] Despite Richard Crane's advantageous position at the State Department, Austro-Hungarian authorities ignored the pleas of Crane's group. Richard sent his father a message explaining that the embassy had no power to intervene in an Austro-Hungarian affair given that Masaryk's wife had finally never been implicated (probably because of her American nationality) and suggested that an appeal could be made at the Austrian embassy in Vienna.[41]

The Alice Masaryková affair was not Masaryk's last call for Crane's help, but rather the start of a steady stream of appeals to make use of Crane's political and journalistic contacts and requests for his financial contribution. From that point onward, Crane found himself closely involved in Masaryk's great cause, the emancipation of "small nations," particularly Bohemia. In a letter written on March 11, 1915, he alluded—in veiled terms due to the censure forced upon the European post—to his status as a dissident in the Austro-Hungarian Empire and to his plans of recruiting a Czechoslovakian national army. He first explained that Austro-Hungarian authorities had quickly singled him out as a dissident when he was still a member of the Austrian Diet and supported Serbian and Croatian movements and regularly criticized the authoritarian and repressive measures taken by the imperial government toward Czecho-Slovak and Serbo-Croatian minorities. Even at that time, he expressed that his future activities during the war would be "to work against Vienna abroad" so that "the Bohemian nation would become free and independent," more specifically informing Crane that he would use his exile to "organize our journalistic and political representations abroad and to be in touch with the politicians of the Triple Entente." It was after having laid out his nationalistic goals to Crane that Masaryk expressed his need for funds to finance his exile, explaining that "We need money not only to relieve the men and families, who become the victims of the military absolutism" but also to "help to organize our journalism abroad and to organize our political representation [...] imagine the costs of the trip."[42] Unable to go into more detail, Masaryk assumed that Crane already had some understanding of what was being alluded to, especially given that this financial request would not surprise a renowned philanthropist like Crane. Crane himself had, after all, recruited Masaryk with the specific intent of involving the Czech revolutionary in his Slavophile activities and putting him in touch with other collaborators such as Milyukov. A letter from Masaryk dated November 15, 1915 mentioned his gratitude following the receipt of a check for $1,000, though it is unclear whether this was the full or partial sum Crane gave his friend to fund his diplomatic exile.

During the war years, Crane took on a more concrete role in Masaryk's nationalist mission. Right before his departure for Moscow as a member of the Root Mission (where he would incidentally be joining Masaryk, there to organize his military recruitment initiative), Crane sent a letter to his daughter Josephine, who was herself interested in the Bohemian cause through her friendship with Alice Masaryková. In the letter, he explained his view of the Czech issue:

> the struggle between the Czechs and the Germans [i.e. the German-speaking majority in Austria-Hungary] has gone on for centuries and has never been more acute than during this war. The Czechs have resisted in every possible way the efforts of their ancient enemies—the Magyars as well as the Germans—to make them fight their friends, the Serbs, the Russians and the French; and they have been cruelly punished for it.

Yet Crane also recognized the complex linguistic and geographic aspects inherent to the Bohemian problem given that "In this country the Bohemians (Czechs) and Germans are mixed everywhere." As mentioned by Crane at the end of his letter, he based his understanding of the conflict on that of Masaryk, particularly as expressed in the articles written by the latter for the press.[43] One notion in particular constituted a typical trait of European (or continental) nationalism: the idea of "ancient enemies," which suggested that an enemy had been "inherited"[44] and pointed to the historical perspective and proportions of a conflict tinged with inevitability. As a humanist, Masaryk generally shied away from this type of narrow and Manichean patriotic fervor which demonized the opponent. It is not impossible, however, for him to have been influenced by this current when pressured by the threats on his life and the lives of his close ones. Even so, the content of his nationalist discourse remained rather moderate across his whole body of work on the Bohemian issue during the war and when mentioning the "Germans" as enemies, he referred to the cruel and decadent Austro-Hungarian regime and Prussian militarism rather than to the German-speaking populations and culture per se. In fact, Masaryk's ideal for a postwar Europe also allowed for Austrian and Hungarian national aspirations, ensuring everyone would be capable of "fully realizing cultural ideas."[45]

Masaryk expressed his understanding of Europe's geopolitical problem in a memorandum titled "Independent Bohemia," published during his stay in London in 1915. Observing that Europe was divided into two parts; the west half made up of large and small nation-states and the east half made up of empires dominating over "small nations," he made the following analysis:

> There is a striking difference between the west and east of Europe in regard to the composition of states and the number of small nations. The west has four (five) great nations and only five small ones, whereas the east has only one great nation and a great number of small ones. In the west the states are formed by one dominant race, in the east they are nationally mixed.

Without ever defining his concept of "nation" and "race," and without specifying his criteria for determining size or geographic limits between the continent's halves (seemingly arbitrary, considering his positioning of Germany in the West), Masaryk formulated his vision of Europe's political future around a reorganization of eastern European territories based on a concept he called "principle of nationality." In the same article, Masaryk denounced what he considered to be the main cause of the war: Germany's dominion and its use of Austria-Hungary to expand its influence toward the East and the Balkans in keeping with the old slogan "Drang nach Osten" (push eastward). To counterbalance Germany's power in Eastern Europe, Masaryk's first step was to accept Russia's historical and "essential" influence over other Slavic nations. But more importantly, he linked other national problems with that of Bohemia, thus reinforcing his argument for a reorganization of territories based on this "principle of nationality." He argued that, when looked at as a whole, these separate destinies highlighted the severity of the crisis—which to him was the leading cause of the conflict—and the potential of his proposed solution, and would lead to what he termed "regenerating Europe." These words evoke the subsequent comments made by Mott to Crane, though in their case, Mott was referring to the multiplication of philanthropic activities and missionary expansion.[46] Yet these men all viewed the war as an opportunity to build a new European civilization based on the freedom of peoples and on harmony rather than on the classic imperial dominion. Masaryk's memo also resembled a comment made by Crane to Wilson a few days after the February Revolution in Russia about the democratization of nations and the bulwark this would form against militaristic autocracies like Germany.[47] To Masaryk and to Crane (who was possibly influenced by Masaryk's analysis as he was in charge of publishing his ideas in the United States), Germany represented the ultimate threat to peace and to the world's democratization which, from Crane's progressive point of view, seemed inevitable. In fact, Germany's power was so threatening that few supported Czech independence before the war, which brought with it the opportunity to fatally wound the Central Powers. Even Masaryk, before the war, was simply campaigning for fairer treatment of Slavic peoples by Austria-Hungary rather than for a complete destruction of the empire. Because an independent Bohemia would have been much more vulnerable to a German takeover, Masaryk's nationalism became more radical only when wartime repression increased and an opportunity to break the imperial system in Central Europe presented itself.[48]

In other memos he published in 1915 and 1916, Masaryk elaborated on the case of Central Europe as a "peculiar ethnological zone" where so many small nations remained under imperial dominion. He deemed that the Allies' main concern should be to pursue "the plan of Central Europe freed from German control" given that "the political organization of this zone is the real task of the present war." There were three aspects to this great task: freeing Poland (a crucial but sensitive topic which Masaryk approached with caution since Russia was still an Allied country), creating Czechoslovakia, and creating a Great Serbia. Only in another memo titled "Pangermanism and the Zone of Small Nations" and published in December of 1916 did Masaryk explain the other national challenges which stemmed from this task, namely, the destinies of the Albanians, the Ukrainians, the Romanians, the Greeks, the Lithuanians, the Latvians, etc. Consolidating this zone based on the principle of nationality with the help of the Allies would serve to block German expansionism and domination.[49]

In Masaryk's eyes, it was the ensuing peace rather than the war itself which would prove an ideal context for the implementation of such a project, and he accordingly led his diplomatic missions in Western democracies rather than in Russia. He reached out particularly to England and the United States and played his trump card with President Wilson, who had already established himself as a champion of small nations and endorsed the idea of self-determination as of 1915. Wilson, particularly through his friendship with Crane, constituted Czech nationalism's best diplomatic hope.

Wilson and the Bohemian Cause: Crane and Masaryk's Contribution

Of his own accord and even before Crane had introduced him to Tomáš Masaryk, Wilson felt obvious sympathy toward the specific issue of Czech and Slovak minorities in the Austro-Hungarian Empire as well as toward Bohemian Americans.[50] On December 5, 1917, the Bohemian National Alliance of America sent Wilson a personal message praising him for his entry into the war against Austria-Hungary and declaring itself in agreement with his rhetoric on the defense of peoples' national destinies:

> Above the thunder of guns, above the storms of war the clear voice of our President resounds throughout the world. Your stern voice declares war upon the family and the ruling German [and] magyer [Magyar] caste now holding down central European peoples. It will encourage these peoples to fight tyrants [...] Like the voice of Lincoln [...] so your voice gives new strength to millions of oppressed, for their fight is now led by the President of the world's premier republic.

The Bohemian National Alliance of America, founded in 1915 in Chicago (where lived the largest number of Czech Americans) and disbanded in 1918 during the war (when Austro-Hungarian repression and nationalistic outrage of minorities had reached its highest point), was a patriotic and separatist organization representing voters in favor of an independent Bohemia.[51] With this message, its leaders strove not only to share their point of view with the president but also to reassure him (essentially on behalf of all Czech Americans) of its constituents' loyalty to the American government's military goals. Fearing above all that Bohemians would be treated like the German Americans, the Bohemian National Alliance of America asked Wilson to grant a special status to the Bohemians who still did not have American citizenship and begged him to spare them the "stigma of enemies," entreating him instead to become their "protector."[52] The very next day, Wilson confessed that the letter sent by the Bohemians had made "a very strong appeal" and forwarded a copy to the Attorney General Thomas Watt Gregory along with an inquiry into the possibility of granting their request. Of particular interest here are not the results of this exchange but rather its arguments and tone, and the mutual sympathy between both parties. Ultimately, everything suggests that Wilson cared, at least to a certain degree, about the Czech cause. The Bohemian separatists, including Masaryk, recognized in him a key to the success of their mission.

The following year, a little over two months after Russia's surrender at Brest-Litovsk, Charles Crane sought for the first time to arrange a meeting between Wilson and Masaryk so that the latter could offer the president "technical" help in the pursuit of his global plan. Attached to this message sent on May 8, 1918 was a memo written by Masaryk. Wilson agreed to read it while indicating that he saw no point in meeting with Masaryk unless he had further information to provide. Richard Crane, from his position at the State Department, relayed another message from his father to Wilson. Crane was asking once again that the president meet with Masaryk, who had just arrived in Washington on May 9, 1918, as he had further details to give about the memo in person. Following his father's recommendations, Richard Crane was very insistent with the president and stressed Masaryk's status and competence in the Slavic issue:

> Professor Masaryk's position as the leader of the Bohemian race, as well as recognized authority on racial and political conditions in Austro-Hungary makes it especially desirable, in view of recent developments in regard to these questions, that he be given an opportunity to see you.

Overwhelmed by these "recent developments" Richard Crane spoke of, Wilson asked his secretary to telephone Crane and postpone the meeting indefinitely.[53] Interestingly, Masaryk was an expert on those very issues as the Allies were then in the process of penning a response to the Bolshevik Revolution and the Treaty of Brest-Litovsk. As emphasized by the historian George F. Kennan, the American government never truly had an opportunity to react to the process leading up to the Brest-Litovsk treaty as it involved, on the one hand, a country with which the United States were at war and on the other hand, a regime they still had not recognized. Wilson, who foresaw general settlements of international scope, naturally deplored the bilateralism of the Brest-Litovsk treaty but he made few private or public declarations to this effect.[54] More worrisome yet to the Allies was the fact that the separate peace with (and to the advantage of) Germany made Russia seem more vulnerable to German influence and penetration, and at greater risk of becoming a satellite state.[55] In Siberia, where Bolshevik presence was still minimal, more moderate groups supported the idea of foreign intervention to keep Vladivostok out of the hands of the Red Army. France and Great Britain supported this scenario of foreign intervention from the Chinese border, accepting that it would be with the cooperation of Japan, which was planning to occupy Siberia's Maritime Provinces. It was believed that Japan would certainly end up crossing swords with the Germans or at least would dissuade them from penetrating into Eastern Russia. House and Wilson, for their part, feared such a plan as it risked displeasing the Bolsheviks and even stirring up the European Slavs "because of the race question." Wilson considered that Russia's situation could improve without Allied military help[56] and he was relatively optimistic about the Revolution's liberalization despite the slew of bad news he received from Crane about the repression of civil liberties, the deteriorating social conditions in Moscow and the spread of the Bolsheviks.[57]

Pressure from Britain and France increased, but Wilson maintained his position and sent both Japan and the Allies a message acknowledging the potential of concerted action but also pointing out its risks and costs.[58] To House and Wilson, the greatest risks appeared to be of a moral nature as such action might destroy the "fine moral position" which Wilson believed his leadership had conferred to the Allied cause, making "our position [...] no better than that of the Germans."[59] In short, Wilson, along with most of his cabinet members and diplomats, feared that intervention would undermine the principle of self-determination of peoples promoted by the United States. Josephus Daniels in particular expressed this sentiment, saying that "nothing should be done that could in any way affect the confidence of the Russian people in our sincere desire to help them establish and maintain government of their own choosing."[60]

As a realist, Masaryk, whose troops had still not been able to leave Russia, opposed an intervention in Siberia not as a matter of moral principles (though he did not disagree with such reasoning) but based on strategic concerns. On April 10, 1918, he sent Crane a "private and confidential" letter in which he laid out his recommendations, in the form of fourteen points, with respect to the issue of minorities in Russia and Central Europe. These recommendations were intended for Wilson, to whom Crane relayed the memo mentioned by his son Richard on May 11, 1918. Firstly, he asked that the Allies recognize the Bolshevik government *de facto* (specifying that *de jure* recognition was not in question at the time) and remain on good terms with it, drawing inspiration from Wilson's self-determination message on March 11, 1918.[61] This apparent abdication in the face of Bolshevik success likely stemmed from his doubts in regard to the potential for democracy of Russia's other moderate parties. Contrary to the assumption of most Allies, Masaryk believed in the longevity of the Soviet regime. Though the Bolsheviks had been weakened by the Brest-Litovsk negotiations, they had garnered support internally according to Masaryk. For this reason, he foresaw the creation of a coalition dominated by Bolsheviks and moving toward a democratic compromise capable of influencing the peoples of Germany and Austria-Hungary which explained, in his eyes, why the Central Powers now adopted such an aggressive stance toward the Revolution despite having been the ones to finance it. He deemed that the small nations of Central and Eastern Europe were in need of a strong and democratic Russia supported by the Allies. Thus, a Republic of Ukraine—the richest part of Russia—would have much to gain from joining a "Russian union" rather than becoming a German satellite of sorts, it being understood that "Russian politics [would] gravitate toward the South." For this reason, the Allies had to draw up a clear plan in support of Revolutionary Russia with the help of Japan which, Masaryk hoped, would be in favor of such a plan. Finally, Masaryk emphasized the necessity of getting the Czechoslovakian legion out of Russia and bringing it to the Western Front, since its strategic and military importance as a "Slavic barrier" was crucial in resisting German hegemony in Central Europe, especially considering the recent retreat of the Russian army.[62] In short, Masaryk's "Fourteen Points" were quite optimistic about Russia's future and profoundly suspicious of Germany's ambition. Masaryk also saw the national destinies of Central Europe and of the Balkans as connected with that of Russia and of its own minorities. He based his project of self-determination of peoples on two keystones: the (democratic) success of the Russian Revolution and the creation of a Czechoslovakian nation-state supported by Western powers and strong enough to "contain" Pan-Germanism.

On another note, it appears that Masaryk's point of view on the Siberian issue differed from that of the Allies, who had a tendency to exaggerate the risk of a German—and Bolshevik—penetration into Siberia. In *Soviet-American Relations*, Kennan criticized the generally ignorant perspective of the Allies (including the United States), who failed to differentiate between the chaos in European Russia and the climate of relative freedom in Siberia. Kennan compared the social climate in Siberia to that of the American frontier, more individualistic and therefore more resistant to collectivist movements. The Bolshevik threat was thus less grave in Vladivostok or Irkutsk—despite some very real confrontations between the Cossacks and the communists—than in

Petrograd. The counter-offensive measures discussed by the Allies, however, were based on an exaggerated assessment of the risk of Bolshevization and especially Germanization of Siberia. According to Kennan, the Allied and American decision-makers' lack of understanding of Siberia's "specific characteristics" (its resemblance to the American frontier) had led to the shoddy policy-making in that region. He wrote that "If considerations based on the specific characteristics of Siberia, as a part of Russia, ever entered into Washington's handling of the Siberian Problem, the record does not show it."

Kennan did not, however, take into account the information Crane and Masaryk regularly sent Wilson, which was aimed precisely at helping him to understand Siberia's unique situation. In his "Fourteen Points," Masaryk emphasized, as if to put to rest the Allies' worries, that "nowhere in Siberia have I seen German and Austrian armed prisoners [which triggered major apprehension in the Allies[63]]; in Siberia there is no greater anarchy than in Russia."[64]

Toward the end of May, in an interview published by the *New York Times*, Masaryk warned the Allies that their presence in Siberia would pose insurmountable logistical problems. He suggested, instead, that economic, administrative, and industrial help be given to the Russian government as a means of combating German anti-Allied propaganda.[65] Yet it was ironically the presence of Masaryk's Czechoslovakian troops in Russia that pushed Wilson to reconsider his stance on American armed intervention in Siberia. After receiving a number of reports about clashes between the Czechoslovakian soldiers and Bolsheviks or groups of former Austro-Hungarian war prisoners, Wilson started viewing the issue as an extension of the war in Europe against the Triple Alliance. Factors like the presence in Russia of Czechoslovakian troops (who represented the Allied cause) as well as the freeing of Austro-Hungarian prisoners after the Brest-Litovsk treaty caused a shift in the way the Siberian issue was perceived by the Wilson Administration. Formerly seen as a civil war with political undertones, it was now being viewed as a new eastern theatre for the Great War and its struggle toward the self-determination of imperial minorities. In this sense, the Siberian issue contributed to Wilson's understanding of his involvement as participation in a liberation war rather than as an intrusion into the internal affairs of a sovereign country.[66] Despite this new and comforting outlook on the Siberian question, it remained true that the Allies were still concerned with "driving back" the Bolsheviks. This included the Wilson Administration, though for six months, the president resisted French and British entreaties to organize a landing in

Vladivostok. In this sense, Siberia had perhaps become, to Wilson, the only hope for a liberal and democratic Russia owing to Cossack resistance and the support of the Allied and Czech forces. In fact, Crane said of the Bohemian army that it was "the only organized thing there [in Siberia]." Almost in confirmation of this belief, Crane later told Wilson of an old Russian tale which predicted that Russia would one day be saved by Siberia.[67]

Though proving his direct involvement is no easy task, it would seem that Masaryk played a non-negligible role in the Wilson Administration's change of heart. He appears to have closely participated in the relay of information about Czechoslovakian troops in Siberia, and his relations with Crane, Wilson, and the members of the State Department seem to complete the chain of events.

Crane took great joy in the Wilson Administration's attitude toward "the small peoples in the Austrian Empire"[68] and continued asking Wilson to personally meet with Masaryk. In a letter written on June 9, 1918, Crane's praise of his protégé was formulated in such a way as to pique the devout president's interest. He described Masaryk as "one of the wisest and best of Christians" and as "the outstanding Slavic leader of the world" given that he was already ranked as "one of the half dozen leading statesmen" of his time. The remainder of Crane's message is perhaps indicative of the type of argument he believed suited to convince Wilson and demonstrated both his profound motivations and the aspirations he had for the future of the world. Believing that the Wilsonian foundations of the coming peace could forge a world in America's Christian (evangelical) image, Crane deemed Masaryk's role a crucial one in the shaping of Europe's future given that the continent's main issue was still, as mentioned previously, the problem of small nations in Central Europe. He affirmed that "As I still hope that Christians—New Testament Christians—will determine the conditions under which peace may come and be maintained for a long time, I believe no one else in Europe could make so valuable a contribution as he."[69]

Despite his distinction between institutional and "authentic" Christianity (likely viewed by him as that original, preclerical New Testament Christianity he alluded to), Crane endorsed the ecumenical view of the Christian mission promoted by his friend John R. Mott, who likewise saw the war as an opportunity to transform the relations between peoples. Given this view of Masaryk, and since Masaryk was a member of the Czech Evangelical Church (ČCE), it comes as no surprise that Crane strove to put him in touch with Woodrow Wilson, his biggest hero in the coming peace.

Without exaggerating the weight of Crane's persistence in securing this meeting and the importance of his role as an intermediary, it is of note that some, like British officer George T. M. Bridges, worried that someone as biased (in terms of his Czech patriotism) as Masaryk would be giving the American president advice about the Siberian issue, which necessarily encompassed the Bohemian issue. Bridges in all likelihood already knew Crane, who had asked him for help in organizing his next trip to Arkhangelsk in Northern Russia, one of the sites of the planned American landing. It is in fact without a doubt the progression of the Siberian question and the rise of the Czechoslovakian legion as a major stake that motivated Wilson to grant Masaryk the long awaited interview. In a letter to Lord Reading, the British ambassador to Washington, Bridges foresaw correctly that "[Masaryk] will carry great weight with the President," this in large part because he had been recommended by Crane "as the best information he is likely to get on the Russian problem."[70]

This time, Wilson responded favorably to the idea of a meeting and wrote in response to Crane's entreaty that "Of course, I will try to see Professor Masaryk."[71] This mention of Masaryk's professional title emphasizes that both men had in common their pursuit of an academic career. In fact, it seems evident that Wilson liked those who resembled him as was the case in his feelings toward Professor Milyukov (detailed in the previous chapter). On June 19, 1918, Tomáš Masaryk met the president at the White House for an exchange that lasted forty-five minutes. Masaryk first mentioned the creation of a Czechoslovakian nation-state but Wilson, though admitting his "sincere interest" in the problems of the Czechs and Slovaks, promptly steered the conversation toward the situation in Russia. After explaining the way the Allied powers planned on using Japanese forces to safeguard Siberia, Wilson asked Masaryk about the military potential of the Czechoslovakian legion. Masaryk seemed to have different information at his disposal about the number of available soldiers and mentioned his worries about the territorial compensation Japan would eventually claim. Wilson had evidently never considered this hypothesis, though he had taken into account Allied funding of a Japanese intervention in Siberia. Overall, neither man seemed particularly enthusiastic about the idea of an intervention, but Masaryk nevertheless got the chance to request support for his Czechoslovakian soldiers, while Wilson admitted that he felt in a way "tied" to the will of the Allies.[72]

That same day, Robert Lansing gave Wilson a message sent by the members of the Kadet Party (Milyukov's party) which assured the president that he had both their support and that of the Russian people, contrary to what had been expressed by the Bolsheviks.[73] Furthermore, though Masaryk had told Wilson that his Czechoslovakian troops were peacefully moving toward Vladivostok and out of Russia, Lansing informed Wilson two days later that they were now being harassed by the Bolsheviks and forced to defend themselves in order to advance. Lansing then asked Wilson: "ought we not to consider whether something cannot be done to support them?" Surprisingly, even Crane seemed to have shared with Wilson opinions in favor of military intervention in Siberia. At the very least, he was probably the one to personally transmit an anonymous memo dated June 17 which promoted such a scheme and which Wilson immediately had analyzed by General Peyton C. March and by the Secretary of War Newton D. Baker. General March quickly refuted its contents by indicating that "all such schemes are absolutely futile." Nevertheless, Crane's position on the matter is hard to deduce simply based on this one document delivered among many others.

Until that point, House and Wilson had both been more concerned with providing Russia with material and humanitarian support as promoted by Masaryk. They considered limiting their contribution to a "Relief Commission" led by Herbert Hoover, who was a champion of the Belgian Relief and director of the Food Administration and who oversaw the efforts of the American Red Cross and of the YMCA (directed by John R. Mott). A few days later, however, British ambassador Reading reported that "Colonel House has certainly changed his views and is distinctly favorable to some definite step being taken immediately by the United States and the Allies in support of Russia." According to Reading, who had evidently contributed to reorienting House's opinion, the best way to convince the president was to suggest the deployment of a protective army for the Relief Commission. Though Wilson's exact train of thought remains unclear, the very next day, a press report was published in the *New York Times* on June 27 announcing a plan to help Russia "without army" while also (paradoxically) stipulating that "Troops might be sent to give protection to the commissioners." One of the plan's aims was to support and protect the creation and consolidation of pro-Allied "local governments," clearly showing that, though America did not want to admit it, its actions would more or less result in a military intervention. At the very least, Wilson rationalized that his plan did not encroach on the self-determination of the Russian population as the commission would only be supporting local initiatives.[74]

Crane, for his part, continued trying to keep Wilson abreast of the situation in Russia. Toward the end of June, he reported having had a few enlightening conversations on this topic with two long-time acquaintances: the economist Edward A. Ross of the University of Wisconsin and James F. Abbott, Japan specialist at the University of Washington and also part of the U.S. Army's Military Intelligence Division. Crane affirmed that both men had come to conclusions "very much in accord with the views of Professor Masaryk," and asked Wilson whether he would be interested in receiving a summary of their notes for his use, to which the president responded favorably.[75] Crane confirmed that he would send these notes and then congratulated Wilson for a statement made by Lansing on June 28, 1918 about America's support for the Slavic peoples which stated that "All branches of the Slav race should be completely freed from German and Austrian rule."[76] Crane also suggested an addition to this statement:

> Sometime you might call the attention to the Slavic people of the damage Germany has done to them and their wonderful mission in the world by keeping them divided [...] and urge them from now on to adjust their differences and bring out the best there is in the whole race."

Crane then explained his view of the United States' role in the preservation of this new era of self-determination, positing that "it will be the duty of the rest of us after this war to see that the various Slavic states are so well established that it will be possible for this to come about."[77] However, three days before Crane sent Ross and Abbott's texts to Wilson on July 9, the president had already decided on his position in regard to the matter and added American units to the inter-Allied intervention in Siberia in order to secure Vladivostok and offer armed support to the Czechoslovakian troops and to Russian counter-revolutionaries.[78] The president nevertheless promised to read the texts and incorporate them in his vision,[79] and Crane congratulated Wilson on having taken the time to reflect on the matter before intervening in Siberia. Crane also once again suggested that his friend Mott accompany the Relief Commission in his capacity as director of the American branch of the YMCA. Wilson, in return, told Crane that "to have any assurance from you that, on the whole, I am handling the things as promptly and as wisely as the circumstances permit gives me the deepest comfort."[80]

Once the July 6 decision was made, Masaryk's friend Emmanuel Viktor Voska, an American of Czech descent and an intelligence officer in the 1917 National Army, proposed a technical solution to help support Czechoslovakian troops in Siberia. Through Masaryk and Frank L. Polk, an advisor to the Secretary of State, Voska suggested that a group of American officers take charge of Russian and Polish volunteer units along with 5,000 American soldiers. He based this suggestion on the idea that Russians generally hated the Japanese and that given the rise of a strong anti-German sentiment in Russia, Czechoslovakian, and American troops would most likely be better received and supported. Voska also opposed the idea of sending Czechoslovakian soldiers to France and Central Europe, recommending instead deploying them in Siberia where they were already more useful. As an introduction to Voska's work, Crane called him the greatest specialist on Slavic issues,[81] which he had also said of Masaryk.

Already at this stage—and undoubtedly in part due to Masaryk's influence—providing military support to Czechoslovakian troops had become a greater priority for the United States than driving back Bolshevism. It was in this sense that Wilson told Masaryk that "Nothing is giving me more concern at present than the position of the Czecho-Slovak forces in Siberia."[82] Masaryk expressed gratitude for Wilson's concern and thanked him for his decision on July 6 "to help our Czechoslovak Army in Russia." He then praised the president's liberal and universal principles:

> you have repeatedly announced [...] the principles of liberated mankind, of the actual equality of nations [...] according to which governments derive all their just power from the consent of the governed [...] it is for these principles that our boys are shedding their blood on the endless plains of Russia and Siberia.

Continuing his praise, Masaryk added that "Your name, Mr. President, [...] is openly cheered in the streets of Prague" and that "our nation will forever be grateful to you and to the people of the United States."[83]A few more exchanges about the Siberian issue followed between Wilson and Masaryk, but after the start of the American intervention, it was primarily discussions about Bohemian independence and Czechoslovakia's gratitude that marked the relationship between Crane, Wilson, and Masaryk as the president of the Czechoslovak National Council.

By Wilson, the Siberian crisis was primarily seen as another aspect of the war and another front which had been created after the signing of the Brest-Litovsk treaty. Crane and Masaryk, however, saw it as pertaining to the larger issue of the Slavs as well as those "small nations" they so often referred to. Undoubtedly in order to bring Wilson further along the path of self-determination, Crane wrote him a long (at least by his own epistolary standards) commentary on the general aspects of the Russian issue and on the role Masaryk would play. Crane's rationale was tinged with religious elements that would help convince Wilson to consider the full extent of the Slavic issue. He first emphasized the new proportions it had taken on, writing that "the present and the future of all the gifted Slavic peoples is perhaps a greater problem for the welfare of the world than the war." Satisfied with having pledged his fortune to such a cause, he also wrote that "Life is found to be worth living and worth giving. Democracy is justifying herself and setting an inspiring example to the ages." Surprisingly, he put little stock by expert advice on the matter since "any understanding of the previous states gives little help in interpreting what is passing at present." Consequently, according to Crane, Wilson was right in not seeking the advice of specialists and instead "pursuing the wisest possible course." He explained that this in particular had earned him Russia's esteem, assessing that "Your prestige is higher than ever there [...] any program you propose will be accepted as the expression of a wisely sympathetic friend." This result he once again attributed to the religious affiliation Wilson and the Russians shared, for "Russia is fundamentally Slavic and also Christian and you have near you the best and wisest of Slavs, Masaryk, and the best and wisest of Christians, Mott, to consult about moves that are more or less technical." Crane thus believed that Wilson, Mott, and Masaryk were key figures in the Slavic issue and told him that "You three are trusted by the whole world—and especially by the slavic world—and will do what is possible as opportunity offers."[84]

Even with the diplomatic recognition of countries like France, Italy, and Great Britain, Bohemia's independence would best be legitimized if it also had the formal recognition of the United States, which was quickly becoming an arbiter in international relations as well as a self-proclaimed beacon of morality. Following the recent events, Lansing advised Wilson that the United States ought to make a formal declaration about Czechoslovakia's fight against the imperial powers. The Secretary of State was against the idea of "fully" recognizing Czechoslovakia's independence as it might force America's hand in regard to the Yugoslavian issue (rather more sensitive because of the rivalry between Yugoslavia and Allied Italy). He also hoped that there would be no mention of specific territories in the declaration as many thorny territorial issues still remained and were waiting to be resolved during the upcoming Versailles conferences. Lansing's suggestion, which Wilson accepted, was to recognize the Czechoslovak National Council, with Masaryk at its head, as a *de facto* "warring" government (Lansing used the term "revolutionary"). It was submitted in the form of an official declaration made on September 3, 1918. The following day, Lansing wrote to Wilson to inform him of Masaryk's financial requirements in the pursuit of independence and gave Masaryk control over the provided funds. The goal was not only to supply Masaryk's independence movement with material support but also to give "substantial evidence of our opinion as to the probable success of the movement and our faith in the repayment of moneys loaned." Wilson, however, opposed the idea of a loan and instead suggested a $1,500,000 donation taken straight from the special war fund managed by Bernard M. Baruch, director of the War Industries Board.[85]With this diplomatic and financial support, Masaryk and his Czechoslovak National Council declared Czechoslovakia's independence on October 18, 1918, at the Independence Hall in Philadelphia.[86]

Afterward, Masaryk confirmed not only Wilson's indubitably crucial role in the success of the Bohemian cause but also the subtle and decisive part played by Charles Crane. In a letter written to Wilson a few days after the American government promised this donation to the Czechoslovak National Council, he began by thanking the president profusely and expressed his "feeling of profound gratitude for the recognition of our Army, the National Council, and the nation." Then, much like the Bohemian National Alliance of America had done the previous year in asking for the president's "protection," Masaryk, inspired by a visit to the Gettysburg Cemetery, compared Wilson's task to the one undertaken by Abraham Lincoln:

> At an historical moment of great significance Lincoln formulated these principles which were to rule the internal policies of the United States,—at a historical moment of world-wide significance you, Mr. President, shaped these principles for the foreign policies of this great Republic as well as those of the other nations.

Masaryk also highlighted the diplomatic results of what he called "[an] act of political generosity." He commended America's recognition of "the justice of our struggle for independence," affirming that "America's recognition will strengthen our armies and our whole nation in their unshakeable decision to sacrifice everything for the liberation of Europe and of mankind." The support pledged by Wilson and the United States gave the newly established country a much needed sense of legitimacy and Masaryk's gratitude seemed to flatter Wilson, who incidentally remarked that "It reassures me to know that you think that I have followed the right course [...] to be of as much service as possible to the Czecho-Slovak peoples," whom he deemed to be "[a] great group of peoples whom you [Masaryk] represent." Wilson also thanked Masaryk for his diplomatic involvement, declaring that "I want you to know how much the Secretary of State and I have valued the counsel and guidance which you have given us."[87]

Crane, for his part, received through his son Richard a no less remarkable testament of Masaryk's gratitude by way of a letter of thanks and of introduction in view of a future trip to Czechoslovakian Siberia, in which he was described as "a good friend of the Czech and Slovak people."[88] The recognition he received from Wilson was even more significant, as the following year, the president appointed Richard Crane first United States ambassador to the new Czechoslovakian Republic.[89] This came in addition to the previously mentioned honor of having Mucha's painting of Josephine Crane featured on Czechoslovakian banknotes. Then, in 1924, Crane's other daughter, Frances Leatherbee, entered into a second marriage with Masaryk's son and Minister of Foreign Affairs Jan Masaryk.[90] Crane returned several times to visit Masaryk, now president of Czechoslovakia, and maintained friendly ties with him and his family. Jan told him many years later that "The whole Masaryk family calls you the godfather of Czechoslovakia."[91]

Even after the Czechoslovakian nation was recognized by all the Allied countries, Lansing, House, and Wilson continued regularly consulting Masaryk about the situation of the Czechoslovakian legion, which was crumbling under Bolshevik pressures in Central Russia. Though occasionally frustrated with the American government, particularly when Austria-Hungary rather absurdly attempted to negotiate with Wilson on the subject of the Bohemian issue[92] despite the fact that the Czechoslovak National Council had already been declared a *de facto* government, Masaryk always maintained the same high esteem for Wilson's "kind sense of freedom and justice," deeming that his ideals were "one with the ideals of our nation."[93]

Overall, the events surrounding the Bohemian issue, which tied in with the situation in Russia, highlighted Charles Crane's dedication to building a postwar world in accordance with Wilson's Christian and philanthropic conception of American democracy. This philanthropic vision was also endorsed by Mott and by Masaryk, who seemed to have more in common with Wilson and House than with other Allied leaders. Ecstatically, Crane affirmed a few days before Czechoslovakia's declaration of independence that "The new America is as different from the old one as can possibly be. The ideals and interests and aims under Wilson's inspiring leadership are most important for the whole world today."[94] Crane evidently attributed this new current in America to Wilson's leadership, expressing that "his authority is spiritual as well as political," that he represented "the highest statesmanship the world has never known" and that he was "acting for the whole world and not for America alone." Despite the international orientation of Wilson's presidency,

Crane insisted that Wilson's leadership was supported by all Americans, thus downplaying the essential tensions that had always existed between the purely patriotic approach to politics (what Crane called "interests" in his commentary) and the internationalist approach (those "ideals" Crane referred to).[95]

Wilson's popularity both worldwide and in the United States, however, was to be sorely tested in the months following the armistice of November, 1918 and over the course of the peace conferences. This would be particularly the case in regard to the implementation of his principle of self-determination, a cornerstone of the Wilsonian project abroad. More specifically, Crane's involvement in one particular facet of this project of self-determination, the Ottoman Empire, illustrates the principles and aspirations of Wilsonianism and demonstrates Crane's attachment to those principles even when applied outside of his usual Slavic field of interest.

Notes

1. *Crane Papers*, "Samuel Harper to Roger H. Williams," October 27, 1918.
2. *Crane Papers*, "P. M. Matthieff to Crane," October 22, November 28, December 15, 1905. At the same time, Matthieff deplored Russia's maneuvers to block Bulgaria's democratic and national reform efforts like it had for Finland and Armenia. He hoped that a new constitutional Russia would act in a more just and transparent manner.
3. Multiple uprisings against the decadence and repression of Hamid II's regime, particularly in military circles, led to the Sultan's forced resignation and the creation of the Young Turk government at the head of the Ottoman Empire in 1908. See Bernard Lewis, *The Emergence of Modern Turkey* (London: Oxford University Press, 1961), 203–5; Taner Akçam, *From Empire to Republic. Turkish Nationalism & the Armenian Genocide* (New York: Zed Books, 2004), 59–114.
4. John Keegan, *The First World War* (New York: Random House, 1998), 48–70. For a more detailed history of the Kingdom of Bulgaria, see Georges Castellan, dir., *Histoire de la Bulgarie des origines à nos jours*. (Paris: Horvath, 1977), 385–8. For their part, socialist groups opposed traditional militarism, whether Triple Alliance or the Triple Entente. As for public opinion, it remained wary of the Entente countries' motives, even though most people wanted to avoid a war.
5. *Crane Papers*, "James L. Barton to CRC," January 8, 1915.
6. *Crane Papers*, "Andrea S. Tsanoff to CRC," October 16 (29), 1914, January 12 (25), 1915.
7. Andrea S. Tsanoff, "Bulgaria's Plea for Peace," *Boston Sunday Globe*, February 28, 1915.
8. *Crane Papers*, "Andrea S. Tsanoff to CRC," June 16 (29), 1915.
9. *Crane Papers*, "Andrea S. Tsanoff to CRC," October 13 (26), 1915. See Victor S. Mamatey, *The United States and East Central Europe, 1914–1918. A Study in Wilsonian Diplomacy and Propaganda* (Princeton: Princeton University Press, 1957), 70–1.
10. *Crane Papers*, "Eleonore [Queen of Bulgaria] to CRC," June 20, 1915.

11. *Crane Papers*, "A. Mitchell-Innes to CRC," August 18, 1915.
12. *Crane Papers*, "Andrea S. Tsanoff to CRC," January 19, 1916.
13. Karel Capek, *Entretiens avec Masaryk* (Éditions de l'aube, 1991 [c. 1936]), 168. It remains a possibility that this first meeting between them took place in 1901 rather than 1902 since their correspondence began circa 1901, as was also approximately dated their first letter exchange. See the *Crane Papers*.
14. Jan Rubes, "Foreword" in Karel Capek, *Entretiens avec Masaryk*, i–iii.
15. Jiri Mucha, *Alphonse Maria Mucha. His Life and Art* (New York: Rozzoli, 1989), 236.
16. Anna Daley, "*Alphonse Mucha in Gilded Age America, 1904–1921*" (Master's diss., Parsons New School for Design, 2007), 52.
17. Mucha, Jiri. *Alphonse Maria Mucha. His Life and Art*, 236–7. This excerpt from Jiri Mucha's account is perhaps—but not necessarily—chronologically erroneous. If Crane himself reports having become acquainted with Wilson during his inauguration as President of Princeton University in 1902, it is more likely that they would have formed ties of friendship during Wilson's selection as candidate for the Democratic nomination toward 1912. See *Crane Papers*, "Memoirs," 152–3. See also the first chapter of this book.
18. *Crane Papers*, "A. Mucha to CRC," December 27, 1914.
19. Jiri Mucha, *Alphonse Maria Mucha. His Life and Art*, 238–9.
20. Jiri Mucha, *Mucha. His Life and Art*, 227. This passage was taken from correspondence between Alphonse Mucha and his wife Maruska and added to his biography by Jiri Mucha.
21. Karel Capek, *Entretiens avec Masaryk*, 238.
22. *Crane Papers*, "CRC to A. G. Gardiner," March 10, 1919.
23. *Crane Papers*, "Mott to CRC," January 11, 1916; "Mott to CRC," August 3, 1916.
24. Hopkins, *John R. Mott, 1865–1955. A Biography*, 463–468. Crane's contribution is documented on a list handwritten by Mott. Cleveland H. Dodge was also part of the donors, and the fund's contributions totaled three million dollars.
25. *Crane Papers*, "Mott to CRC," September 18, 1914.
26. *Crane Papers*, "CRC to John O. Crane," September 30, 1914.
27. *FRUS, 1915, World War* (U. S. State Department), 85.
28. *Crane Papers*, "CRC to Josephine Crane Bradley," May 31, 1916.
29. *PWW*, "CRC to WW," Vol. 32, January 10, 1915, 52–3. Crane's letter to Wilson mentions this January 6 meeting where they talked with Mott.
30. On January 22, 1917, after telegraphing the message to the warring entities, Wilson made his famous "Peace without Victory" speech before the Senate. Claiming to speak for the silent masses of the world, Wilson called for an egalitarian, spoil-free peace and pressed the warring countries to state their causes for war in an effort to undermine the legitimacy of each side's urge to fight and to arouse a worldwide campaign for peace. See Link, *Woodrow Wilson and the Progressive Era, 1910–1917*, 264–6.
31. *Crane Papers*, "Lady Elinor Grogan to CRC," December 22, 1916.
32. *Crane Papers*, "F. Hernan Gade to Roger Williams," November 5, 1917.
33. *Crane Papers*, "Memoirs," 208.
34. To thank him for his welcome, Crane sent him a shipment of Russian tea. *Crane Papers*, "J. J. Pershing to CRC," November 14, 1917.

35. Karel Capek, *Entretiens avec Masaryk*, 225–33. Samuel Harper claimed that Crane had accompanied Masaryk on his voyage to recruit the Czech Druzhina on the eastern front, but there is no mention of this in either his memoirs or his correspondence, and Masaryk also never referred to it. See S. Harper, *The Russia I believe In: The Memoirs of Samuel N. Harper* (Chicago: University of Chicago Press, 1945), 107. For a detailed study of the Czechoslovakian legion in Russia as a counter-revolutionary force and of the American involvement in this effort, see George F. Kennan, *Soviet-American Relations, 1917–1920*, Vol. 2, *The Decision to Intervene* (Princeton: Princeton University Press, 1958). See Chapters 6 and 12. For a divergent interpretation, see Eugene P. Trani, "Woodrow Wilson and the Decision to Intervene in Russia: A Reconsideration", *The Journal of Modern History*, 48, 3 (1976): 440–2. The most complete account of the birth and significance of the Czech Legion remains Betty M. Unterberger's *The United States, Revolutionary Russia, and the Rise of Czechoslovakia* (Texas: A&M University Press, 2000).
36. Karel Capek, *Entretiens avec Masaryk*, 193–195, 206.
37. *Crane Papers*, "Mary McDowell to CRC," February 26, 1915.
38. As a matter of fact, Masaryk feared that Alice's arrest would lead to the arrest of his wife, the American Charlotte Garrigue, in which case the American embassy would have to intervene.
39. *Crane Papers*, "CRC to Josephine Crane Bradley," April 20, 1916.
40. Betty Unterberger, "The Arrest of Alice Masaryk," *Slavic Review*, 33 (1974): 98–9. Unterberger shows Crane's effort as both motivated by his affection for Alice Masaryk whom he admired (he later compared her to Joan of Arc and said that she had "the most beautiful woman's expression I know of," *Crane Papers*, "CRC to JCB," May 9, 1919), and also by the chance it gave him to boost American sympathy for Czech nationalism by demonizing Austrian repression. In fact, both Crane and Masaryk viewed Alice's arrest as a tactic meant to quash her father's proindependence activities, given that an Austro-Hungarian arrest warrant was issued for him on the grounds of high treason.
41. *Crane Papers*, "Richard Crane to CRC," April 24, 1916.
42. *Crane Papers*, "Tomas Masaryk to CRC," March 11, 1915.
43. *Crane Papers*, "CRC to Josephine Crane Bradley," February 14, 1917.
44. This term is naturally problematic because it is primarily associated with the vengeful spirit and rivalry between France and Germany between 1870 and 1945. Nevertheless, there is no doubt that the strongly ethnocultural nationalism of the Balkan and Austro-Hungarian peoples was imbued with an ancient, even inexorable enmity toward imperial authorities or toward competing neighbors. See Guy Hermet, *Histoire des nations et du nationalisme en Europe* (Paris: Seuil, 1996), 128–9; Bernard Michel, *Nations et nationalismes en Europe Centrale, XIXe-XXe siècle* (Paris: Aubier, 1995). On the subject of more radical elements in the Czech version of ethnocultural nationalism, see John F. N. Bradley, *Czech Nationalism in the Nineteenth Century* (New York: Columbia University Press, 1984), 33–5.
45. John F. N. Bradley, *Czech Nationalism in the Nineteenth Century*, 98.
46. *Crane Papers*, "Mott to CRC," August 3, 1916.
47. *Crane Papers*, "CRC to WW," March 28, 1917. For a personal analysis of this message, see the previous chapter.

48. René Girault, *Diplomatie européenne. Nations et impérialisme, 1871–1914* (Paris: Armand Colin, 1995), 247. The evolution of Masaryk's nationalist thought is problematic because he could express fairly radical thoughts while also staying away from antimonarchical conspiracies. To be clear, before the war, Masaryk was saying that the system would crumble on its own if it was not reformed. See Bradley, *Czech Nationalism in the Nineteenth Century*, 99–100.
49. These memos written by Masaryk during his exile to convince public opinion and Western leaders can be found in R. W. Seton-Watson, *Masaryk in England* (Cambridge: Cambridge University Press, 1943), 116–202. The last one mentioned, "Pangermanism," appeared in the journal *New Europe* created by T. Masaryk. The same ideas can also be found in a book published later, *The New Europe. The Slav Standpoint* (Lewisburg: Bucknell University Press, (1972 [c. 1918]), 158–62.
50. The Thirteenth Census of 1910 showed 539 392 Bohemian (or Moravian) nationals in the United States. More than half of the Americans originally from Bohemia lived in the Midwestern states, and Illinois alone housed close to 125 000 (110 000 of them in Chicago). Texas and cities on the east coast also harbored a significant Czech population. See Thomas Čapek, *The Čechs (Bohemians) in America* (New York, Arno Press, 1969 [c. 1920]), 59–63.
51. Many other organizations for a free Bohemia emerged in various cities across the United States, but the *Bohemian National Alliance* became truly "national" owing to its 350 or so branches spread across the whole country. See Thomas Čapek, *The Čechs (Bohemians) in America*, 266–7.
52. *PWW*, "Bohemian National Alliance of America (Ludvik J. Fisher, president) to WW," Vol. 45, December 5, 1917, 223–4.
53. *PWW*, "CRC to WW", Vol. 47, May 8, 1918, 561; "Richard Crane to WW," May 11, 1918, 610; "WW note," Vol. 47, May 11, 1918, 611.
54. George F. Kennan, *Soviet-American Relations, 1917–1920*, Vol. 1, *Russia Leaves the War*, 372–6.
55. On the same day the treaty was signed, March 3, 1918, the US General Consul in Moscow, Maddin Summers, called it an "ignominious and unconditional peace." Summers also pleaded for an Allied intervention to fight off the German presence. *FRUS*, Vol. 2, *1918, Russia*, 65. Kennan for his part points out that Allied fears about a German "invasion" of Russia stemmed from the particular situation in Western Russia, whereas nothing foreshadowed such a move in Siberia. Similarly, the war in Europe, a motivating force for the Allies, was a distant factor to Japanese and Chinese leaders as well as to the Siberian populations. See Kennan, *Soviet-American Relations, 1917–1920*, Vol. 2, *The Decision to Intervene*, 63.
56. Kennan, *Soviet-American Relations, 1917–1920*, Vol. 1, *Russia Leaves the War*, 459–65. Furthermore, some of Crane's collaborators such as his friend Thomas F. Millard, China specialist, were indignant about the Japanese presence in Manchuria which went against the principle of Chinese sovereignty. Millard in fact wrote two letters denouncing the 1917 Lansing-Ishii Agreement and asking Crane to intervene with Wilson. See *Crane Papers*, "Millard to CRC," March 11 and 12, 1918. Nothing indicates that Crane reacted

to these entreaties, though one can suppose his opposition to this agreement given his distrust of Japanese expansionism.

57. *PWW*, "CRC to Tumulty," Vol. 46, February 21, 1918, 411. Crane gave him two telegrams reproduced in the *New York Times*: "Moscow is become a city of despair" and "Russia expiring under Red's rule," dated February 13 and 18. Wilson called this news "distressing" and relayed them, as asked by Crane, to Postmaster General Albert S. Burleson (Vol. 46, February 23, 1918, 422).
58. *FRUS*, Vol. 2, *1918*, *Russia*, 67. Wilson's note was sent on March 5, 1918, two days after the signing of the Brest-Litovsk Treaty, to American ambassador Roland S. Morris in Tokyo so that he might read it to the Japanese government.
59. Charles, Seymour, ed., *Intimate Papers of Colonel House*, Vol. 3 (London: Ernest Benn, 1928), 393–4. In private, Wilson and House detested the idea of Japan leading the intervention in Siberia, and clarified their diplomatic position by declaring their general opposition to the military plan of action while specifying that Japan, in the case of its intervention, should a priori disclose its agreed upon intentions (namely, to push back Germany). See p. 482.
60. Quoted in Kennan, *Soviet-American Relations, 1917–1920*, Vol. 2, *The Decision to Intervene*, 98. Countless opinions and commentaries stemmed from Wilson and his collaborators. As will be shown later, Crane supported Wilson's initial position for self-determination, though he entertained little hope about the possibility of a Bolshevik democracy.
61. *PWW*, "WW to the Fourth All-Russian Congress of Soviets," Vol. 46, March 11, 1918, 598. There, Wilson declared that "The whole heart of the people of the United States is with the people of Russia in the attempt to free themselves forever from autocratic government and become the masters of their own life." Incidentally, Crane thanked and warmly congratulated Wilson for this message which he deemed "well directed and at the right moment." *PWW*, "CRC to WW via Tumulty," Vol. 46, March 12, 1918, 619.
62. *PWW*, "Private and confidential. Letter from Professor T. Masaryk to Charles R. Crane," Vol. 47, April 10, 1918, 549–52.
63. It was namely feared that these Austro-Hungarian prisoners, fed on communist propaganda, would become a force for the Bolshevik's use against Cossack insurgents, as had happened in Irkutsk in March. (*FRUS*, Vol. 2, *Russia*, *1918*, 92–3). Kennan nevertheless emphasizes that the danger was exaggerated given that the majority of prisoners were not German but rather Slovak, Serb or Magyar. In fact, even Masaryk did not believe in the likelihood of such a threat. Another fear was that these armed and trained groups would be sent back to the western front and pitted against the Allied armies. From a Bolshevik standpoint, recruiting Austro-Hungarian prisoners was the only way to fend off the Cossacks in Manchuria, the Japanese in Vladivostok and the Czechoslovakian troops spread out across Central Asia and struggling to leave through Siberia and reach the western front. Kennan, *Soviet-American Relations, 1917–1920*, Vol. 2, *The Decision to Intervene*, 402.
64. *PWW*, "Private and confidential. Letter from Professor T. Masaryk to Charles R. Crane," Vol. 47, April 10, 1918, 550. Masaryk was still in Russia when he sent this message intended for Wilson.

65. *PWW*, "Telegram from Jusserand to Pichon," Vol. 48, May 29, 1918, 202–3. The interview in question was published in the May 27, 1918 edition of the *New York Times*.
66. Historians debated much on the subject of Wilson's motivations in regard to the intervention in Siberia. For some (Link, *WW. War, Revolution, and Peace* (1979); Kennan, *Soviet-American Relations* (1958); etc.), Wilson's hesitation demonstrates the extent to which his democratic ideals—and chronic indecisiveness—prevented him from enthusiastically following the strategy chosen by France and Britain, while for others, (Williams, *The Tragedy of American Diplomacy* (1959); Arno J. Mayer, *Politics and Diplomacy of Peace Making: Containment and Counterrevolution at Versailles, 1918–1919.* (1967); Levin, *WW and World Politics* (1968); Calhoun, *The Uses of Force and Wilsonian Foreign Policy* (1993); etc.), it constituted proof that he was trying to find a distinctly American position allowing him to establish the United States' preponderance in view of the concept of collective security delineated in the Fourteen Points. Generally, these discussions follow the historiographical pattern presented in the introduction. For an alternative interpretation, see Eugene P. Trani, "Woodrow Wilson and the Decision to Intervene in Russia: A Reconsideration," *The Journal of Modern History*, Vol. 48, 3 (1976): 440–61. Trani argued that to Wilson, the double problem of the Siberian issue and the Czechoslovakian Legion was only a marginal aspect of the war's overall strategy, along with the primacy of the Western Front. This would explain why he submitted to the Allies' decisions even though he did not approve of interference with the Revolution.
67. *PWW*, "CRC to WW," Vol. 49, August 1, 1918, 154.
68. *Crane Papers*, "CRC to Tumulty," May 30, 1918. Crane was doubtlessly reacting to a favorable decision by the Wilson Administration in regard to the "struggling races [...] fearfully shattered Slavic peoples." On May 29, 1918, the State Department declared America's official support to the peoples of Austria-Hungary seeking their national independence. See Victor S. Mamatey, *The United States and East Central Europe, 1914–1918. A Study in Wilsonian Diplomacy and Propaganda*, 252–61.
69. *Crane Papers*, "CRC to WW," June 9, 1918.
70. *PWW*, "George Tom M. Bridges to Lord Reading," Vol. 48, June 18, 1918, 352–3. Bridges was specifically referring to the fact that it was Crane who had introduced Masaryk to Wilson and that as a result, Wilson would place his faith in Masaryk.
71. *PWW*, "WW to CRC," Vol. 48, June 11, 1918, 283.
72. Mamatey, *The United States and East Central Europe, 1914–1918*, 285–6. This book contains the only account, based on a short note in Czech handwritten by Masaryk, of the meeting on June 19, 1918. Also cited in *PWW*, Vol. 48, June 19, 1918, 358.
73. *PWW*, "Robert Lansing to WW," Vol. 48, June 19, 1918, 364–5.
74. *PWW*, "Robert Lansing to WW," Vol. 48, June 23, 1918, 398; "Peyton C. March to Newton D. Baker," Vol. 48, June 24, 1918, 419; "House to WW," Vol. 48, June 21, 1918, 390–1; "Lord Reading to Arthur J. Balfour," Vol. 48, June 25, 1918, 430; "A News Report," Vol. 48, June 26, 1918, 432–4.
75. *PWW*, "CRC to WW" and "WW to CRC," Vol. 48, June 27 and 28, 1918, 450–1, 7.
76. *FRUS*, Vol. 1, *1918, World War, Supplement*, 816.
77. *Crane Papers*, "CRC to WW," July 2, 1918.

78. *PWW*, "A Memorandum by Robert Lansing," Vol. 48, July 6, 1918, 542–3. Wilson made this decision at the cost of great torment which he shared with House: "I have been sweating blood over the question what it is right and feasible to do in Russia." See July 8, 1918, 550.
79. *PWW*, "WW to CRC," Vol. 48, July 11, 1918, 590.
80. *PWW*, "CRC to WW" and "WW to CRC," Vol. 49, July 23 and 29, 1918, 62–3, 122.
81. *PWW*, "Frank L. Polk to WW (enclosure)," Vol. 49, July 20 (17), 1918, 41–2.
82. *PWW*, "WW to Masaryk," Vol. 49, July 22, 1918, 53. Wilson was then replying to a memo that Masaryk had sent him on July 20 and which came from the British consulate in Vladivostok (p. 44).
83. *PWW*, "Masaryk to WW," Vol. 49, August 5, 1918, 185. In *The United States and East Central Europe, 1914–1918*, Victor S. Mamatey points out that before World War II, many monuments stood in Prague in honor of Woodrow Wilson, including the station of the Orient Express, across it Wilson Square, a park called Wilson and a statue of the president, this not even including all the Woodrow Wilson avenues in Prague, around Czechoslovakia and in the countries formerly belonging to the Austro-Hungarian Empire (vii).
84. *Crane Papers*, "CRC to WW," August 1, 1918.
85. *PWW*, "Robert Lansing to WW" and "WW to RL," Vol. 49, August 19 and 22, 1918, 287–9, 313; "RL to WW" et "WW to RL," Vol. 49, September 4 and 5, 1918, 434–435, 446–447; Vol. 51, September 17, 1918, 26.
86. For the official declaration, see *FRUS*, Vol. 1, *1918*, *World War*, *Supplement*, 824.
87. *PWW*, "Masaryk to WW" and "WW to Masaryk," Vol. 49, September 7 and 10, 1918, 485–6, 511–2.
88. *Crane Papers*, "Memoirs," 210.
89. *PWW*, "Robert Lansing to Frank L. Polk (for Richard Crane)," Vol. 57, April 15, 1919, 374. Richard Crane was officially named ambassador in Czechoslovakia on April 23, 1919.
90. Strangely enough, this marriage only lasted a few years since Jan and Frances divorced in 1931. Sadder yet, Jan Masaryk was found dead in the courtyard of the Ministry of Foreign Affairs in 1948, having fallen from his bathroom window. Many theories about the cause of death spread as the various investigations were carried out, but Frances Crane as well as Jan's sister Alice believed it to have been a suicide. A more recent verdict (2004), however, ruled out suicide and instead seemed to confirm the possibility of a communist plot against Jan. See *New York Times*, "Sylvia E Crane: Masaryk, a Suicide?," January 28, 1990. There, Sylvia Crane affirmed that "All members of our immediate family in the United States, including Frances, Jan's former wife, believed at the time that he died by suicide. We were joined in this verdict by Jan's sister, Alice Masaryk."
91. *Crane Papers*, "Jan Masaryk to CRC," August 7, 1928.
92. *PWW*, "Masaryk to Lansing," Vol. 51, October 20, 1918, 506–8.
93. *PWW*, "Masaryk to WW," Vol. 53, January 2, 1919, 590.
94. This excerpt inevitably reminds us of international Wilsonianism as explained by the historian Akira Iriye. In *From Nationalism to Internationalism. U.S. Foreign Policy to 1914* (London: Routledge, 2002), Iriye explains that Wilson succeeded in bringing together different American understandings of international relations from the beginnings of the republic, including defensive ideas reacting to European imperialism and moral ideals

involving the myth of American exceptionalism and messianism as well as considerations linked to national interest. See pp. 233–237. In this sense, Crane seemed to have grasped what made Wilson unique in this period of diplomatic (re)structuring in the United States.

95. *PWW*, "Richard Crane to WW (enclosure)," Vol. 53, November 30, 1918, 258–9. Richard Crane had attached one of his father's letters (he was then visiting Japan) to Prince Georgy Lvov, exiled head of the Russian Provisional Government, dated October 7 and presenting Wilson as an ally of the anti-Bolshevik cause. Lvov met with Wilson on November 21, 1918, where the president assured him that the United States remained at the service of Russia, more particularly where resisting Bolshevism was concerned. Integrating Lvov in the discussions about Russia had been part of Crane's plan as well as that of his group of Slavophile friends, as indicated by Samuel Harper in a letter written in October 1918 through his mention of the efforts in this direction made by the former members of the Root Mission. *Crane Papers*, "Harper to Roger H. Williams and CRC," October 27, 1918.

Bibliography

Archives

Charles Richard Crane Papers, 1869–1967. Rare Books & Manuscript Library, University of Columbia.

Published Primary Sources

Baker, Ray S. and William E. Dodd, ed. *The Public Papers of Woodrow Wilson*. New York: Harper, 1925–26.

Baker, Ray S. *Woodrow Wilson: Life and Letters*. Garden City, NY: Doubleday, 1927–39.

Baruch, Bernard M. *Baruch*. New York: H. Holt, 1957–1960.

Capek, Karel. *Entretiens avec Masaryk*. Paris: Éditions de l'aube, 1991 [c.1936].

Daniels, Josephus. *The Wilson Era*. Chapel Hill: University of North Carolina Press, 1946.

Harper, Samuel N. *The Russia I Believe In: The Memoirs of Samuel N. Harper*. Chicago: University of Chicago Press, 1945.

Hart, Albert B. *The War in Europe. Its Causes and Results*. New York: D. Appleton, 1914.

House, Edward M and Charles Seymour. *What Really Happened at Paris: The Story of the Peace Conference, 1918–1919, by American Delegates*. New York: Scribner's, 1921.

Houston, David F. *Eight Years with Wilson's Cabinet, 1913–1920*. Garden City, NY: Doubleday, 1926.

Lansing, Robert. *The Peace Negotiations: A Personal Narrative*. Kessinger Publishers, 2004 [c.1921].

Link, Arthur S., ed. *Papers of Woodrow Wilson*. Princeton, NJ: Princeton University Press, 1966–92.

Mantoux, Paul. *Les délibérations du Conseil des Quatre, 24 mars-28 juin 1919. Notes de l'officier Interprète Paul Mantoux*. Paris: Ed. CNRS, 1955.

Masaryk, Tomas G. *The New Europe: The Slav Standpoint*. Lewisburg: Bucknell University Press, 1972 [c.1918].

Mucha, Jiri. *Alphonse Maria Mucha. His Life and Art*. New York: Rozzoli, 1989.

Seton-Watson, R. W. *Masaryk in England*. Cambridge: Cambridge University Press, 1943.

Seymour, Charles, ed. *The Intimate Papers of Colonel House Arranged as a Narrative*. London: Ernest Benn, 1926–28.

Tumulty, Joseph P. *Woodrow Wilson as I Know Him*. Garden City: Doubleday, 1921.

U.S. State Department. *Papers Relating to the Foreign Relations of the United States*.

Bibliographic Guides

Buckingham, Peter H. *Woodrow Wilson: A Bibliography of His Times and Presidency*. Wilmington, DE: Scholarly Resources, 1990.

Beisner, Robert L. and Hanson Kurt W., ed. *American Foreign Relations since 1600. A Guide to the Literature*. Santa Barbara, CA: ABC-CLIO, 2003.

Bellot, Hugh Hale. *American History and American Historians: A Review of Recent Contributions to the Interpretation of the History of the United States*. Norman: University of Oklahoma Press, 1952.

Haines, G. K. and J. S. Walker, ed. *American Foreign Relations. A Historiographical Review*. Westport, CT: Greenwood Press, 1981.

Parish, Peter J., ed. *Reader's Guide to American History*. Chicago: Fitzroy Publishers, 1997.

Encyclopedias

Balmer, Randall Herbert. *Encyclopedia of Evangelicalism*. Louisville, KY: John Knox Press, 2002.

Monographies

Akçam, Taner. *From Empire to Republic. Turkish Nationalism and the Armenian Genocide*. London: Zed Books, 2004.

Allerfeldt, Kristofer, ed. *The Progressive Era in the USA: 1890–1921*. Burlington, VT: Ashgate, 2007.

Ambrosius, Lloyd E. *Woodrow Wilson and the American Diplomatic Tradition: The Treaty Fight in Perspective*. Cambridge: Cambridge University Press, 1987.

———. *Wilsonian Statecraft: Theory and Practice of Liberal Internationalism during World War I*. Lanham, MD: SR Books, 1991.

———. *Wilsonianism: Woodrow Wilson and His Legacy in American Foreign Relations*. New York: Palgrave Macmillan, 2002.

Bell, Sidney. *Righteous Conquest. Woodrow Wilson and the Evolution of the New Diplomacy*. Port Washington, NY: Kennikat Press, 1972.

Blum, John M. *Woodrow Wilson and the Politics of Morality*. Boston: Little, Brown & Co., 1956.

Bradley, John F. N. *Czech Nationalism in the Nineteenth Century*. New York: Columbia University Press, 1984.

Bu, Liping. *Making the World Like Us: Education, Cultural Expansion, and the American Century*. Westport, CT: Praeger, 2003.

Calhoun, Frederick S. *Uses of Force and Wilsonian Foreign Policy*. Kent, OH: Kent State University Press, 1993.

Čapek, Thomas. *The Čechs (Bohemians) in America*. New York: Arno Press, 1969 [c.1920].

Clements, Kendrick A. *William Jennings Bryan, Missionary Isolationist*. Knoxville, TE: University of Tennessee Press, 1982.

———. *The Presidency of Woodrow Wilson*. Lawrence, KA: University Press of Kansas, 1992.

Curti, Merle E. *American Philanthropy Abroad*. New Brunswick, NJ: Rutgers University Press, 1963.

Davis, Donald E. and Eugene P. Trani. *The First Cold War. The Legacy of Woodrow Wilson in U.S.-Soviet Relations*. Columbia: University of Missouri Press, 2002.

Duroselle, Jean-Baptiste. *Histoire diplomatique de 1919 à nos jours*, 11th ed. Paris: Éditions Dalloz, 1993.

Ferrell, Robert H. *Woodrow Wilson and World War I, 1917–1921*. New York: Harper & Row, 1985.

Figes, Orlando *A People's Tragedy. The Russian Revolution, 1891–1924*. New York, Penguin Books, 1996.

Gardner, Lloyd C. *Safe for Democracy. The Anglo-American Response to Revolution, 1913–1923*. New York: Oxford University Press. 1984.

Gerson, Louis L. *Woodrow Wilson and the Rebirth of Poland 1914–1920. A Study in the Influence on American Policy of Minority Groups of Foreign Origin*. Hamden, CT: Archon Books, 1972 [c.1953].

Girault, René. *Diplomatie européenne. Nations et impérialisme, 1871–1914*. Paris: Armand Colin, 1995.

Hansen, Jonathan M. *The Lost Promise of Patriotism. Debating American Identity, 1890–1920*. Chicago: University of Chicago Press, 2003.

Hapgood, David. *Charles R. Crane. The Man Who Bet on People*. New York: ICWA, 2000.

Hays, Samuel P. *American Political History as Social Analysis*. Knoxville: University of Tennessee Press, 1980.

Hermet, Guy. *Histoire des nations et du nationalisme en Europe*. Paris: Seuil, 1996.

Holmes, James R. *Theodore Roosevelt and World Order. Police Power in International Relations*. Washington: Potomac Books, 2006.

Hopkins, Charles H. *John R. Mott, 1865–1955: A Biography*. Grand Rapids: Eerdmans, 1979.

Iriye, Akira. *From Nationalism to Internationalism. U.S. Foreign Policy to 1914*. London: Routledge, 2002.

Keegan, John. *The First World War*. New York: Random House, 1998.

Kennan, George F. *American Diplomacy, 1900–1950*. New York: New American Library, 1954.

———. *The Soviet-American Relations, 1917–1920*. Princeton, NJ: Princeton University Press, 1956.

Kennedy, David M. *Over Here. The First World War and American Society*. New York: Oxford University Press, 1980.

Knock, Thomas J. *To End all Wars. Woodrow Wilson and the Quest for a New World Order*. New York: Oxford University Press, 1992.

LaFeber, Walter. *The New Empire. An Interpretation of American Expansion, 1860–1898*. Ithaca, NY: Cornell University Press, 1963.

Lasch, Christopher. *The American Liberals and the Russian Revolution*. New York: McGraw, 1962.

———. *The New Radicalism in America. The Intellectual as a Social Type*. New York: Knopf, 1965.

Laserson, Max M. *The American Impact in Russia, 1784–1917*. New York: Collier, 1950.

Levin, Norman G. *Woodrow Wilson and World Politics: America's Response to War and Revolution*. New York: Oxford University Press, 1968.

Link, Arthur S. *Wilson*. Princeton, NJ: Princeton University Press, 1947.

———. *Woodrow Wilson and the Progressive Era, 1910–1917*. New York: Harper & Brothers, 1954.

———. *Wilson the Diplomatist. A Look at His Major Foreign Policies*. Baltimore: Johns Hopkins Press, 1957.

———. *Woodrow Wilson. Revolution, War, and Peace*. Arlington Heights, IL: Harlan Davidson, 1979.

Lippmann, Walter. *U.S Foreign Policy, Shield of the Republic*. Boston: Little & Brown, 1943.

Livermore, Seward W. *Woodrow Wilson and the War Congress 1916–1918*. New York: Octagon Books, 1968 [c. 1957].

Mamatey, Victor S. *The United States and East Central Europe, 1914–1918. A Study in Wilsonian Diplomacy and Propaganda*. Princeton, NJ: Princeton University Press, 1957.

Manela, Erez. *The Wilsonian Moment: Self-Determination and the International Origins of Anticolonial Nationalism, 1917–1920*. New York: Oxford University Press, 2007.

May, Ernest. *The World War and American Isolation, 1914–1917*. Cambridge: Harvard University Press, 1966 [c.1959].

———. *Imperial Democracy. The Emergence of America as a Great Power*. New York: Harper & Row, 1973.

Mayer, Arno. *Politics and Diplomacy of Peacemaking: Containment and Counterrevolution at Versailles, 1918–1919*. New York: Knopf, 1967.

McCartney, Paul T. *Power and Progress: American National Identity, the War of 1898, and the Rise of American Imperialism*. Baton Rouge: Louisiana University Press, 2006.

McLoughlin, William G. *Revivals, Awakenings, and Reform. An Essay on Religion and Social Change in America, 1607–1977*. Chicago: The Chicago University Press, 1978.

Michel, Bernard. *Nations et nationalismes en Europe centrale, XIXe-XXe siècle*. Paris: Aubier, 1995.

Muukkonen, Martti. *Ecumenism of the Laity. Continuity and Change in the Mission View of the World's Alliance of YMCA, 1855–1955*. Joensuu: University of Joensuu Publications in Theology, 2002.

Noble, David W. *The Paradox of Progressive Thought*. Minneapolis: University of Minnesota Press, 1958.

———. *The Progressive Mind, 1890–1917*. Minneapolis: Burgess, 1981.

Nordholdt, Jan W. S. *Woodrow Wilson: A Life for World Peace*. Berkeley: University of California Press, 1991.

Notter, Harley. *The Origins of the Foreign Policy of Woodrow Wilson*. New York: Russell & Russell, 1965.

Osgood, Robert E. *Ideals and Self-Interests in America's Foreign Relations. The Great Transformation of the Twentieth Century*. Chicago: University of Chicago, 1964 [c.1953].

Saul, Norman E. *The Life and Times of Charles R. Crane, 1858–1939. American Businessman, Philanthropist, and a Founder of Russian Studies in America*. Lexington Books, 2013.

Smith, Neil. *American Empire: Roosevelt's Geographer and the Prelude to Globalization*. Berkeley: University of California Press, 2003.

Soutou, Georges-Henri. *L'or et le sang. Les buts de guerre économiques de la Première Guerre mondiale*. Paris: Fayard, 1989.

Steel, Ronald. *Walter Lippmann and the American Century*. Boston: Little, Brown & Co. 1980.

Temperley, H. W. V, ed. *A History of the Peace Conference of Paris*. London: Oxford University Press, 1969 [c.1920].

Trask, David F. *Victory without Peace. American Foreign Relations in the Twentieth Century*. Huntington, New York: Robert E. Krieger Publishing Company, 1975.

Unterberger, Betty M. *The United States, Revolutionary Russia, and the Rise of Czechoslovakia*. Texas A&M University Press, 2000.

Van Alstyne, Richard W. *The Rising American Empire*. Oxford: Oxford University Press, 1960.

Walworth, Arthur. *Wilson and His Peacemakers. American Diplomacy at the Paris Peace Conference, 1919*. New York: Norton, 1986.

Weinstein, Edwin A. *Woodrow Wilson: a Medical and Psychological Biography*. Princeton, NJ: Princeton University Press, 1981.

Williams, William A. *The Tragedy of American Diplomacy*. New York: Dell Publishing, 1972 [c.1959].

Theses and Memoirs

Bocage, Leo J. "The Public Career of Charles R. Crane." Ph.D. diss., Fordham University, 1962.

Daley, Anna. "Alphonse Mucha in Gilded Age America, 1904–1921." M.A. diss., Parsons New School for Design, 2007.

Sulzbach, Jacob John, Jr. "Charles R. Crane, Woodrow Wilson, and Progressive Reform: 1909–1921." Ph.D. diss., Texas A&M University, 1994.

Journal Articles

Ahonen, Risto. "John R. Mott as an Ecumenical Leader. What Was Mott's Vision?" *The Finnish Evangelical Lutheran Mission*, 2010, 1–5.

Anghie, Antony. "Cultural Differences in International Law: the League of Nations and Two Visions of Nation-State." *International Center for Comparative Law and Politics Review*, 5, 2002, 4–13.

Beloff, Max. "Self-Determination Reconsidered," In *Confluence*, 5, 1956, 195–203.

Leuchtenburg, William E. "Progressivism and Imperialism: The Progressive Movement and American Foreign Policy, 1898–1916." *The Mississippi Valley Historical Review*, 39, 3, 1952, 483–504.

Osgood, Robert E. "Woodrow Wilson, Collective Security, and the Lessons of History." *Confluence*, 5, 1957, 341–354.

Parry, Albert. "Charles R. Crane, Friend of Russia." *Russian Review*, 6, 2, 1947, 20–36.

Pomerance, Michla. "Methods of Self-determination and the Argument of Primitiveness." *Canadian Yearbook of International Law*, 12, 1974, 38–66.

———. "The United States and Self-determination: Perspectives on the Wilsonian Conception." *The American Journal of International Law*, 70, 1, 1976, 1–27.

Saito, Natsu T. "Crossing the Border: The Interdependence of Foreign Policy and Racial Justice in the United States." *Yale Human Rights and Development Law Journal*, 1, 1998, 53–84.

Smith, Daniel M. "National Interest and American Intervention, 1917: A Historiographical Appraisal." *The Journal of American History*, 52, 1, 1965, 5–24.

Trani, Eugene P. "Woodrow Wilson and the Decision to Intervene in Russia: A Reconsideration." *The Journal of Modern History*, 48, 3, 1976, 440–2.

Unterberger, Betty. "The Arrest of Alice Masaryk." *Slavic Review*, 33, 1, 1974, 91–106.

Van Alstyne, Richard W. "Woodrow Wilson and the Idea of Nation-State." *International Affairs*, 37, 1961, 293–308.

· 5 ·

CHARLES R. CRANE AND VERSAILLES: TOWARD THE EMANCIPATION OF THE OTTOMAN PEOPLES, 1919

Crane and America's Reaction to the Armenian Issue

Charles Crane cast his first glance at the non-European world through a prism tinged with both religious and political considerations. An avid tourist since the end of the 1870s, the young Crane had come to perceive the Ottoman Empire as a nemesis of the Slavs and Christians of Europe. He owed this view to the Russian-Turkish rivalry in Crimea and the tensions caused by Ottoman and Muslim dominance over the Balkans. Having witnessed multiple conflicts between the Ottoman Empire and the Slavic peoples of Russia and of the Balkans, Crane later interpreted the 14–18 war partly as a war against the Ottoman encroachment upon Europe, which was abetted by the scheming Central Powers. However, what he feared above all, as expressed in a letter to President Wilson, was "that Asia is growing rapidly in political power. With that situation facing the Christian world, for it to engage in this fearful war is to run the risk of placing Europe at the mercy of Asia."[1]

This impression formed in the late 1870s did not, however, prevent him from becoming voluntarily involved in the field of education in the Ottoman Empire as of 1910. He made donations to the Robert College of Constantinople and to the Constantinople College for Girls and became a member of the board of both overseas American schools in 1910.[2] This effectively made him an icon of the American school system's expansion movement, and it was even suggested in 1919 that the American College for Girls (called Constantinople College) be renamed Crane College or Crane University in his honor, though this plan was never executed for reasons unknown.[3]

Yet for Crane, the Ottoman case did not simply boil down to a rivalry between civilizations—that would be much too simplistic an analysis—and the issue was rife with its own internal difficulties which he also observed through the lens of the principle of nationalities. As early as 1878, at the age of twenty, Crane had traveled to Cairo, Jerusalem, and Damascus, and then up through Turkey to Smyrna and to the Balkans, where Europe's nationalism issue, described in the previous chapter, first came to his attention. Then, in 1909, he spent a whole year in the Arab world with his wife Cornelia, reportedly in the exclusive company of Muslims, many of whom he befriended despite the fact that, according to him, they did not open up easily to others.[4] It was in 1915, however, that Crane truly developed a profound interest in the fate of the various nationalities spread across the Ottoman Empire when he caught wind of stories about the massacre of Armenians and Greeks by Ottoman soldiers and Kurdish and Turkish civilians. These accounts reached him through the personal contacts he had among American missionaries, philanthropists, diplomats, and educators. As he had done with the "American Friends of a New Middle Europe," Crane became involved with a sort of clique made up of people who sympathized with the fate of Armenians in Turkey, which also included many of Wilson's close friends and supporters of the Democratic Party. Among Crane's main allies in America's response to the Armenian problem was Cleveland H. Dodge, one of Wilson's closest friends, his classmate from Princeton in 1879 and a contributor and organizer of the 1912 and 1916 campaigns. They were also aided in their efforts by the missionary James Levi Barton, director of the American Board of Commissioners for Foreign Missions (ABCFM). The information they received first came from the U.S. ambassador in Constantinople, Henry Morgenthau, Sr., (the father of the United States Secretary of Treasury under Franklin D. Roosevelt), a democratic New York Jew born in Germany. Crane saw Morgenthau as a "deserving" Jew and a "great power" in Turkish affairs,[5] and he was appointed to the ambassadorial post specifically for his Jewish origin.[6] The Wilson Administration, which considered Constantinople a crossroads between the East and the West, believed western Jews to be particularly suited to such diplomatic positions. In fact, when Morgenthau left his diplomatic post to help organize Wilson's 1916 campaign[7] and his successor, another Jew named Abram Elkus, was selected, Crane commented that "a Jewish Ambassador does better at Constantinople than elsewhere [...] The Jews seem to be a natural bridge between Europe and Asia."[8]

As horrific reports from consuls and missionaries confirmed the atrocities carried out against Armenian populations in Anatolia and attested to Talaat Pasha's shameless acknowledgment thereof, Morgenthau proposed both the application of diplomatic pressure and the creation of a massive aid program for the victims.[9] The idea of organizing humanitarian relief had already emerged in missionary and educational circles, but Morgenthau took upon himself the task of asking Secretary of State Lansing to "suggest to Cleveland Dodge, Charles Crane, John R. Mott, Stephen Wise, and others to form committees to raise funds and provide means to save some of the Armenians and assist the poorer ones to emigrate."[10] The Armenian Relief Committee (originally named American Committee on Armenian Atrocities) was thus created during their first meeting on September 16, 1915 in Cleveland Dodge's office in New York, with Barton as its president and Crane acting as treasurer.

Crane mentioned this first key meeting in a letter to his daughter Josephine:

> a number of us interested in the affairs of the Levant—in missionary work and in education—had a strong appeal from our friend the Ambassador to Turkey, Mr. Morgenthau, to do all possible to save and to relieve the poor Armenians. We had a fine meeting of men representing these various activities at the office of Cleveland.

The committee then asked Crane and Barton to travel to Washington in order to look over the official documentation Morgenthau had sent the State Department. This proved to be a crucial step as, despite the echoes that had reached them previously, Crane reported that "the material we found at the State Department more than confirmed our worst fears."[11]

Shortly after the meeting on September 16, Crane received a letter from his good British friend, Viscount James Bryce, a renowned politician, diplomat, and historian who congratulated him on his appointment as treasurer. Bryce, himself involved in Britain's relief effort, wrote that "We are extremely glad to know you have taken charge of Armenian Relief to be sent from America" and approved of America's initiative, which to him confirmed that "America is indeed the land of humanity and generosity."[12] Such a comment was hardly trivial as it came from a great expert on American society and its institutions. Indeed, in 1888, James Bryce had published *The American Commonwealth*, a great classic which even garnered Wilson's praise at the start of his academic career. Bryce had also written a report on the atrocities committed by the Germans in Belgium and, as a specialist on the Armenian people since the 1880s, had been selected by the British government to conduct a field survey on the Armenian massacre in Turkey. He was accompanied on this mission by the young but soon-to-be eminent historian Arnold Toynbee, and together, they published a parliamentary document in 1916 called *Blue Book: The Treatment of the Armenians in the Ottoman Empire, 1915–1916*.[13]

To these first echoes corroborating the State Department's diplomatic and consular documents was added the testimony of a certain Haigazoun H. Topakyan, a Persian consul of Armenian descent. Topakyan, then a carpet merchant and entrepreneur living in New York, wrote a letter directly to Wilson on October 22, 1915 in which he attested to the deportations and murders of thousands of Armenian families carried out by "fanatical Moslems." In his reply, Wilson assured Topakyan both of his awareness and of his worry in regard to the situation and declared that he was willing to use diplomatic influence in Turkey to put an end to the violence against the Armenians.[14] In December, William Nesbitt Chambers, an American missionary working in Turkey for the ABCFM, also wrote Wilson (whom he knew from the Princeton Class of 1876) a poignant letter urging the president to take an official stance on the massacres carried out by the Turks. Though writing in a personal capacity, Chambers expressed views that aligned with the position adopted by several other representatives of the missionary world. To broach the topic that concerned him, namely the fate of the Armenians, Chambers first described his idea of America's role in world affairs:

> I stood with one hand on a great gun, and in the other was the Gospel—the one made for the destruction of men and the other revealed for their life and peace. I could satisfy myself only with the thought that the world needs them both. In the hands of such men as yourself the one would be used to restrain evil and the other to develop righteousness and good-will to men.

Though the example's fierceness seems to clash with its peaceful conclusion, Chambers undoubtedly saw the use of force as a viable approach to stopping crimes against humanity:

> The Armenian situation in Turkey is so appalling in its awful cruelty and relentless extermination of that people that one could wish that such a power as the United States should become so strong on land and sea that such a government as Turkey would never dare to commit such a horrible crime.[15]

Chambers evidently hoped to see the United States use the necessary dissuasive force to prevent crimes against humanity like those committed in Turkey. Wilson, who was still a staunch believer in neutrality, sent a warm response but also strove to curb his old classmates' ardor. Thanking him for the "personal" part of his letter where Chambers confirmed that he had safely left Turkey, Wilson assured him that he was equally horrified by the Armenian massacres, but also added that "We have been doing everything that is diplomatically possible to check the terrible business." Though Crane acknowledged Chambers's part in rousing sympathy for the Armenians,[16] neither he nor the Armenian Relief Committee supported the missionary's belligerent position. Crane, Dodge, Barton, and Mott not only (initially) endorsed neutrality in the European conflict but they also slowly built a sort of lobby opposed to any form of military action in Turkey even after the United States had gone to war against Germany and Austria-Hungary. Such an attitude stemmed primarily from their belief that America's missionary and educational presence in Turkey was too important to risk being compromised if the United States made an enemy out of the Ottoman Empire. The committee's purpose thus became diplomatic as well as humanitarian, and its work extended beyond the Armenian issue, which, however, remained a central concern.

The committee's primary goal was to help the Armenians, who due to their religious kinship with America were viewed as a Christian minority oppressed by Muslim authorities. Yet it also worked toward the rescue of other victims of Turkish persecution, even those of Muslim faith like the Syrians and other groups ruled by the Ottomans. Its name was thus changed first to American Committee for Armenian and (As)syrian Relief (ACASR) and then to Near East Relief (NER), which was to be its formal title from 1919 (the year of its officialization by Congress) until 1930, when it was renamed Near East Foundation. When the NER was incorporated in August, 1919 by the 66th Congress, its board of directors included Crane, Dodge, Barton, Mott, and Morgenthau as well as many other major personalities of the time like Elihu Root, Charles E. Hughes, and Charles W. Eliot.

The ACASR, sometimes also informally called the Dodge Committee in its earlier days, belonged to the old Protestant philanthropic tradition, and Cleveland Dodge himself was described by the writer and historian Peter Balakian as a "distinguished American philanthropist in the old mugwump tradition of civic-minded entrepreneurs."[17] In this regard, he rather resembled Crane, who also fit into this tradition as the first chapter has shown. Yet Crane and Dodge, influenced by social gospel ethics, had brought with them a new and characteristically progressive way of doing things. They combined fundraising, public relations, and administrative skills with sound academic knowledge, in this case precisely about the peoples and regions they geared their aid campaign toward. Suzanne E. Moranian in particular remarked that "The Social Gospelers [...] drew upon the dynamic, twentieth century ideas of bureaucracy and rationalization [...] Goodness and efficiency became synonymous."[18]

Moreover, one of the Armenian Relief Committee's greatest assets at the time was certainly the close relationship its members had with President Wilson. In fact, while arguing before Talaat and Enver Pasha that American missionary interests in Turkey were linked with the fate of the Armenians (the primary beneficiaries of American philanthropy in Turkey), Ambassador Morgenthau impressed upon the Turkish triumvirate that Wilson himself was a friend of the missionaries and philanthropists who led the relief campaign. Morgenthau then added that these people, specifically referring to Crane and Dodge, "represent what is best in America and the fine altruistic spirit which in our country accumulates wealth and then uses it to found colleges and schools."[19] James Barton also recognized Crane and Dodge's proximity to the president as a key factor in the committee's success, affirming that "President Wilson was keenly alive to the situation and eager that America should do its part in the humanitarian effort" and that "through his personal friendship with Mr. Dodge and Mr. Crane he assured the Committee of his interest in the Near East."[20]

Wilson, Dodge, and Crane, along with James Barton and sometimes John Mott, made up what the historian Joseph L. Grabill called an "unofficial cabinet."[21] Though this statement may be somewhat of an embellishment, it shows Wilson's tendency to prefer the loyalty of informal advisors and representatives to more traditional diplomatic lines of communication. As an example of their collaboration, it was Dodge who covered the committee's administrative expenses until 1917, when Barton succeeded in getting Congress to issue a resolution of sympathy and Wilson called a special fundraiser on October 22, 1916.[22]

From an American perspective, the fate of the Armenians in the Ottoman Empire, a belligerent state that was part of the Triple Alliance, naturally fit into the larger issue of neutrality in regard to the war in Europe. As seen in the previous chapters, the choice to remain neutral or join the war was intertwined with the question of the Russian Revolution, which had in fact greatly contributed to America's increasingly favorable stance toward intervention and affected its way of perceiving the conflict in Europe. The

Ottoman issue, generally viewed through the lens of the events as reported by American nationals in the Middle East, in some way also became part of the national debate on neutrality. The members of missionary and philanthropic circles, for their part, strove in their own way to influence the American government's position on the war and on relations with the Ottoman Empire.

Like Crane and Mott, Dodge also endorsed Wilsonian neutrality between 1914 and 1917,[23] though according to Wilson, some of his humanitarian activities seemed—outwardly, at least—to compromise American neutrality. As part of these activities, Dodge strove to unify various American humanitarian organizations like the Red Cross, the YMCA, the Armenian (and Syrian) Relief Committee (ACASR), and the Belgian Relief Committee under Wilson's supervision. His efforts were first met with the president's hesitation and then with his outright refusal as Wilson, afraid of betraying his own principle of neutrality, refused to be associated with one camp or the other. House explained more precisely in his journal that "The President is willing to help but not take the lead, because he is afraid some criticism might arise on account of the critical condition of foreign affairs" and asserted that "if he took the lead in a general relief plan someone would be certain to say that he sympathized with one side or the other."[24]

This large national humanitarian empire directed by Dodge, Mott, and Crane fell within the framework of "preparedness," a movement Wilson initially opposed but which he began viewing more favorably after the sinking of the *Lusitania* in 1915. A telegram probably written on February 3, 1917 or slightly earlier and signed, among others, by Mott, Dodge, and Hoover (Crane's name does not feature on the telegram but Dodge signed on behalf of the Armenian Relief Commission) assured Wilson that "it would be very desirable, as a matter of preparedness, to take early steps for the formation of a great national relief fund." Wilson responded with gratitude that he saw in their venture "the spirit of America itself" and that it reassured him in his fragile position of "preparedness" which remained an aspect of neutrality.[25] This view of humanitarian aid in the context of military preparedness and national defense might seem paradoxical. Yet charitable action fit into the larger and increasingly important idea of a war against chaos and imperial tyranny, associated with Prussian militarism or with the Turkish cruelty deplored by philanthropists in the context of the Armenian massacres. It also intersected with the idea of "new" international relations founded on sympathy and charity formulated and promoted by Crane and Mott and explored in the previous chapters.

At the same time, the philanthropists' readiness to accept the possibility of America's participation in the war (as long as this participation was fuelled by righteous reasons) meant that Wilson had their unwavering support in his war effort against Germany and Austria-Hungary following his War Message of April 2, 1917. The day after Wilson's speech to Congress, Dodge hastened to congratulate him. "[M]ay God grant that your great declaration may have the effect of bringing the awful war to a speedy end,"[26] Dodge wrote, expressing in a sense the idea that American participation in the conflict served a noble and pacifistic cause.

However, though the members of the ACASR took no issue with a confrontation between the United States and the Austro-German alliance, they hoped to avoid a declaration of war against the Ottoman Empire at all costs. Many varied strategies and arguments were employed to deter Wilson from succumbing to the (Allied) temptation of confronting the Ottoman Empire. With occasional help from Crane and with the support of Barton and of the missionary world, Dodge led a lobby against military intervention in Turkey. Even before America's entry into the war against Germany and Austria-Hungary, the Dodge-Crane committee, on behalf of the ACASR and the ABCFM, sent Barton to deliver an official caution against the war in Turkey to Lansing at the State Department, who then relayed the message to Wilson.[27]

Firstly, it was Morgenthau who, contrary to the ACASR's usual depiction of the Turks in its pro-Armenian fundraising campaigns, emphasized the respect Turkish leaders had for Americans, and particularly for him as a U.S. ambassador.[28] Wilson had always displayed the greatest sympathy toward Armenians and regularly asked about the conditions of American nationals in Turkey, especially those in missionary circles like Cleveland Dodge's son, who was a constant conveyor of news. In a letter where he unsuccessfully offered Dodge a post at the British embassy, Wilson also inquired about the missionary situation in Turkey, writing that "I have thought more than once of your dear ones in Turkey with a pang of apprehension that was very deep." More generally, Wilson wished to act with a certain amount of caution to ensure that "there will be no real danger to the lives of our people abroad."[29] Dodge reassured Wilson on this account, affirming that "the Turks are treating the Americans well," and then reminded the president of the situation's severity by adding "the suffering of the peoples [primarily Armenians, Greeks, and Syrians] are indescribably awful." Wilson replied that he was "grateful to God that at least some element of prudence toward America has been planted in the heart of the Turk,"[30] implying, perhaps, that lack of "prudence" in the treatment of Americans on Turkish soil would result in dire consequences for the Ottoman Empire. Nevertheless, Wilson's declaration of war on April 2, 1917 concerned only Germany. Wilson did not extend America's war effort to the Ottoman Empire, though it remains unclear whether this decision was made deliberately and whether Dodge's influence played any part in the president's choice.

Yet Wilson continued being pressured to declare war on the Ottomans even by contributors and militants within the Armenian Relief (Theodore Roosevelt, for instance). It was Dodge who took on the task of pleading with Wilson against the war with Turkey. Recognizing the "biased" nature of his arguments given his position in the educational and philanthropic movement, he explained that:

> Those of us who are interested in the great educational, missionary and relief work, in the Turkish Empire are worried over the possibility that the anomalous but friendly relations that now exist between this country and Turkey may be changed by a declaration of war, which would be fatal to our interests.

Dodge reported that his arguments stemmed from conversations with Barton (of the ABCFM), with Crane (as a trustee of the Constantinople colleges and manager of the ACASR), and with ex-ambassador Morgenthau and his successor Abram Elkus. Though he assured Wilson that "we all feel that our selfish interests should not stand in the way of what you think it best to do in carrying out your great purposes to end the war," Dodge insisted that:

> It is the unanimous feeling of all, that war with Turkey would be a serious blow to these great American enterprises & would jeopardize many American lives besides stopping the work we are doing in saving the lives of hundreds of thousands of natives.

More specifically, Dodge and his collaborators hoped that the Americans in Turkey would not be repatriated so that they could continue providing aid to the oppressed minorities, especially considering that "the Turks are treating our people with great & actually friendly considerations [...] they want peace badly & have no love for the Germans." Interestingly, Dodge included Bulgaria in his argument against the war, asserting that American missionary presence there would suffer just as much as missionary presence in Turkey as a result of any belligerent action.[31]

In his response, Wilson confirmed his full agreement with Dodge's missionary and philanthropic arguments but also mentioned the pressures he was facing from Congress: "I sympathize with every word of your letter [...] and am trying to hold the Congress back from following its inclination to include all the allies of Germany in a declaration of a state of war."[32] Indeed, in his message to Congress on December 4, 1917 (two days after Dodge's intervention), Wilson motioned to include Austria-Hungary in the state of war but continued to exclude Bulgaria and Turkey for, as he explained, they "do not yet stand in the direct path of our necessary action."[33] The pragmatism of this argument was perhaps tailored to his target audience (Congress), but it is also quite possible that Wilson purposefully avoided mentioning other lines of reasoning for not seeking a confrontation with Turkey.

It thus remains difficult to prove that Dodge and his lobby had a direct hand in America's decision to stay out of the conflict with the Ottoman Empire. It even appears that the United States at one point considered military action against Turkey and Bulgaria as the State Department had requested advice from the British Foreign Office on the soundness of a joint declaration of war against Bulgaria and the Ottoman Empire.[34] In response, London prepared an argument which was presented by Walter Hines Page, the American ambassador to Great Britain and a friend of both Crane and Wilson. Page advanced that such a decision would play "a significant role for the United States at the peace table in regard to the settlements to be reached concerning the Near East and Middle East." This argument's decidedly realist spin did not appeal to Wilson, who had never viewed the war as a means of strategically promoting America's national interests. Yet London presented other arguments concerning the fate of Armenian and Greek minorities in Turkey which were more likely to sway Wilson. Great Britain argued that these minorities would certainly benefit from American military opposition to the Ottoman regime due to the dissuasive effect it would have on the massacres.[35] While transmitting London's response to Wilson, Lansing took the opportunity to describe the idea as "unwise" without, however, explaining the reasoning behind this assessment. Evidently, the Eastern Front was losing steam and very little would result from a declaration of war against Turkey, from a tactical perspective, given the obvious degeneracy of the Ottoman regime and the vulnerability of its army. Wilson's pragmatic December 4 arguments had thus not been shaken by Great Britain's input, yet whether they were the only thing standing in the way of a conflict with the Ottoman Empire remains to be seen.

A few other hints, this from British sources, serve to confirm the part played by Dodge, Crane, and the missionary circles in America's decision not to declare war on Turkey. William Wiseman (1885–1962), a British spy who served as a liaison between Wilson and Great Britain during World War I, discussed the potential of a war against Turkey with House and Wilson and wrote a report of the conversation which he then sent to London. Wiseman's assessment reveals that Wilson's understanding of the Ottoman issue had been influenced by the missionary circles:

> He [Wilson] has no sympathy or liking for the Turks, but he believes that the presence of American missionaries and others has up to now prevented massacres and atrocities which would otherwise have occurred. Advisers whom he trusts (mostly connected with various educational and religious organizations in Turkey) have convinced him that a terrible outburst of savagery would follow on a declaration of war. This reason, a curious one I admit, added to the fact that he cannot see any direct military advantage to be gained and only an indirect political one, make him definitely opposed to the idea.[36]

Wiseman only summarized a few elements of Dodge's argument, omitting, for instance, the idea that a state of war would endanger American institutions in Turkey. Yet the account he made of his conversation with Wilson makes it hard not to attribute the president's ruling against military action in Turkey to these "advisers whom he trusts," primarily Dodge, Crane, Barton, and Mott. The excerpt also sheds light on what was possibly one of Wilson's (and Crane's, given his involvement with the same organizations as Dodge) greatest concerns: America's prominent philanthropic role and its humanitarian presence overseas. Regardless of the extent to which Dodge and his committee influenced America's decision, Dodge commended Wilson on his policy of neutrality in regard to these two allies of Germany whose population saw American institutions in such a favorable light. He wrote, a few weeks before the armistice, that "I realize now more than ever before how wise your policy has been toward Bulgaria & Turkey." Moreover, having financed the ACASR's running costs himself in the first few years of its existence, Dodge and his wife had taken a personal interest in the organization. In view of the fact that their children were working in Constantinople as missionaries and educators, Wilson's decision was all the more important to Dodge, who wrote in his letter that "It means so much to Grace and myself." Dodge's opinion in regard to the situation in Bulgaria also matched the one shared by Wilson and Crane about the Balkans. Expressing his faith in a future of self-determination with settlements based on national identity and states managed technocratically by the international community, Dodge wrote that "If the Balkan states would now make peace and leave the settlement of their vexed boundaries &

nationalities to a disinterested tribunal after the war is ended, there would be some hope for a permanent peace in that unhappy peninsula."[37]

Yet beyond the undeniably fundamental Armenian case, Wilson, Crane, and the Dodge Committee were concerned with other questions relating to the Ottoman Empire at the end of the war. With America now elevated in the diplomatic hierarchy, its leaders and influencers began planning the postwar world order, with particular emphasis on the protection of minorities in the Turkish Empire.

Preparations for the King-Crane Commission and the Self-Determination of the Ottoman Peoples: "To Reconstitute the Turkish Empire in an American way"

Previous chapters in this book have demonstrated Crane and Wilson's interest in the fate of "small nations," as proven namely by their support of Masaryk's efforts in bringing about the emancipation of the Czech nation. Austria-Hungary's destruction and the neutralization of German military power had been the primary stakes of the war and of America's intervention. The postwar settlements, however, would concern the Ottoman Empire just as much as Central Europe. Charles Crane, in this regard, was to play an official part in the proceedings, though his involvement would yield no tangible political results. Crane was appointed by Wilson to co-lead a commission of inquiry on minorities living in the former Ottoman Empire. Its purpose was to help the Big Four at the Versailles Conference determine the new national boundaries for these territories. Consequently, Crane joined the president on the American Commission to Negotiate Peace, to which the Inter-Allied Commission on Mandates in Turkey was accountable.[38] Crane's journey to the Middle East to become better acquainted with the state of mind and sense of allegeance of the populations—once again in accordance with the very delicate principle of nationalities—touched on many themes close to his heart. The Armenian question naturally featured among these, but there was also the thorny Syro-Palestinian problem and, to a lesser degree, the Zionist movement and the Jewish issue. All of these issues fit into the larger context of a shattered imperial order replaced by a system of mandates administrated by the victorious Allies. The situation was complicated by the outrageous "old diplomacy" which persisted at the heart of this current of international reform.

Crane approached the commissioner's task assigned to him by Wilson like a missionary follows his calling. He did not need compensation for the work and refused the provided salary, unlike his colleague Henry C. King, who earned a modest living as a teacher.[39] In a way, the commission represented for Crane the political culmination of his philanthropic and educational activities in the East and he considered it quite natural and even commendable (though he never seemed to be boastful on this account) to volunteer without remuneration. Wilson, incidentally, had a similar conception of his own political work in Versailles, where he was recognized by all—to Georges Clemenceau's great displeasure—as a messiah at the diplomats' table. Crane did not disagree with this vision and in fact believed that there was a missionary dimension to Wilson's involvement in the Versailles negotiations. As he expressed in a letter to his eldest son Richard shortly after the armistice, Wilson's whole first term in its focus on the New Freedom had been devoted to making "Christian principles prevail in political life," an effort which according to Crane had been crowned with success. Wilsonian diplomacy, therefore, constituted in Crane's eyes the international application of this same effort of Christianization since "the principles which will be established there [in Versailles] and the methods of carrying them out must also be entirely in accord with Christianity." The Paris Peace Conference, for Crane, had thus taken on the same missionary character as his previous involvement in the Root Mission or his support of a free and democratic Bohemia. Furthermore, he looked once again to his two favorite collaborators in these past endeavors for help in promoting Wilsonian (and Christian) principles, writing that "I hope Masaryk and Mott will have important roles in carrying them [the Christian principles] out."[40] Such was Crane's state of mind when he followed Wilson to Versailles and when he set out for the Middle East as part of the Commission on Mandates in Turkey.

Even before leading his country into the war, Wilson, for his part, had taken up a clear stance in favor of the political autonomy and sometimes even of the liberation of imperial minorities. Much like philanthropists and many other Americans, Wilson had come to see the Armenian case as a prime example of the imperialist oppression he strove to destroy. In his 1916 campaign, the president expressed the following view emphasizing America's role in the quest for political rights for the small nations:

> You know the feeling of this nation towards those unorganized people who have no political standing in Europe, like the Armenians [...] America does not believe in the rights of small nations merely because they are small, [...] because we are big [...] and

> the big ought not impose upon the helpless. But we believe in them because, when we think of the sufferings of mankind, we forget where political boundaries lie, and say "These people are the flesh and blood of mankind, and America is made up out of the peoples of the world".[41]

This speech serves as a representation of Wilson's decidedly humanistic point of view. It shows his way of drawing parallels between other populations and the ethnic melting pot that was America, bringing these various peoples together under the umbrella of a shared humanity. Autonomy, Wilson believed, was not owed to small nations simply through a protective, paternalistic reflex, but because those nations were home to human beings on par with all other human beings in the world. Though only one element in a much larger election speech in Ohio, this principle remained central and meaningful in Wilsonian thought and guided the president during the imperial settlements, particularly with regard to the Armenians living in the Ottoman Empire. They represented the "small nations" Wilson referred to while advocating their political emancipation from the imperial system.

Even during the first months of the ACASR's existence, Armenian authorities rightly recognized Wilson's importance in America's help to Armenian victims and applauded his speech in support of national destinies. The bishop of the Armenian Apostolic Church of America Arsene Vehouni sent Wilson a letter in the name of the patriarch of the Armenian Church and of all Armenians thanking him for his "humane and generous interest" toward the Armenian people. To this, Wilson replied that the services rendered by his "representatives" (in this case, the Dodge Committee clique including Crane, Barton, and Mott) were spurred by hearts "full of sympathy" and were the expression of America's feelings toward the Armenian people.[42]

Though it was only one of the aspects covered by the King-Crane Commission, Armenia's fate as a country was cast into sharper focus and interest in it was renewed as the armistice drew closer. At the start of the Paris Peace Conference in January of 1919, many factors combined to make a settlement in the Ottoman Empire more difficult than anticipated. First among them was the problem of Allied diplomacy during the war, which was founded on the colonial logic of spheres of interest. The Allies took for granted that the Ottoman Empire, where several important battles had taken place, would be divvied up for the benefit of the victorious powers. This resulted in various secret inter-Allied agreements and outlines of sometimes completely contradictory negotiations with the concerned regions. In April of 1915, the Triple Entente secured Italy's support by promising it a share in Asia Minor. The following year, it was Russia's turn to be awarded "rights" over part of Armenia and a chunk of northern Anatolia, while the Sykes-Picot Agreement concluded in May of 1916 essentially handed Syria to France and Mesopotamia and Baghdad to Great Britain. Simultaneously, Britain was bargaining with different Arab kingdoms about the possibility of political autonomy if they in exchange revolted against the Ottoman power. An agreement was thus concluded with Emir Hussein, Faisal's father, while the British government of India was negotiating with Emir Ibn Saud about Saudi sovereignty in those very same regions. These war strategies were also complicated by the Zionist position endorsed by Great Britain throught the Balfour Declaration made on November 2, 1917. Though Emir Hussein appeared sympathetic toward the Zionist movement, the Balfour Declaration posed a significant obstacle to a viable settlement when it came to dividing the Ottoman Empire during the Versailles Negotiations.

Wilson made this jumble of territorial and political agreements even more complex with his historic Fourteen Points speech pronounced on January 8, 1918. Its twelfth point advocated limiting the Ottoman power to Turkish regions only and promoted autonomy for Ottoman imperial minorities as well as free access to the Dardanelles under international supervision. More information about this twelfth point was soon added to the early draft by American commentors. They now included international jurisdiction over Constantinople, the disappearance of Turkey's European portion (eastern Thrace), a Greek mandate over Greek-speaking regions of Asia Minor's coastline, as well as an independent Armenia with access to both the Black Sea and the Mediterranean, also called "Wilsonian Armenia."[43]

Though the project of a commission of inquiry in the Ottoman Empire took shape during the Big Four's first discussions in March of 1919, the idea itself had been suggested earlier by a representative of the missionary world in the Middle East. Howard Bliss, the president of the American University of Beirut, argued in favor of an inquiry into local opinions in Syria before the Council of Ten on February 13, 1919.[44] While Clemenceau and David Lloyd George tried to organize the territory based on the secret treaties they had made during the war, Wilson insisted that since all involved parties had already agreed to the mandate system which accompanied the principle of self-determination, one now had to inquire into questions like "whether the French were really wanted in Syria and the British in Mesopotamia."[45]

Wilson was aware of the fundamental conflict between this diplomacy of secret agreements based on the colonialist concept of "spheres of interest" and the system of mandates which revolved around the idea of self-determination. He proposed the establishment of an inter-Allied commission which would gather facts pertaining to the implementation of the mandates and determine "the state of opinion and the soil to be worked on by any mandatory." A few days later, Wilson published his general instructions for the commissioners even though the list of participants had not yet been finalized. Their aim would be to define "the sentiments of the people of those regions [...] with the social, racial, and economic conditions, a knowledge of which might serve to guide the judgement of the Conference [...] of the divisions of territory and assignment of mandates." Such a system would be "most likely to promote the order, peace and development of those peoples and countries."[46]

Wilson personally chose the commission's two leaders, though it would seem that Ray Stannard Baker, a member of the delegation in Versailles and one of the president's future biographers, played a prominent role in Henry C. King's nomination. King was a professor at the Oberlin College in Ohio and was also, like Crane, involved in philanthropy. Though he was no more an expert in foreign policy than Crane, it was thought that his biblical studies (King was, above all, a Congregationalist theologian) had familiarized him with the Holy Land, even though the Jewish Palestine of biblical times bore no resemblance to the largely Muslim and Arab Palestine of the twentieth century. King had also participated in humanitarian relief with the YMCA under command of the American Expeditionary Forces starting in August of 1918. Under King and Crane's leadership, a team of "technical advisors," which included several engineers, teachers, and clergymen as well as a secretary, two interpreters, one business manager, and two stenographers, was formed to assist in the commission's investigations.[47]

The commission did not start on time, however, due to a long delay caused by hesitation on the part of the French and the British that lasted almost all of April and May of 1919. It seemed that settlements had already been decided—at least in principle—during the discussions that had begun in Paris between the Allies. The main concern had been to respect the spirit of the Sykes-Picot Agreement and organize the mandated territories in accordance with preexisting spheres of influence. Furthermore, the two commissioners' presumed anti-Zionist stance and the potential impact of a report based strictly on demographic data worried the World Zionist Organization (WZO) led by Chaim Weizmann. The WZO insisted that the Balfour Declaration had already determined the (Jewish) future of Palestine and that it was unnecessary to carry out such an investigation, especially considering that the

French were also opposed to an inquiry into Syria's perspective. "To go or not to go"[48] neatly summarized the commission's existential status at that time.

During these deliberations concerning the fate of the King-Crane Commission, missionaries in Turkey involved in the Near East Relief were trying to use their own diplomatic resources to influence Wilson, the American Commission to Negotiate Peace (ACNP) and the Allied leaders. Opinions differed vastly on various topics like the validity of the commission, the issue of Armenia in a Turkish context, or the Balfour Declaration and its impact on the situation in Palestine. Despite being profoundly sympathetic toward the idea of an independent Great Armenia, James Barton was reminded of his position by his colleagues who demanded that the Foreign Mission Board (ABCFM) remain neutral in the countries where it had deployed its staff. The historian Joseph L. Grabill explains that neutrality (in regard to the state and to foreign relations) had historically been the norm for missionaries. However, the expansion of the social gospel movement at the turn of the twentieth century along with the rise of an outward-looking American patriotism merging with Protestant missionary ethics had created "almost a national revival campaign" which in turn bolstered the Armenophile movement.[49] Yet missionary institutions in Turkey knew that their interests and longevity would best be protected by maintaining the status quo and consequently feared the idea that a non-Protestant power like France, Italy, or Greece might be awarded a mandate over the Ottoman Empire's territory. As an ironic consequence, the project of an independent Armenia was opposed precisely by the American Armenophile movement and primarily by Barton himself. What is more, Barton, like Caleb F. Gates, posited that the demographic composition of the Anatolian region meant that if it achieved independence, the Christian Armenia would be completely boxed in by its "natural" Muslim rivals. Barton and Gates also worried about the fate of the Turkish majority living in an independent Armenia as delineated by the Armenian delegation in Versailles and by the American Committee for an Independent Armenia (ACIA), just as they worried about the fate of Armenian minorities living in the rest of Turkey.[50] However, while Gates believed that the delays preventing the launch of the commission constituted proof of its futility in view of the decisions already made in Paris, Barton remained staunchly in favor of a field survey in Turkey, Syria, and Palestine.

These deliberations and delays, for their part, had occurred while—and partially because—the Peace Conference was temporarily "on the fritz." Indeed, after opening the first sessions at the start of 1919, Wilson returned to the United States and stayed there for a full month, from mid-February to mid-March. This brought the negotiations to an almost complete standstill and instead made way for a slew of doubts about the merit of the commission.[51]

Crane, in the meanwhile, made good use of the time freed by these delays to promote Wilsonian diplomacy and the principles of the Fourteen Points in Paris's socialist and radical bourgeois salons while keeping abreast of the deliberations between the various plenipotentiary national commissions. He considered himself an "interpreter" of Wilsonianism in high society, citing as an example an instance when he, along with two of his compatriots, the muckrakers Ida Tarbell and William Allen White, were received by Madame Ménard d'Orient,[52] whom he called the "queen of all the socialites." There, Crane strove to convince his French friends of Wilson's "genuine interest in the everyday people." He also occasionally met with Wilson and his wife, and had succeeded in placing his own private secretary, Walter S. Rogers, inside the ACNP in the wire communications department (headed by George Creel's Committee on Public Information) where, according to Crane, he made a powerful impression.[53] Rogers proved to be a significant source of regular internal information on the Versailles Conference for Crane. He was in direct and constant contact with House, who acted as the primary intermediary between Wilson and the Allied leaders (Clemenceau even said that he preferred dealing with House rather than Wilson[54]). With information provided by this invaluable source, Crane became aware that establishing a peace modeled after Wilson's principle of self-determination was becoming increasingly difficult due in large part to the proliferation of secret colonial agreements between the Allied countries. Crane grew pessimistic about the outcome of the negotiations and, in a telegram to the *New York Times* sent while he awaited his departure for Constantinople, lamented that the "Problems to be solved are extremely complex [and […]] vastly increased by all kinds [of] secret treaties made during war." To him, these "secret treaties [were a] serious menace" and threatened to compromise not only the peace but also the safety of the peoples struggling for autonomy. He remarked that "These people look to America as their only friend and any failure […] will reflect on us," judging that the heavy duty of standing up to the colonial ambitions of the European powers fell on the United States. In order to not let these "helpless people" down, he assessed that the "Doctrine [of] self-determination [of] peoples must be given life and carried out in an intelligent way by men who know something of peoples with whom they have to deal." The Wilsonian project, and particularly the Fourteen Points, seemed to Crane a crucial substitute for the ignominious secret treaties, even if it had to be "relentlessly" imposed on the Allies by the American delegation.[55] By "secret treaties," Crane was naturally referring to the 1916 Sykes-Picot Agreement which, as previously demonstrated, split the eastern part of the Ottoman Empire into French and British zones of influence and which constituted the greatest impediment to the commission on mandates in Turkey. After waiting for more than two months in Paris, Crane was bursting with desire to leave and in a gloomier mood than ever, especially in regard to delegates from other countries. With an abundance of time at his disposal to write detailed missives, he shared in another letter to Cornelia that "I am having quite a time with our own Commission and others about Balkan affairs and am unhappy about them. On the whole I am glad Richard is not here." Richard, to Crane's relief, was busy with the State Department and had not accompanied Lansing to Paris.[56] His dissatisfaction with his own commission was most probably caused by his two technical advisors, William Yale and George R. Montgomery, who reported to the ACNP delegate Westermann and who, like their superior, still opposed a commission in the Middle East. Westermann, what is more, believed that Paris already had sufficient data for the settlements. Crane, in turn, replied that in addition to gathering much-needed information, America's presence in the Middle East would serve to generate an unparalleled degree of enthusiasm and hope.[57] With even greater melancholy, he complained to Mildred Nelson Page, a New York missionary who worked in Japan, that "One feels the hopeless inadequacy of human in the face of such human upheaval. And one feels the great limitation of reaching conclusions by purely intellectual processes," then adding with uncanny foresight that "Under the surface there is the same kind of petty political intriguing going on that takes place at all peace conferences and which produce no peace at all but only bring an armistice with greater wars in prospect."[58] Crane was naturally referring to the other peace negotiations he had observed in the past, particularly those that had led to the disastrous Treaty of San Stefano in 1878 following the Russo-Turkish war, which had also been Crane's first experience with warfare as mentioned in the previous chapter. On this subject, he said: "I was greatly dismayed at the settlement […] in regard to the Balkans," and though he spoke here of one region, Crane applied the same concept ubiquitously:

> An essential condition for bringing about a peace [in the Balkans] is a sincere and full application of the doctrine of the self-determination of peoples […] If this doctrine does not apply to the little people of the Balkans, it certainly has no value elsewhere in the world.

Though this seems to indicate that the principle had to first be applied in the Balkans, the formula he posited suggests equivalence with the Middle East, in the sense that if peace could not be achieved in Europe, it would be hard to hope for its establishment elsewhere. With dismay, Crane was forced to admit that the governing powers had thus far disregarded self-determination as a general guideline in their proposed settlements, commenting that "I certainly see no evidence of the application of this principle."[59]

By mid-March, Crane had had enough and was planning on departing for Constantinople whether the commission was confirmed or not in order to visit the colleges where he acted as a trustee. House, however, begged him to remain in Paris with the president, who had just returned from his stay in the United States, until the commission's status could be determined by the Big Four. Crane's everyday work would be "seeing people who can be helpful and who want to understand the President and "stand by" in case they can aid."[60] Nevertheless, this conversation with House which took place during a long walk they went on together and which he described to his daughter Josephine, seemed to be of slight comfort to him.

Despite rumors of King's withdrawal from his post as commissioner, Wilson's return to the Peace Conference put some wind back in the commission's sails, with the added help of an appeal by General Allenby in its favor. In mid-April, Wilson extended a supper invitation to Crane and to the members of the ACNP. Vance C. McCormick (unrelated to Crane's friend Cyrus H. McCormick, Jr.), also present at the reception, wrote in his diary that Wilson spoke at length with his guests after the meal and that it was "a nice informal time."[61] Westermann, who also attended the event, made an interesting mention in his diary of some intelligence Crane shared about a French telegram intercepted by the Americans which spoke of deliberate Allied attempts to prevent the commission in Turkey in order to protect the traditional zones of influence and the Sykes-Picot Agreement.[62] Strangely enough, it would seem that discussions during this meeting on April 18 marked the end of the commission, or at least, that is what Wilson, House, and his guests seemed to have agreed on. Yet Crane related in his memoirs that Allenby's appeal had a great impact in favor of the commission's reestablishment, as did an appeal by Prince Faisal to Wilson.[63]

In spite of this, Crane wrote to his wife saying that he was overwhelmed by "things [moving] so rapidly and in so chaotic a fashion." He believed his own observations to be already outdated "fifteen minutes after [they were] written" given the speed at which changes succeeded one another, and "the world of yesterday," to him, seemed "to have no historical introduction to the world of today and certainly no relationship to the world of tomorrow." These pessimistic comments, rare for Crane at least where his writings were concerned, undoubtedly betrayed some of his anxiety in regard to the consequences of the peace settlements. Even the war had not led Crane to have so little optimism about the world's future, except perhaps when the Bolshevik forces came into power in Russia. Incidentally, bad news on that front undeniably intensified his worries. He explained, however, that "the central difficulty is that all of the men with whom and through whom the president has to work are not only inadequate from every point of view but they are all the authors of the secret treaties, are trying in every way to keep them secret and still make them work."

Worse still, these old school diplomats seemed to "have no understanding of the Fourteen Points or real sympathy with them" and were incapable of comprehending the Wilsonian principles.[64] In typically American terms and with a clearly spiritual outlook, Crane affirmed that a sort of "great awakening" would be necessary for the project to truly work.[65] Given the reprehensible attitude of the Allied delegates, Crane considered the president's position to be quite a difficult one:

> The Great Virginian here has had a very difficult task [...] He has been alone in his ideals and his aspirations and had to work through this human morass made up of Foreign Office men who have been building up this abominable structure through what is called "diplomacy".[66]

Crane admitted, however, that Wilson had unfortunately already made too many compromises—such as Chinese concessions to the Japanese—in order to get the other members of the Big Four to accept the League of Nations.

In any event, a decision had to be made in regard to the commission in Turkey. By May, it had been settled that it would indeed take place, but as an American rather than an inter-Allied venture. Yet Crane, disheartened by the long wait and by the powers' shameless scheming, had little hope that the politicians would make adequate use of the commission's findings and seemed already resigned to the failure of the Wilsonian project:

> We have an excellent commission nominated to go into the Levant to determine how the dark meat and the light meat of the Turkey is to be divided. The doctrine of the self-determination of peoples, like the doctrine of secret treaties, has not been conspicuous in resolving the fates of the little peoples. Indeed one hears little of the Fourteen Points which cheered the world and exalted the soldiers.[67]

This private comment made to his son John just a few weeks before his departure for Constantinople and cynically describing Europe's grotesque dispute over the carcass of the Middle East shows Crane's growing skepticism about the inquiry's pertinence. Crane was not yet so defeated, however, that he stopped trying to keep the president abreast of topics he deemed important. On one occasion, he sent Wilson an article about political and religious strife within Islam written by a specialist of the Muslim world, Christiaan Snouck Hurgronje (1857–1936). Hurgronje, originally from Holland, had converted to Islam and spent the larger part of his career in the Dutch East Indies and in the Ottoman Empire. Wilson, who had forgotten his name when he appeared before the members of the ACNP to share his point of view, even mistook him for a Muslim Indian.[68] Hurgronje's article, though written from a pro-Allied perspective, pleaded for the respect of the wishes and religious and ethnic diversity of the Arab populations in the concerned region. It was sent as a response to Crane's inquiry, the day before his departure for Constantinople, concerning rumors he had heard about the restoration of a Turkish caliphate in Constantinople. Given the impending dissolution of the Ottoman Empire, the article explained that a caliphate, which claimed the legitimacy of the unity of religious power, was not intrinsic to Islam and to the development of Muslim peoples. Hurgronje argued that a caliphate would only fuel Islamic fanaticism and compromise both world peace and the well-being of Muslims. He wrote that "the only *raison d'être* of a caliph being his leadership in a war of Islam against the rest of mankind with aims that are no more capable of being realized," a caliphate would only serve "to disturb the minds of the masses of Mohammedan nations to the prejudice of their own interests and of universal peace." "[T]he utopian idea of the caliphate," as he called it, was according to him considered "absurd by anybody acquainted with the incongruous mentalities of the Arabic populations." More generally, Hurgronje supported the principle of self-determination and also agreed with a system of mandates as endorsed by Wilson and Crane. He thus proposed that Muslim countries be placed under the control of Western governments "in their own interests," and then be given as much autonomy as possible until they achieved internal stability.[69] However, though Hurgronje's arguments were both pro-Allied and Wilsonian in regard to a Turkish caliphate and to the Arab people, his position implicitly rejected the idea of an autonomous Jewish homeland right in the middle of an Arab and Muslim Palestine. By recommending this type of reading material, *a priori* in agreement with Wilsonian principles but also discussing a topic less familiar to the president, Crane was possibly trying to prepare Wilson for the pro-Arab report that would be issued by the commission, which, though it had not yet set out, would be departing shortly.

Near the end of May, Crane and Wilson finally had a last meal together when the latter invited Crane to dine with King, the president's wife and his physician, Admiral Cary T. Grayson. King's departure was planned for May 29 but Crane, completely autonomous in his travels, wished to spend more time visiting "his" colleges in Constantinople and set out alone, probably in the days that followed his last supper in Paris. On May 26, therefore, Crane was on his way to Bucharest. From Milan, he wrote Cornelia a letter praising his partner King, whom he called a "fine associate" and with whom he declared being "quite in accord." He then mentioned comments made by Gates, who had previously been invited to Paris to expose his "federative" view of Turkish affairs before the Supreme Council. As explained previously, Gates was opposed to an independent Great Armenia because of the demographic and geographic issues that would follow from its creation and because of his doubt in the Armenians' ability to govern such a large area. It does not appear that Crane ever contested this view, and though Gates was reluctant to accept even the idea of a commission in Turkey, Crane seemed to support a federative vision of Anatolia which respected its ethnic components (Turks, Armenians, Kurds, Arabs, Greeks, etc.) since the start of the commission. He affirmed that Gates had painted a very interesting and very useful portrait of this idea given the Big Four's lack of knowledge about this topic:

> He […] made some wise suggestions regarding the future of Turkey, which I hope will prevent serious mistakes being made by the Virginian [Woodrow Wilson], the Welshman [David Lloyd George] and the Frenchman [Georges Clemenceau], no one of whom has much knowledge or sympathetic understanding of Moslems.[70]

On the one hand, this comment about his hope that Gates's idea would guide the Big Four in his absence betrayed some of the apprehension Crane felt about the commission not producing results quickly enough to inform the decisions made in Versailles. On the other hand, his acknowledgement that Wilson and the other plenipotentiary delegates were lacking information in their decisions presupposed the necessity of expert input and confirmed the relevance of a commission of inquiry.

On a personal level, Crane's departure from Paris and his journey through the Balkans, so reminiscent of his previous travels, seemed to put a new spring in his step. "I am thoroughly enjoying this little excursion," he wrote to his wife, with whom he had visited the region nine years earlier. Travelling also gave him some respite from his "task of trying to repair the damage done to the world by [...] the Foreign offices."[71] Additionally, his passage through Bulgaria allowed him to appear at various social gatherings and attend several Bulgarian ecclesiastical choir performances.[72] Once he had reached Constantinople and looked back at the months spent in Paris during the Peace Conference, however, he could not help but once again confide in his missionary friend Mildred N. Page that "I do not like to be pessimistic [...] but I cannot conceive of great good coming out of [the Peace Conference]." He also recollected morosely that the president had had to concede on a great number of issues in order to salvage the essence of his League of Nations project. The ending of his letter reveals an outlook that was both personal and also characteristic of the status and mentality of many American Progressives on the challenge posed by the Turkish question for the United States in Versailles. Despite his worries and the difficulties, he knew the United States would have to contend with, Crane hoped "that we may accomplish something" in regard to the Wilsonian project, but added that "it is a difficult matter to reconstitute the Turkish Empire in an American way."[73] First, this passage supports the theory that Crane now subscribed to the idea of a federated Turkey—no doubt convinced by Gates's arguments—and had thus abandoned the project of an independent Great Armenia. "Turkish empire," with no further elaboration, refers most probably to Anatolia—including Armenia—and consequently would exclude Mesopotamia and the Syro-Palestinian corridor, for which the commission would eventually offer specific recommendations. Finally, his mention of an "American way" of doing things, certainly a testament to his prevailing cultural bias, in all likelihood designates America's role in the new mandate system and alludes to the liberal and democratic structure Crane hoped to see implemented in the new states created by Versailles.

His recent conviction that an independent Great Armenia would survive inside a majoritarily Muslim and Turkish-speaking peninsula (almost a continent) was perhaps solidified by news he received about the situation in Turkey from a certain Halide Edib. Edib was a Turkish humanitarian worker and teacher with whom Crane corresponded regularly during the commission. Having studied, among other places, at the Constantinople College for Girls, she had maintained close ties with many members of America's missionary world, including James Barton and Howard Bliss, who had inspired the commission. Cultivated, modern, and fluent in various languages, Halide Edib was at once a feminist and a nationalist. In this regard, she had some common ground with the Young Turk regime, but her humanist spirit opposed the violence encouraged and sometimes even provoked by the Committee of Union and Progress. In her memoirs, published in two volumes over the span of several years, she recounted many conversations with Djemal and Enver Pasha about the ill treatment of Armenians, but also mentioned the increasing collaboration between American missionary institutions and the Turkish government, particularly in the humanitarian domain. She also knew Cleveland H. Dodge and his family, who were actively involved with the Armenian relief effort and more largely with the Turkish world of education, and she wrote in praise that "the self-sacrificing life [of the Dodge family is] a thing to be proud of."[74]

In preparation for his upcoming arrival in Palestine for the eastern portion of the commission, Crane thus gathered information for his audiences with the local populations by commissioning various studies on the historical, socioeconomic and political foundations of the regions involved. As shown by this useful correspondence he had with Halide Edib, Crane's unique and characteristic way of proceeding stemmed both from his understanding that the issues at hand were complex and required adequate documentation and from the fact that he had at his disposal the considerable human resources which he had amassed over the course of his travels. Here as well, his talents as an intermediary played a large part in his behavior and his methodology.

The King-Crane Commission in Syria-Palestine: Crane, Zionism, a Great Syria, and Self-Determination for the Arabs

Though the commission's itinerary had been planned in a purely logistical way, the fact that its first audiences took place in the Holy Land serves as a reminder of the prominence of the Jewish question in the settlement of the Ottoman issue. There is no need to go into detail about each step of these audiences or analyze each aspect of the preliminary report issued by the chief commissioners: descriptions of these proceedings can be found in Harry Howard's *The King-Crane Commission* (1963). Our aim will instead be to pinpoint Crane's specific perspective as well as his personal contribution to the direction taken by the commission, namely, in light of his correspondence (omitted by Howard), of the commission's documents and of his previously analyzed antecedents.

After having briefly reunited with his fellow commissioners in Constantinople and reached out to a few of his collaborators like Mary Mills Patrick (of the Constantinople College for Girls) and Halide Edib (this, apparently, was the first time they met in person), Crane set out for Jerusalem. Still separate from and ahead of his colleagues, he arranged to meet one of his Muslim friends from Cairo, Gafir Waly Pasha, who, Crane was proud to report, confided in him as though he were a Muslim himself. Waly warned him in advance that no Arab in Syria or Palestine was in favor of a French mandate, which Crane was able to personally confirm after attending several audiences. His first impression upon arriving in the Holy Land was that the Arab peoples seemed to hold Americans in high esteem, this, he explained, due to the missionary work carried out by American educational institutions, among them the American University of Beirut. Crane proudly reported that the Syrians at the college—in fact, even the desert Bedouins—had declared their hope that the United States would do in Syria what they had previously done in the Philippines.[75] Surprising and dubious though such a flattering claim may seem, it would appear that the Arab peoples were indeed extremely impressed with the promises of Wilsonianism, at least during the first months of the Paris Peace Conference.[76]

Furthermore, Crane affirmed that "There was a marvelous movement all through Palestine and Syria," with as its aim the destruction of the colonial system. From a chronological standpoint, however, it seems that Crane's recollections may have been somewhat inaccurate. He remembered the commission's first audiences as having taken place on June 6 in Beersheba (to the southwest of Jerusalem), whereas Howard described them as having taken place on June 11 in Jaffa (to the northwest of Jerusalem, on the Mediterranean).[77] In any case, Crane reported being pleased at the number of people and delegations that were in attendance and impressed with their orderly behavior. At the end of the Syro-Palestinian part of the commission, Crane concluded that the Arab peoples as well as the Christian and Jewish minorities in the area preferred a British or an American mandate to a French one.

Yet besides the question of mandates, the audiences also examined the crucial issue of a Jewish State in Palestine, which was supported by the Allies in accordance with Great Britain's Balfour Declaration of 1917 and which later also became endorsed by the United States.[78] Crane himself, a few days before the first audiences, said that the Syro-Palestinian problem was a Muslim (here used almost synonymously with "Arab") issue, given that, as corroborated by the commission, eighty percent of the population adhered to Islam. This was another way of saying that the Jewish question in Palestine ought not to be pursued, at least in view of the principle of nationalities. In fact, most of the Arab, Christian, and Muslim delegations, as well as pre-Zionist Jewish groups, openly opposed the Balfour Declaration.[79]

Crane's own attitude toward Zionism and toward Jewish-Muslim relations in Palestine remains rather difficult to interpret, particularly given the many weak claims made on this subject. One thing is certain, however: since his voyages in the Middle East in 1909 and 1910, Crane had developed a marked appreciation for the Arab peoples and for Islamic culture in general. In the context of the trips that followed his revoked nomination to the diplomatic post in China in 1909, Crane had taken the time to become better informed, through contacts provided by his friend James Bryce, about the various Arab and Muslim nationalist movements in Egypt.[80] Crane also seemed to admire Muslim wisdom and enjoyed repeating various anecdotes and jokes to illustrate the vivacity of the Arab spirit, often at Wilson's request.[81] And as he had done for Slavic culture, though to a lesser extent, Crane had already invested, before Versailles and the King-Crane Commission, in the promotion of Oriental and Islamic culture. In 1911, for instance, he contributed 5,000 francs to the *Encyclopedia of Islam*, a collective work most likely directed by C. Snouck Hurgronje and published in 1913.[82]

On the other hand, his experience in America, where the positions and activities of some American Jews went against his own goals, elicited from him a discourse which was often anti-Semitic in tone and appearance. As seen in the third chapter, the treatment of Jews in Russia and the Jewish reaction to this treatment in the United States inconvenienced those who, like Crane and his collaborators (Samuel Harper, for instance), endeavored to forge better commercial and cultural relations with Russia. His written exchanges with the president of Harvard University Charles W. Eliot and with James Bryce showed a very critical stance on the "Jewish lobby," particularly that of the pro-Japanese and pro-German New York banker Jacob H. Schiff, who Crane said had "for [a] long time controlled the bridge between Russia and America."[83] More generally, Crane mentioned this lobby when referring to the New York Jews (also called East Siders or Manhattan Jews), to Jews of German descent (nicknamed Hamburg Jews) and to the republican Jews. The Jewish lobby remained a constant theme in his correspondence after the Russo-Japanese War of 1905.

Despite this bias, it cannot be denied that Crane had many Jewish friends and collaborators over the years, as this book demonstrates. Brandeis, who also happened to be extensively involved in the Zionist movement, featured among them, as did Stephen S. Wise, the rabbi of the New York Free Synagogue where Crane himself was occasionally invited, sometimes along with Wilson. Morgenthau, ambassador in Constantinople during the creation of the ACASR and organizer of Wilson's electoral campaigns, was also a Jew who collaborated with Crane and remained one of his long-time friends. Richard Gottheil, a professor at Columbia and a Zionist leader, was upon his wife Emma Gottheil's request warmly recommended by Crane to Wilson for a diplomatic post.[84] Crane in fact called him "a man of the highest possible character" and pointed out that he benefited from the support of the "best American Jews." Richard Gottheil himself criticized some Zionist Jews and complained to Crane about this "small clique of snobs"[85] trying to gain the president's favor for the advancement of their movement (ironically, it was their friend Brandeis who later approached the president to discuss Zionism). Gottheil and Crane even considered thoroughly unpatriotic the lobby efforts of some Zionist Americans, particularly Jacob Schiff and New York's Republican Jews. In this regard, Crane believed Brandeis had the merit of being an American first and a Jew second.[86] Crane had seemingly also advised him, at Gottheil's behest, to not cease his involvement in Zionist affairs after his appointment to the Supreme Court even despite the criticism this would incur.[87] In fact, many signs point to the idea that Crane was favorable to a "settlement" of the Jewish issue through the creation of a Jewish State in Palestine, at least before the commission in the Ottoman Empire. As of 1914, it would seem that Crane and Wilson began discussing the fate of the European Jews after the war and though the details of these conversations remain unknown, it would appear that Brandeis, newly elected at the head of the Zionist Organization of America, was also present.[88] Not only had Crane noticed that, for the most part, the Jewish populations of Palestine and Turkey assimilated easily and coexisted peacefully with the Muslim populations, but he also remarked that they seemed to be treated more cordially by Turkish authorities than by the European powers.[89]

Crane was, nevertheless, used to making the distinction between "good" Jews and "bad" Jews, the latter category necessarily including those who opposed his activities. This binary perspective, coupled with an almost mechanical impulse to notice a person's Jewishness before any other characteristic, perhaps revealed Crane's subconscious view of Jews as forever outsiders in the American Protestant and Anglo-Saxon society. His comments were never hateful despite their occasional harshness, but they showed a propensity to quickly disqualify any "undeserving" Jew, though he was also quick to admire Jews who like Brandeis demonstrated patriotism, competency, and progressive values. Thus, even in his compliments, he could not help himself from distinguishing between the Anglo-Protestant and the Jewish American, saying, for instance, about Lillian Wald, a renowned Progressive involved with the settlement houses in New York, that "I often think of her [Lillian Wald] as the finest flower of the Jewish race as I think of Miss [Jane] Addams as the finest flower of the Puritan stock."[90] Upon his arrival at the Paris Peace Conference, therefore, Crane paradoxically displayed both a degree of sympathy toward Zionism as a potential solution to the Jewish situation in Europe (nothing, in fact, indicated that he opposed the Balfour Declaration) and a racial Anglo-Saxon bias (which he shared with many of his peers) even in his appreciation of his Jewish friends and collaborators.

Oddly enough, in a preliminary report written before their departure for Constantinople, King and Crane proposed a mandate in Anatolia, Greek possessions in Asia Minor, a part of Constantinople under American mandate, and a Great Armenia stretching "from sea to sea" (also under American mandate), but made no mention of the Jewish issue in Palestine or of the Balfour Declaration. Their final report, on the other hand, clearly established that the commissioners had set forth "with minds predisposed in [Zionism's] favor,"[91] and that this issue played a central part in the audiences as well as in their final assessment. To be sure, the topic was inevitably an intrinsic part of any settlement concerning the Arabic Middle East and the commissioners, Crane included, were aware of its importance. What they did not yet suspect, however, was the amount of resistance to Zionism they would encounter throughout their stay in Syria-Palestine.

During his stay in the Balkans before reaching Constantinople, Crane visited a Jewish school where everyone knew Brandeis and hoped that the Versailles Treaty would bring about the creation of a Jewish republic with Brandeis at its head.[92] Crane's comments carried no negative connotation and were neither reproachful nor displeased when he described this visit to his wife. He even befriended a five-year-old girl, "a most charming little miss," whom he invited to study at "his" college in Constantinople when she was older. After his arrival in Palestine, Crane took pleasure in visiting various other schools and Jewish colonies, including one on Mount Carmel, which he praised for its prosperity, its good management, and the quality of the wine it produced (which, incidentally, seems to have been the one he usually consumed).[93]

When he presided over an audience before a crowd of delegations and groups of interest, Crane generally began by listing the president's instructions in Arabic. He then modeled his questions on those asked by Mott during the 1917 audiences in Russia, namely, to determine, first what the attendees would most readily agree to, and secondly, to discover what they most strongly feared. In regard to these questions, the answers almost unanimously pointed, according to Crane, to the population's overall acceptance of a political union between Syria and Palestine and to its fear of "any extensive Jewish immigration." The key word here was "extensive," and attendees generally clarified that "their relations with the old Jews who had lived here for years and for spiritual reasons were always satisfactory and friendly." Crane therefore began drawing a distinction between the old Jewish tradition of a return to the Promised Land and the modern and politicized wave of Zionism which had become more radicalized after the Great War and the Balfour Declaration, explaining that "there is a clear feeling of menace about the modern, pushing Jew." Anti-Zionist responses greeted the commission wherever it went, and some delegations even travelled great distances to share their views. The Bedouin caravans in particular greatly impressed Crane and he was once, to his immense amusement, serenaded by a group of impassioned Arab separatists with "fine arab songs."[94] Crane's participation in the Commission on Mandates in Turkey was thus marked with a growing opposition to the Balfour Declaration. It stemmed, in part, from an increasing awareness of internal relations in Palestine as presented to him during the audiences, yet it was also fuelled by a rather romanticized view of the Holy Land. Indeed, Crane had always appreciated and admired the exoticism—in other words, the Orientalism—of the Arab populations and of the Bedouin tribes (whose immutability over the course of a millennium filled him with awe) just as he had always admired the old Christian monasteries and the pre-Zionist Russian Jewish colonies. The modern Zionist movement, on the other hand, had brought with it changes that affected the very landscapes of the places Crane adored, and he wrote regretfully to Cornelia that:

> The Mediterranean was beautiful in its expanse and color and with all the traditional clinging about the mountain and the history of the colonies at its foot which have so much impressed the world [...] But the Palestine of trains and automobiles and Jews distresses me. I prefer the horses, tents and Russian pilgrims. The old color and glory have gone.[95]

Postbellum Zionism, in this sense, seemed to ruin the beauty and meaning of the holy places in Crane's eyes. The country's modernization, partially set into motion by the Zionist newcomers, also tarnished his nostalgic view of this perfect little piece of the Eastern world. Naturally, this paradoxical perspective was in direct contradiction with the designs he had always had for the Muslim world and which revolved around Christian education. He even recognized, not without a touch of regret, that the inexorable western influence of American, British, and French schools had already initiated a cultural transformation of the Islamic peoples.[96] He thus began viewing extensive Jewish presence in Palestine as inappropriate and unfavorable to the area's ideal development.

Despite what some believed,[97] Crane's change of heart in regard to the Zionist issue did not stem from some pathological dislike for Jews in general. It was fuelled, rather, by a concern for the region's largely Arab and Muslim demographic makeup and by an idealized, Orientalist, and backward-looking view of pre-Zionist Palestine. The demographic argument, for its part, directly connected with the Wilsonian principle of self-determination and came within the scope of the commission, whose purpose was to determine the will of the communities involved. American Zionist leaders like Felix Frankfurter naturally raised objections to this but Wilson remained unmoved.[98] Brandeis, who was also in the Middle East and closely followed the progress of the commission in Palestine, took the initiative to interrogate some of the delegations. Crane encouraged those attending to share their true opinions with Brandeis, whom Crane considered to be "entitled to the fullest confidence" and who, he believed, "would want nothing but the truth."[99] In fact, Crane, who saw Brandeis as a reasonable man open to rational arguments, hoped that his friend could be swayed by the views of the Arab Palestinian perspective and would come to temper his strong Zionist position. It does not appear, however, that Brandeis's stay in Palestine or his encounters with the delegations had any effect on his Zionist involvement.[100]

Shortly afterward, the commission continued on its itinerary to Syria, where the fate of the Syro-Palestinian region was to be decided. There, Crane spent some time with Prince Faisal and even stayed with him in Damascus after the commission had returned to Constantinople. At the very beginning of the Paris Peace Conference, the Arab world, at least the part of it represented by Faisal, as well as the World Zionist Organization, agreed on a possible coexistence of Arab and Zionist political wills in Palestine in accordance with the January, 1919 Faisal-Weizmann Agreement.[101] After the start of the audiences in Syria, however, Faisal declared the Zionist project's inadmissibility in view of Arab aspirations for Syria-Palestine. Always enthusiastic about meeting interesting "characteristic" people, Crane asked Faisal to put him in touch with "an outstanding Moslem […] whose judgment and opinion [he trusted]." The prince thus introduced him to an Arab sheik from Damascus who confirmed, at Crane's request, the facts already demonstrated during previous audiences, namely, that all Arab and many Christian and Jewish communities in Syria-Palestine abhorred the idea of a French mandate and that the Zionist project would be detrimental to the Arab and Muslim character of the region. Crane explained that "They want a united Syria and Palestine as their country, with the Arabic language as the official one, no zionism and no French mandate, and the country to become a colony of no country."[102] In short, his final assessment of the situation in Syria-Palestine completely contradicted not only the colonial spirit of the Sykes-Picot Agreement but also the Paris Peace Conference's plan to offer France the mandate over Syria.

Knowing this, Crane sent Wilson an encrypted telegram with the first draft of his report covering this initial stage of the commission. To it, he attached a personal message which provided one of the rare descriptions of his criteria for self-determination. Underscoring the commission's usefulness, Crane affirmed that "The every-day people are sober, industrious and intelligent" and summarized the three national aspects that defined the Arab people of Syria-Palestine: "1) the rich and beautiful Arabic language; 2) both Christian and Moslem faiths; 3) the ancient and interesting culture."[103] By establishing a national unity based on language, religion, and history, Crane included the region's ancient Christians (Latin and Maronite) while also tacitly excluding the recent and future Jewish settlers. In the report itself, Crane reiterated these comments on Syro-Palestinian unity and reaffirmed its essential Arab and Muslim character as well as its hostility toward a French presence. He emphasized the population's gratitude to President Wilson and to the United States, explaining why, should a mandate be issued for the region, America would be the people's first choice. He also boasted of the population's "considerable political insight" and "unexpectedly strong expressions of national feeling," citing in example the Bedouin caravans mentioned previously which had journeyed for thirty hours to take part in the audiences. Then, with extraordinary foresight, Crane predicted that a "[French Mandate] would precipitate warfare between Arabs and French and force Great Britain to [a] dangerous alternative." For once, Crane's prediction was correct, as a conflict broke out only a few months after the creation of the Kingdom of

Syria (including Palestine) in 1920. Crane ended his telegram with a vigorous defense of Faisal, whom he viewed as the future leader of a Great Syria:

> Emir Faisal, despite limitations of education, has become unique outstanding figure, capable of rendering greatest service for world peace. He is the heart of the Moslem world, with enormous prestige and popularity, confirmed believer in Anglo-Saxon race, really great lover of Christianity.

Given Faisal's qualities and his authority, Crane believed that he would be able "to reconcile Christianity and Islam" and that he deserved the support of the United States and of its allies. As proof, Crane mentioned that Faisal had in his presence even expressed the wish that an "American College for Women" be set up in Mecca. Recounting this event in a letter to Mildred N. Page, Crane concluded: "So the world is moving."[104] These words very neatly summarize the missionary dimension of Wilsonian diplomacy and the historic opportunity presented by the war and the ensuing peace efforts for the emancipation of peoples and for the extension of America's spiritual and cultural influence. For Crane and Wilson, this missionary dimension fit into and even underpinned their geopolitical goals. Interestingly, Faisal also had faith in Wilson, and on the same day that Crane sent his telegram to the president, Faisal wrote to him directly begging him to free his people from the "paws of the devourers" in accordance with the principles he had expressed as well as those endorsed by the "honorable commission" codirected by Crane.[105] By "devourers," Faisal naturally referred to the French (in their quest for a mandate to formalize their sphere of influence) and to the Zionists.

Crane's impressions after his return from Syria concerned, on the one hand, his personal discoveries in terms of the "rare human experiences" he had had and, on the other hand, his sense of personal responsibility toward the people he had met and whom it would "be tragic to disappoint [...] in any material degree." Crane seemed to implicitly recognize that the commission's journey through Syria-Palestine had changed his position in regard to Zionism, which he does not seem to have opposed previously. He admitted that "We are not sending in a very enthusiastic report of the possibilities of the Zionist program being easily carried out. The feeling all through Palestine and Syria against it was very strong." This assessment is particularly striking given that the commission, as we have seen, had set out with an open mind toward Zionism.

Thus, Crane's attitude toward Zionism and even toward Jews in general soured as of late 1919. He began to complain about their undue influence in politics and even within largely Christian philanthropic organizations. Referring to Zionist interference in the Rockefeller Foundation, Crane promised Charles W. Eliot to speak to John D. Rockefeller, Jr. personally. Writing that the Jews were a "race which I profoundly distrust," Crane declared himself against their involvement with Christian philanthropy, stating that "There are certainly enough fine Christian men around."[106] Even though he still praised some exceptional Jews associated with the Wilson Administration like Bernard Baruch and Henry Morgenthau, he had begun viewing the "chosen people" as a constant lobby in search of political openings to promote the Zionist cause.[107] In his writings, Crane generally stopped distinguishing between "Jewish" and "Zionist," which were becoming interchangeable and even synonymous.

The preliminary report he sent to Wilson, for its part, made Crane a hero to the Arabs in Syria-Palestine. A few days after leaving Syria, he received a letter praising his work as commissioner from a certain Abdel-Koder Masaphen, president of the Arabic Association and a delegate of Palestine in Versailles. Masaphen wrote:

> The Arab inhabitants of Syria and Palestine will never forget your kind deeds, for presenting their rights to the American nation, and changing to good the general idea of West concerning our cause. They esteem highly the report of your mission [...] You are a perfection of human generosity [...] the pioneer of justice, so that humanity will get rid of the policy of unjust colonization.[108]

The King-Crane Commission in Constantinople: At the Heart of the Turkish Problem

The commission's second portion centered on the Anatolian part of the Ottoman Empire and also concerned the decisive region of Constantinople and of the Dardanelles. Due to lack of time and financial constraints, the commissioners stationed themselves in Constantinople to collect the necessary documentation and to receive the delegations. They were thus deprived of a stay in Armenia and in the Anatolian plateau and contented themselves with visits of Adana, Tarsus, and Mersin in southern Asia Minor, previously reached via Syria. To Crane, this part of the commission seemed more concrete than the one in Syria-Palestine, at least in regard to Allied interests, since it encompassed a particularly difficult international dimension: the Dardanelles and the Bosporus (Constantinople) in their capacity as crucial commercial seaways. As Crane explained to Mildred N. Page, these central straits "ought not to be controlled by any one power" and instead must be kept open to international commerce in accordance with the Fourteen Points.[109] Such was the premise at the basis of the commission. Yet rather paradoxically, this did not constitute the main issue during the second portion of the commission. Instead, the most complex aspects of the Anatolian question concerned the Greek and Armenian situation within a Turko-Muslim environment as well as the issue of the Turkish majority's political status.

On the subject of Greek minorities in Asia Minor, Crane sent Wilson a private and very specific message severely criticizing Greece's goals and diplomacy during the Paris Peace Conference. He wished to warn Wilson that Prime Minister Eleftherios Venizelos would compromise peace in the Balkans and in Asia Minor if his ambitions were not promptly checked. In Crane's eyes, the Big Four's suggestion of a Greek mandate over Asia Minor was an error of judgment given the civil unrest in Greece. Crane even commented that "As an example of a self-governing race, the Greeks have been far from a success." In regard to the criteria for self-determination, however, the Greek issue in Asia Minor and Thrace was primarily demographic according to Crane. After alerting Wilson to his suspicion that the demographic data produced by the Greek delegation were erroneous, Crane argued that the geographic dispersion of Greek populations in (western) Thrace and in Ionia (the region of Smyrna) made it difficult to attach them to Greece. He rejected the "historical" arguments for a cumulation of ancient boundaries posited in Venizelos's "Great Idea." Crane believed that by approving the Greek expedition to Smyrna and the occupation of Bulgarian Thrace, "The Peace Commission precipitated one embryo war" and that "The League of Nations ought not to be charged with the carrying out of an arrangement so unnatural and unjust."[110]

It is hard to tell whether this message from Crane to Wilson had any impact on the president's opinion, diminished as he was by disease, but the King-Crane Commission's final report reflected the opinions Crane had already expressed to Wilson. It recommended "[that] no independent territory be set off for the Greeks; though local autonomy be granted to that portion of the sanjak of Smyrna which has a decided majority of Greeks, but the general mandate for Turkey." This solution, which owed its complexity to the geographic dispersion of Greek populations in Turkey and to their isolation from Greece, aimed to reconcile the right to autonomy of the Ottoman Greeks with Turkey's right to an Anatolian state. Each antagonistic group demanded that it benefit from the same right to self-determination based on the principle of nationality, but the geographic and linguistic reality of the region forced this type of compromise.

Armenia's demands, for their part, undeniably garnered Crane's sympathy. In theory, the idea of an independent Armenia met all the criteria set by supporters of self-determination like Wilson and Crane: linguistic, historical, and religious specificity, a strong national conscience, and a (presumed) predisposition for self-government. Furthermore, the Armenians stood as an indomitable Christian people under siege and constantly resisting Muslim assimilation and oppression, which earned it America's support and admiration, especially in the context of the aid given to the victims in 1915 and 1916. Having played a central role in the coordination and dissemination of the Armenophile movement, Crane unsurprisingly supported the Armenian delegation's nationalist objectives in Versailles from the start. Yet the commission's report, with recommendations particularly skewed toward the Armenians and strict in regard to the Turks, did not fully reflect Crane's more nuanced position.

As with the Zionists in Palestine and the Greeks in Asia Minor and Thrace, Crane expressed doubt about the argument of cumulated "historical" borders. The "historical Armenia" described in the final report did not correspond perfectly with the Armenian delegation's cumulative version which stretched "from the Black Sea to the Mediterranean." It was in fact much smaller and took into account the extent to which Armenian populations were scattered across eastern Anatolia.[111] The fact remains, however, that the report was written very much in support of Armenia and considered the Turks incapable of governing such a multiethnic state. Though Crane had implicitly ratified this pro-Armenian compromise, several elements hint to the fact that he may have condemned Turkey less by 1919 than he had several years prior during the Armenian crisis. For one, it would appear that some of the commissioners (among them Captain Donald M. Brodie, one of Crane's closest partners in the commission whom he maintained an important correspondence with later on) as well as many missionaries like Caleb Gates and James L. Barton (namely, for the institutional and political reasons mentioned previously) progressively took on a harsher view of their Armenian protégés. A draft fragment in Henry C. King's archives contains an anonymous crossed-out note mentioning this shift in the Armenophile philanthropic movement and even questioning the assumption that the Turks were exclusively responsible for the conflict with the Armenians.[112] The note's author remains unknown, but the statements made about Armenia rather reflect Halide Edib's arguments to Crane.

Crane had asked Edib to produce a biographical analysis of the major figures in the Young Turk Party then in power, a sort of political "who's who" which he only received on August 20, 1919, just a bit over a week before the completion of the commission's final report. In a letter to Cornelia, Crane described Edib as "that wonderful Turkish woman [...] and the heart of Turkey."[113] As she had been the first to graduate from the Constantinople College for Girls (which Crane called "our college"), Crane invited her, no doubt through his friend Mary Mills Patrick, a teacher and missionary at that same college, to act as an interpreter during the Anatolian portion of the commission. Edib was part of a small group of young and increasingly influential militants opposed to the Enver, Talaat, and Djemal triumvirate and who would eventually spearhead the Kemalist movement. In his memoirs, Crane said of them that "Perhaps the most significant delegation we saw was a little group which afterward became the nucleus of the Angora government."[114] Halide Edib's analysis, for its part, implicitly admitted the reality of the Armenian extermination, which she ascribed to Nazim Bey and in a lesser capacity to Enver Pasha. It also documented the rise in power and popularity of Mustapha Kemal as Enver Pasha's political rival and as an educated, moderate, and patriotic politician. The introduction of her analysis is of particular interest, however, as it shows her faith in the commissioners' favorable disposition toward the Turks. She affirmed that "Human suffering is the same and never changes with race or creed. I am humanly proud to see that your commission has taken the same attitude of mind. *Nothing but truth and humanity*," and added that "the outcome of American culture and ideals" led to this attitude. Thus, Edib rejoiced at the fact that the commission had not entered the audiences with the intention of berating the Turkish people but rather with a mind bent on finding viable solutions for all of Anatolia, Thrace, and the straits. Her faith in an American approach to the settlements was certainly a result of her education in an American missionary establishment. She concluded by writing that "Christians, Moslems and others all are doomed to suffering unless the present conditions are removed and we see only America in a position to remove the conditions of misery and carnage and begin construction for the future."[115]

In her memoirs, Edib also mentioned her collaboration with Crane during his participation in the commission. Her account thereof, which goes unmentioned in the historiography that concerned Crane or the King-Crane

Commission, concerned the commission's arrival in Constantinople and described her work as an interpreter for Turkish regional leaders during the audiences led by King and Crane. Her recollections of these first audiences, which featured a Turkish delegation from Thrace come to oppose Greek control of a predominantly Turkish-speaking region, show both Crane's singular sympathy within a commission largely indifferent to the Turkish cause and the despair of a defeated group of people come to plead for its future before a hostile "judge":

> It was not pleasant. I felt as if everything had come to an end as I walked up the stairs of the American embassy [...] There they sat. Any man sitting at a big table with a green cover is imposing, and there were five of them, all looking ominous. It made one feel bewildered and hurt to be obliged to defend national rights before an embassy [...] The interview was extremely painful to me. I was very much aware of the somewhat unsympathetic attitude of the commission at my left, sitting at an enormous table [...] If it had not been for the Moslem-like understanding and benevolence of that old man's face in the middle, I could not have borne it. The Moslem-like understanding face belonged to Mr. Crane.[116]

It appears, if one is to trust Halide Edib's account, that Crane played a significant part in ensuring that the report did not rule as harshly as expected against the Turks. Shortly after the report's publication and its suggestion of an American mandate in Turkey, Edib wrote to Crane to express her satisfaction with its content but also to share her apprehension about its potential political outcome:

> The American Commission and the possibility of America's coming out here to bring peace and a constructive period unchained all the political passions. Mr. Lloyd George's declaration for Turkey was the danger signal [...] I do not dare to imagine things out here if America, the unique power in which we believe, retires and leaves the field to ambition and imperialism.[117]

Though he had already accepted the inevitable destruction of the Ottoman imperial system, Crane showed some sensitivity toward the realities of the defeated peoples and some awareness of the human hardships caused by geopolitical reorganization. In a private comment to Cornelia, he wrote that "It is a great tragedy, this breaking up of an ancient empire and it is very hard for simple humans to make any plans for regrouping the old fragments," adding, however, that "with Russia smashed, Austria smashed, Germany smashed, Turkey's position is not a unique one." Though this affirmation was tinged with nostalgia for the old disappearing world, it also showed a cold resignation to the inescapable task in which he was—albeit modestly—involved.

To Crane, the destruction of empires only made sense if the imperial system was replaced by the Fourteen Points. In the Arab and Muslim world, these Wilsonian principles could potentially help mend the bridges between civilizations. This way of thinking was reflected in a discussion Crane had with a religious leader of the Senussi sect some ten days before the submission of the report. The encounter, described in detail to Cornelia, had been made possible by Halide Edib, whom he this time called "the most influential person in the Empire."[118] When Crane told him that he was President Wilson's close friend, Sheik Ahmed al-Senussi informed him that he had already had all of Wilson's speeches translated into Arabic. According to Crane, the sheik even knew the Fourteen Points by heart, and Crane explained that "He also quite accepted my own doctrine that an entire understanding and accommodation of interests is possible between the Moslem and the Christian worlds through the full acceptance of the [Fourteen] Points."[119] The sheik even presented Crane with his belt and harness as well as his ancestral pistols as a gift.

Crane's particular interest in the Senussi sect dated back to his voyage across the Middle East in 1910, when a meeting with their supreme leader made a strong impression on him. Interestingly enough, in a speech given many years later about Crane's role in the commission, Captain Donald M. Brodie remarked that the final report was written primarily by Henry King, and that Crane had insisted only on the inclusion of one short paragraph about the Senussi's social and spiritual contributions to Islam as an example of cultural vitality.[120] In this excerpt, Crane pleaded for the safeguard and political autonomy of regions controlled by the Senussi:

> As illustrative of the spiritual values still resident in Islam, for example, may be mentioned the remarkable and inspiring achievements of the Senussi sect, in establishing a vast state in a most barren, unpromising land, and in up-lifting, organizing, and harmonizing a most backward and degenerated population in the heart of Africa within a comparatively few years, and under influences purely Moslem. Such a state should not be needlessly encroached upon. It rather affords ample warrant for expecting that under new democratic processes and in due time the Moslems will prove themselves able to build up and manage their own states in the Arabian and Anatolian peninsulas. If the Entente powers are sincere in their declarations not further to harass the Moslem world and so give excuse for a pan-Islamic movement, they should also at once definitely and publicly renounce all further political encroachments on that world, and outline a clear policy of uplifting the Moslems, already subject to their control, by enlarged opportunities both in education and in public service.[121]

Crane, in short, saw the Senussi as the progressives of the Muslim world and therefore considered them best suited to self-determination. He gathered his information not only from his meeting with the sheik but also from a study he commissioned about the history and organization of the Senussi's Muslim branch. A certain Dr. Abdussalem Mustapha of Tripoli sent him a condensed history and an analysis of the movement's structure, which he described as "founded for the distinct purpose of civilization." He also sent Crane a list of the movement's achievements: a network of legal and theological schools, trade associations, land reform, creation of a government, charitable actions, hospitals, legal education, and establishment of courts of law. Thus, the studied region, previously steeped in obscurantism, had become a beacon of the Arab civilization, "a center of helpfulness and of progress," through the work of the "great and humanitarian organization" that was the Senussi movement.[122] Whatever the status of this Mustapha—perhaps he was even a Senussi himself—or the precision of his analysis, one cannot fail to notice the similarities between this movement and the current of the social gospel in America. Crane's enthusiasm for it was quite natural, therefore, and he used the commission's final report as a platform to defend the movement's integrity and sustainability.

A few days after the final report's submission on August 28, 1919, Crane wrote Wilson a summary of his personal understanding of the report's meaning, probably foreseeing that the president's illness would prevent him from perusing it carefully. Crane certified that the report was "well founded on vital human facts" while admitting that its conclusions were "not in harmony with many things the Allies are doing." Trusting the American public's just and humanitarian spirit, Crane then suggested that Wilson publish the report immediately in order to stimulate his electoral campaign on the basis of the internationalist project, the system of mandates, and the League of Nations. Crane deemed that "Outside of Armenia and Constantinople the former Turkish state must be kept for the Moslem world or there will be no peace there or in any other part of the world," and the report could thus play a significant role in the reorganization of the Ottoman Empire.[123]

However, already foreseeing European and Zionist opposition to the report, which only increased his mistrust, Crane confessed to Mildred N. Page that "I am quite content about them [our reports]. They are worth while but will not make us any friends."[124] Indeed, once submitted to Wilson and the delegates in Paris, the report quickly fell into disgrace and was more or less forgotten. It was published only in December of 1922, with Wilson's authorization.[125] Crane shared his disappointment in the report's reception, particularly by the European diplomats, with his partner Henry C. King, writing that "It is most important that it should come out, and I feel would do much to clear the air," and adding that "The last two months there has been very dangerous drifting, and the people in Syria do not know what to make of the apparent lack of interest in our work."[126]

The Treaty of Versailles, which put an end to these crucial war years which had initially been so promising where Wilsonian reformism was concerned, had already been signed during the report's submission, and Crane quickly began thinking of it as the work of the world's greatest egoists. In his opinion, "the best over there had gone to the front and had been shot off, leaving the reconstruction of the world to the selfish, the stay-at-home and the profiteers."[127]

While Henry King had done most of the writing, Crane's less tangible part in the report's completion was summarized by Donald Brodie, who wrote that "Mr. Crane, through his prestige and personal friendships [...] not only added greatly to the interest of their travels but assisted the others in understanding the peoples of the Near East."[128] As an example, Brodie mentioned Crane's crucial role in establishing close ties with Faisal and being invited to witness the most sacred Arab ceremonies. This in addition to his considerable documentation work before and during the commission, as demonstrated by the studies he commissioned from specialists like Christiaan Snouck Hurgronje and from "natives" like Halide Edib and Abdussalem Mustapha, as well as interviews with local chiefs like Ahmed al-Senussi, the Sheik of Damascus (whom he had been introduced to by Faisal) or his long-time Egyptian friend Gafir Waly Pasha. Relaying information to his fellow commissioners, to Allied advisors, to delegates in Versailles, and even to the president himself, Crane believed—until the very end and despite his constant criticism and complaints about the persistence of "old diplomacy"—that an examination of "vital human facts" pertaining to the Middle East would help implement the Fourteen Points and build a Wilsonian peace and a new world order with the decisive and "benevolent" collaboration of the United States. From his first steps in the Middle East in 1878 and 1910 all the way until his central involvement in the Near East Relief and his work for the King-Crane Commission, philanthropy, education, and Wilsonian diplomacy were intertwined in Charles R. Crane's progressive mind. That was what he meant when he exclaimed "So the world is moving!" while remembering Faisal's interest in American schools.

Ultimately, the commission had a greater impact on Crane's career than on politics strictly speaking. The sympathy he earned for his anti-Zionist leanings allowed him to serve American interests by building relations and eventually obtaining the first oil concessions in the 1930s, and he personally invested in the technological and structural developments of the region. He was already sixty-one years old when he submitted the King-Crane Commission's report, but this would not be his last camel ride or his last crossing in a flimsy fisherman's boat. He still had enough desire to travel that, after his return to America, Wilson appointed him to the post of Minister Plenipotentiary to China. There, he went on to carry out his greatest humanitarian undertaking, showing once again that in his mind, politics and philanthropy went hand in hand.

Notes

1. *Crane Papers*, "CRC to WW," August 4, 1914.
2. *Crane Papers*, "Memoirs," 273. An editorial note shows that Crane was part of the Board of Trustees of the Constantinople College for Girls from December 1910 to November 12, 1932, and was president of the board from December 15, 1915 until October 10, 1928. He was also on the Board of Trustees of the Robert College of Constantinople from April 22, 1915 to November 21, 1932. This long term voluntary engagement in American education overseas which also involved missionaries like Mary M. Patrick, the Dodge family and Howard Bliss, demonstrates Crane's faith in social progress through education, particularly Christian education, among the peoples of the Orient. Constantinople, in this regard, was a cultural crossroads between Europe and Asia.
3. *Crane Papers*, "Mary Mills Patrick to CRC," January 19, 1919.
4. *Crane Papers*, "Memoirs," 232. Crane's recollection of the timing in his memoirs was inaccurate, however. His correspondence reveals that his stay in the Muslim world most likely happened between December of 1909 (in Cairo) and spring of 1911 (in Constantinople) and spanned across Egypt, Palestine, Lebanon, Syria, and Turkey.
5. *Crane Papers*, "CRC to WW," September 25, 1914. Crane told Wilson that Turkey [i.e., the Ottoman Empire] had successfully remained neutral until August of 1914 owing to Morgenthau's influence on the members of the Young Turk government. This perspective had been shared with him by an American missionary, Mary Mills Patrick, then a teacher at the Constantinople American College for Girls. Curiously, Crane did not mention the recent alliance between the Ottomans and the Central Powers.
6. Like Crane, he had met Wilson in 1911—while the latter was Governor of New Jersey—during the Free Synagogue's fourth anniversary celebration in New York, which both Morgenthau and Wilson had been invited to attend by the rabbi Stephen Wise. According to the historian Peter Balakian, this event was a turning point in Morgenthau's political career, as he offered Wilson his moral and financial support. See Peter Balakian, *The*

Burning Tigris. The Armenian Genocide and America's Response (New York: Harper Collins, 2003), 219–23.

7. Above all, Morgenthau was appalled at having to rub shoulders, on a daily basis, with men who had the blood of almost a million Armenians on their hands. Constantinople had become a place of horror. Merrill D. Peterson, *Starving Armenians. America and the Armenian Genocide, 1915–1930 and After* (University of Virginia Press, 2004), 11.
8. *Crane Papers*, "CRC to Josephine Crane Bradley," March 2, 1916.
9. Simon Payaslian, *United States Policy Toward the Armenian Question and the Armenian Genocide* (New York: Palgrave, 2005), 84–9. Payaslian explains that the Wilson Administration preferred humanitarian aid over diplomatic or military courses of action due to its commitment to neutrality. This also demonstrates a certain willingness on the part of the American government "to accept a *fait accompli*."
10. *FRUS, Supplement, The World War, 1918*, "Morgenthau to Lansing," April 27, July 20, August 11, 1915, 980–8.
11. *Crane Papers*, "CRC to Josephine C. Bradley," October 5, 1915.
12. *Crane Papers*, "James Bryce to CRC," November 5, 1915.
13. Balakian, *The Burning Tigris*, 117–9; James Bryce, *Le livre bleu du Gouvernement britannique concernant le traitement des Arméniens de l'Empire ottoman, 1915–1916* (Paris: Payot, 1987 [c.1916]).
14. *PWW*, "H. H. Topakyan to WW" and "WW to Topakyan," Vol. 35, October 22 and 28, 1915, 104–5, 119.
15. *PWW*, "William Nesbitt Chambers to WW," Vol. 35, December 10, 1915, 337.
16. *Crane Papers*, "CRC to Josephine C. Bradley," October 5, 1915.
17. Balakian, *The Burning Tigris*, 279.
18. Suzanne E. Moranian, "The American Missionary and the Armenian Question, 1915–1927," (Ph. D. diss., University of Wisconsin, 1994), 191–3. Moranian based her interpretation of the role played by members of philanthropic circles and Foreign missions on the interpretation made by Richard Hofstadter and Robert Wiebe according to which, rather than crumbling under the structural changes implemented in industrial America, Protestant missionaries and their social gospel collaborators embraced the efficiency movement in order to reestablish their position while fulfilling their duty to do good. To Moranian, Dodge and Barton's efforts served as characteristic examples of this trend.
19. Henry Morgenthau, *Ambassador Morgenthau Story* (Toronto: McClellan, Goodchild & Stewart, 1918), 118.
20. James L. Barton, *Story of the Near East Relief* (New York: MacMillan, 1930), 381.
21. Joseph L. Grabill, *Protestant Diplomacy and the Near East. Missionary Influence on American Policy, 1810–1927* (Minneapolis: University of Minnesota Press, 1971), 80.
22. Joseph L. Grabill, "Cleveland H. Dodge, Woodrow Wilson, and the Near East," *Journal of Presbyterian History*, 48 (1970): 254–5. Generally, Grabill interprets the Dodge Committee's influence on Wilson as an effort by Barton and the missionaries to use the ACASR "to strengthen government commitment to missionary and relief interests."
23. In fact, Dodge had applauded Wilson's "Peace without Victory" speech in which the president urged the warring countries to sign the armistice and to renounce any claims or spoils. *PWW*, "Cleveland H. Dodge to WW," Vol. 41, January 24, 1917, 6–7.

24. *PWW*, "Diary of Colonel House," Vol. 40, January 5, 1917, 418–9.
25. *PWW*, "WW to Mott," Vol. 41, February 3, 1917, 113.
26. *PWW*, "C. H. Dodge to WW," Vol. 41, April 3, 1917, 539.
27. *ABCFM*, "Barton to Lansing," February 8, 1917, ABC 3.2.
28. *PWW*, "Morgenthau to WW," Vol. 42, June 7, 1917, 462–3.
29. *PWW*, "WW to C. H. Dodge," Vol. 41, February 6, 1917, 133.
30. *PWW*, "C. H. Dodge to WW" and "WW to C. H. Dodge," Vol. 44, August 30, September 1, 1917, 93, 119.
31. *PWW*, "C. H. Dodge to WW," Vol. 45, December 2, 1917, 185–6.
32. *PWW*, "WW to C. H. Dodge," Vol. 45, December 5, 1917, 215.
33. *PWW*, "Annual Message on the State of the Union," Vol. 45, December 4, 1917, 200.
34. *FRUS*, *Supplement*, *The World War, 1918*, "Lansing to Walter Hines Page," May 3, 1918, 222.
35. *FRUS*, *Supplement*, *The World War, 1918*, "Walter Hines Page to Lansing," May 17, 1918, 232–233. The French government, for its part, also hoped that the United States would declare war against the allies of Germany and Austria-Hungary, but feared the impact this might have on America's crucial presence on the Western Front (*FRUS*, *Supplement*, *The World War, 1918*, 7 May 1918, 228).
36. *PWW*, "Sir William Wiseman to Sir Eric Drummond," Vol. 49, August 27, 1918, 365. If Wiseman had expressed skepticism in regard to Wilson's "missionary" point of view, his correspondent from the Foreign Office, Eric Drummond, refuted Wilson's "untenable" position outright by rightly emphasizing that from 1915 until then, missionary presence had had no success in preventing the massacres.
37. *PWW*, "C. H. Dodge to WW," Vol. 51, September 28, 1918, 151–2.
38. Though he was chosen much earlier (possibly around the beginning of March), Crane's official nomination was only communicated to him in a letter on April 30, 1919, primarily because of the delays due to slow negotiations in Versailles, as shall be explained later. Crane's copy of the letter features in the *Crane Papers*.
39. Harry N. Howard, *The King-Crane Commission. An American Inquiry in the Middle East* (Beirut: Khayats, 1963), 54. This information does not feature in the *Crane Papers*, and Howard instead takes it from the archives of Henry C. King. See also *FRUS*, *1919*, *Paris Peace Conference*, Vol. 11, 164–6, 170. King received a yearly salary of $8,000 for the time he spent on the commission.
40. *Crane Papers*, "CRC to RC," November 13, 1918.
41. *PWW*, "A Non-partisan Address in Cincinnati," Vol. 38, October 26, 1916, 539. For other references to Crane and Wilson's affection toward what they called "small nations," see Crane's May 29, 1916 letter to Wilson: "I am especially happy about your declaration regarding the smaller nations [...] I have been much among the small nations and feel very close to them." *Crane Papers*, "CRC to WW," May 29, 1916.
42. *PWW*, "Arsene Vehouni to WW," "WW to Arsene Vehouni," Vol. 40, November 29, December 21, 1916, 105–6, 311.
43. Lawrence Evans, *U.S. Policy and the Partition of Turkey, 1914–1924* (Baltimore: Johns Hopkins University Press, 1965), 43; Harry N. Howard, *The King-Crane Commission. An American Inquiry in the Middle East*, 4–6.

44. *FRUS, 1919, Paris Peace Conference*, Vol. 3, 1013–20; *Crane Papers*, "Memoirs," 229. Crane described Bliss's appeal as a determining element for the commission. He also mentioned that Howard Bliss had first met with Wilson, who had from the start been open to the proposal, before appearing before the Council of Ten.
45. *PWW*, "Council of Four," Vol. 56, March 20, 1919, 112.
46. *FRUS, 1919, Paris Peace Conference*, Vol. 11, 128. Crane's personal and secret copy appears in the *Crane Papers*, "American Commission to Negotiate Peace: Future Administration of Certain Portions of the Turkish Empire under the Mandatory System," (March 25, 1919).
47. Harry N. Howard, *The King-Crane Commission*, 38–41.
48. Howard, *The King-Crane Commission*, 50, 84. The expression stems from Howard and refers to the long period of confusion before the implementation and departure of the commission. Many incidents caused drastic changes in opinion on this topic. On the one hand, there came a request by British general Edmund Allenby (stationed in Cairo) to send the commission forthwith, but there was also reluctance from Caleb F. Gates, a missionary in Turkey invited to share his point of view in Versailles, and of William L. Westermann (a member of the ACNP and in charge of two of the commission's members!), who argued that the Allies already possessed all the necessary information in Paris and that such a delegation would get in the way of a quick peace settlement.
49. Grabill, *Protestant Diplomacy and the Near East*, 188–9.
50. Howard, *The King-Crane Commission*, 71.
51. Historiography attached great importance to this diplomatic hiatus during which House acted as Wilson's replacement in the role of first plenipotentiary American delegate. This focus on the subject results from diverging interpretations proposed by two historians who had accompanied Wilson as part of the ACNP in Paris. Ray S. Baker (author of *Woodrow Wilson and World Settlement*, 1922) claimed that House, co-opted by the Europeans, had betrayed Wilson and the Fourteen Points, whereas Charles Seymour (author of *Woodrow Wilson and the World War*, 1921, 278–9; and editor of *The Intimate Papers of Colonel House*, 1928) pointed out that House had diligently maintained contact with Wilson during his absence, that the president had accepted the Council of Three's advances (with House) and that nothing seemed to indicate that House's influence had decreased for this reason. Indeed, House's fall from grace occurred a bit later, in April, when Wilson suffered from an (undiagnosed) heart attack. His cerebral and emotional capabilities continued to deteriorate and limited his leadership in Versailles. See Gene Smith, *When the Cheering Stopped* (New York: Morrow, 1964) and Edwin A. Weinstein, *Woodrow Wilson: A Medical and Psychological Biography* (Princeton: Princeton University Press, 1981).
52. She was nicknamed "d'Orient" as play on words on her full name, Pauline Ménard-Dorian.
53. *Crane Papers*, "CRC to CSC," February 26, 1919. Crane was writing from Paris to his wife who had stayed in the United States.
54. In fact, Clemenceau once told House that he understood him well whereas with Wilson, he felt like he was dealing with a sort of Jesus Christ. Clemenceau then added: "The Almighty gave us Ten Commandments, but Wilson has given us Fourteen." *PWW*, "House Diary," Vol. 58, April 28, 1919, 186.
55. *Crane Papers*, "CRC to John H. Miller (*New York Times*)," March 3, 1919 (from Paris).

56. *Crane Papers*, "CRC to CSC," March 9, 1919 (from Paris).
57. Howard, *The King-Crane Commission*, 48.
58. *Crane Papers*, "CRC to Mildred Nelson Page," March 9, 1919 (from Paris). Crane reiterated these same comments about the limits of human understanding in regard to the complexity of the issues brought forward in Versailles in a letter to M. N. Page written on March 20, 1919.
59. *Crane Papers*, "CRC to A. G. Gardner," March 10, 1919 (from Paris).
60. *Crane Papers*, "CRC to JCB," March 16, 1919 (from Paris).
61. *PWW*, "Vance C. McCormick Diary," Vol. 57, April 16, 1919, 391.
62. *PWW*, "Westermann Diary," Vol. 57, April 18, 1919, 468. This episode is also mentioned in Howard, *The King-Crane Commission*, 48–9. Curiously, Vance McCormick's diary seems to place this meeting two days earlier.
63. *Crane Papers*, "Memoirs," 220–32 (interesting fact: Crane seems to be the only person to have mentioned Allenby's appeal); Howard, *The King-Crane Commission*, 49–51; *PWW*, "Feisal to WW," Vol. 57, April 20, 1919, 525–6.
64. As an example, Crane mentioned Italy's claims over the region of Fiume, illustrating how territorial pursuits and the concept of "war booty" overpowered Wilson's recommendations, which were based on the principle of self-determination.
65. *Crane Papers*, "CRC to CSC," April 28, 1919 (from Paris). Crane made similar comments to his son John O. Crane: "I shall feel that the age of miracles is not yet past if any great secure good comes out of it," May 10, 1919.
66. *Crane Papers*, "CRC to M. N. Page," May 1, 1919 (from Paris).
67. *Crane Papers*, "CRC to JOC," May 10, 1919 (from Paris).
68. *PWW*, "Diary of William L. Westermann," Vol. 59, May 22, 1919, 376. This incident was told by the commissioner Westermann, and he mentioned that Crane was the one who had transmitted Hurgronje's text to Wilson. The *Wilson Papers* contain neither Crane's letter nor the text attached to it, which was declared missing, but both are included in the *Crane Papers*, along with a confirmation of receipt and a short comment written by Wilson on May 22, 1919 indicating that he had indeed read it. The missive also contained a note from Crane expressing that Hurgronje was "the foremost Moslem authority in the world," which probably led to Wilson's confusion about the professor's origin.
69. *Crane Papers*, "C. Snouck Hurgronje to CRC," May 9, 1919.
70. *Crane Papers*, "CRC to CSC," May 26, 1919.
71. *Crane Papers*, "CRC to CSC," May 31, 1919 (from Pleven, Bulgaria).
72. *Crane Papers*, "Memoirs," 230.
73. *Crane Papers*, "CRC to M. N. Page," June 1, 1919 (from Constantinople).
74. Halide Edib, *Memoirs of Halide Edib* (New York: The Century, 1926), 455.
75. *Crane Papers*, "Memoirs," 231–2.
76. Erez Manela, *The Wilsonian Moment: Self-determination and the International Origins of Anticolonial Nationalism, 1917–1920* (Oxford: Oxford University Press, 2007), 106–60. Manela did not specifically discuss the Syrian and Palestinian issues, but he did give the example of Egypt's anticolonial movement (Egypt then being *de jure* under the Ottoman Empire's dominion while also being under British protectorate). The movement was greatly influenced by Wilsonian self-determination rhetoric, and it would seem that before

Franco-British schemes prevailed over the Fourteen Points, the Arab people, those of Egypt, in this case, had admired Wilson and used his arguments when rejecting imperialism. Manela also wrote that the Wilsonian message was primarily adopted by the educated classes, at whom the CPI's Fourteen Points "propaganda" was directed. It comes as no surprise, therefore, that American educational environments became platforms for Wilson's liberal message to those who were educated there, as Crane had implied.

77. *Crane Papers*, "Memoirs," 232; Howard, *The King-Crane Commission*, 91.
78. Richard Ned Lebow, "Woodrow Wilson and the Balfour Declaration," *The Journal of Modern History*, 40, 4 (1968): 501–23. It would seem that though Wilson was personally favorably disposed toward Zionism for moral and ideological reasons and in accordance with the principle of self-determination based on nationality, the fact that the United States were not at war against the Ottoman Empire made House and Wilson decide to postpone any public support for the Zionist project (though they privately assured Britain of their sympathy for it). Wilson also felt responsible for American interests in Turkey, namely for the missionary institutions which would very likely suffer from a conflict between the two countries.
79. Howard, *The King-Crane Commission*, 93; *Crane Papers*, "Memoirs," 231.
80. *Crane Papers*, "J. Bryce to CRC," 13 December 1909.
81. *Crane Papers*, "Memoirs," 228–9.
82. *Crane Papers*, "Snouck Hurgronje to CRC," 23 October 1911.
83. *Crane Papers*, "CRC to JCB," 5 April 1916. Comment previously quoted in Chapter 3.
84. *Crane Papers*, "Emma Gottheil to CRC," 26 January 1913; "CRC to WW," 24 March 1913.
85. *Crane Papers*, "R. Gottheil to CRC," 5 July 1913.
86. *PWW*, "CRC to WW," vol. 27, 10 February 1913, 107–8. Crane told Wilson that "Brandeis is the only important Jew who is first American and then Jew." This praise came before Brandeis's involvement with Zionism, but Brandeis himself articulated a Zionist position which was compatible with patriotism and American social justice values, which he also found inside Judaism: "To be good Americans, we must be better Jews, and to be better Jews, we must become Zionist." Brandeis had even come to see an opportunity to build American-style Jewish democracy, another "new Jerusalem," inside a Zionist Palestine. See Melvin I. Urofsky, *Louis D. Brandeis and the Progressive Tradition*, 93.
87. *Crane Papers*, "CRC to JCB," 23 July 1916.
88. *Crane Papers*, "CRC to JOC," 30 September 1914.
89. *Crane Papers*, "CRC to JCB," 2 March 1916.
90. *Crane Papers*, "CRC to JOC," 15 October 1916. Crane wrote this passage to his son John in order to celebrate the fact that Wald and Addams, both from Roosevelt's camp in 1912, had declared their support for Wilson. In the same letter, Crane also mentioned the rise of Walter Lippmann, "that brilliant young Jew," a writer for the New Republic and who had now also joined Wilson's camp and had begun drawing inspiration from Brandeis.
91. Howard, *The King-Crane Commission*, 59–62, 349.
92. *Crane Papers*, "CRC to CSC," 31 May 1919; "Memoirs," 230.
93. *Crane Papers*, "CRC to CSC," 15 June 1919.
94. *Crane Papers*, "CRC to CSC," 19 June 1919, 24 June 1919.

95. *Crane Papers*, "CRC to CSC," 24 June 1919.
96. *Crane Papers*, "Memoirs," 233.
97. Robert D. Kaplan, *The Arabists. The Romance of an American Elite* (New York: The Free Press, 1993), 69–72; and F. W. Brecher, "Charles R. Crane's Crusade for the Arabs, 1919–39," *Middle Eastern Studies*, 24, 1 (1988): 42–55. Kaplan described a caricatural Crane who nursed a visceral hatred toward the Jews without ever taking into account Crane's lasting friendships with several Zionist Jews. Though Brecher paints a more nuanced portrait focusing on the twenty years following the commission, he still presents Crane as fixated on the idea of Jewish conspiracies. Brecher puts excessive emphasis on comments made in the specific context of the Russian-Japanese war and of the Bolshevik Revolution, and especially on his praise of Hitler a few years before his death.
98. Howard, *The King-Crane Commission*, 72–4. Frankfurter demanded that Wilson not send the commission to Palestine given that the Balfour Declaration, supported by the Allies, would already in principle feature among the future settlements in the Ottoman Empire. He asked instead that the commissioners limit their inquiry to Syria, Mesopotamia and Anatolia. Wilson refused to implement any modifications to the itinerary, replying that there was "no ground for discouragement" in the pursuit of a resolution that would be satisfactory to all.
99. *Crane Papers*, "CRC to CSC," 27 July 1919.
100. Alpheus T. Mason, *Brandeis: a Free Man's Life*, 456–7.
101. This agreement on a "mutual friendship" between Jews and Arabs stipulated that Faisal would accept the Balfour Declaration in exchange for the Arab independence which had previously been promised by the British. See Howard, *The King-Crane Commission*, 23.
102. *Crane Papers*, "CRC to CSC," 9 July 1919.
103. *Crane Papers*, "CRC to WW," 10 July 1919; *PWW*, "CRC to WW," (enclosure), vol. 61, 10 July 1919, 442–4.
104. *Crane Papers*, "Cabled Text of Report from the American Section, International Commission of Mandates in Turkey," 8 July 1919; "CRC to M. N. Page," 29 July 1919.
105. *PWW*,"Feisal to WW," vol. 61, 9 July 1919, 409.
106. *Crane Papers*, "CRC to Eliot," 5 May 1920.
107. *Crane Papers*, "CRC to Eliot," 5, 12 February 1921. Crane specified that Baruch was a southerner before he was a Jew. Indeed, his Jewish ancestry was rather distant and his father, a German-speaking immigrant from Bohemia, had been a doctor in the Confederate army despite his aversion to slavery. See Bernard Mannes Baruch, *Baruch*,vol. 1, *My Own Story* (New York: Henry Holt, 1957), 1–12.
108. *Crane Papers*, "Abdel-Koder Masaphen to CRC," [Date not specified but the letter was received between July 10 and 15, 1919].
109. *Crane Papers*, "CRC to M. N. Page," 29 July 1919.
110. *Crane Papers*, "CRC to WW," 2 August 1919.
111. The commission's full report stated: "the large Armenia would never become an Armenian State at all [...] On the contrary, an Armenia reduced to the Armenian highlands in both Turkey and Russia, with an outlet on the Black sea, would have a good chance of establishment and continuance [...] The Turks and Kurds could not rightfully

complain of such an area, because it is the historical Armenia…" See *Oberlin College Archives*, "King-Crane Commission Report," Digital Collection, 28 August 1919, 101. (On-line).

112. *Oberlin College Archives*, "Fragments of a Report on the King-Crane Commission," Digital Collection, unknown date, 12–18. (On-line). The text said that "The Turk is an agreeable surprise. Instead of a blood-thirsty bandit with a black beard […] the Turk of today, the better-class Turk […] is a carefully groomed gentleman." On the subject of the massacres, the text granted that Bryce's report was authentic and that the Turks had proven to be poor imperial rulers, but argued that though America had naturally favored the Christian Armenian minority, some in the humanitarian world had changed their mind on the issue and that "something of a pro-Turkish, anti-Armenian sentiment has been gaining ground." In short, "The Armenian is not quite such a worthy fellow after all." These harsh statements were not, however, made by the note's author and were instead reported as "hearsay" to document these evolving opinions. Strangely enough, the statements were crossed out of the final report by the commission's members. They nevertheless serve as a good illustration of the type of testimony that contributed to shaping Crane's opinion, as well as that of other commissioners, in favor of a sovereign Turkish state under an American mandate.
113. *Crane Papers*, "CRC to CSC," 3 August 1919.
114. *Crane Papers*, "Memoirs," 234.
115. *Crane Papers*, "Halide Edib Adnan to CRC," 20 August 1919.
116. Halide Edib, *The Turkish Ordeal. Being the Further Memoirs of Halide Edib* (New York: Century Co., 1928), 42–3.
117. *Crane Paper*, "Halide Edib to CRC," 16 September 1919.
118. Crane maintained a good relationship with Halide Edib long after the end of the commission. He even took charge of her children's university education in the United States when their future appeared to be endangered in their home country. See *Crane Papers*, "Edib to CRC," 16 September, 27 November 1919.
119. *Crane Papers*, "CRC to CSC," 19 August 1919.
120. *Crane Papers*, "Charles R. Crane as Mandate Commissioner, by D. M. Brodie," 1940.
121. *Oberlin College Archives*, "King-Crane Commission Report," 28 August 1919.
122. *Crane Papers*, "Dr. Abdussalem Mustapha to CRC," 19 August 1919.
123. *Crane Papers*, "CRC to WW," 31 August 1919.
124. *Crane Papers*, "CRC to Mildred N. Page," 3 September 1919.
125. Bruce Murphy, *The Brandeis/Frankfurter Connection. The Secret Political Activities of Two Supreme Court Justices* (New York: Oxford University Press, 1982), 63. The judicial historian Bruce Murphy claimed that Brandeis had convinced Wilson to disregard the King-Crane Commission's final report due to the suggested restrictions on Jewish immigration to Palestine and the proposed idea of a Great Syria. The *Wilson Papers*, however, contain no proof that Brandeis exerted this sort of influence over the president.
126. *Crane Papers*, "CRC to Henry C. King," 3 December 1919.
127. *Crane Papers*, "CRC to Eliot," 7 November 1920.
128. *Crane Papers*, "Charles R. Crane as Mandate Commissioner, by D. M. Brodie," 1940.

Bibliography

Archives

American Board of Commissioners for Foreign Mission Papers. Houghton Library, Harvard University.

Charles Richard Crane Papers, 1869–1967. Rare Books & Manuscript Library, University of Columbia.

Oberlin College Archives. King-Crane Commission Digital Collection: www.oberlin.edu/library/digital/king-crane/

Published Primary Sources

Baker, Ray S. and William E. Dodd, ed. *The Public Papers of Woodrow Wilson*. New York: Harper, 1925–26.

Baker, Ray S. *Woodrow Wilson: Life and Letters*. Garden City, NY: Doubleday, 1927–39.

Barton, James L. *Story of Near East Relief*. New York: Macmillan, 1930.

Baruch, Bernard M. *Baruch*. New York: H. Holt, 1957–1960.

Bryce, James and Arnold J. Toynbee. *Le livre bleu du Gouvernement britannique concernant le traitement des Arméniens de l'Empire ottoman, 1915–1916*. Paris: Payot, 1987 [c.1916].

Burnett, Philip M. *Reparation at the Paris Peace Conference, from the Standpoint of the American Delegation*. New York: Octagon Books, 1965 [c.1940].

Daniels, Josephus. *The Wilson Era*. Chapel Hill: University of North Carolina Press, 1946.

Edib, Halide. *Memoirs of Halide Edib*. New York: The Century, 1926.

———. *The Turkish Ordeal. Being the Further Memoirs of Halide Edib*. New York: The Century, 1928.

House, Edward M and Charles Seymour. *What Really Happened at Paris: The Story of the Peace Conference, 1918–1919, by American Delegates*. New York: Scribner's, 1921.

Houston, David F. *Eight Years with Wilson's Cabinet, 1913–1920*. Garden City, NY: Doubleday, 1926.

Lansing, Robert. *The Peace Negotiations: A Personal Narrative*. Kessinger Publishers, 2004 [c.1921].

Link, Arthur S., ed. *Papers of Woodrow Wilson*. Princeton, NJ: Princeton University Press, 1966–92.

Mantoux, Paul. *Les délibérations du Conseil des Quatre, 24 mars-28 juin 1919. Notes de l'officier Interprète Paul Mantoux*. Paris: Ed. CNRS, 1955.

Morgenthau, Henry. *Ambassador Morgenthau's story*. Detroit: Wayne State University Press, 2003 [c.1918].

Seymour, Charles, ed. *The Intimate Papers of Colonel House Arranged as a Narrative*. London: Ernest Benn, 1926–28.

Tumulty, Joseph P. *Woodrow Wilson as I Know Him*. Garden City: Doubleday, 1921.
U.S. State Department. *Papers Relating to the Foreign Relations of the United States*.

Bibliographic Guides

Buckingham, Peter H. *Woodrow Wilson: A Bibliography of His Times and Presidency*. Wilmington, DE: Scholarly Resources, 1990.
Beisner, Robert L. and Hanson Kurt W., ed. *American Foreign Relations since 1600. A Guide to the Literature*. Santa Barbara, CA: ABC-CLIO, 2003.
Bellot, Hugh Hale. *American History and American Historians: A Review of Recent Contributions to the Interpretation of the History of the United States*. Norman: University of Oklahoma Press, 1952.
Parish, Peter J., ed. *Reader's Guide to American History*. Chicago: Fitzroy Publishers, 1997.

Encyclopedias

Balmer, Randall Herbert. *Encyclopedia of Evangelicalism*. Louisville, KY: John Knox Press, 2002.
Shelton, Dinah L., ed. *Encyclopedia of Genocide and Crimes against Humanity*. Detroit: Macmillan Reference USA, 2004.

Monographies

Akçam, Taner. *From Empire to Republic. Turkish Nationalism and the Armenian Genocide*. London: Zed Books, 2004.
Ambrosius, Lloyd E. *Woodrow Wilson and the American Diplomatic Tradition: The Treaty Fight in Perspective*. Cambridge: Cambridge University Press, 1987.
———. *Wilsonian Statecraft: Theory and Practice of Liberal Internationalism during World War I*. Lanham, MD: SR Books, 1991.
———. *Wilsonianism: Woodrow Wilson and His Legacy in American Foreign Relations*. New York: Palgrave Macmillan, 2002.
Balakian, Peter. *The Burning Tigris: The Armenian Genocide and America's Response*. New York: Harper Collins, 2003.
Bailey, Thomas A. *Woodrow Wilson and the Lost Peace*. New York: Macmillan, 1944.
———. *Woodrow Wilson and the Great Betrayal*. Chicago: Quadrangle Books, 1945.
Baker, Ray S. *Woodrow Wilson and World Settlement*. Garden City, NY: Doubleday, 1922.
Bell, Sidney. *Righteous Conquest. Woodrow Wilson and the Evolution of the New Diplomacy*. Port Washington, NY: Kennikat Press, 1972.
Berlin, William S. *On the Edge of Politics. The Roots of Jewish Political Thought in America*. Westport, CT: Greenwood Press, 1978.
Blum, John M. *Woodrow Wilson and the Politics of Morality*. Boston: Little, Brown & Co., 1956.

Bouchard, Carl. *Le citoyen et l'ordre mondial. Le rêve d'une paix durable au lendemain de la Grande Guerre*. Paris: Éditions A. Pedone, 2008.

Bu, Liping. *Making the World Like Us: Education, Cultural Expansion, and the American Century*. Westport, CT: Praeger, 2003.

Burns, James M. *The Workshop of Democracy. From the Emancipation Proclamation to the Era of the New Deal*. New York: Vintage Book, 1985.

Calhoun, Frederick S. *Uses of Force and Wilsonian Foreign Policy*. Kent, OH: Kent State University Press, 1993.

Clements, Kendrick A. *William Jennings Bryan, Missionary Isolationist*. Knoxville, TE: University of Tennessee Press, 1982.

———. *The Presidency of Woodrow Wilson*. Lawrence, KA: University Press of Kansas, 1992.

Cooper, John M. *The Vanity of Power. American Isolationism and the First World War, 1914–1917*. Westport, CT: Greenwood Publishing Corp., 1969.

———. *The Warrior and the Priest*. Cambridge: Harvard University Press, 1983.

———. *Woodrow Wilson*. New York: Alfred A. Knopf, 2009.

Cranston, Alan. *The Killing of the Peace*. New York: The Viking Press, 1945.

Curti, Merle E. *American Philanthropy Abroad*. New Brunswick, NJ: Rutgers University Press, 1963.

Denovo, John. *American Interests and Politics in the Middle East: 1900–1939*. Minneapolis: The University of Minnesota Press, 1963.

Duroselle, Jean-Baptiste. *Histoire diplomatique de 1919 à nos jours*, 11th ed. Paris: Éditions Dalloz, 1993.

Evans, Lawrence. *United States Policy and the Partition of Turkey, 1914–1924*. Baltimore: The Johns Hopkins University Press, 1965.

Feingold, Henry L. *Zion in America*. New York: Twayne Publishers Inc., 1974.

Ferrell, Robert H. *Woodrow Wilson and World War I, 1917–1921*. New York: Harper & Row, 1985.

Fromkin, David. *A Peace to End All Peace. Creating the Modern Middle East, 1914–1922*. New York: Holt, 1989.

Gardner, Lloyd C. *Safe for Democracy. The Anglo-American Response to Revolution, 1913–1923*. New York: Oxford University Press. 1984.

Gidney, James. B. *A Mandate for Armenia*. Kent, OH: Kent State University Press, 1967.

Grabill, Joseph L. *Protestant Diplomacy in the Near East. Missionary Influence on American Policy, 1810–1927*. Minneapolis: University of Minnesota Press, 1971.

Hansen, Jonathan M. *The Lost Promise of Patriotism. Debating American Identity, 1890–1920*. Chicago: University of Chicago Press, 2003.

Hapgood, David. *Charles R. Crane. The Man Who Bet on People*. New York: ICWA, 2000.

Holmes, James R. *Theodore Roosevelt and World Order. Police Power in International Relations*. Washington: Potomac Books, 2006.

Hopkins, Charles H. *John R. Mott, 1865–1955: A Biography*. Grand Rapids: Eerdmans, 1979.

Howard, Harry. *The King-Crane Commission. An American Inquiry in the Middle-East*. Beyrouth: Kayats, 1963.

Iriye, Akira. *From Nationalism to Internationalism. U.S. Foreign Policy to 1914*. London: Routledge, 2002.

Israel, Jerry. *Progressivism and the Open Door. America and China, 1905–1921*. Pittsburgh: University of Pittsburgh Press, 1971.

Kaplan, Robert D. *The Arabists. The Romance of an American Elite*. New York: The Free Press, 1993.

Keegan, John. *The First World War*. New York: Random House, 1998.

Kennedy, David M. *Over Here. The First World War and American Society*. New York: Oxford University Press, 1980.

Keynes, John Maynard. *Les conséquences économiques de la Paix*. Paris: Nouvelle Revue Française, 1920.

Kitsikis, Dimitri. *Le rôle des experts à la Conférence de la Paix de 1919. Gestation d'une technocratie en politique internationale*. Ottawa: Éditions de l'Université d'Ottawa, 1972.

Knock, Thomas J. *To End all Wars. Woodrow Wilson and the Quest for a New World Order*. New York: Oxford University Press, 1992.

LaFeber, Walter. *The New Empire. An Interpretation of American Expansion, 1860–1898*. Ithaca, NY: Cornell University Press, 1963.

Lasch, Christopher. *The American Liberals and the Russian Revolution*. New York: McGraw, 1962.

———. *The New Radicalism in America. The Intellectual as a Social Type*. New York: Knopf, 1965.

Levin, Norman G. *Woodrow Wilson and World Politics: America's Response to War and Revolution*. New York: Oxford University Press, 1968.

Lewis, Bernard. *The Emergence of Modern Turkey*. London: Oxford University Press, 1961.

Link, Arthur S. *Wilson*. Princeton, NJ: Princeton University Press, 1947.

———. *Woodrow Wilson and the Progressive Era, 1910–1917*. New York: Harper & Brothers, 1954.

———. *Wilson the Diplomatist. A Look at His Major Foreign Policies*. Baltimore: Johns Hopkins Press, 1957.

———. *Woodrow Wilson. Revolution, War, and Peace*. Arlington Heights, IL: Harlan Davidson, 1979.

Livermore, Seward W. *Woodrow Wilson and the War Congress 1916–1918*. New York: Octagon Books, 1968 [c. 1957].

Mamatey, Victor S. *The United States and East Central Europe, 1914–1918. A Study in Wilsonian Diplomacy and Propaganda*. Princeton, NJ: Princeton University Press, 1957.

Manela, Erez. *The Wilsonian Moment: Self-Determination and the International Origins of Anticolonial Nationalism, 1917–1920*. New York: Oxford University Press, 2007.

Mason, Alpheus T. *Brandeis: A Free Man's Life*. New York: Viking Press, 1946.

May, Ernest. *The World War and American Isolation, 1914–1917*. Cambridge: Harvard University Press, 1966 [c.1959].

———. *Imperial Democracy. The Emergence of America as a Great Power*. New York: Harper & Row, 1973.

May, Henry F. *The End of American Innocence. The First Years of Our Own Times, 1912–1917*. New York: Oxford University Press, 1959.

Mayer, Arno. *Politics and Diplomacy of Peacemaking: Containment and Counterrevolution at Versailles, 1918–1919*. New York: Knopf, 1967.

McCartney, Paul T. *Power and Progress: American National Identity, the War of 1898, and the Rise of American Imperialism*. Baton Rouge: Louisiana University Press, 2006.

McLoughlin, William G. *Revivals, Awakenings, and Reform. An Essay on Religion and Social Change in America, 1607–1977*. Chicago: The Chicago University Press, 1978.

Michel, Bernard. *Nations et nationalismes en Europe centrale, XIXe-XXe siècle*. Paris: Aubier, 1995.

Murphy, Bruce. *The Brandeis/Frankfurter Connection. The Secret Political Activities of Two Supreme Court Justices*. New York: Oxford University Press, 1982.

Muukkonen, Martti. *Ecumenism of the Laity. Continuity and Change in the Mission View of the World's Alliance of YMCA, 1855–1955*. Joensuu: University of Joensuu Publications in Theology, 2002.

Noble, David W. *The Paradox of Progressive Thought*. Minneapolis: University of Minnesota Press, 1958.

———. *The Progressive Mind, 1890–1917*. Minneapolis: Burgess, 1981.

Nordholdt, Jan W. S. *Woodrow Wilson: A Life for World Peace*. Berkeley: University of California Press, 1991.

Notter, Harley. *The Origins of the Foreign Policy of Woodrow Wilson*. New York: Russell & Russell, 1965.

O'Neill, William L. *The Progressive Years. America Comes of Age*. New York: Dodd, Mead and Company, 1975.

Osgood, Robert E. *Ideals and Self-Interests in America's Foreign Relations. The Great Transformation of the Twentieth Century*. Chicago: University of Chicago, 1964 [c.1953].

Payaslian, Simon. *United States Policy toward the Armenian Question and the Armenian Genocide*. New York: Palgrave, 2005.

Pérennès, Roger. *La Palestine et la Décadence de l'Empire Ottoman, 1820–1920*. Nantes: Ouest Éditions & Université Permanente de Nantes, 1999.

Peterson, Merrill D. *Starving Armenians. America and the Armenian Genocide, 1915–1930 and After*. Charlottesville: University of Virginia Press, 2004.

Saul, Norman E. *The Life and Times of Charles R. Crane, 1858–1939. American Businessman, Philanthropist, and a Founder of Russian Studies in America*. Lexington Books, 2013.

Smith, Gene. *When the Cheering Stopped: The Last Years of Woodrow Wilson*. New York: Morrow, 1964.

Smith, Neil. *American Empire: Roosevelt's Geographer and the Prelude to Globalization*. Berkeley: University of California Press, 2003.

Soutou, Georges-Henri. *L'or et le sang. Les buts de guerre économiques de la Première Guerre mondiale*. Paris: Fayard, 1989.

Steel, Ronald. *Walter Lippmann and the American Century*. Boston: Little, Brown & Co. 1980.

Thorsen, Niels A. *The Political Thought of Woodrow Wilson, 1875–1910*. Princeton, NJ: Princeton University Press, 1988.

Trachtenberg, Alan. *The Incorporation of America. Culture and Society in the Gilded Age*. New York: Hill & Wang, 1982.

Trask, David F. *Victory without Peace. American Foreign Relations in the Twentieth Century*. Huntington, New York: Robert E. Krieger Publishing Company, 1975.

Urofksy, Melvin I. *Louis D. Brandeis and the Progressive Tradition*. Boston: Little, Brown & Co., 1981.

Van Alstyne, Richard W. *The Rising American Empire*. Oxford: Oxford University Press, 1960.

Walworth, Arthur. *Wilson and His Peacemakers. American Diplomacy at the Paris Peace Conference, 1919*. New York: Norton, 1986.

Weinstein, Edwin A. *Woodrow Wilson: A Medical and Psychological Biography*. Princeton, NJ: Princeton University Press, 1981.

Williams, William A. *The Tragedy of American Diplomacy*. New York: Dell Publishing, 1972 [c.1959].

Wright, Quincy. *Mandates under the League of Nations*. New York: Greenwood Press, 1968 [c.1930].

Theses

Bocage, Leo J. "The Public Career of Charles R. Crane." Ph.D. diss., Fordham University, 1962.

Moranian, Suzanne E. "The American Missionary and the Armenian Question, 1915–1927." Ph.D. diss., University of Wisconsin, 1994.

Sulzbach, Jacob John, Jr. "Charles R. Crane, Woodrow Wilson, and Progressive Reform: 1909–1921." Ph.D. diss., Texas A&M University, 1994.

Journal Articles

Ahonen, Risto. "John R. Mott as an Ecumenical Leader. What Was Mott's Vision?" *The Finnish Evangelical Lutheran Mission*, 2010, 1–5.

Anghie, Antony. "Cultural Differences in International Law: The League of Nations and Two Visions of Nation-State." *International Center for Comparative Law and Politics Review*, 5, 2002, 4–13.

Beloff, Max. "Self-Determination Reconsidered," In *Confluence*, 5, 1956, 195–203.

Bloxham, Donald. "Three Imperialisms and a Turkish Nationalism: International Stresses, Imperial Disintegration and the Armenian Genocide" *Patterns of Prejudice*, 36, 4, 2002, 37–58.

Blumenthal, Henry. "Woodrow Wilson and the Race Question." *The Journal of Negro History*, 48, 1, 1963, 1–21.

Brecher, F. W. "Charles R. Crane's Crusade for the Arabs, 1919–1939." *Middle Eastern Studies*, 24, 1, 1988, 42–55.

Grabill, Joseph L. "Cleveland H. Dodge, Woodrow Wilson, and the Near East." *Journal of Presbyterian History*, 48, 1970, 249–264.

Leblanc, Lawrence J. "United States Foreign Policies toward Genocide and Crimes against Humanity." *Encyclopedia of Genocide and Crimes against Humanity*, Vol. 2. New York: Macmillan Reference USA, 2004, 1107–1116.

Lebow, Richard N. "Woodrow Wilson and the Balfour Declaration." *The Journal of Modern History*, 40, 4, 1968, 501–523.

Leuchtenburg, William E. "Progressivism and Imperialism: The Progressive Movement and American Foreign Policy, 1898–1916." *The Mississippi Valley Historical Review*, 39, 3, 1952, 483–504.

Malkasian, Mark. "The Disintegration of the Armenian Cause in the United States, 1918–1927." *International Journal of Middle East Studies*, 16, 3, 1984, 349–365.

Osgood, Robert E. "Woodrow Wilson, Collective Security, and the Lessons of History." *Confluence*, 5, 1957, 341–354.

Pomerance, Michla. "Methods of Self-determination and the Argument of Primitiveness." *Canadian Yearbook of International Law*, 12, 1974, 38–66.

———. "The United States and Self-determination: Perspectives on the Wilsonian Conception." *The American Journal of International Law*, 70, 1, 1976, 1–27.

Saito, Natsu T. "Crossing the Border: The Interdependence of Foreign Policy and Racial Justice in the United States." *Yale Human Rights and Development Law Journal*, 1, 1998, 53–84.

Smith, Daniel M. "National Interest and American Intervention, 1917: A Historiographical Appraisal." *The Journal of American History*, 52, 1, 1965, 5–24.

Van Alstyne, Richard W. "Woodrow Wilson and the Idea of Nation-State." *International Affairs*, 37, 1961, 293–308.

Collective Works

Allerfeldt, Kristofer, ed. *The Progressive Era in the USA: 1890–1921*. Burlington, VT: Ashgate, 2007.

Braeman, John, ed. *Wilson*. Englewood Cliffs, NJ: Prentice-Hall, 1972.

Carlier, C. and Georges-Henri Soutou, dir. *1918–1925, comment faire la paix?* Paris: Ed. Economica, 2001.

Castellan, Georges, dir. *Histoire de la Bulgarie des origines à nos jours*. Paris: Horvath, 1977.

Haines, G. K. and J. S. Walker, ed. *American Foreign Relations. A Historiographical Review*. Westport, CT: Greenwood Press, 1981.

Nash, Stephen E. and Gary M. Feinman, ed. *Curators, Collections, and Contexts: Anthropology at the Field Museum, 1893–2002*. Chicago: Fieldiana Anthropology, 2003.

Temperley, H. W. V, ed. *A History of the Peace Conference of Paris*. London: Oxford University Press, 1969 [c.1920].

Winter, Jay, dir. *America and the Armenian Genocide of 1915*. Cambridge: Cambridge University Press, 2003.

· 6 ·

CHARLES R. CRANE'S MINISTERSHIP IN CHINA: "TO PROMOTE CHINESE-AMERICAN FRIENDSHIP," 1920–1921

Crane and the Crushing of Reform by the Powers in China

As was the case with the Ottoman Empire and Central Europe, China's issues, in Crane's mind, fit into a larger battle against the imperialistic policies of the great powers. Since the Russian-Japanese War of 1905, Japan's presence in Manchuria and in the Shandong Peninsula seemed to him as an intolerable encroachment upon China's sovereignty. Though he criticized Japan disproportionately while ignoring Russia's even greater presence in Manchuria before 1905, Crane expressed his disgust at these rivalries over control of the opium trade and of the railway networks. In his inclination to side with China against Japan, he stood apart from his American peers even in progressive circles.[1]

In *Progressivism and the Open Door*, Jerry Israel presents two general views of Chinese affairs in America. Proponents of the first view, which was defended by the majority of the population, advocated cooperation with the other powers (mainly with Japan). Adherents of the second view, supported by a minority in which Israel includes Crane, sought an independent course for American policy in China that favored competition instead of cooperation. As we shall see, Crane would in fact successively endorse both strategies depending on circumstances while uncompromisingly stressing the importance of soliciting Chinese participation in the modernizing process that many Americans wished to generate in China.[2] In the months that followed the 1912 presidential election, while the Wilson Administration was still in the process of formulating its policy toward China and as Crane was gaining influence in the president's entourage, the Chinese Revolution of 1911 as well as the Boxer Rebellion of 1900 remained fresh in his mind. These social and nationalist movements had emerged in response to foreign imperialist invasion and contributed to crippling the Manchu Qing Dynasty which was then reigning over China. The West's response to the 1900 uprising, with the support of a subjugated Manchu government, was reminiscent of the crusades for some observers of the times as it constituted yet another western intrusion in Asia. Still, many worried about the violence perpetrated by these queue-wearing Chinese, and a western bias in certain narrations of the events and in their media coverage increased racial prejudice and fear of this "Yellow Peril" in Europe and in the United States[3]. It was in this singular atmosphere that Crane developed a distinctive, history-based perspective on the Chinese issue. In January of 1912—right in the middle of the Chinese Revolution and just a few days before the last emperor's abdication—Crane delivered a speech at the City Club of Chicago where he criticized (though with some moderation) the imperial forces vying for control over China:

> There is a revolution going on all over the world, and all sorts of political powers are being very carefully and very thoroughly examined. Countries governing other countries must show that they are doing this for the benefit of the governed and not for themselves. This is particularly true in Asia at the moment.

Interestingly, the excerpt suggests that in 1912, Crane still accepted, at least as a necessary evil, a certain degree of colonialism, albeit indirect colonialism like that inflicted upon the Chinese government. Crane did not go so far as to extend the Republican principle of "consent of the governed" to the Chinese, suggesting instead that they stood to "benefit" from being governed.[4]

He continued his speech by outlining what he considered to be the historical precedents of the Chinese Revolution. First, Crane resented the fact that the Taiping rebellion had been repressed with the help of Great Britain. This uprising against the Qing monarchy which had taken place between 1851 and 1864 had resulted in the creation of a vast kingdom in southeastern

China. It drew inspiration partially from Christianity's egalitarian doctrine as well as from the Protestant notion of temperance promoted in China by the missionaries. Guided by such principles, the Taiping rebels had revolted against the alcohol and opium trade (which benefited British and, to a lesser extent, American interests) while rejecting both their Manchu leaders and the western forces controlling them from the outside.[5] Crane recognized that the insurgents had rebelled primarily against the Qing government and the Manchus who "were governing then just as badly as they are governing now" and who had "not helped China at all for a century past, if they ever did." However, he also believed that through its rage at imperialism, the Taiping movement had foreshadowed and even caused the Boxer Rebellion in 1900. Britain and America's illegitimate involvement in the Chinese civil war seemed deplorable to him, and he deemed that their eagerness "to have the Tai-ping movement stopped" had indirectly led to the subsequent Boxer Rebellion, since "If that movement had been allowed to go through fifty or sixty years ago, it would not have to be gone through with again." Concerning interests in the opium trade, which was linked to the crushing of the Taiping who opposed it, Crane reacted with equal vehemence against the Anglo-American interference, calling it a "very serious matter" and "probably the most disgraceful thing that was ever done."[6] The opium wars, in this case specifically the Second Opium War lasting from 1856 to 1860 and involving the United States (to Crane's great dismay), had culminated in the defeat of the Qing. China, as a result, was forced to give Hong Kong up to Great Britain and accept the legalization of the opium trade as well as an unfair commercial treaty favoring British and American exports. The ensuing decline of the Manchu Dynasty and the impact of foreign dominion over Chinese affairs thus played a part in fuelling the Taiping and Boxer rebellions and, finally, the 1911–12 Revolution. In Crane's mind, the foreign powers' disgraceful interference in China's political evolution as well as the Protestant missionary effort in China had at least had the merit of unleashing some indigenous reformist energies which could henceforth free China from imperialist infringements. More generally, he associated China's desire for reform with the growing international wave of emancipation from colonialism. Thus, as early as 1912, well before the beginning of World War I and the formulation of Woodrow Wilson's principle of self-determination, Crane interpreted the Chinese Revolution as a prelude to the collapse of imperialism. Crane was undoubtedly observing both the development of the new republican regime in China and the effect of the Balkan Wars on world affairs and concluded that it was becoming increasingly difficult for imperialism to survive in this current of popular and national emancipation.

Wilson and China: The "Proud Position" of the Open Door

It was under such circumstances that the Wilson Administration first formulated its policy toward China. Wilson, like Crane, viewed China's struggle against foreign control in a favorable light. Soon after his inauguration, Wilson undertook to remove America from the six-power consortium involving Great Britain, France, Germany, Russia, and Japan which had been constituted in 1911 for the purpose of financing the construction of the Huguang Railroads through a 125 million dollar loan to the Chinese government. Taft had encouraged several American banks to join the consortium in 1909, but American banking interests balked and sought to withdraw from their commitment after the late admission of Russia and Japan. Only a few days after he took up his post in the White House in March of 1913, Wilson conferred with a group of American bankers to discuss and implement this retreat. Many interpreted Wilson's decision as some Machiavellian strategy to curry favor with China, but Arthur S. Link countered that this suspicion "credited Wilson with a sophistication in foreign affairs that he did not yet possess." Indeed, Link noted that "There seems [...] to have been no serious consideration by the new administration of these larger economic and strategic interests, only the moral judgment that, as the President told the Cabinet, 'we ought to help China in some better way.'"[7] Furthermore, according to Link, "the overwhelming approval of missionaries and [of] the American religious press was good evidence that Wilson and Bryan had simply voiced the revulsion all moralists felt against what seemed to be a conspiracy to control the government of China."[8] A few weeks later and without consulting his own cabinet or his foreign allies, Wilson unilaterally extended formal diplomatic recognition to the new Republic of China. Satisfied that he had succeeded in keeping out of the European powers' machinations, Wilson told his cabinet that by staying in the consortium, "we would have got nothing but mere influence in China and lost the proud position which America secured when Secretary Hay stood for the open door."[9]

Crane was jubilant over these decisions. To him, Wilson's administration had passed this first test of its foreign policy with flying colors. He promptly wrote to the president with effusive praise: "I cannot tell you how happy I am about your declaration published this morning regarding your position on our affairs in China. It is wonderfully wise and sympathetic and will do much to restore us to the old place we occupied five years ago."

By "five years ago," Crane was referring to the Roosevelt era, before Taft's request to join the banking consortium in 1909, when the United States promoted free access to the Chinese market instead of monopolistic influence over the Manchu government. Crane, like Wilson, agreed with John Hay's model of an open-door policy founded on nondiscriminatory access to markets abroad and protected from external political control. He shared Wilson's belief that the preferential loan rights granted to the banking consortium infringed on the principle of the open door and saw the whole situation as a lobby-like attempt by the creditor countries to permanently secure negotiating power in China. A few days later, Crane sent Wilson another message of encouragement, this time a short telegram about the Chinese issue, writing that "Your Chinese policy is wise, American and popular and recent changes in the [State] Department will aid you greatly in quickly righting ourselves." Changes had indeed been necessary, as Crane believed that the Taft Administration was "entirely Steel Trust." The State Department required "extensive reorganization" and Crane had advised Wilson to ensure that Bryan staffed it with men who were in complete accord with the president's vision of diplomacy and of international trade. He was visibly satisfied with the changes implemented by Wilson and felt confident in America's ability to turn a new page after its involvement with the consortium had done such a disservice to its position in China, for "At no time has the dismemberment of China proceeded so rapidly as since the formation of the Six-Power group."[10]

Interestingly enough, even a high-ranking official like Huntington Wilson, Secretary of State Bryan's assistant who had been nominated by Taft in 1909, was so shocked by Wilson's acknowledgment of China's new regime and by his decision in regard to the consortium that he angrily resigned from his post in protest. Ironically, Crane had already advised Wilson to fire this disloyal lackey and he commented humorously that the "problem" had resolved itself.[11]

Crane, therefore, saw the consortium's strategy as a foreign intrusion into Chinese affairs which would result in the "dismantlement" of China's sovereignty and unity and its division based on zones of influence by its creditors. His interpretation of the Chinese issue and his way of expressing it after the creation of the new republic matched Wilson's, who rejoiced in Crane's approval of his policy toward China.[12] Though not as explicitly critical as he would become during the war and especially during the Paris Peace Conference, Crane deplored the powers' colonial forays into China even though he, like Wilson, believed in free access to trade.

Wilson's humanitarian view of diplomacy was also apparent in his wish, when he entered the White House in 1913 and while Crane was being offered the ambassadorship in Russia (as seen in Chapter 3), to send John R. Mott to China. This choice was supported by Cleveland Dodge, Crane, and other major philanthropists in the president's entourage. Wilson had initially considered the president of Harvard University, Charles W. Eliot, another of Crane and Wilson's mutual friends. Mott, however, appeared an even finer selection considering Wilson's humanitarian approach to diplomacy. He sought to "find exceptional men, out of the common run, for all the chief posts [...] Men who will see and think," and Mott, with his close ties to social development in China through his work in the YMCA ("which is doing so much to bring about reform in China"[13]), was evidently such a man. Wilson explained the philanthropic reasoning behind his decision to his Secretary of State Bryan:

> The thing most prominent in my mind is that the men now most active in establishing a new government and a new regime for China are many of them members of the YMCA, and many of them also trained in American universities. The Christian influence, direct or indirect, is very prominently at the front and I need not say, ought to be kept there. Mr. John R. Mott, whom I know very well and who has as many of the qualities of statesman as many of my acquaintance, is very familiar with the situation in China, not only that, but he enjoys the confidence of men of the finest influence all over the Christian world.[14]

Coincidentally, Mott was already in China at that very moment on a philanthropic mission with the YMCA. Wilson hoped that he would stay there and take up the diplomatic post immediately, telling him in a telegram that "You must understand your own influence and how intimately you can tie yourself in with all the best things that are going on in the new Republic." Wilson's mind seemed to be completely set on Mott's appointment and he wrote: "I beg with all my heart that you will accept this mission which seems to me so important for China and for the world."[15]

It might seem surprising that Mott, even after such an impassioned entreaty, resisted the prestige of the post in Peking, but as he explained to his wife, he "could not fulfill serious obligations already assumed and do justice to

[the] new position."[16] Despite this refusal, Mott took an interest in America's relations with China during his stay there, namely, by pressing Wilson to recognize the Republic of China, which the president quickly accomplished.[17] Though it was ultimately unsuccessful, Wilson's plan to give Mott an ambassadorial role in China bore testimony to his conviction that China's interests were linked with those of the Christian world. The president hoped that a Christian missionary like Mott would become the official representative of the relations between the two countries. Wilson's comments and his offer of the ministerial position to Crane seven years later must consequently be analyzed in light of these first diplomatic selections.

Crane, Philanthropy, and the Advance of Democracy in China

Crane's interest in China's sovereignty and democratization manifested itself in several ways and over a long span of time. Much like what he had done in the Ottoman Empire and in the Balkans, he participated in China's social reform efforts by funding various educational causes. In 1913, for instance, he donated $50,000 for the construction of a new Harvard Medical School in Shanghai, a project developed under the leadership of Charles W. Eliot. For unknown reasons, Crane asked Eliot not to publicize this gesture in the United States.[18]

During this time, Crane also took an interest in the development of publishing and journalism in China. In a letter to Wilson written on April 8, for instance, he mentioned his contribution to the *China Press*, a daily newspaper published in Shanghai which Crane deemed "the best newspaper in the Far East." Ever keen to keep the president informed on various topics, Crane even urged him to read an article in this newspaper on current Chinese events written by a professor at the University of Chicago, Charles R. Henderson.[19] Crane also had shares in a "Sinophile" and anti-imperialist journal called *Millard's Review of the Far East* (1917–1922). Both newspapers were edited by the journalist Thomas F. Millard, with whom Crane would collaborate for many years to come. Millard, best placed to understand and express Crane's importance in the promotion of overseas publications, described him as "a firm believer in the press as a means of improving relations among nations and creating a better understanding between different races and peoples." Crane's sinological work was certainly reminiscent of his previous efforts in the field of Slavic studies and tied in with his educational activities at the University of Chicago, in the Balkans, in Constantinople, and at the Harvard Medical School of Shanghai. Millard explained that Crane "regarded the press primarily as an educational power" and that he was "especially interested in helping to develop a free and independent press conducted on American lines in the Far East." Through its tendency to foster diversity of opinion, confrontation between different viewpoints, and normative rigor in writing and presentation, formal journalism education (naturally following the American model) seemed to Crane the best way of disseminating democracy in China. He therefore offered financial assistance to many Chinese journalism students in American schools like the University of Missouri-Columbia (which hosted the Missouri School of Journalism, founded in 1908) and funded the creation of journalism schools in Chinese universities.[20]

Interested in the propagation of knowledge about Chinese culture and history, Crane also supported the Chicago Field Museum. More specifically, he financially assisted Berthold Laufer, an anthropologist and sinologist of German Jewish descent, in the publication of his encyclopedic work *Sino-Iranica*. Laufer, one of the few doctors specializing in eastern languages in the United States, acknowledged Crane's contribution to his research by promising to mention him in his book and told him that he appreciated his "kind *esprit de noblesse* and [his] devotion to the advancement of science." Knowing that Crane was in China at the time, Laufer entrusted him with a scientific "errand" of sorts and asked him to bring back several copies of books from the Tibetan library which, according to Laufer, had not yet attracted the notice of scholars in the United States.[21]

When Wilson appointed Paul Reinsch, a Progressive and a professor at the University of Wisconsin, to the post of minister to China,[22] Crane congratulated him profusely and used his rapport with Reinsch to help forge closer bonds between the two countries. Reinsch also used his relationship with Crane as well as the latter's close ties with many important American and European politicians to help his own acquaintances further their diplomatic causes. One such acquaintance was a certain Dr. Koo, about whom Reinsch wrote Crane a very complimentary letter of introduction from Peking.[23] He described Koo, who had just been named Chinese minister to Mexico, as "the ablest among younger Chinese statesmen" and hoped that Crane would put him in contact with his best political associates. Reinsch spoke highly of Koo, writing that "He has at heart the development of closer relations between our country and China."[24] He and Crane were manifestly made to get along, and

Koo even began communicating with Wilson, possibly as early as 1917, and cultivated a cordial relationship with the president, particularly during the 1919 Paris Peace Conference.

Crane Prepares Versailles: The Reality of the War and the Promises of the Fourteen Points, 1917–1919

In early 1917, Wilson's position of neutrality began to erode under the pressures created by Germany's intensified submarine warfare and by the Russian Revolution and Crane, also a partisan of neutrality, was forced to acknowledge America's impending participation in the war. China thus served to Crane as an example in his argument that national independence could act as a bulwark against imperialist expansion. In an excerpt from a letter written to Wilson and already cited in Chapter 3, Crane explained that "With Russia and China directed by their people we shall not have to concern ourselves so much about the military autocracies of Germany and Japan." Consequently, argued Crane, America ought to support their governments and maintain direct relations with these two reformist regimes.

Though Crane did not know China's leaders as well as those of Russia's Provisional Government, he urged the Wilson Administration to adopt a pro-Chinese stance right before America's entry into the war. He reasoned that "With China we must keep entirely clear of anything that gives Japan the slightest leverage for a claim to suzerainty" and affirmed that "The silent and invisible power of Chinese sympathy and solidarity is now with us and it is the greatest force in that country."[25]

Crane was still in Russia in November of 1917 after the Root Mission when, despite his arguments, the United States signed the infamous Lansing-Ishii Agreement. Cleverly playing on the fears of the United States, Viscount Ishii had told Secretary of State Lansing about repeated attempts by Germany to lure Japan away from the Allied cause. He thus succeeded in concluding an ambiguous agreement which reaffirmed Japan's adherence to the open door while also, with disconcerting duplicity, recognizing its claims over Manchuria and Shandong. Japan's dishonesty in this matter as well as in its subsequent cunning translation of the document into Chinese[26] and its dissemination in China was equaled only by the naivety of an American government anxious to secure Japan's collaboration during the Paris Peace Conference.

This secret and exclusively bilateral protocol, which inherently went against the Wilsonian principles of transparency and diplomatic nonexclusivity, was apparently first made public by the Bolshevik government. By 1918, as seen in Chapter 4, the Bolsheviks were being threatened with foreign intervention under the pretext of freeing the Czechoslovakian Legion and halting German penetration into Central Asia and Siberia. They feared that this new accord might nullify the mutual assistance treaty in case of an attack by a third party concluded between Russia and Japan in 1916. In a series of letters written to Crane in March of 1918, Thomas Millard asserted that "If the combination of conditions and circumstances exhibited by these revelations do not display secret diplomacy at its worst, I cannot conceive any." Millard candidly admitted that he was "trying by indirection to get some points to the attention of our Government" and hoped that Crane might "be able to attract attention where I would fail." Millard then added that a Siberian intervention involving Japan was not pertinent to the problem of Austro-Hungarian and German prisoners as they had only congregated west of Lake Baikal. An Allied occupation of Manchuria thus became solely a response to the spread of communism in the area rather than a means of checking German expansion in Russia. Millard argued that allowing Japanese influence to spread across China for the purpose of creating an anti-Bolshevik buffer zone would not be consistent with Wilsonian principles, writing that "If Japan is given a free hand to act in that region, China cannot but feel that her interests are not only ignored, but are distinctly threatened." The United States were thus faced with a decision, either to continue playing Japan's diplomatic game to the detriment of Chinese sovereignty or to uphold that original Wilsonian spirit which had motivated the president's withdrawal from the consortium in 1913. What is more, Millard used terms reminiscent of those employed by Wilson and Crane when they discussed the consortium in China in 1913 to connect America's dilemma with the very purpose of its involvement in the war, namely, Wilsonianism. He wrote that "America has a chance not only to restore Chinese confidence in us, but to aid the general cause which we are presumed to be at war to sustain," advocating, more precisely, that the United States finance China's military effort to occupy and defend Manchuria. Millard insisted that such a gesture would also quickly expose Japan's true motives if, as he supposed, the Japanese leaders expressed any objections. However, Millard warned that if Wilson did not select the right course, "American prestige in China and the East [would] get another serious set-back."[27]

Millard was not the only one in Crane's circle to criticize Wilson's involvement in the Lansing-Ishii Agreement, as Charles W. Eliot also mentioned his disapproval of the American government's "secrecy"[28] in a message sent to Crane while the latter was preparing his next trip to China. Crane had informed Eliot of the upcoming journey in a previous letter, explaining that his aim for such a trip was to "settle down in Peking for several months to study the social and political conditions of that part of the world." He had long dreamed of embarking on this extended voyage which was not unlike the one—mentioned in the previous chapter—which he had undertaken in the Arab world between 1909 and 1911. His deep-rooted interest in the conditions in China stemmed from the "unique social revolution, as well as [the] political one" which was taking place there, and he was eager to "study" these changes.[29]

Crane mentioned his own unease about the Lansing-Ishii Agreement to Wilson in a letter explaining the reasons for his voyage sent two weeks before his departure for Asia. Though careful with his words, Crane asked Wilson to "please remember the kind of people I shall be seeing during the next few months who will be intensely interested to know in which direction you are thinking." He also requested a special audience before his departure to discuss several topics and to record a presidential message which he could then relay to the people of China.[30] One week later, on August 27, 1918, Crane's request was granted and he dined with the president and his physician Cary T. Grayson at the White House.[31]

After a peaceful crossing of the Pacific Ocean with Paul Reinsch and several members of various charitable organizations,[32] Crane spent the last three months of 1918 in the Far East. He first travelled to Japan, then to Korea (which at the time lay under Japan's sphere of influence), and finally stayed over a month in China, his tour's primary destination. Driven by his self-imposed task of spreading the Wilsonian principle of self-determination, Crane gave many speeches in Peking and Shanghai, where he also met a few Korean nationalists right after the Armistice. He in fact received regular invitations to make public appearances in Shanghai, where he was seen as a direct representative of the American president, very much in consonance with Crane's own belief that he was carrying a message to the Chinese on the president's behalf.[33] One speech in particular, pronounced during a banquet held in his honor by the Chinese authorities and heard by the Korean nationalists, is not mentioned in either Crane's memoirs or correspondence but can be found in Korean sources.[34] It would appear that a Korean educator and activist, Yo

Unhyong, was so impressed with Crane's words about self-determination that he congratulated the philanthropist and brought up his desire for an independent Korea. According to Yo's account, the conversation helped convince Crane that the principle of self-determination could be applied to Korea and Crane even offered to defend this position in Versailles. The optimism likely inspired by Crane then led Yo Unhyong and his collaborators to write a petition pleading for Korea's independence. It described Korea's ill-treatment by Japan and asked for America's support in implementing the Fourteen Points on Korean soil. Manela reports that one copy of this petition was given to Crane and another one to Millard so that it would be sure to reach the American delegates in Versailles,[35] but history has no record of it ever reaching them and cannot confirm whether Crane even completed the task which Yo Unhyong affirmed having entrusted him with. In any event, Crane's trip to China made him known to the Korean nationalists and to the Chinese government as an ally in their quest for self-determination at the Paris Peace Conference in 1919.

The young Republic of China continued to suffer many setbacks on its quest for self-determination, however, and had to contend with numerous uprisings and local coups aiming to revive the Qing dynasty. The power in Peking struggled to support itself, and the death in 1916 of President Yuan Shikai, successor of Sun Yat-sen and a favorite in the United States, had created a political vacuum which worked to the benefit of the warlords. There began a decade of war and political instability in the midst of which Crane was contacted by Tseng-Chu-tu, a representative of Xu Shichang's presidential cabinet, to inform him of China's adherence to Wilsonian principles. Explaining that his country had regrettably not been able to take a greater part in the Allied war effort due to the internal rivalries between "the Military Leaders, who have usurped complete control in the Provinces," Tseng Chu-tu implored the Allies to be patient in regard to the consolidation of the Republic of China. At the same time, Tseng hoped that China would take on the role of "chief among the weak nations" in the postwar period, explaining that the Peking government wished to increase the country's openness to the world by abolishing extraterritorial rights and westernizing its legal system. Tseng then asked Crane, Reinsch, and the American government for advice on the position to adopt in Versailles and informed Crane that a special bureau had been created in China to compile the Conference's documents and translate all of President Wilson's speeches and addresses.[36]

Among those who admired Woodrow Wilson in China was its former president and spiritual father of the Revolution of 1911, Sun Yat-sen,[37] who had hosted Crane during his stay in Shanghai in November of 1918. Right after the Armistice, the Chinese revolutionary sent Wilson a telegram, which he mentioned in a message to Crane, commenting on the events in China and detailing his aspirations. In this telegram, he admitted his initial reluctance to follow Wilson's call to arms against Germany out of fear of the military opportunism that might ensue (his concerns were in fact confirmed in the months that followed China's entry into the war, and the Manchu monarchy was even briefly restored that same year). Sun also corrected a simplistic western interpretation of the civil war brought on by this era of warlords as a struggle between the North (fighting for a Manchu revival) and the southern militaries. He instead framed this conflict to Wilson as a confrontation between military forces of another era, primarily Manchu, and modern, pro-democratic revolutionary forces stationed in the south. What Sun Yat-sen asked of Wilson, in short, was for the president to make use of his "bully pulpit" in Versailles to recognize, as he had in 1913, the parliament dissolved by Yuan Shikai and which Sun was striving to reinstate.[38] Wilson, for his part, seemed wary of Sun, who had been repudiated by the Peking government. On the same day he received the telegram, he confided to Lansing that he preferred not to communicate directly with Sun Yat-sen even though he had "sometimes sympathized with his professed principles and objects."[39] Even in 1913, Wilson had not trusted Sun, to whom he had at the time preferred Yuan Shikai, due to Sun's compromised principles in his dealings with various warlords from Canton in an attempt to regain the upper hand in the revolution and bring to fruition his federative and nationalistic ideals.[40] Yuan eventually turned out to be as much a disappointment for America as Sun had been, but Wilson never lost his sympathy for China's struggle for sovereignty in the face of both the collaborative and the competitive imperialistic efforts of the foreign powers.

Crane, for his part, continued gathering documentation about the Chinese situation until the end of 1918. He received, among other testimonies, a letter written by Li-Chun-huang, a representative of the warlord Tang Jiyao, containing an (inherently biased due to its author's political affiliations) analysis of the political forces at play. Li-Chun-huang's constitutional viewpoint was also shared by the southern generals associated with Sun Yat-sen, and he promoted democratic goals while affirming the sustainability of the revolution. He argued that "the South is fighting for democracy and justice. The militarism of the North is menacing China's newly won Democracy." Seeking Wilson's support, he used Wilsonian rhetoric to defend the Chinese cause:

> Under the leadership of President Wilson America fought because she wanted to "make the world safe for democracy". We are fighting because we want to make China safe for Democracy. And therefore we are but following the lead of America.

With this wording, Li-Chun-huang was attempting to endow China's cause with the same kind of moral legitimacy Wilson had conferred to the Allied cause by elevating it to the level of a struggle for the development of democracy and self-determination. After congratulating Wilson on his victory in combat against militarism and brutality, Li added: "We ask your Great President to use his good office in upholding our cause." This compliment was intended directly for Wilson, since Li asked Crane to send the president a copy of the document along with an expression of China's admiration.[41] The *Wilson Papers*, however, bear no evidence that this letter ever reached Wilson or that Crane relayed it to the president directly. What we do know is that Wilson was sympathetic to the cause of Chinese sovereignty as it presented itself in the months following the Armistice.

After his return to the United States, Crane's work in China was praised by a missionary from the YMCA, Eugene E. Barnett, who was greatly impressed with China's response to Wilsonianism:

> Your visit in Hangchow has left a permanent impression. It was superlatively worthwhile from the standpoint of increasing the feeling of good will toward America which exists among the Chinese here. The hold President Wilson has on the imagination and the confidence of the people is remarkable; he is quoted as though he were a veritable modern Confucius.

An overconfident Barnett even claimed that Wilsonianism was destined for success, barring of course a "complete collapse of his whole program" which to Barnett seemed "unthinkable." This optimism was in fact shared by most Americans on the eve of the Paris Peace Conference. Barnett also added—with more realism this time—that if Wilson succeeded in implementing even half of his program, all international relations would be lastingly transformed. This proved to be a reassuring thought given his fear that the Chinese "might pin extravagant hopes on America and on President Wilson in connection with the Paris Peace Conference," a tendency which he had observed both among the Chinese and among Americans living in China while he himself was working there.[42] Once again, it seems that philanthropists and missionaries like Crane and Barnett staunchly believed that America was the object of universal admiration.

China at Versailles: Wilson, Koo, and the Denial of the Fourteen Points

Crane did not speak much of the Chinese question during the Paris Peace Conference as his attention was fully devoted to the Ottoman issue and to the commission he would be leading in the Middle East. Yet the relationship Wellington Koo (who was Paul Reinsch's and indirectly Crane's protégé) forged with the American delegates and with President Wilson became particularly cordial even though China ultimately benefited least among the Allied nations from the settlements in Versailles. Had Crane interfered on behalf of China, the country might have been spared such a disadvantageous outcome, but Japan's weight in the strategic balance of the Versailles settlements sufficed to drive China out of the treaty. However, emboldened by Wilson's undeniable sympathy, Koo and the Chinese delegation had legitimate reasons to hope for concrete results in favor of their national objectives during the Paris Peace Conference.

Shortly before the American delegations departure for Paris on November 26, 1918, Koo was granted a fifteen-minute interview with Wilson during which he hastened to express China's hopes that the president would make himself the defender of Chinese sovereignty in Paris. Koo reported that "He [Wilson] had always felt sympathy for China and was interested in the problems of the Far East, for in his opinion peace was more likely to be endangered there than in other parts of the world," and that "He agreed with me that the ideals of China and the United States were along the same lines and said he would gladly do his best to support China at the Paris Peace Conference." Curiously, Wilson mentioned the secret treaties (the latest of which had been concluded by Wilson's own administration) of his own accord, saying that they were "injurious to China" in regard to its fate in Versailles.[43] Wilson and Koo only indirectly alluded to the Lansing-Ishii Agreement during their meeting, however. Caution most likely prevented Koo from discussing it further, more so because Wilson seemed to interpret the agreement as recognition of Chinese sovereignty. In spite of this, their conversation allowed Koo to leave for Paris with the conviction that he had a sizeable ally at his side.[44]

Doctor Cary T. Grayson's personal diary offers a distinctive insight into Wilson's position on China during the opening sessions of the Council of Ten in January of 1919. Grayson's explanation accurately reflected the report on the January 28 conference, but the doctor also added that the president "Naturally [...] sympathized with the Chinese viewpoint." According to Grayson, Wilson "found himself in an absolute minority" when he opposed the Allies' idea of redistributing the Shandong colonies taken from Germany primarily to Japan and then having the decision ratified by the League of Nations. During the January 28 conference, Makino, Japan's representative, cited a prior agreement concluded between his government and China about an assumed retrocession of the Kiaochow (Jiaozhou) Bay on the southern coast of the Shandong Peninsula once the area was rid of its German occupants. When Wilson demanded evidence of this secret agreement, Koo readily agreed to provide the necessary documents. Makino, on the other hand, attempted to stall and claimed that he had to run the request by his government owing to the fact that the Japanese had already established a foothold in Shandong by conquest and believed they had the right to wait for Germany's official cession of the lease to them. Wilson sharply retorted that all German possessions were under review and that Germany would play no part in the process, thereby invalidating Makino's hesitation to display evidence of the presumed agreement before the Council of Ten.[45] It seemed, in short, that Japan sought to be given rights over Jiaozhou and the whole Shandong Peninsula by Germany, claiming that it then had every intention of returning this territory to China. Neither the Chinese nor the American delegations were fooled, and Wilson's retort implied that, if Japan truly intended to hold up its end of the bargain, it would not need permission from Germany to do so.

The Japanese were not pleased with Koo's readiness to show the Council of Ten documents pertaining to the "agreement." Shortly after these events, Lansing warned the president that the Japanese government was attempting to intimidate the Chinese government into pulling Koo out of Versailles. Lansing had received this information in a confidential telegram sent by his assistant Frank L. Polk, a member of the American Commission to Negotiate Peace. Polk specified that the agreement centered on control over the Tsingtao (Qingdao) railway and the transfer of Germany's rights to the Japanese, but that nothing had been ratified by the Japanese government. Perhaps this explained why Koo had no scruples about exhibiting the requested "proof," thereby revealing Japan's devious strategy.[46] In addition to unequivocally defending Koo and the Chinese government, Wilson acknowledged

Japan's attempts to intimidate the Chinese government. He charged Reinsch with the task of advising the government in Peking to stand firm in the face of Japan's influence and manipulation. Wilson also asked the ambassador to Japan Roland S. Morris to intervene in Tokyo and "have a friendly conversation with the Minister of Foreign Affairs about this matter and disclose our knowledge of what is going on in Peking." As for Koo, Wilson suggested that he act freely and "follow the course that he thinks right."[47] Japan's schemes clearly chagrined Wilson as they demonstrated the country's "unwillingness to trust the fairness and justness of the Peace Conference," and that very day, Lansing sent the president's instructions out to all concerned parties.[48]

During a private meeting with the Chinese delegates on March 24, 1919, Wilson shared with Koo that he did not consider Shandong, and more precisely the Bay of Jiaozhou, to be a German colony like those in Africa and in the South Pacific. Instead, the Bay of Jiaozhou was a concession granted by China, and China ultimately held real and final rights over the region. Both Wilson and Koo suspected that, in demanding Germany's cession of the area to Japan, the Japanese were striving to maintain control over the railways and hoped to lay down conditions such as the establishment of a Japanese enclave before returning the territory to China. Such an arrangement, according to Wilson and Koo, would be no better than the iniquitous position of the British in Hong Kong: an empire within an empire. Koo also took this opportunity to explain the importance of the railroad crossing the peninsula and connecting it to Peking in the matter of China's sovereignty. Following this discussion, Wilson professed having a very clear understanding of the situation in Shandong and cordially concluded the meeting.[49]

Just over two weeks later, Koo sent Wilson a memorandum covering the issues discussed on March 24, this time displaying concern about the direction taken by the Conference in regard to the Shandong case. The memo's aim was to encourage Wilson to use his full influence in the Council of Four, which had now replaced the Council of Ten, in order to hasten the matter's resolution. The copy of Koo's message included in the *Wilson Papers* shows passages underlined by Wilson himself which corresponded to the topics they had already discussed. Koo deplored the fact that "that denial of China's claim would jeopardize her political independence, territorial integrity and economic welfare." Knowing how important the open door policy was for the United States and, to a lesser extent, for Great Britain and other foreign powers, Koo pointed out that such a settlement would work against the interests of commercial powers in China. The Shandong peninsula, explained

Koo, was one of the country's best strategic and economic crossroads. Whoever controlled Shandong also controlled the capital as well as all of northern China. What is more, observed Wilson, the Japanese were attempting to claim for themselves and exclude from an eventual retrocession those very regions which conveniently proved to be the most profitable. The Chinese government consequently demanded that the Conference reject this plan of indirect restitution and dismissed Japan's Twenty-One Demands (a set of conditions formulated as of 1915) due to the climate of instability and internal rivalry reigning in China. Attempting to bind China to its previous illegitimate commitments in this context amounted to depriving it of control over its foreign policy and went directly against the principles of the Fourteen Points endorsed by the Allies, though it must be noted that France, Italy, and Great Britain still supported Japan in its objectives.[50]

In addition to these memos, Koo produced a detailed eighty-seven-page description of Germany and Japan's occupation of Shandong between 1898 and 1918. In this longer and better-documented iteration of the ideas he had shared with Wilson previously, Koo once again pleaded for the direct restitution of the peninsula to China. Despite the repetition, Wilson received the document and arranged a second private meeting with Koo on April 17, 1919 to discuss its contents.[51]

Wilson continued his defense of the Chinese position before Clemenceau, George, and Orlando at the meeting of the Council of Four on April 22. Yet in the presence of Koo, who also made a temporary appearance, Wilson admitted that, unlike agreements made with the defeated countries, China's acceptance of the Twenty-One Demands (under the threat of an ultimatum, argued Koo) which bound it to Japan could not be withdrawn after the war. In theory, both China and Japan were in league with the Allies—though as Japan took pleasure in remarking, China's participation in the war effort had been negligible and hardly earned it a place at the negotiating table with the other victorious nations. To resolve this impasse and restore China's sovereignty despite its previous ties with Japan, Wilson appealed to Japan's goodwill rather than dictating terms. He proposed that all countries at the Conference renounce their privileges in China so as not to encroach on the nation's right to self-determination. His choice of such a delicate approach stemmed from an understanding that Japan's cooperation was just as vital as China's in forging sustainable world peace. The minutes of the council meeting confirm that "[President Wilson] had emphasized the great need of trust and friendship between Japan and China, which he regarded as essential to peace in the Far

East," and that he was "above all concerned not to create a chasm between the East and the West." Good relations had to be maintained with Japan even at the cost of disappointing its more vulnerable neighbor.

Though very critical of Japan's underhanded imperialist maneuvers, Koo was more amenable to other proposals put forward by the Japanese delegation. For instance, he approved of Japan's motion to have the notion of equality of nations written into the text of the League of Nations Covenant.[52] On the other hand, he was wary of Wilson's demand that the recognition of the Monroe Doctrine also be included in the Covenant. The proposed wording, reminiscent of the spheres of interest mentality, described the Monroe Doctrine as a "regional understanding [...] for securing the maintenance of peace."[53] Koo's worry naturally lay in the potential for generalization of this doctrine, which would confer undue legitimacy upon Japan's interference in China. While the independence of China's positions suggests that Koo had made himself the advocate of China's cooperation with both Japan and the West, he also strove to warn the Allies that it would be dangerous to neglect China's rights. Recognizing that some groups in China favored the establishment of closer ties with Japan, Koo explained that the Chinese government "believed in the justice of the West and [that] their future lay there," and insinuated that "If they failed to get justice there, the consequential re-action might be very great."[54] Though he did not know it yet, Koo's statement prophesied the coming of the May Fourth Movement in China, which will be examined later in this chapter.

Lu Tseng-Tsiang, the head of the Chinese delegation, proposed a compromise in response to Japan's aggressive negotiation. He asked that Japan return the occupied territories to China no later than a year after the signing of the treaty. In exchange, China would provide monetary compensation as a reward for Japan's victory over the Germans in Qingdao and would agree to open Jiaozhou Bay to international trade.[55]

Wilson, for his part, found himself in a rather awkward position. On the one hand, he had supported China's demands and had become friendly with Wellington Koo. Historian and member of the ACNP Ray Stannard Baker in fact indicated in his diary that "There is no possible doubt as to where the President's sympathies lie: he is for the Chinese." On the other hand, Wilson acknowledged the importance of not losing Japan's approval. When Baker insisted that China was favored by the whole world, Wilson replied that he could easily decide for the Chinese and go home, yet it would only win him temporary popularity before the storm broke. With Italy already out,[56] it would be calamitous if Japan also chose to withdraw from the treaty. Therefore, after making the strongest case he could for the Chinese cause, Wilson had no choice but to adopt the Allied stance on enforcing previous treaties while hoping that Japan would act in good faith and restore China's sovereign rights over Shandong. Despite Wilson's ability to approach the issue rationally, Baker observed that the Japanese-Chinese question troubled the president considerably.[57]

Wilson had had to choose the lesser of two evils, and he was comforted in this choice by none other than House. Regarding the Conference's new pro-Japanese mindset, House admitted that while the situation was "all bad," they had best "clean up a lot of old rubbish with the least amount of friction, and let the League of Nations and the new era do the rest." He had such faith in this "new era" that he believed in the potential of an emerging public opinion forged by Wilsonian rhetoric to "push" powers like France, Great Britain, and Japan out of China. House's perspective was based primarily on Britain's opinion as expressed by Lord Balfour, who had confidence in Japan's good faith in its dealings with China. Balfour believed that Japan would limit itself to only keeping the economic benefits connected with its enclave in the port of Jiaozhou and with Qingdao's railway network while handing the rest of the peninsula over to China.[58] Of course, such an arrangement completely contradicted the American delegation's original attitude toward the issue and butchered Chinese sovereignty to satisfy Japan's demands. Britain's stance was also fuelled more by its diplomatic interest in securing Japan's assistance with other matters than by true faith in Japan's commitment to self-determination.[59]

The following day, Koo sent Wilson a personal message reminding the president with some urgency that the Twenty-One Demands had been forced on China by means of an ultimatum coupled with threats of invasion. The decision to repeal them now lay in the Conference's hands. Koo also reminded Wilson of Lu Tseng-Tsiang's proposed compromise sent on April 24 and argued that China's declaration of war against Germany in 1917 signified that China now deserved to have its concessions returned without Japan's involvement following the Allied victory.[60]

Unfortunately for Koo, no response came from Wilson, whose health had sharply declined on the morning of April 28. "The President is tired & looks worn," described Ray S. Baker after seeing him the following day. Having spent the month already weakened by what was diagnosed as a possible case of influenza but which, according to Edwin Weinstein, turned out to be encephalitis, Wilson had also suffered multiple aneurysms since 1906, which had been treated only more or less adequately. This combined with his high blood pressure in Versailles led to various complications and to a major stroke that left him incapacitated and prevented him from defending the Treaty in the United States.[61]

After spending a restless night with his mind "so full of the Japanese-Chinese controversy," as he told Doctor Grayson, Wilson attended the decisive conference of the Council of Four (now whittled down to three after Orlando's departure) on April 30.[62] There, the "Holy Trinity" (as Lansing liked to call them) decided entirely in favor of Japan without even mentioning Japan's promise to eventually return the Shandong Peninsula to China.[63]

Koo had warned the Americans about China's reaction to such a disappointment, and his predictions were quickly confirmed once news of the draft treaty put together by the Council reached China. The May Fourth Movement, led primarily by students and intellectuals, emerged in protest of the unilateral cession of Shandong to the Japanese and expressed the population's disillusionment with Wilsonianism,[64] which had been the source of high hopes particularly following Crane's fervent promotion of its tenets in 1918.

A message from the State Department sent on May 4 but which only reached Wilson four days later informed the president of the uprisings in China. It reported a student attack in Peking on the Chinese ambassador to Japan as well as the burning down of several houses around Peking, Shandong, and Shanghai. Robert Lansing asked that Wilson, as a figure of authority, address the issue in a formal message to the Chinese population and explain the reasons behind such a humiliating settlement in Versailles to the uncomprehending masses. He suspected that the May Fourth Movement might escalate into a full blown civil war and perhaps even result in a coup d'état.[65]

Koo and the other Chinese delegates, for their part, protested against the unfavorable settlement by refusing to ratify the Treaty of Versailles, which had effectively betrayed them. Despite their disappointment, they approached Clemenceau, the president of the Conference, and offered to sign the treaty with some reservations, hoping namely to reaffirm Lu Tseng-Tsiang's aforementioned compromise. Unsurprisingly, Clemenceau declared that reservations were inadmissible but that he would accept a declaration after the signing of the treaty, which the Chinese delegates deemed unacceptable. Koo turned once more to Wilson, his sincerest and perhaps only ally, beseeching him to "exercise [his] friendly influence with a view to enabling the Chinese Delegates to sign the treaty without sacrificing their sense of national honor and pride."[66] Receiving no response, Koo and his fellow delegates finally refused to sign the Treaty of Versailles, which was ratified on June 29, 1919.[67]

Afterward, Wellington Koo regained his post as China's minister to the United States while Crane, in an interesting reversal, became the United States minister to China. Despite their identical positions, they do not seem to have continued their correspondence. Yet this episode and the part Wilson played in the failure of China's program in Versailles help to set the context of Crane's first appearance as an official emissary of the Wilson Administration.

Crane and Humanitarian Diplomacy: Ministership in China, 1920–1921

It was thus in the wake of China's national humiliation in Versailles that Crane was appointed minister plenipotentiary in Peking by Wilson. Leo Bocage's thesis already covers the entirety of Crane's term as minister there, but a few central characteristics of Crane's work and diplomatic outlook seem to have escaped the notice of historians like Bocage, Hapgood, Sulzbach, and Saul. In the following pages, we will attempt to bring to light the lesser-known aspects and context of Crane's term in China and their relevance within the larger framework of his previous thoughts and accomplishments.

After the signing of the Treaty of Versailles and before Crane was appointed minister to China, Wilson's physical and mental state drastically deteriorated, particularly as a result of his western tour during which he suffered a severe aneurysm. Given the distance that had grown between him and House, his closest advisor, it was his wife Edith Bolling Wilson who—in a manner of speaking—took the reins after the Paris Peace Conference. Wilson was now only president *de jure* and Crane advised Edith to choose as her right-hand man the Secretary of Agriculture David F. Houston, whose "loyalty, wisdom and experience" Crane deemed "unquestionably supreme."[68] As part of a greater reorganization of the Wilson Administration in its last months, Houston was moved from Agriculture to the Treasury so that he could take on greater responsibilities and place "his great wisdom, experience and loyalty [...] more conspicuously at the disposal of the President."[69]

Paul S. Reinsch having tendered his resignation as minister in response to the disappointing outcome of the Shandong issue,[70] a diplomatic post was now open in China. To fill it, Edith followed an order issued by Wilson himself and asked Robert Lansing, on January 19, 1920, to appoint Crane, "whose familiarity with oriental affairs is unrivaled and whose experience in dealing with oriental questions qualifies him as no one else is qualified." Lansing confirmed this selection several days later and assumed that Wilson had already reached out to Crane about this matter.[71] Crane had indeed been invited to dine at the White House at the beginning of February with Edith, McAdoo and his wife Eleanor (the president's daughter), and Doctor Grayson, who remarked to Crane that Wilson often asked about him. The dinner was followed by a discussion of various government affairs and then, with Grayson's approval, Crane paid a short visit to Wilson[72] during which one can suppose that the two men talked in a preliminary manner about Crane's upcoming work in China. Crane received his formal directives from Wilson right before his departure for Peking in April of 1920, perhaps even resolving that his diplomatic aim there would be "to promote Chinese-American friendship" (as recorded by his personal secretary Donald M. Brodie) during that encounter.[73] This nomination, understood by Crane as being based on humanitarian considerations, is reminiscent of Wilson's previous attempted appointment of Mott in 1913 which also seemed to be informed by philanthropic concerns and was in keeping with his desire to foster closer ties between the peoples of the world. Confused at first by this nomination and even doubtful given the opposition of several Republican members of congress back in 1909, Crane was somewhat heartened by his conversation with the president. Thankful but by no means jubilant, Crane offered his house in Woods Hole, Massachusetts as a summer home for the use of the presidential couple during his absence.[74]

Crane's discussion with Wilson at the end of April about the diplomatic appointment lasted approximately an hour. Afterward, he made a detailed account of the meeting to his friend Charles W. Eliot during his stay in San Francisco before the impending departure for Peking. Crane's impressions of the president's health were favorable compared to his previous assessments, and he reported being "quite amazed at the extent and accuracy of his understanding of the processes of the Far East," adding that "the President's mind is working perfectly well." Above all, Crane rejoiced in the contrast between his present appointment and the prematurely terminated mission in 1909, especially in terms of Wilson's outlook on diplomacy which coincided with his own. "I am going to my post with a great deal of satisfaction about this harmony in ideals and methods," he announced, mentioning also that conversely, "Secretary of State Knox had no kind of sympathy with altruistic politics." These comments effectively summarized his understanding of Wilsonian diplomacy and by extension of his own "altruistic politics," which is the subject of this book's analysis.

To familiarize Crane with the ins and outs of the Chinese issue in the wake of the Versailles Treaty, Wilson turned to the minutes of the Council in Paris to expose the "maneuvers of the Japanese delegates." Obviously annoyed with Japan's diplomacy in Paris, Crane, who had devoted little attention to the Shandong issue during the Conference, received from Wilson a strong warning against Japanese imperialism. Though sometimes hard to separate from Crane's own opinions, Wilson's statements as reported in a letter from Crane to Eliot were in keeping with the ideas he had already expressed during the Council meetings (both Council of Ten and Council of Four) in 1919. With Europe weakened by the war, the Japanese were now, according to Wilson, "staking out a vast empire," and "while assenting verbally to the doctrines of the open door," they had "not the slightest idea of applying it." By framing the situation in this manner, Wilson seemed to suggest that Crane's task as minister to China would be to win back the country's gratitude and friendship, a conclusion Crane had already come to during their previous meeting in April of 1920 in resolving "to promote Chinese-American friendship."

Crane did not harbor much optimism about the world's potential for peace, confessing that he was "leaving the country in a good deal of dismay over the political situation." His thoughts on the 1920 presidential campaign were equally bleak, for "no man [seemed] to stand out who [had] the necessary qualifications."[75] Crane did not fear the Democratic Party's defeat, however, asserting that "history is with us." Victory did not seem so impossible when, according to Crane, ordinary people understood and liked Wilsonian principles and approved of the president's achievements, chiefly that of "freeing the government in general and the treasury in particular from the control of Wall Street." According to Crane, the Democratic Party under Wilson had also made itself the party of morality, of effective tariff policies, and of business and entrepreneurship, thus successfully appropriating three of the Republican Party's greatest traits.[76]

In any case, Crane seemed to find new purpose in the ministerial position after his discussions with Wilson. Just like Wilson, Crane approached his upcoming work with a humanitarian mindset and a growing enthusiasm replaced his initial confusion on the eve of his departure. In San Francisco, Crane held a farewell banquet attended among others by a Chinese delegation (most likely from California). In a farewell telegram to Wilson, he also expressed his hope of meeting with the American ambassador to Japan,

Roland S. Morris, in order to "get the keys of the situation in the East" before taking office in Peking.[77]

Arriving in Shanghai on May 19, 1920 after a peaceful crossing on the SS *Nanking* and some sightseeing, Charles and Cornelia Crane were warmly welcomed by the local American "colony," by several members of the YMCA, and by a few Chinese friends. They settled in Peking in the American minister's quarters and Crane happily took to "shepperding" his American flock composed of missionaries, teachers, merchants, and correspondents.[78]

Even though he was stationed in China, Crane admitted that he was "glad to have a few friends in Japan who know that my chief concern in accepting the new post out here is to have peace, real peace in the Pacific (!)" and added that he believed this to also be "the sincere wish of President Wilson." In regard to his very public criticism of Japan over the years, Crane explained that "that does not at all mean I am anti-Japanese." After all, he had also criticized Great Britain's politics and yet never been an enemy of the British.[79]

Crane certainly had his own way of going about his duties in Peking. When Wilson named him minister plenipotentiary and head of American diplomacy in China, Crane warned the president that he would take on the position for a year at most. He also made the rather unusual decision of using the library rather than the minister's office for his work. What is more, Donald M. Brodie, who had accompanied him in the Middle East in 1919, wrote that "He also told the Legation secretaries that he did not intend to be concerned with the routine details." Crane evidently preferred to delegate the regular task of relaying intelligence incumbent upon the chief minister to his legation officers and secretaries, devoting himself instead to "cultivating the acquaintance and friendship of government leaders, army and navy officials, business men, educators, missionaries, students, craftmen, etc." Brodie reported that "He visited all kinds of institutions […] frequently making simple little talks,"[80] and this diplomatic style earned Crane an exaggerated reputation as a nonconformist, even a dilettante, in the exercise of his diplomatic duties.[81]

Well aware of Wilson's physical condition and hoping to spare the president as much work and worry as possible, Crane reported his first impressions about the state of affairs in China to the new Secretary of Treasury David F. Houston in a message written three months or so after his arrival. Crane's views had changed since the time of the Russian Revolution, and he wrote regarding the radicalism in China that he had "never been enthusiastic about revolutions as a mode of progress" and that "even in the mild form that it exists in China it is not working very well." Despite what many believed about him, Crane took no pleasure in fostering rebellions around the world[82] unless they served to strengthen local liberal democratic movements. And even so, Crane preferred to promote social, scientific, and technical development as a means of encouraging self-determination rather than financing one faction or the other in a reformist movement, especially in China, where the "progressivism" of the central government and of the various factions struggling for control remained hard to ascertain. He had in fact tried to remedy this situation in part through his previous initiatives to develop journalism in China. Having inherited a strong entrepreneurial tradition from his father, Crane believed that fostering a free enterprise culture in China constituted a first and fundamental step toward a prosperous, peaceful, and democratic society. All of his prior work in China was in keeping with this objective to "represent the latest and best practice in American business methods." His work there would also serve to help put an end to the harm inflicted on China by other countries, and he declared that "It is not going to make any country popular that menaces the integrity of China, corrupts her officials or poisons her people."[83] He wrote to Houston that "We have a great role to play here; it is all perfectly clear; it is a role that we can play, and a role that is entirely American and cannot be counterfeited by any other nation." This role was essentially philanthropic and centered on a progressive approach to civilizing the Chinese population. Crane believed that "American science and engineering can do much to lift the fearful burden pressing down on the Chinese people; American medicine can do much to diminish the suffering; and the American educators and missionaries can do much to brighten their spirit."[84]

Crane was soon forced to once again face the reality of a revolutionary China. A coup was staged by Duan Qirui in July of 1920 and Crane blamed the Japanese who he believed had instigated this failed and rather "amateurish" rebellion, considering it further evidence of "the weakness of [Japan's] policies toward China." By contrast, he thought that "The methods and lives of our missionaries, of our businessmen, and of our educational and medical men, as well as the consistently sympathetic attitude of our legation, have won the hearts and secured the confidence of the Chinese people." Hard though it may be to determine the accuracy of this statement, Crane's reports to the State Department provided ample documentation on the context of the civil war in China. The conflict lay between the Zhili faction led by General Zhang Zuolin and the pro-Japanese Anhui faction (with the Anfu Club as its military branch) led by Duan Qirui, who was supported by the dissident Canton government.[85] Crane, as demonstrated by his previous comments about the ineffectiveness of revolutions, saw the situation with pessimism. In keeping with his orientalist and "bourgeois" mindset, he regretted the destruction of Peking's architectural heritage through something "so unladylike as dropping bombs on so fine an old city."[86] This characteristic reaction did not, however, prevent him from also considering the humanitarian and social consequences of the civil war. In fact, Crane personally played a part in the relaying of information as shown by the reports he sent to the State Department throughout the civil war and up until his departure from China in July of 1921. More involved in his administrative duties than he had hoped to be, Crane even complained on several occasions about the weight of the task at hand and how much this ministership differed from his usual leisurely travels.[87]

Despite these complaints, Crane made his greatest contribution in China precisely in the humanitarian domain, which had always been central to his career, and all other aspects of his work stemmed from this involvement in philanthropy. Interestingly, this humanitarian work was carried out in response to a completely unexpected event at the beginning of Crane's ministership—the great North China famine of 1920 which put significant social and economic strain on the population.[88] Judging the situation to be grave enough that Wilson ought to be informed, Crane sent the president a long telegram about the crisis and the humanitarian aid he proposed. The famine, of historic proportions due to its extent and severity, affected no less than five provinces and was the worst of its kind in forty years. Striving to emphasize that it was not a result of China's moral decadence, Crane insisted that the "region is almost oldest human settlement" and that "Industrious people for several thousand years worked out satisfactory social system lasting longest, peaceful, unmilitary, multiplying fruits of earth, making family life altar happiness. To it we owe tea, porcelain, silk."

The famine was primarily caused by the regions climate and geography. Periodic floods inundated the Yellow River plain and the last one had struck three years prior, decimating food reserves despite local drainage techniques. Furthermore, floods were generally followed by periods of drought, and insufficient rainfall in the years following the last flood had thus culminated in "total crop failure" in 1920.[89] Many of Crane's American colleagues, however, considered relief efforts futile in the face of this cyclical natural phenomenon. "[O]f course it is a great famine," they responded, "but you haven't been out here long; you don't know much about China." They advised Crane that "This is the sort of thing that goes on all of the time and people are used to it; leave it alone and the thing will take care of itself." To those who claimed that fundraisers in the United States would not be as successful as they had been before the war, Crane replied that he could not imagine that American society would turn its back on a good cause.[90]

Curiously, it was not Crane but rather Graham Patterson of the *Christian Herald* and Thomas W. Lamont of J.P. Morgan & Co. who asked for Wilson's direct involvement in the matter. In November of 1920, Patterson requested that Wilson, who had already been informed of the food shortages in China by Crane, pronounce a few words of encouragement for the Chinese cause and personally select a few members for a national famine relief committee. Though declining to participate in the selection process due to his poor health, Wilson promised to nominate whoever was suggested to him and affirmed that "the attempts you are making to raise funds for the relief of the distress in China has my most hearty approval and applause [...] I hope with all my heart that it may be successful in every way."[91] Another letter was sent to the president by Lamont asking that he publicly declare his allegiance to the famine relief movement and urging him to call for the American population's involvement. Patterson had made a similar call for contributions in the *Christian Herald*, and his appeal risked being "greatly handicapped" if it was not supported by the president. Lamont also attempted to convince Wilson to select members for the future relief committee, but finally resigned himself to sending him a list of 128 suggested names. Wilson then sent out invitations to all the people listed. Patterson and Lamont did, however, succeed in getting Wilson to make a public declaration, and Lamont proposed a text which Wilson ended up repeating almost word for word.[92]

Wilson's declaration was published on December 9, 1920. It described the legation's role in reporting information about the famine and explained to the American public that neither China's government nor its humanitarian agencies were equipped to deal with a crisis of such magnitude. Though aware that America's philanthropic resources had already been spread quite thin by the war, Wilson described China's cause as "especially worthy." The United States had already showed China, through its previous missionary, educational, and philanthropic work, that it could act as a strong pillar of support, and had consequently earned the Chinese peoples' gratitude and devotion. In the name of this friendship, Wilson called on America to mobilize once again. To better manage the donations, he appointed Lamont director of the committee and chose as its treasurer the Under (and then Acting) Secretary of State Norman H. Davis.[93]

Lamont himself admitted that the public's response to Wilson's call for help was modest, and he strove to find other ways to raise funds for the relief effort in China. His suggestion was to tap into some of the Department of Agriculture's unused funds as part of the Food Administration and donate them to the China Famine Relief National Committee. This plan was rejected by Secretary of the Treasury Houston, and Wilson candidly explained to Lamont that he had searched for such an "available" sum to no avail.[94] Lamont persisted, this time proposing to use other "dormant" funds in the Department of Treasury under the auspices of the United War Work Committee. Unfortunately for him, this idea was also vetoed, this time by Raymond Blaine Fosdick, former member of the provisional committee of the League of Nations and a philanthropist associated with Wilson's government. Wilson, following Fosdick's advice, was once again forced to disappoint Lamont, especially since he now found that Congress was "ready to treat everything [the president suggested] with something less than consideration."[95] Despite this, Wilson constantly supported Lamont in his humanitarian activities and congratulated him profusely even after the end of his presidency.[96]

Though Crane had been the first to bring the famine in China to Wilson's attention, he was not the first American to launch a plan of assistance for its victims. Indeed, an organized response to the catastrophe in northern China had already been initiated by the Peking chapter of the American Red Cross. However, as noted by John Earl Baker in a Red Cross report on famine relief from 1920 to 1921, Crane was the first to suggest cooperation between the various international humanitarian efforts and pushed to centralize their oversight. He also involved the American government and the other legations in China in this collaborative effort. Crane's intervention allowed the Red Cross to then take charge of the operations in the field, which had been made possible by what had now become a whole movement and "inaugurated a campaign." Baker explained that "Mr. Crane's idea for an International organization was accepted by other Legations and an International Foreign Committee was formed." Crane also reached out to the State Department, which in turn charged a certain Emmet W. White, director of foreign missions for the American Red Cross, with conducting further investigations into China's situation. He was also told to appoint Baker manager of the relief program, and the State Department requested a donation of 500,000 gold dollars from the Red Cross. According to Baker, Crane's involvement had been essential since "This cable and gift of five hundred thousand dollars were the result of representations made to Washington by the American Minister."[97]

By writing to its president H. P. Davison, Crane thus helped convince the Red Cross in New York to intervene in China. He sent two telegrams, the second being the one mentioned by Baker in which Crane suggested that the Red Cross take "full charge of [its] own expenditures" by way of a $500,000 donation spread over a span of ten months in $50,000 installments, all of this under Baker's personal oversight.[98] In his first telegram, Crane praised the remarkable cooperation between locals and foreign communities in China as a result of humanitarian efforts there, affirming that "All disputes are dropped." He argued that "The movement should be promptly and generously encouraged as it is the most hopeful sign of internal and international peace out here and through it we must try to work into a new spirit." The famine relief efforts he promoted so assiduously in China thus seemed to be a direct application of his often expressed view of international philanthropy and Christian charity as the basis for new relations between countries. At the very least, this seemed to be Crane's way of understanding the mission he had undertaken. Crane also described the more technical details of the work done in China. It had finally rained over the drought-ridden region in the fall and seeds had to be bought in sufficient quantities to ensure a plentiful harvest for the following year, especially given the risk of a snowless winter and of a dry spring. Furthermore, Crane insisted that "road and canal work should be provided at once as ground freezes over in three months," adding that "Our engineers' canal plans are ready for constructive work and millions of men are glad to work."[99] Difficult though it would be to complete this work before the arrival of winter, the project provided an excellent solution to the major problem of homelessness by employing men who had lost everything during previous floods, which had damaged and even swept away whole houses and large amounts of farm equipment.[100] Crane also encouraged other relief efforts, such as sending engineers from the Shanxi region, one of the five that had been struck by famine, to teach Governor Yan Xishan's demobilized soldiers how to dig artesian wells.[101] Furthermore, Crane left—of his own accord—on a tour to promote the idea of a "China Relief" and to generate more enthusiasm for unity and cooperation across China and particularly in the hostile regions near Peking and in the north.[102]

Though well aware of the geographic and societal causes of the famine, Crane bent his mind to the wider problems that prevented China from managing its weaknesses and turning them into strengths. Always comparing China to the United States in terms of size, demographics and history, Crane considered its greatest weakness to be that "She lacks men of power, foresight and prestige to carry her along." He seemed to lay the blame for this unfortunate situation on foreign powers, which had supported men with little ability and who could be easily controlled in order to protect their own interests in China, adding that "the present world would not tolerate men of that kind in important positions for any great length of time." There was hope, however, and Crane affirmed that "After centuries of isolation China has been drawn into the world by irresistible forces and both she and the world will have to take the consequences."[103] Crane believed that philanthropic engagement represented an opportunity to participate in China's modernization through this road and canal work which would alter the very structure of China's landscape, economy, and trade relations.

A considerable amount of readily available capital was required to undertake a project of this scope. A new banking consortium was being created and Crane, in his capacity as diplomatic envoy of the United States, had already had it ratified by the Chinese government. Using his privileged diplomatic position, Crane now busied himself with trying to enlist its help in aiding China with famine relief. Since its establishment, the consortium, which was led by J.P. Morgan & Co. and involved several French and British banks, had already had to face demands from Japan[104] and some misbehavior on the part of the Chinese government. Indeed, though Peking was constantly on the brink of bankruptcy and therefore unable to pay its debts, its monetary needs continued to grow. One such debt, which the Chinese government had refused to pay to its German creditors in 1919 on the grounds of their status as enemies, was uncovered during negotiations over an emergency loan from the members of the consortium. This debt, still unpaid in the summer of 1920, constituted an obstacle which threatened to derail the consortium if not for the solution proposed with Crane's help by the United States. Acting through Thomas W. Lamont (its envoy in China) and through the State Department, J.P. Morgan & Co. impressed upon the Chinese Minister of Communications that though China's position might be tenable, failure to repay Germany's loan for the construction of the Hukuang railway would affect the New York and London markets and greatly damage China's credit rating.[105] Of course, even the soundest reasoning would be of no use if Peking had no means of paying its dues. Crane was the one to propose a way out of this impasse, suggesting that the consortium advance part of the loan, allowing China to pay its debt. On September 9, Crane communicated the urgency of the situation to the State Department by explaining that the "Minister of Finance is clearly in desperate condition [...] his tenure of office depends on result of this negotiation more especially as his Ministry is entirely without funds." This issue also tied in with the food crisis, and Crane pushed for a quick ratification of the loan contract so that China could use part of the borrowed sum to create an "official board of famine relief." Under secretary of State Norman H. Davis had asked Crane to "adequately impress upon the [Chinese] Government the necessity of prompt and full compliance with its obligations." In October of 1920, after some reluctance on the part of the Chinese government, Crane was able to report to the State Department that such a board had been created by the Chinese Minister of Finance. Crane, who had the government's trust, was asked to assist with the implementation of this famine relief effort and help the Chinese government to manage its financial responsibilities.[106]

The consortium, however, did not see the matter in such simple terms and gave itself the right to oversee China's use of the loan, much to the Chinese government's dismay. China's anticonsortium press even depicted this "right" as a stratagem to decrease China's sovereignty over its own economy and to make it even more vulnerable to the rivalries of the warring factions.[107] However, though this imperialistic and "interventionist" approach did, in principle, limit China's sovereignty, its motivations were partly humanitarian. Representing the American branch of the consortium, J.P. Morgan & Co. advised the State Department that the loan should be used by China for "constructive purposes" rather than for administrative purposes per se. According to Lamont, this stance had been adopted for the "upbuilding of China."[108]

At the same time, another matter shows that the position of the United States as China's credit and trading partner was based in part on humanitarian considerations. Near the end of 1920, the Chinese government resolved to implement a ten-percent increase in customs tariffs applicable on incoming and outgoing products to help finance the famine relief program. While France, Great Britain, and Japan all refused to ratify this proposal, the United States, through Crane, decided that "On this understanding and in view of humanitarian purposes for which funds are to be used the Department will interpose no objection to the proposed surtax." Given the other countries' refusal to support this motion, however, the State Department stipulated that the tariff increase should apply to everyone equally. In the end, an agreement on the terms of the customs surtax was only reached in January of 1921. Crane informed the State Department that the surtax would come into effect on March 1, 1921 and be applied to all of China's trade partners. In reality, however, the surtax only affected the four main powers with interests in China, namely, the United States, Great Britain, France, and Japan. In exchange for their adherence to this provisional surtax treaty, the latter three imposed a special oversight committee composed of six Chinese and six foreign members. The committee held a right of scrutiny over all of the Chinese government's public expenses and over another loan granted by the consortium, a four million dollar advance on the increased customs payments. China's weakness thus served, to these powers, as an excellent opportunity to extend their economic reach inside the country.[109]

As for Crane's opinion on the matter, it was not represented in the State Department's documents because he limited himself to relaying information. When talking with his colleagues, he took care to express America's official position in a curt and factual way. In view of the harsh comments he had made previously about the "rapacious" behavior of the foreign powers and his own adherence to "altruistic politics," however, his written correspondence shows the way in which he prioritized humanitarian aid over other economic considerations (the consortium, negotiation of loans, the safety of the railroad system for foreign nationals, new customs tariffs, etc.) In any case, all of these things fell under the scope of the relief effort, or so it appeared to him and certainly also to the new Secretary of State Bainbridge Colby, who had succeeded Robert Lansing in 1920. In a letter to Charles W. Eliot written in the last months of his term in China, Crane underscored this priority by affirming that "Out here we are all more concerned with famine relief than anything else this winter." He then explained the way in which the Red Cross and the consortium both worked to alleviate the food crisis:

> The Red Cross is being well directed here by Mr. Baker and is setting an example of effective relief work [...] We have had an interesting time building up an international organization to handle all the general relief work [...] The present organization is an excellent one, covers all the areas and is being well managed by the best possible men representing the various communities, furnishing the main part of the money through the Consortium banks.

Crane deemed these efforts "the best constructive work in China" and hoped that they would "form the nucleus of a movement for unifying China politically." He reasoned that "The various Chinese groups from different parts of the country first held off from cooperating with Peking but are now taking part," and counted on such cooperation in response to a vital common cause to foster the social cohesion and socioeconomic development necessary to build a peaceful and prosperous republic.[110]

Many other tasks kept Crane occupied during his time as minister to China, though most of them centered on adequately managing the famine relief efforts. The safety of American nationals in China, for instance, constituted one of the concerns incumbent on the minister plenipotentiary. Many times, Crane had to intervene in order to petition the Chinese government for better protection for American missionaries, businessmen, and goods. Several incidents detrimental to American commercial interests, particularly in regions adjacent to the Yangtze River, were mentioned in various consular reports and the State Department called on Crane to lodge a complaint with the Chinese government. Unfortunately, Crane could only reply by informing his superiors that the country was slipping further into chaos despite all that had been accomplished by the famine relief movement. The central government simply could not guarantee adequate protection for American interests from the damage caused by the civil war. Crane even recommended that the American government "take steps to supply with its own forces such protection to its citizens as may be possible."

Such an infringement on China's sovereign rights seemed justifiable given its government's inability to harness its own power and to dispense justice on its territory. In fact, the United States even refused to let China revoke the extraterritorial rights that had been imposed on it after the Boxer Rebellion in response to various violations against foreign people and belongings on Chinese territory. China's legal system was considered too unstable, unreasonable, and unpredictable to be imposed on foreign nationals. The powers had therefore claimed the right to independently try the crimes their citizens committed in China. Asked by the Chinese to reconsider extraterritoriality, the American government concluded that "we could not feel that the Chinese Government had yet made sufficient progress" toward self-determination in this domain.[111] Crane did not seem to object in any way to this additional incursion on China's sovereign rights, perhaps because he had himself witnessed examples of China's failure in this regard. Among other instances, Crane once had to inform the State Department of the kidnapping of an American doctor and missionary, A. L. Shelton, by bandits. On another occasion, he found himself having to report the murder of another missionary, William A. Reimert, by militiamen opposed to the Peking government.[112] Crane even recounted in his memoirs an instance where he heroically saved two American engineers captured by social bandits in Inner Mongolia after a rebellion had taken place there.[113]

Though the last story remains uncorroborated, protecting his fellow citizens was clearly a crucial part of Crane's diplomatic work. It was also closely linked to the social development he contributed to through his humanitarian role in the famine relief effort. For example, Crane at one point had to reach out to Zhang Zuolin, who had by then become governor of Manchuria (composed of three northeastern provinces), about safety along the railroads. Manchuria had been luckier than its southern neighbors and even enjoyed a certain degree of prosperity and agricultural surplus resulting from a good harvest. While listing the security and transport issues encountered along the railroads, therefore, Crane also wrote Zhang Zuolin a long letter both formal and friendly in tone describing the collective famine relief effort in China. He went as far as including Wilson's appeal, the declaration made on December 9, 1920 calling upon America's generosity in contributing to humanitarian aid in China:

> We are trying in every way to relieve the great suffering; we are purchasing the surplus grain in Manchuria for distribution here. There seems to be some difficulty in procuring railway cars for shipping this grain down here, and I hope you will do everything in your power to assist and encourage this good work.

Crane also asked that the military attaché he had sent to Manchuria to assess the situation there, Major Philcon, be treated with consideration, writing that "I shall much appreciate any courtesy your subordinate officers may show him." Wishing to end his request on a less official note, Crane wrote about his own son, John, who was then, in the purest paternal tradition, also in China conducting "a study of political and social conditions." Crane expressed a desire that their sons—Zhang's son was one of his generals—engage in an exchange of experiences for the benefit of their respective countries.[114] Though Zhang's response remains unknown, the episode serves primarily to show how once again in Crane's life the political, humanitarian, and even personal aspects of his diplomatic position melded together, all the more since the chaos and destruction caused by the civil war often interfered with his humanitarian activities.

In preparation for his withdrawal from public affairs,[115] Crane wrote to Wilson before tendering his resignation in January of 1921 to make a strong case for his attaché Charles D. Tenney, who had worked in China first as a missionary and then as a diplomat for thirty-eight years. Tenney was going to leave his position, but considering his presence invaluable, Crane asked Wilson to help convince Tenney to finish his term in Peking.[116] Crane was so certain of Tenney's expertise that he even wrote to the new president-elect Senator Harding in December of 1920 to recommend Tenney as an advisor for the Republican Administration if the latter refused to take over the position in Peking after Crane's departure.[117]

During his last months as minister, Crane also helped the YMCA purchase a new building in Shanghai. Besides making his own financial contribution and securing a donation from Baker, Crane obtained a loan from the banking consortium with the help of his good friend John R. Mott.[118] In addition to this, he donated to the YMCA for the China Relief and was thanked profusely by one of the organization's representatives.[119]

Crane was evidently kept very busy with various diplomatic, humanitarian, and even personal occupations. He shared his impressions in a letter to Mildred N. Page:

> The *vie* here is rather intense. There are many formal things and many routine things which take up much of one's time and strength [...] There is however a great difference between being here as a formal official with a dual responsibility and being here as a free traveler at liberty to see anyone and everyone and not obliged to waste time and energy on heavy functions and light people.

As demonstrated by his description of this forced acquaintance with "light people" during his time in China, Crane clearly still felt some of the same disdain for traditional diplomacy already expressed in Versailles. Yet he had to admit at the end of his term that "we have not had one disagreeable or unsympathetic experience, not even in the diplomatic body which usually looks out for the worst rather than the best interests," and that all career diplomats were not part of an oppressive "human morass."[120] Both the excerpt and a glance at his work in China as minister plenipotentiary demonstrate that, on the whole, he was proud of having "served officially under Woodrow Wilson," as he confessed to his daughter Josephine. Even though "Diplomatically it has not been of historical importance," he commented in regard to his own goal, described earlier, of establishing closer ties between the world's peoples that "our relations with all kinds of people here and especially with the Chinese, have been well worth while."

Crane thus departed from China content with his humanitarian work and proud of his more symbolic than concrete role within Wilsonian diplomacy, which he had served in keeping with the philanthropic principles so often mentioned during his public career. Though his ministership did not have any tangible impact on the ensuing political events in China, one can suppose that his significant and particularly active role there might have helped shape Sino-American diplomatic relations.[121] It certainly seems to have had an impact on future legations and embassies, eventually encouraging the American government to upgrade the legation in China to an embassy in 1935. Otherwise, however, his greatest contribution, namely, the famine relief effort and his work with the State Department, with the consortium, and with various humanitarian organizations, proved to be largely circumstantial and primarily affected only the victims of the food crisis. And ironically, by the time Crane officially became part of Wilson's administration, Wilson himself was no longer able to carry out his own diplomacy or to act as his own Secretary of State as had been his habit.

Crane left China greatly impressed with its people and culture, judging that "there is a profound element of permanent wisdom in people who have endured so long and carry their heavy burden with so much serenity as the Chinese."[122] He held this view even despite the often distressing portrait which, in his capacity as minister plenipotentiary, he had painted of the chaos in China and which had led him to conclude that China owed its problems to its vastness, echoing the same reasoning that had, under Brandeis's influence, shaped his opinion about trusts in 1912. A Jeffersonian at heart, Crane wrote in reference primarily to China and Russia that "the great states of the world have outgrown the brain capacity of the men who were responsible for their politics." America and Britain, he explained, were exceptions to this trend due to their decentralization.[123]

Though he might have had Jeffersonian views, the methods that distinguished Crane during his time as a diplomat were distinctly Hamiltonian and he considered his time in China to have been the culminating point of his political career, writing that "it seems as though all our previous experiences had been preparing us [him and Cornelia] for this year."[124] He explained to Eliot that "the most important things going on, religious, educational, scientific [and] political" during his term in China "were exactly the sort of things we had been doing all our lives at Chicago." Among these activities, it was undeniably the food crisis and his work putting together a relief effort which set him apart during his term as minister to China, and Crane wrote that "when the famine came along I felt that there was something really worth while doing." Despite the fact that "there was very much pessimism when [he] started the movement," Crane viewed it not only as an opportunity to "take care of the famine" but also "to give a kind of full dress rehearsal of the Consortium principles." Despite the lukewarm reaction to

Wilson's call for assistance in the United States, Crane believed that "the results were entirely sufficient to carry out the work to the fullest extent." More importantly still given Crane's diplomatic goals, he rejoiced in the gratitude and admiration he thought the Chinese now felt for America. Though the relief movement received international support, Crane took pleasure in the idea that "The Chinese nevertheless are convinced that it is essentially an American proceeding and insist on giving us the main credit."[125]

Again, Crane's ministership in China exemplifies President Woodrow Wilson's aim to use philanthropy as a means of transforming international relations. By favoring humanitarian action, despite the obvious and sometime confusing mingling of private investment and charity it involved, over imperialist penetration as a weapon of policy, Wilson and Crane attempted to depart from the established means by which the powers conducted diplomacy toward weaker nations like China. They sought to build up a new "direct" relationship, as Crane once said, between a power and a developing country. In Crane's mind as well as in Wilson's, this "new diplomacy" was to spring from cooperation and generosity rooted in the Anglo-Protestant tradition, a major foundation of the social gospel and of the Progressive movement in America. In the case of Crane's ministership in China, "altruistic politics," aiming at "promoting Chinese-American friendship," formed the cornerstone, albeit an unacknowledged one, of Wilson's particular brand of international progressivism. This sympathy toward Christian missionaries and toward philanthropy was also the foundation of their friendship and collaboration. In that sense, Crane's very presence and role in Wilsonian diplomacy, as exemplified by his leading part in the China Relief, illustrates the importance of the humanitarian factor in Wilson's thought and politics.

It was with a light heart that Crane left Peking in June of 1921. He was departing with his son John, who Crane proudly remarked was "getting well trained as a traveler,"[126] and the two would be taking a longer route back through northern China, Siberia, and Europe.[127] Before his departure, Crane even requested to take with him a cargo of medicine and medical equipment provided by a doctor from the Rockefeller Foundation. His goal was to distribute it in Russia during his voyage as "there is nothing the people of Russia are more in need of."[128] Crane would be turning sixty-three in less than two months.

Notes

1. Let us note that Theodore Roosevelt had clearly expressed his approval and admiration for Japan. He also despised Chinese society, as demonstrated by his use of the word "chink" to describe those whom he disliked. After the start of the Russo-Japanese War, progressives generally sided with Japan. Crane worked relentlessly to shift public opinion in favor of Russia and, by extension, of China. See Michael Schaller, *The United States and China in the Twentieth Century* (Oxford: Oxford University Press, 1979), 32; Warren I. Cohen, *America's Response to China. An Interpretive History of Sino-American Relations*, 4th ed. (New York: Wiley, 1971), 66–75.
2. Michael Schaller, *The United States and China in the Twentieth Century*, 32; Warren I. Cohen, *America's Response to China. A History of Sino-American Relations*, 4th ed., 55–60; Jerry Israel, *Progressivism and the Open Door. America and China, 1905–1921* (Pittsburgh: University of Pittsburgh Press, 1971), 56, 86; Michael H. Hunt, "1898: The Onset of America's Troubled Asian Century," *OAH Magazine of History*, 12, 3 (Spring, 1998): 30–36.
3. Diana Preston, *The Boxer Rebellion. China's War on Foreigners, 1900* (London: Robinson, 1999), xx–xxii. Also see John K. Fairbank, *The United States and China* (Cambridge: Harvard University Press, 1979) 210–1; and Cohen, Warren I. *America's Response to China*, pp. 54–60. Cohen notes that Americans seemed better disposed to understand and justify China's anti-imperialist rebellion than the Europeans. Nevertheless, the United States officially collaborated with other powers in promoting repressive policies (such as imposing indemnities and maintaining extraterritorial jurisdiction) and its actions were geared more toward trying to steal a march on the other powers than toward respecting China's sovereign rights.
4. The historian Stephen G. Craft defines relations between China and foreign powers as semicolonial. See *V. K. Wellington Koo and the Emergence of Modern China* (Lexington: University of Kentucky Press, 2004), 3.
5. John K. Fairbank, *The United States and China*, 181–9. For a compelling account and interpretation of the Taiping War, see Stephen R. Platt, *Autumn in the Heavenly Kingdom. China, the West, and the Epic Story of the Taiping Civil War* (New York: Vintage Books, 2012), xxvi–xxvii, 13–20. Platt writes: "As regards the participation of foreigners beyond just military personnel, the events of that period are a reminder of just how fine the line is that separates humanitarian intervention from imperialism." As for the Christian influence upon the Taiping, Platt explains that the founder of the Taiping movement, Hong Xiuquan, "converted" to Christianity—he in fact claimed to be Jesus' brother—after a mental breakdown and an episode of religious delusion which was part of a personal rebellion against Confucianism.
6. *Crane Papers*, "CRC Address, City Club of Chicago," January 27, 1912.
7. Arthur S. Link, *Woodrow Wilson and the Progressive Era, 1910–1917*, 82–3. This quote, attributed to Wilson, features in Secretary of the Navy Josephus Daniels's personal journal. See *PWW*, "Daniels Diary," Vol. 27, March 13, 1913, 174–5.
8. Link, *Woodrow Wilson and the Progressive Era*, 83–4. The policy Wilson adopted with regard to China fit into a movement that Link called "missionary diplomacy." Not to be understood in the technical sense as diplomacy centered on protecting the interests

of churches and missions abroad, Wilson's missionary diplomacy was simply motivated by a desire to help other nations. The New Left, for its part, interpreted Wilson's withdrawal from the consortium as his way of breaking with traditional imperialism as argued by Norman G. Levin: "The ultimate Wilsonian hope was to use America's expanding commercial and political influence to establish on a worldwide scale the type of liberal-capitalist order of commercial freedom which had been the goal of his concern for American moral and material expansion in China." See *Woodrow Wilson and World Politics. America's Response to War and Revolution*, 22. This interpretation, however, was based on the assumption that Wilson did not fully grasp the potential clash between America's material and moral interests and once again credited Wilson with a mastery of diplomatic strategy which, according to Link, he did not possess.

9. *PWW*, "Daniels Diary," Vol. 27, March 28, 1913, 237.
10. *Crane Papers*, "CRC to WW," March 19, 1913; "CRC to WW," March 21, 1913.
11. *Crane Papers*, "CRC to WW," March 24, 1913. Also see Cohen, *America's Response to China*, 88–9.
12. *Crane Papers*, "WW to CRC," March 21, 1913.
13. *PWW*, "House Diary," "WW to Bryan," Vol. 27, February 13 and 14, 1913, 110, 112.
14. *PWW*, "WW to Bryan," Vol. 27, February 21, 1913, 124.
15. *PWW*, "WW to Dodge," Vol. 27, February 24, 1913, 131.
16. Quoted from C. Howard Hopkins, *John R. Mott, 1865–1955. A Biography*, 400. The *Wilson Papers* do not document Mott's response to Wilson's offer. An editorial note reports that the telegram had been lost, but that Mott had sent his answer to Wilson via Dodge (*PWW*, Vol. 27, 167).
17. *PWW*, "Mott to Dodge," Vol. 27, March 1, 1913, 144–5. Mott had sent Dodge a telegram to be relayed to Wilson. This telegram exposed, in seven points, the political situation in China, which he deemed stable and promising, and outlined several arguments for recognizing Yuan Shikai's government.
18. *Crane Papers*, "CRC to Charles W. Eliot," January 11, 1913; "Eliot to CRC," February 7, 1914. In this last letter, Eliot reminded Crane that his first payment should have been made before February 1. Crane recognized his mistake and proceeded to send the money. See "Eliot to CRC," December 14, 1914, September 13, 1915.
19. *Crane Papers*, "CRC to WW," April 8, 1913.
20. *Crane Papers*, "Charles R. Crane, by Thomas F. Millard," October 27, 1939. Millard made these comments in Shanghai during a speech in Crane's honor after the philanthropist's death. Around the same time, John B. Powell, a journalist who had worked with Crane and Millard, mentioned Crane's substantial contribution to the *China Press*, of which he also became the director. John B. Powell, *My Twenty-Five Years in China* (New York: Macmillan, 1945), 10.
21. *Crane Papers*, "B. Laufer to CRC," November 11, 1918. The dedication recognizing Crane's generosity does indeed feature in the introduction of Laufer's work, *Sino-Iranica. Chinese Contributions to the History of Civilization in Ancient Iran* (Field Museum of Chicago, 1919), 207. For more on the subject of B. Laufer, see Stephen E. Nash, and Gary M. Feinman, ed. *Curators, Collections, and Contexts: Anthropology at the Field Museum*,

1893–2002 (Fieldiana Anthropology, 2003). Chapter 9 (from page 117 to 126), written by Bennet Bronson, concerns the life and work of Berthold Laufer.

22. *Crane Papers*, "CRC to WW," October 1, 1913.
23. V. K. Wellington Koo, who completed his Ph. D. at the University of Columbia in 1912, served as Chinese ambassador in Mexico, Cuba, and in the United States before becoming China's plenipotentiary delegate in Versailles. See Stephen G. Craft, *V. K. Wellington Koo and the Emergence of Modern China* (Lexington: University of Kentucky Press, 2004).
24. *Crane Papers*, "Paul S. Reinsch to CRC," September 9, 1915.
25. *Crane Papers*. "CRC to WW," March 28, 1917.
26. Wilson's reaction to the Lansing-Ishii Agreement is not documented in the *Wilson Papers*. For an analysis of this agreement, see Robert H. Ferrell, *Woodrow Wilson & World War I, 1917–1921* (New York: Harper & Row Publishers, 1985), 120; Cohen, *America's Response to China*, 96–7. Cohen claims that Wilson viewed this treaty as a "great stroke on behalf of Chinese as well as of American interests" but provides no supporting data for this interpretation.
27. *Crane Papers*, "Thomas F. Millard to CRC," March 11 and 12, 1918.
28. *Crane Papers*, "Eliot to CRC," August 26, 1918.
29. *Crane Papers*, "CRC to Eliot," August 12, 1918.
30. *Crane Papers*, "CRC to WW," August 20, 1918.
31. *Crane Papers*, "CRC to WW," August 20, 1918; *PWW*, "CRC to WW," August 20, 1918. An editorial note mentions that a supper with Crane and Grayson was on the president's schedule on August 27, 1918. There remains no record of this conversation, but one can assume that they were discussing the situation in China and Crane's upcoming trip.
32. *Crane Papers*, "CRC to Cornelia S. Crane," September 17, 1918.
33. John K. Fairbank, ed., *The Cambridge History of China. Republican China 1912–1949. Part I*,.Vol. 12. (Cambridge: Cambridge University Press, 1983), 766.
34. This information does not feature in the works of Leo Bocage or of Jacob Sulzbach, or in the book written by David Hapgood. Instead, Erez Manela, who used Chinese and Korean sources, helps shed light on the matter in *The Wilsonian Moment: Self-determination and the International Origins of Anticolonial Nationalism, 1917–1920*, 290.
35. Manela, *The Wilsonian Moment*, 291.
36. *Crane Papers*, "Tseng Chu Tu to CRC," November 3, 1918.
37. See Sun Yat-sen, *Souvenirs d'un révolutionnaire chinois* (Paris: Éditions d'aujourd'hui, 1983).
38. *PWW*, "Sun-Yat-sen to WW," Vol. 53, November 20, 1918, 138–40. In fact, Sun Yat-sen emphasized that "this very parliament was first recognized by the United States through your own good self" in reference to Wilson's personal and perhaps even unilateral involvement in the recognition of the new republican regime in 1913.
39. *PWW*, "WW to Robert Lansing," Vol. 53, November 20, 1918, 138.
40. Fairbank, *The United States and China*, 220–37. Also see Cohen, *America's Response to China*, 108.
41. *Crane Papers*, "Li-Chun-huang to CRC," December 14, 1918.
42. *Crane Papers*, "Eugene E. Barnett to CRC," January 28, 1919. Barnett's description of China's enthusiasm for the Fourteen Points, especially in intellectual circles, aligns with

various other studies on the impact of Wilsonianism in China. See Manela, *The Wilsonian Moment*, 218–71; Cohen, *America's Response to China*, 100–101.

43. *PWW*, "Memorandum of a conversation at an audience with the President of the United States, Woodrow Wilson, at the White House," Vol. 57, November 26, 1918, 632–4.
44. This passage can be interpreted quite literally, as Wellington Koo traveled to Paris with Wilson and the American delegates aboard the *George Washington*. See Manela, *The Wilsonian Moment*, 251.
45. *PWW*, "Meetings of Council of Ten," Vol. 54, January 28, 1919, 314–6.
46. *PWW*, "Robert Lansing to WW" and "Frank L. Polk to RL," Vol. 54, February 4, 1919, 474–5. It seems, however, that Koo was not yet aware, at that point in time, of the negotiations between Japan and the Chinese warlords, which shows his willingness to present the diplomatic evidence in a different light.
47. *PWW*, "WW to Lansing," Vol. 54, February 7, 1919, 548.
48. *PWW*, "Lansing to Frank. L. Polk," Vol. 54, February 7, 1919, 549.
49. *PWW*, "Memorandum of an audience with President Wilson," Vol. 57, March 24, 1919, 635–7.
50. *PWW*, "A Memorandum by Vi Kyuin Wellington Koo," Vol. 57, April 12 (8), 1919, 298–301.
51. *PWW*, "Koo to WW," Vol. 57, April 17, 1919, 431.
52. *PWW*, "Meeting of the League of Nations Commission," Vol. 57, April 11, 1919, 263–70. Wilson, who presided over the meeting, rejected Baron Makino's proposal on the grounds that it had not gotten unanimous support during the vote (it had received eleven out of seventeen votes). When Makino insisted that the results of the vote should at the very least be recorded in the League of Nations Covenant, Wilson replied that the proposal would not be approved in the United States. It would be better not to press the issue, especially considering that the racial equality clause was already part of the League of Nations Covenant and did not need to be defined any further. Besides, had the racial equality clause been sustained in the Covenant, it goes without saying that Wilson could have foretold the even more immediate rejection of the treaty in America. As a Southern president who had allowed segregation in the Federal administration, Wilson could not discuss racial matters at Versailles without a degree of discomfort.
53. *PWW*, "Meeting of the League of Nations Commission," Vol. 57, April 10, 1919, 226–9.
54. *PWW*, "Meeting of Council of Four," Vol. 57, April 22, 1919, 615–26.
55. *PWW*, "Lu Tseng-Tiang to WW," Vol. 58, April 24, 1919, 68–70.
56. After vehemently protesting Wilson's intention to make a public declaration about Fiume, Vittorio Orlando temporarily left the conference. *PWW*, "A News Report. Orlando Makes Protest," Vol. 58, April 24, 1919, 97–101.
57. *PWW*, "Diary of Ray S. Baker," Vol. 58, April 29, 1919, 229.
58. *PWW*, "Balfour to WW" and "House to WW," Vol. 58, April 29, 1919, 228–9.
59. Chow Tse-tsung, *The May Fourth Movement. Intellectual Revolution in Modern China.* (Cambridge: Harvard University Press, 1960), 86.
60. *PWW*, "Koo to WW," Vol. 58, April 30, 1919, 247.
61. *PWW*, "Appendix: Wilson's Neurologic Illness at Paris," Vol. 58, 607–40. Interpretations differ considerably about the nature of Wilson's health issues and their impact on his

performance as a statesman in Versailles and afterward. Even Doctor Weinstein, leading expert on this subject, had to revise some of the ideas posited in his *Woodrow Wilson: a Medical and Psychological Biography* (Princeton (NJ): Princeton University Press, 1981). However, most experts came to the consensus that Wilson's personality and behavior had been altered by his illness and that a form of dementia led him to act in uncharacteristic ways and be more vulnerable to outside pressures. He was even sometimes confused about his own principles, once admitting to Ray S. Baker that he had forgotten the content of the Fourteen Points. His unlikely compromises with regard to the Shandong issue based on the idea of respecting preexisting Sino-Japanese treaties were not consistent with his often expressed aversion to secret treaties.

62. *PWW*, "Diary of Dr. Grayson," Vol. 58, April 30, 1919, 244.
63. *PWW*, "Meeting of the Council of Four," Vol. 58, April 30, 1919, 257–61.
64. Chow Tse-tsung, *The May Fourth Movement*, 84–116; King Wunsz, *China at the Paris Peace Conference in 1919* (New York: St-John's University Press, 1961), 27–8. Oddly enough, most of the anger and violence was directed at Japan and its sympathizers. It would appear that Wilson did not lose his aura of infallibility in China's eyes.
65. *PWW*, "RL to WW (enclosure)," Vol. 58, May 8 (4), 1919, 552–4.
66. *PWW*, "Wellington Koo to WW," Vol. 61, June 27, 1919, 288–9.
67. The May Fourth Movement and China's refusal to sign the Treaty of Versailles are generally seen as catalysts for the rise of communism in China. See Chow Tse-tsung, *The May Fourth Movement* and King Wunsz, *China at the Paris Peace Conference in 1919*; Manela, *The Wilsonian Moment*, 267; Schaller, *The United States and China in the Twentieth Century*, 35–6.
68. *PWW*, "CRC to Edith B. Wilson," Vol. 64, January 9, 1920, 262–3.
69. *Crane Papers*, "CRC to JCB," February 7, 1920.
70. Reinsch fiercely opposed Allied diplomacy in Paris and supported the May Fourth Movement to such an extent that the Japanese even falsely accused him of funding the student protest. See Chow Tse-tsung, *The May Fourth Movement*, 198–9; Manela, *The Wilsonian Moment*, 258–9.
71. *PWW*, "Edith B. Wilson to Lansing," Vol. 64, January 19, 1920, 296; "Lansing to Edith B. Wilson," Vol. 64, January 23, 1920, 317.
72. *Crane Papers*, "CRC to JCB," February 7, 1920.
73. *Crane Papers*, "Charles R. Crane's Ministership to China, 1920–21 by D. M. Brodie," 1940.
74. *PWW*, "CRC to Edith B. Wilson," Vol. 64, February 13, 1920, 317. One can assume that Wilson and his wife accepted Crane's offer since Edith refused another offer made by Breckinridge Long, specifically mentioning Crane's invitation in the process. "Edith B. Wilson to Breckinridge Long," Vol. 65, March 21, 1920, 110.
75. *Crane Papers*, "CRC to Eliot," April 28, 1919. Crane seemed to agree with those who, like Edith, wanted to get Wilson back on his feet for the "solemn referendum" in 1920, or at the very least, he believed that the Democratic Party "should rest solidly and squarely upon the principles so widely proclaimed by President Wilson." However, Crane added that he would prefer to have Republicans in power rather than to compromise the principles of the Treaty of Versailles. In the end, the idea of nominating Wilson for a third

term was opposed by his personal secretary Joseph Tumulty and by Doctor Grayson, who declared: "save the life and fame of this great man from the juggling of false friends." See Kendrick A Clements, *The Presidency of Woodrow Wilson*, 202–3.

76. *Crane Papers*, "CRC to Gavin McNab," May 4, 1920. These comments were part of an argument against Bryan's idea of making prohibition part of the Democratic platform. Crane deemed that there was no need to steal the Republican Party's "dry" position as the Democratic Party had already borrowed sufficiently from their rhetoric.
77. *Crane Papers*, "CRC to WW," April 29, 1920.
78. *Crane Papers*, "CRC to D. F. Houston," July 19, 1920.
79. *Crane Papers*, "CRC to Mildred N. Page" and "CRC to Yo Uchida," May 31, June 11, 1920.
80. *Crane Papers*, "Charles R. Crane's Ministership to China, 1920–21 by D. M. Brodie," 1940.
81. See David Hapgood, *Charles R. Crane. The Man Who Bet on People*, 63–5.
82. Besides Hapgood, see Robert D. Kaplan, *The Arabists. The Romance of an American Elite*, 68–71.
83. These words echoed the speech Crane gave in Shanghai on May 29 upon taking up his ministerial duties, which served as a very clear warning to the foreign powers: "From now on it will not make any Government popular to try to harass this new Chinese democracy by following the old menacing process of corruption, poisoning and interfering with its internal affairs." *FRUS, 1920*, Vol. 1, 434.
84. *Crane Papers*, "CRC to D. F. Houston," July 19, 1920.
85. *FRUS*, 1920, Vol. 1, 434–97.
86. *Crane Papers*, "CRC to Eliot," August 11, 1920.
87. *Crane Papers*, "CRC to William Kent," July 6, 1920. Having agreed to do Kent a favor, Crane asked not to be solicited excessively from that point onward since "this job out here in the East [...] is straining all my resources." Later, during the last months of his term as minister, Crane added to this by comparing his extensive administrative duties with his previous touristic visits. Luckily, his helpers were able to take care of a large part of the work. "CRC to Mildred N. Page," February 10, 1921. Unfortunately, the demands of his position in Peking were such that he had to renounce his chair at the head of the board of the Constantinople College for Girls. See "R. H. Malone to Sam C. Darling," November 26, 1920.
88. There is, to this day, very little documentation on the famine of 1920. The existing documentation naturally favored a Western treatment of the subject since it stemmed primarily from western sources (diplomatic and missionary documents). This bias, of a documentary nature, resulted in the omission of local perspectives on the famine relief efforts. See Pierre Fuller, "North China Famine Revisited: Unsung Native Relief in the Warlord Era, 1920–1921," *Modern Asian Studies* (August 2012). This article, which focuses on China's own response to international relief efforts during the food crisis, only briefly mentions the part played by Crane and Wilson.
89. Crane's explanations to Wilson were probably based on technical observations made by the Red Cross in a report written by its Director of Operations John E. Baker. According to the report, farmers living in western Shandong between Peking and Suzhou counted

on (occasional) snow melts and on a few spring showers for a first summer harvest, then, more importantly, on the summer monsoon for a second harvest in the fall. If either of these water sources failed, the farmers living near the Yellow River automatically became the most vulnerable as they had neither sufficient food stores nor effective transport methods to survive the drought. Indeed, animals consumed as much food as they could carry and river transport depended on various factors and presented considerable topographical and hydrographical difficulties. The 1920 famine was thus the result of a monsoon that never came between June and August and of the devastation caused by previous floods. The most urgent priorities in northeastern China, other than emergency food distribution, were the establishment of an irrigation and drainage network (to channel water in case of a flood and to help irrigate the fields in case of a drought) and the development of roads and railway networks to facilitate the exchange of supplies and to foster cooperation between the different regions. See John Earl Baker, *Report of the China Famine Relief. American Red Cross. October 1920–September 1921* (Ithaca: Cornell University Library, 1921), 1–6.

90. *Crane Papers*, "Memoirs," 239–43. Crane repeated these thoughts the following year after his return to the United States during a speech at the University of Wisconsin. *Crane Papers*, "Charles R. Crane Speech at "Wisconsin in China"," January 10, 1922, 3. Unfortunately for Crane, the Chinese relief conflicted with Herbert Hoover's feeding plan in Europe.
91. *PWW*, "Graham Patterson to WW," Vol. 66, November 5, 1920; "WW to Patterson," Vol. 66, November 8, 1920, 327, 38.
92. *PWW*, "Lamont to WW," Vol. 66, November, 26, December 3 and 7, 1920; "WW to Lamont," Vol. 66, November 29, 1920; "WW to Edward Nash Hurley," Vol. 66, December 9, 1920, 424, 443, 467, 491–2, 497.
93. *PWW*, "A Statement on Chinese Famine Relief," Vol. 66, December 9, 1920, 495–46.
94. *PWW*, "Lamont to WW," Vol. 66, December 14, 1920; "Houston to WW," Vol. 66, December 17, 1920; "WW to Lamont," December 18, 1920, 509–10, 529–30, 532.
95. *PWW*, "Lamont to WW," Vol. 67, January 17 and 21, 1921; "R. B. Fosdick to WW," Vol. 67, January 24, 1921; "WW to Lamont," Vol. 67, January 28 and 30, 1921, 75, 80, 87–8, 96, 105.
96. *PWW*, "WW to Lamont," Vol. 67, July 4, 1921, 342.
97. John E. Baker, *Report of the China Famine Relief. American Red Cross. October 1920–September 1921*, 6–7. Crane also mentioned this key moment in his September 22 telegram to Wilson. *Crane Papers*, "CRC to WW," September 22, 1920.
98. *Crane Papers*, "CRC to American Red Cross," October 1920.
99. *Crane Papers*, "CRC to H. P. Davison, Red Cross, New York," October 1920.
100. Baker, *Report of the China Famine Relief*, 4–5.
101. *Crane Papers*, "CRC to Chang Tso-lin," December 15, 1920.
102. *Crane Papers*, "CRC to Eliot," June 21, 1921. One of Crane's arguments to the Chinese was the importance of the Yellow River region as the cradle of Chinese civilization and of Confucianism. He insisted that love of their nation should help the opposing factions put their quarrels to rest when it came to saving their peers.
103. *Crane Papers*, "CRC to Eliot," November 7, 1920.

104. Three conditions were set by Japan in exchange for its approval of the consortium. The Japanese asked that the conference in Shanghai be reopened and the Shandong issue be revisited. They also called for the demobilization of China's "superfluous" troops in Manchuria. Finally, they insisted on Japanese supervision of China's finances following its loans from the consortium. See *FRUS, 1920*, Vol. 1, 621.
105. *FRUS, 1920*, Vol. 1, 640, 644–7. These repeated warnings as well as China's response came between April and June of 1920.
106. *FRUS, 1920*, Vol. 1, 659–60, 663–4.
107. *FRUS, 1920*, Vol. 1, 665–9.
108. *FRUS, 1920*, Vol. 1, 671–2.
109. *FRUS, 1920*, Vol. 1, 727–31. Crane also mentioned this in the *Crane Papers*, "CRC to Eliot," June 21, 1921.
110. *Crane Papers*, "CRC to Eliot," February 5, 1921. Similar sentiments are also expressed in "CRC to Bainbridge Colby (Secretary of State)," December 17, 1920.
111. *FRUS, 1921*, Vol. 1, 505, 519–22.
112. *FRUS, 1920*, Vol. 1, 793–4, 806–914.
113. *Crane Papers*, "Memoirs," 243. After the Chinese government refused to send a rescue mission, Crane himself sent a team made of four marines and one officer, who it would seem rescued the engineers and returned them safe and sound. This story is also told by Leo Bocage in "The Public Career of Charles R. Crane," 259, though it has not been corroborated by other sources.
114. *Crane Papers*, "CRC to Chang Tso-lin," December 15, 1920. Whether or not Manchurian militiamen actually disrupted railway facilities used for the famine relief, the problem Crane referred to was a common one in the Warlord Era, especially in Zhang Zuolin's Manchuria. See Fairbank, *The Cambridge History of China*, 303–4. On the other hand, Zhang Zuolin, whose humanitarianism has been overlooked by historians, is reported to have dispatched grain and money to relieve food shortage in the famine-stricken area. See Pierre Fuller, "North China Famine Revisited", 9, 25–27. Crane also drew Zhang Zuolin's attention to some elements of modernization for Manchuria, though it was one of the most developed regions of China—mainly because of Japanese investment in infrastructure and industry. He showed, for example, how the automobile had transformed America during the war years by causing a competition with the railroads and by leading to the development of the road networks. All of this, Crane affirmed, had favored the growth of communication and trade, as well as a reduction in transportation costs within the country. Crane's argument was part of an account he gave Zhang of his own work with the famine relief effort, which he viewed as an opportunity to modernize Chinese society's social and economic structure.
115. The new Secretary of State Charles Evans Hughes accepted Crane's resignation a few days after Harding moved into the White House on the condition that a successor would be found for the position before Crane's departure. *Crane Papers*, "Hughes to CRC," March 12, 1921.
116. *PWW*, "CRC to WW," Vol. 66, August 30, 1920, 78–9.
117. *Crane Papers*, "CRC to Sen. Harding," December 25, 1920.
118. *Crane Papers*, "CRC to Roger Williams," January 7, 1921.

119. *Crane Papers*, "J. Harold Dollar to CRC," March 16, 1921.
120. *Crane Papers*, "CRC to M. N. Page," May 1, 1919 (from Paris). Excerpt quoted in Chapter 5.
121. Jerry Israel, *Progressivism and the Open Door*, 185. Israel argues that Crane's leadership with the consortium and his humanitarian and financial strategy had a structuring effect on Chinese-American relations.
122. *Crane Papers*, "CRC to JCB," June 12, 1921.
123. *Crane Papers*, "CRC to N. Hapgood," December 10, 1920. Crane mentioned this theory several times, particularly to Charles W. Eliot (February 5, March 10, 1921). Eliot rightly suggested that the difference between China and the United States possibly lay in the latter's efficient and far-reaching communication networks (telegram, telephone, radio, roads, railways, national post system, etc.).
124. *Crane Papers*, "CRC to JCB," June 12, 1921.
125. *Crane Papers*, "CRC to Eliot," June 21, 1921.
126. *Crane Papers*, "CRC to JCB," June 12, 1921.
127. Zhang Zuolin, the governor of Manchuria, helped Crane plan this trip by providing information about the itinerary and giving him a safe-conduct for the railway networks in northern China. Crane's representation during the famine might have earned him these favors afterward. See *Crane Papers*, "Interview between General Chang Tso-lin, Mr. Chu Shao-yang and the American Minister, Charles R. Crane, re Conditions in Siberia and Russia. Interpreted by Willys R. Peck," January 8, 1921.
128. *Crane Papers*, "CRC to Eliot," June 21, 1921; "CRC to JCB," June 21, 1921.

Bibliography

Archives

Charles Richard Crane Papers, 1869–1967. Rare Books & Manuscript Library, University of Columbia.

Published Primary Sources

Baker, John E. *Report of the China Famine Relief. American Red Cross. October 1920–September 1921*. Cornell University Library, 1921.

Baker, Ray S. and William E. Dodd, ed. *The Public Papers of Woodrow Wilson*. New York: Harper, 1925–26.

Baker, Ray S. *Woodrow Wilson: Life and Letters*. Garden City, NY: Doubleday, 1927–39.

Baruch, Bernard M. *Baruch*. New York: H. Holt, 1957–1960.

Burnett, Philip M. *Reparation at the Paris Peace Conference, from the Standpoint of the American Delegation*. New York: Octagon Books, 1965 [c.1940].

Daniels, Josephus. *The Wilson Era*. Chapel Hill: University of North Carolina Press, 1946.
House, Edward M and Charles Seymour. *What Really Happened at Paris: The Story of the Peace Conference, 1918–1919, by American Delegates*. New York: Scribner's, 1921.
Houston, David F. *Eight Years with Wilson's Cabinet, 1913–1920*. Garden City, NY: Doubleday, 1926.
Lansing, Robert. *The Peace Negotiations: A Personal Narrative*. Boston, MA: Houghton Miffli, 1921.
Laufer, Berthold. *Sino-Iranica. Chinese Contributions to the History of Civilization in Ancient Iran.* Field Museum of Chicago, 1919.
Link, Arthur S., ed. *Papers of Woodrow Wilson*. Princeton, NJ: Princeton University Press, 1966–92.
Mantoux, Paul. *Les délibérations du Conseil des Quatre, 24 mars-28 juin 1919. Notes de l'officier-Interprète Paul Mantoux*. Paris: Ed. CNRS, 1955.
Powell, John B. *My Twenty-Five Years in China*. New York: Macmillan, 1945.
Seymour, Charles, ed. *The Intimate Papers of Colonel House Arranged as a Narrative*. London: Ernest Benn, 1926–28.
Sun Yat-sen, *Souvenirs d'un révolutionnaire chinois*. Paris: Éditions d'aujourd'hui, 1983 [c.1920].
Tumulty, Joseph P. *Woodrow Wilson as I Know Him*. Garden City: Doubleday, 1921.
U.S. State Department. *Papers Relating to the Foreign Relations of the United States*.

Bibliographic Guides

Buckingham, Peter H. *Woodrow Wilson: A Bibliography of His Times and Presidency*. Wilmington, DE: Scholarly Resources, 1990.
Beisner, Robert L. and Hanson Kurt W., ed. *American Foreign Relations since 1600. A Guide to the Literature*. Santa Barbara, CA: ABC-CLIO, 2003.
Bellot, Hugh Hale. *American History and American Historians: A Review of Recent Contributions to the Interpretation of the History of the United States*. Norman: University of Oklahoma Press, 1952.
Parish, Peter J., ed. *Reader's Guide to American History*. Chicago: Fitzroy Publishers, 1997.

Encyclopedias

Balmer, Randall Herbert. *Encyclopedia of Evangelicalism*. Louisville, KY: John Knox Press, 2002.

Monographies

Ambrosius, Lloyd E. *Woodrow Wilson and the American Diplomatic Tradition: The Treaty Fight in Perspective*. Cambridge: Cambridge University Press, 1987.
———. *Wilsonian Statecraft: Theory and Practice of Liberal Internationalism during World War I*. Lanham, MD: SR Books, 1991.

———. *Wilsonianism: Woodrow Wilson and His Legacy in American Foreign Relations*. New York: Palgrave Macmillan, 2002.

Bailey, Thomas A. *Woodrow Wilson and the Lost Peace*. New York: Macmillan, 1944.

———. *Woodrow Wilson and the Great Betrayal*. Chicago: Quadrangle Books, 1945.

Baker, Ray S. *Woodrow Wilson and World Settlement*. Garden City, NY: Doubleday, 1922.

Bell, Sidney. *Righteous Conquest. Woodrow Wilson and the Evolution of the New Diplomacy*. Port Washington, NY: Kennikat Press, 1972.

Blum, John M. *Woodrow Wilson and the Politics of Morality*. Boston: Little, Brown & Co., 1956.

Bouchard, Carl. *Le citoyen et l'ordre mondial. Le rêve d'une paix durable au lendemain de la Grande Guerre*. Paris: Éditions A. Pedone, 2008.

Bu, Liping. *Making the World Like Us: Education, Cultural Expansion, and the American Century*. Westport, CT: Praeger, 2003.

Calhoun, Frederick S. *Uses of Force and Wilsonian Foreign Policy*. Kent, OH: Kent State University Press, 1993.

Chow Tse-tsung. *The May Fourth Movement: Intellectual Revolution in Modern China*. Cambridge: Harvard University Press, 1960.

Clements, Kendrick A. *William Jennings Bryan, Missionary Isolationist*. Knoxville, TE: University of Tennessee Press, 1982.

———. *The Presidency of Woodrow Wilson*. Lawrence, KA: University Press of Kansas, 1992.

Cohen, Warren I. *America's Response to China. An Interpretative History of Sino-American Relations*. New York: Wiley, 1971.

———. *Empire Without Tears: America's Foreign Relations, 1921–1933*. New York: Knopf, 1987.

Cooper, John M. *The Vanity of Power. American Isolationism and the First World War, 1914–1917*. Westport, CT: Greenwood Publishing Corp., 1969.

———. *The Warrior and the Priest*. Cambridge: Harvard University Press, 1983.

———. *Woodrow Wilson*. New York: Alfred A. Knopf, 2009.

Craft, Stephen G. *V. K. Wellington Koo and the Emergence of Modern China*. Lexington: University of Kentucky Press, 2004.

Cranston, Alan. *The Killing of the Peace*. New York: The Viking Press, 1945.

Curti, Merle E. *American Philanthropy Abroad*. New Brunswick, NJ: Rutgers University Press, 1963.

Diamond, William. *The Economic Thought of Woodrow Wilson*. Baltimore: The Johns Hopkins Press, 1943.

Duroselle, Jean-Baptiste. *Histoire diplomatique de 1919 à nos jours*, 11th ed. Paris: Éditions Dalloz, 1993.

Eckes, Alfred E. *Opening America's Market. U.S. Foreign Trade Policy Since 1776*. Chapel Hill: University of North Carolina Press, 1995.

Fairbank, John K. *The United States and China*. Cambridge: Harvard University Press, 1979.

———. *The Cambridge History of China. Vol. 12, Republican China, 1912–1949*. Cambridge: Cambridge University Press, 1983.

Ferrell, Robert H. *Woodrow Wilson and World War I, 1917–1921*. New York: Harper & Row, 1985.

Figes, Orlando A *People's Tragedy. The Russian Revolution, 1891–1924*. New York, Penguin Books, 1996.

Gardner, Lloyd C. *Safe for Democracy. The Anglo-American Response to Revolution, 1913–1923*. New York: Oxford University Press. 1984.

Goldstein, Judith. *Ideas, Interests, and American Trade Policy*. Ithaca, NY: Cornell University Press, 1993.

Hansen, Jonathan M. *The Lost Promise of Patriotism. Debating American Identity, 1890–1920*. Chicago: University of Chicago Press, 2003.

Hapgood, David. *Charles R. Crane. The Man Who Bet on People*. New York: ICWA, 2000.

Holmes, James R. *Theodore Roosevelt and World Order. Police Power in International Relations*. Washington: Potomac Books, 2006.

Hopkins, Charles H. *John R. Mott, 1865–1955: A Biography*. Grand Rapids: Eerdmans, 1979.

Iriye, Akira. *From Nationalism to Internationalism. U.S. Foreign Policy to 1914*. London: Routledge, 2002.

Israel, Jerry. *Progressivism and the Open Door. America and China, 1905–1921*. Pittsburgh: University of Pittsburgh Press, 1971.

Keegan, John. *The First World War*. New York: Random House, 1998.

Kennan, George F. *American Diplomacy, 1900–1950*. New York: New American Library, 1954.

Kennedy, David M. *Over Here. The First World War and American Society*. New York: Oxford University Press, 1980.

Keynes, John Maynard. *Les conséquences économiques de la Paix*. Paris: Nouvelle Revue Française, 1920.

King, Wunsz. *China at the Paris Peace Conference in 1919*. New York: St-John's University Press, 1961.

Kitsikis, Dimitri. *Le rôle des experts à la Conférence de la Paix de 1919. Gestation d'une technocratie en politique internationale*. Ottawa: Éditions de l'Université d'Ottawa, 1972.

Knock, Thomas J. *To End all Wars. Woodrow Wilson and the Quest for a New World Order*. New York: Oxford University Press, 1992.

LaFeber, Walter. *The New Empire. An Interpretation of American Expansion, 1860–1898*. Ithaca, NY: Cornell University Press, 1963.

Lake, David A. *Power, Protection, and Free Trade. International Sources of U.S. Commercial Strategy, 1887–1939*. Ithaca, NY: Cornell University Press, 1988.

Levin, Norman G. *Woodrow Wilson and World Politics: America's Response to War and Revolution*. New York: Oxford University Press, 1968.

Link, Arthur S. *Wilson*. Princeton, NJ: Princeton University Press, 1947.

———. *Woodrow Wilson and the Progressive Era, 1910–1917*. New York: Harper & Brothers, 1954.

———. *Wilson the Diplomatist. A Look at His Major Foreign Policies*. Baltimore: Johns Hopkins Press, 1957.

———. *Woodrow Wilson. Revolution, War, and Peace*. Arlington Heights, IL: Harlan Davidson, 1979.

Lippmann, Walter. *U.S. Foreign Policy, Shield of the Republic*. Boston: Little & Brown, 1943.

Livermore, Seward W. *Woodrow Wilson and the War Congress 1916–1918*. New York: Octagon Books, 1968 [c. 1957].

Manela, Erez. *The Wilsonian Moment: Self-Determination and the International Origins of Anticolonial Nationalism, 1917–1920*. New York: Oxford University Press, 2007.

May, Ernest. *The World War and American Isolation, 1914–1917*. Cambridge: Harvard University Press, 1966 [c.1959].

———. *Imperial Democracy. The Emergence of America as a Great Power*. New York: Harper & Row, 1973.

May, Henry F. *The End of American Innocence. The First Years of Our Own Times, 1912–1917*. New York: Oxford University Press, 1959.

Mayer, Arno. *Politics and Diplomacy of Peacemaking: Containment and Counterrevolution at Versailles, 1918–1919*. New York: Knopf, 1967.

McCartney, Paul T. *Power and Progress: American National Identity, the War of 1898, and the Rise of American Imperialism*. Baton Rouge: Louisiana University Press, 2006.

McGerr, Michael. *A Fierce Discontent. The Rise and Fall of the Progressive Movement in America, 1870–1920*. Oxford: Oxford University Press, 2003.

McLoughlin, William G. *Revivals, Awakenings, and Reform. An Essay on Religion and Social Change in America, 1607–1977*. Chicago: The Chicago University Press, 1978.

Muukkonen, Martti. *Ecumenism of the Laity. Continuity and Change in the Mission View of the World's Alliance of YMCA, 1855–1955*. Joensuu: University of Joensuu Publications in Theology, 2002.

Noble, David W. *The Paradox of Progressive Thought*. Minneapolis: University of Minnesota Press, 1958.

———. *The Progressive Mind, 1890–1917*. Minneapolis: Burgess, 1981.

Nordholdt, Jan W. S. *Woodrow Wilson: A Life for World Peace*. Berkeley: University of California Press, 1991.

Notter, Harley. *The Origins of the Foreign Policy of Woodrow Wilson*. New York: Russell & Russell, 1965.

O'Neill, William L. *The Progressive Years. America Comes of Age*. New York: Dodd, Mead and Company, 1975.

Osgood, Robert E. *Ideals and Self-Interests in America's Foreign Relations. The Great Transformation of the Twentieth Century*. Chicago: University of Chicago, 1964 [c.1953].

Platt, Stephen R. *Autumn in the Heavenly Kingdom. China, the West, and the Epic Story of the Taiping Civil War*. New York: Vintage Books, 2012.

Preston, Diana. *The Boxer Rebellion. China's War on Foreigners, 1900*. London: Robinson, 1999.

Saul, Norman E. *The Life and Times of Charles R. Crane, 1858–1939. American Businessman, Philanthropist, and a Founder of Russian Studies in America*. Lanham, MD: Lexington Books, 2013.

Schaller, Michael. *The United States and China in the Twentieth Century*. New York: Oxford University Press, 1979.

Smith, Gene. *When the Cheering Stopped: The Last Years of Woodrow Wilson*. New York: Morrow, 1964.

Smith, Neil. *American Empire: Roosevelt's Geographer and the Prelude to Globalization*. Berkeley: University of California Press, 2003.

Soutou, Georges-Henri. *L'or et le sang. Les buts de guerre économiques de la Première Guerre mondiale*. Paris: Fayard, 1989.

Steel, Ronald. *Walter Lippmann and the American Century*. Boston: Little, Brown & Co. 1980.

Thorsen, Niels A. *The Political Thought of Woodrow Wilson, 1875–1910*. Princeton, NJ: Princeton University Press, 1988.

Trachtenberg, Alan. *The Incorporation of America. Culture and Society in the Gilded Age*. New York: Hill & Wang, 1982.

Trask, David F. *Victory without Peace. American Foreign Relations in the Twentieth Century*. Huntington, New York: Robert E. Krieger Publishing Company, 1975.

Van Alstyne, Richard W. *The Rising American Empire*. Oxford: Oxford University Press, 1960.

Walworth, Arthur. *Wilson and His Peacemakers. American Diplomacy at the Paris Peace Conference, 1919*. New York: Norton, 1986.

Weinstein, Edwin A. *Woodrow Wilson: A Medical and Psychological Biography*. Princeton, NJ: Princeton University Press, 1981.

Wiebe, Robert H. *Businessmen and Reform. A Study of the Progressive Movement*. Cambridge: Cambridge University Press, 1989 [c.1962].

———. *The Search for Order, 1877–1920*. London: Macmillan, 1967.

Williams, William A. *The Tragedy of American Diplomacy*. New York: Dell Publishing, 1972 [c.1959].

Theses

Bocage, Leo J. "The Public Career of Charles R. Crane." Ph.D. diss., Fordham University, 1962.

Sulzbach, Jacob John, Jr. "Charles R. Crane, Woodrow Wilson, and Progressive Reform: 1909–1921." Ph.D. diss., Texas A&M University, 1994.

Journal Articles

Ahonen, Risto. "John R. Mott as an Ecumenical Leader. What Was Mott's Vision?" *The Finnish Evangelical Lutheran Mission*, 2010, 1–5.

Anghie, Antony. "Cultural Differences in International Law: The League of Nations and Two Visions of Nation-State." *International Center for Comparative Law and Politics Review*, 5, 2002, 4–13.

Beloff, Max. "Self-Determination Reconsidered," In *Confluence*, 5, 1956, 195–203.

Blumenthal, Henry. "Woodrow Wilson and the Race Question." *The Journal of Negro History*, 48, 1, 1963, 1–21.

Fuller, Pierre. "North China Famine Revisited: Unsung Native Relief in the Warlord Era, 1920–1921." *Modern Asian Studies*, 2012, 1–31.

Hunt, Michael H. "1898: The Onset of America's Troubled Asian Century." *OAH Magazine of History*, 12, 3 (Spring 1998): 30–36.

Leuchtenburg, William E. "Progressivism and Imperialism: The Progressive Movement and American Foreign Policy, 1898–1916." *The Mississippi Valley Historical Review*, 39, 3, 1952, 483–504.

Osgood, Robert E. "Woodrow Wilson, Collective Security, and the Lessons of History." *Confluence*, 5, 1957, 341–354.

Pomerance, Michla. "Methods of Self-determination and the Argument of Primitiveness." *Canadian Yearbook of International Law*, 12, 1974, 38–66.

———. "The United States and Self-determination: Perspectives on the Wilsonian Conception." *The American Journal of International Law*, 70, 1, 1976, 1–27.

Saito, Natsu T. "Crossing the Border: The Interdependence of Foreign Policy and Racial Justice in the United States." *Yale Human Rights and Development Law Journal*, 1, 1998, 53–84.

Van Alstyne, Richard W. "Woodrow Wilson and the Idea of Nation-State." *International Affairs*, 37, 1961, 293–308.

Collective Works

Allerfeldt, Kristofer, ed. *The Progressive Era in the USA: 1890–1921*. Burlington, VT: Ashgate, 2007.

Braeman, John, ed. *Wilson*. Englewood Cliffs, NJ: Prentice-Hall, 1972.

Carlier, C. and Georges-Henri Soutou, dir. *1918–1925, comment faire la paix?* Paris: Ed. Economica, 2001.

Haines, G. K. and J. S. Walker, ed. *American Foreign Relations. A Historiographical Review*. Westport, CT: Greenwood Press, 1981.

Nash, Stephen E. and Gary M. Feinman, ed. *Curators, Collections, and Contexts: Anthropology at the Field Museum, 1893–2002*. Chicago: Fieldiana Anthropology, 2003.

Temperley, H. W. V, ed. *A History of the Peace Conference of Paris*. London: Oxford University Press, 1969 [c.1920].

CONCLUSION: CHARLES R. CRANE IN A POST-WILSONIAN ERA

After China

Charles Crane left China in 1921 and spent the summer visiting Lake Baikal, a few Siberian villages, the Urals, and Moscow. Afterward, he stopped in Prague to see his son Richard, then United States ambassador to Czechoslovakia, and to pay a visit to President Tomáš Masaryk. He stayed a few days in the company of Masaryk and of his daughter Alice, whom Crane greatly admired and whom he had most likely helped free in 1916, in the president's summer home, where he deemed that Masaryk was living "quite like a king."During one of these days, he also took a leisurely drive with his wife Cornelia, who had joined him in Prague, their children John and Frances as well as Masaryk's children, Alice and Jan (who would go on to marry Frances Crane in 1924). By the end of the afternoon, they were also joined by Richard. Crane rejoiced to see the president so well surrounded, with at his side the Minister of Foreign Affairs Edvard Beneš as well as Alice and Jan, who acted as their father's personal secretaries. "Jan," Crane assessed with satisfaction, "is developing finely and by tact, industry and judgment helps very much his father and his state."Crane was also requested to describe his travels and happily regaled this little congregation with accounts of his voyage through Russia.[1]

Crane's reputation had evidently spread beyond America, Czechoslovakia and the Arab world, for upon leaving Masaryk he received an invitation to visit none other than the Pope himself.[2] But even after all these pilgrimages there was no quenching Crane's thirst for adventure, and new travel plans had already begun taking shape in his mind when he finally returned to the United States after an absence of over a year.

The following years, however, proved to be inauspicious for travel as many regions were now plagued by social unrest which compromised the safety of foreigners. Crane was even forced to indefinitely postpone a visit to the Middle East he had been planning to undertake directly after his return owing to "the feeling of resentment against Westerners" which had been "growing so rapidly" there. He thus settled for only sojourning in Syria and Turkey and used the opportunity to visit "his" colleges in Constantinople. Though he still returned to the Middle East several times, Crane was never quite able to shake the impression that the Eastern world was becoming more hostile toward Westerners after the failure in Versailles, particularly marked by the mandate given to France over Syria.[3] He perceived this as a sign that the Wilsonian spirit he had witnessed during the King-Crane Commission had at least temporarily been abandoned and wrote that it would "probably be all of a generation before the Moslem world [returned] to the spirit that it was in three years ago." To Crane, these events potentially foreshadowed the radicalization of the colonial world, perhaps even its eventual collapse and partitioning based on national identity, and he became increasingly pessimistic, maybe even cynical, about the immediate success of the postwar settlements which he had modestly contributed to. "Perhaps we cannot continue to mix so successfully our former excellent salad of Turks, Bulgarians, Armenians and Greeks," Crane mused, and he confided rather derisively to his friend Charles W. Eliot that "My enthusiasm is not uncontrolled about political affairs either abroad or at home."[4]

Preserving Wilson's Memory and Legacy

Charles Crane's dedication to promoting Wilsonianism did not waver after the end of the president's term and even remained constant following the latter's death in 1924. Yet Crane did not consider himself to be a simple collaborator. He was also the president's friend, and as a friend, he worried about what would become of a battered and disheartened Wilson no longer in a fit state to earn a living after leaving the White House. To Cleveland H. Dodge, Crane wrote in November of 1920: "I am concerned about what our friend will do after the 4th of March. Please keep him as serene as possible [...] and assure him of our constant and continuing interest in him."[5] This concern about the president's wellbeing after his retirement in turn encouraged Dodge to raise funds for the purchase of a new house that could accommodate Wilson and his wife. Though Arthur S. Link tells us that the idea for this purchase originated from Doctor Grayson, it remains entirely possible that Crane's letter acted as the inspiration behind this generous gesture. Among those donating money was Dodge with a $20,000 contribution, the McCormick family, Bernard Baruch, as well as other republicans, and likely Crane himself. The house, located at 2340 S Street in Washington, was chosen by Edith. Wilson lived out his last days there before his death in 1924 without ever discovering the extent of his friends' generosity.[6]

Having contributed to Wilson's present comfort, Crane turned an eye toward the future. He was certain that, Wilson's health allowing, the former president ought to put his brilliant thoughts into writing. The task that lay ahead was to "get his materials together and formulate and restate the principles that he, himself, has been acting upon and believes to be necessary for the future, not only of our people but the people of the world." By the end of 1920, Crane insisted that the publication of Wilson's work would constitute "a very precious contribution to humanity." He believed that much in the same way Confucius had shaped Chinese thought, Wilson's influence "on the rising generation in this part of the world [China], by his thoughts and actions, is very profound."[7] Not long afterward, Crane also started believing in the importance of publishing a history of Wilson's presidency. He encouraged his favorite member of Wilson's cabinet, David F. Houston, to take on this task, knowing that Houston also had the merit and the advantage of having been present during the entirety of Wilson's two terms. Houston's contribution appeared all the more essential to Crane because Lansing, who had fallen out of Wilson's good graces, had just published his own version of the fiasco in Versailles in a book called "*The Peace Negotiations: A Personal Narrative*" (1921). In it, Lansing defended his sometimes grudging loyalty to Wilson, whom he depicted as the sole responsible party in the unsuccessful dealings with European diplomacy.[8] In response to Lansing's book, Ray Stannard Baker, who had been the president's press secretary in Paris, reached out to Wilson to ask for his collaboration in putting together a personal history of the events at the Paris Peace Conference. Not particularly keen, however, on competing with Lansing, Baker asked Wilson whether he intended to read the version published by the former secretary of state. With some irony, the president replied that he had no desire to read it, but as far as it being published, he declared that "I think I can stand it if Lansing can!" Unlike Lansing, Baker had remained a staunch believer in Wilsonian diplomacy as a legitimate basis for foreign policy. With this project, he aimed "to lay a sound foundation of knowledge of what happened at Paris, as a basis upon which our future foreign diplomacy might be built,"[9] and the product of his work was a book titled *Woodrow Wilson and World Settlement* (1922). Following Crane's request and with his support, Baker also simultaneously prepared an anthology of Wilson's speeches and writings. Crane then had the anthology translated into Arabic and distributed in the Muslim world, where, according to him, the manuscript was greeted with immense gratitude. Later, Crane tasked his secretary Donald Brodie with also making the text available in Persian, Hindustani, Russian, and Chinese.[10] Historian William E. Dodd who, it seems, had also contributed to the idea of publishing Wilson's texts in the Middle East, helped Baker with the compilation process. A professor at the University of Chicago and future United States ambassador to Nazi Germany, Dodd sent Crane a list of twenty-one essential texts in a letter written on August 14, 1922 asking his opinion and requesting that he also share the list with Baker.[11] Crane himself took care of distributing the texts to the various translators he had found and in January of 1923 during a trip to Egypt, he informed Wilson that the texts had reached Cairo where they had been "received with great appreciation."[12] Several years later, Dodd and Baker worked together once again to compile the *Public Papers of Woodrow Wilson*, and Baker then published a biography of Wilson's life in eight volumes which was completed in 1940. Baker even found several of Crane's letters in the Wilson Papers while working on his biography and, commenting on the crucial and personal role Crane had played in Wilson's life and presidency, he noted that they "must have been of great help and encouragement to a hard-driven president." He also added: "I know now better than I did before I saw his record how much he prized the confidence and support of sincere friends" and graciously sent Crane the letters as a memento.

Part of this effort to document Wilson's thoughts for posterity also concerned the publication of the King-Crane Commission's report. His illness having progressed, Wilson was no longer able to defend the commission's conclusions against French and Zionist pressures. The report was almost completely forgotten, especially after America's withdrawal from the mandate project rendered its recommendations obsolete. Even the U.S. State Department, paralyzed as it was by the president's inability to fulfill his duties, never acknowledged receipt of the report nor commented on it in any way. According to Brodie, Wilson himself might never have read it.[13] With Baker's help, Crane strove to rectify this situation by finally publishing the report over which he and King had labored with such dedication. Following a phone call from Crane, Wilson agreed to have Baker coordinate the report's editing and publication and added that "Indeed, I think this is a very timely moment for its publication."[14] Though his reasons for making such a comment were never explained, it can certainly be noted that the report which had at first been suppressed could now no longer provoke any controversy domestically or abroad. The die had already been cast, and Crane's present battle pertained only to the memory and preservation of Wilsonianism.

As far as the United States' position in international relations was concerned, Crane viewed the Republican Party's return to power as a decidedly backward-looking impulse on the part of the American population and even wondered what "Teddy," who had died in 1919, would think of such a regression. Furthermore, he viewed this normalcy in foreign relations as penance, writing that "We are fortunate to have had eight years of Wilson but we have to suffer for it now and even up [...] having a Chinese wall around the U.S."[15] In retrospect, however, Crane claimed he was "entirely content with the interest we have had in the Wilson administration, and the support we have given it." He held fast to the belief that the last eight years of Wilsonian diplomacy had successfully spread the message to people around the globe and that Wilson's work, similar to that of other great prophets like Confucius, would shape the world in an enduring way:

> The actual achievements of the Wilson administration in a constructive way will pass into history. The principles proclaimed by the President in national and international affairs have gone out into the remotest corners of the world; the seed is sown and the harvest will be very great at some time.

This harvest of almost biblical proportions foreseen by Crane and stemming from the seed planted by Wilson depended on a return to Wilsonianism, as "The world will not get back on any kind of satisfactory working basis until it goes back to [Wilson's] principles."[16] Already "accepted" by the world itself, these principles had nevertheless been betrayed by the world's leaders. Crane's disillusionment was not uncommon in the postwar period and was particularly widespread in progressive circles. Yet Crane never called into question

Wilson's performance as a leader, the validity of his principles, or even their relevance and their applicability. Instead, he directed his disappointment at the world's political and diplomatic leaders. The magnitude of the war and the severity of the failure in Versailles were such that he believed himself to be witnessing no less than "the collapse of the Christian world," which to him appeared "vastly greater than the fall of the Roman Empire" as "it was accomplished in five years instead of five centuries."[17]

The decline of progressivism after the war constitutes a complex and multifaceted issue. The great scholar of Wilsonianism, Arthur S. Link, explained that strong progressive elements persisted in national policy during the 1920s. Yet Wilson's 1916 coalition, spurred on by the war's difficult circumstances, had been inherently short-lived. The absence of a capable leader after the deaths of Roosevelt and Wilson as well as growing tensions within the movement contributed to stalling the wave of reform that had previously washed over America. Many other demographic, social, and cultural factors also came into play to explain this political regression.[18] Overall, one will find that the causes of the decline listed by Link align with Crane's own observations and discover that Crane himself gradually became reactionary in certain regards, particularly where foreign policy was concerned.[19]

At Wilson's death in 1924, Crane broke the news to his son John who was in Prague visiting Masaryk at the time, writing to him that "Our friend has passed into history and his memory will inspire humanity down the age." Crane also charged John with informing Masaryk and asking him to write a passage about his relationship with Wilson, which Crane then planned to use in a speech he would be giving at the William and Mary College. He added that a simple, private funeral had initially been planned by Wilson's family but that the people of Washington had quickly gotten involved and the event had taken on national proportions.[20] Faithful to the friendship between her deceased husband and Crane, Edith Bolling Wilson asked him to be an honorary pallbearer at the funeral.[21] Theodore Roosevelt having died in 1919, this latest loss left Crane and the Progressive movement metaphorically bereft of its "parents," for though Crane never particularly liked Roosevelt, it cannot be denied that he and Wilson were both great leaders who had risen to national and international renown. With their death, America had lost "her two greatest leaders in the last generation" and felt "helpless" in the face of this bereavement.[22]

Though Crane had already retired from his political activities by the end of Wilson's presidency, Wilson's death several years later truly marked the end of an era. Nevertheless, Crane did not cease his private voyages and philanthropic pursuits both in America and abroad and particularly continued promoting social and technological development. He repeatedly traveled to Syria, Egypt, Mesopotamia, and Arabia, where he invested in industrial development and prospecting. In 1929, with the consent of Imam Yahya of Yemen, Crane hired Karl S. Twitchell, an American mining engineer, to execute several public works projects, among them the famous erection of the Arabian Peninsula's first steel truss bridge. In 1931, Crane offered Twitchell's services free of charge to King Ibn Saud, who then developed the first oil concessions in Arabia with funds provided by the Standard Oil Company.[23] This breakthrough had required patience, however, as tribal clashes in the area meant that Crane had to wait several years before meeting Ibn Saud. Furthermore, Crane's involvement in the Near East did not come risk-free as it had resulted in the death of his driver, fatally shot by rebel fighters during a drive across the Arabian Desert.[24]

Despite these technology-centric investments geared at modernizing society, Crane was primarily drawn to Arabia's isolation and its preservation of ancient traditions. It was thus rather ironic that he helped usher modernity into a region whose greatest charms for him were its ancestral customs, its history of prophets and sects, and its fascinating desert lifestyle. He admired Ibn Saud's "rustic" nature much as he appreciated the way Andrew Furuseth's character was "unspoiled by education."[25] Odd though they may seem coming from someone who contributed so much to American education in the United States and abroad, these words, "unspoiled by education," perfectly sum up the paradoxical nature of Crane's progressivism, which was simultaneously anti-intellectual and positivist.[26]

Yet as much as he appreciated minds naturally guided by experience rather than abstraction (having received little formal intellectual instruction himself), Crane deplored what he viewed as either the generalized ignorance or the biased knowledge Americans believed they had about foreign cultures and policies. To remedy this situation, Crane personally created and invested in two foundations, The Friendship Fund and the Institute of Current World Affairs. The Friendship Fund, inaugurated in 1920 with a personal donation of two million dollars for the education of his grandchildren, was also noteworthy because part of the funds had been set aside by Crane for the education of other people of their choosing. This gesture was both a testimony to the care he always had for his family's wellbeing and simultaneously demonstrated the deep-rooted interest he had inherited from his father (see Chapter 1) in offering advancement opportunities to those who needed them. The Institute of Current World Affairs, for its part, had far greater historical significance. Established in 1925, it served to train a host of specialists in international relations and awarded diplomas to men like George Antonius, a Christian Palestinian intellectual who would later go on to help Crane and act as his interpreter, particularly during his meetings with Ibn Saud.[27]

Crane was also very invested in the resolution of the territorial conflict between the imam of Yemen and the king of Arabia, warmly congratulating Ibn Saud when the latter finally succeeded in making peace with his enemy. The king's diplomatic talents seemed to have greatly impressed him, and with bitterness about the failings of Christian civilization (at least where nominal, institutional Christianity was concerned and particularly since the fiasco in Versailles), Crane commented that "There was certainly more of Jesus in Ibn Saud's treatment of his enemies than there was in France's treatment of Germany."[28] In fact, Crane believed that Jesus, having been an Easterner himself, was better understood by other Easterners, frequently citing Gandhi as an example.[29] He regretted only that the Christian world had not sufficiently absorbed the teachings of Christ.

Charles R. Crane's Role in the Progressive Movement and in Wilsonian Diplomacy

Even after the downfall of Wilsonianism, Crane remained committed to the idea of self-determination for colonized peoples and for populations under foreign influence or dominion. The war, in his mind, had at the very least succeeded in weakening the Anglo-Japanese alliance while bringing America and Great Britain closer together. It had also allowed Ireland to win its independence, which gave Crane immense pleasure. A great admirer of Gandhi, whom he compared to Wilson and Confucius, Crane eventually began promoting the liberation of India and astutely remarked that it was British interests in India that had provoked those very opium wars that had then wreaked such havoc in China.[30] His criticism of imperialist diplomacy was, in this respect, considerably more specific than some historians of the New Left like Christopher Lasch had previously concluded,[31] and it was rooted in a more or less exhaustive analysis of history.

Despite his complaints about the limitations of reformism and the obstacles posed by conservative forces, Crane's reaction to Wilson's defeat resembled that of other Progressives who, in many cases, lost the reformist ardor that had driven them in the first two decades of the twentieth century. Crane's retreat from public life in the 1920s acted as a small-scale reflection of progressivism's fate in that decade, much like his public career had been a reflection of the Progressive movement itself. In fact, he embodied many facets of progressivism throughout his lifetime. He was an agent of progressive action from his earliest days as an anticorruption and anti-vice reformer, then as a patron of the arts, an educator, and a philanthropist associated with the settlement houses and with the modernization of universities. He remained true to his progressive ideals while working as a campaigner and intermediary for La Follette and for Woodrow Wilson. Then, as a sometimes official and sometimes unofficial representative of self-determination in Wilsonian diplomacy, he continued spreading his progressive message through his participation in the Root Mission, his involvement in the Czech issue and in the King-Crane Commission, and finally through his work as a "humanitarian" diplomat in China. He was exceptional not only in his passion for exotic places and foreign cultures but also in his ample financial resources (as remarked by Richard Hofstadter in *The Age of Reform* when discussing his unusual economic status for a reformer of his time[32]). Moreover, the vast amount of collaborators and acquaintances he had, their political and social importance, and the lasting bonds he was able to forge with most of them demonstrates how diverse his activities were and how powerfully his subtle influence affected the world around him.

Wilson endorsed a type of self-determination that had many complex and perhaps even subjective meanings and modes of implementation. Without necessarily positing that anyone could aspire to complete political autonomy, Wilsonian diplomacy, especially as promoted by Crane's work, distinguished itself by a heightened sensitivity to social and ethnic diversity in regions that strove to achieve self-determination. Despite some limitations and prejudice, Wilson preferred to take this diversity into account in his approach rather than letting himself be guided by the standards of an official diplomacy based on "spheres of interest." Due in part to the information and comments relayed by Crane to the Wilson Administration, American policy during Wilson's years in power was more often geared toward respecting local uprisings even at the risk of chaos rather than conforming to the "old diplomacy," which prized stability and equilibrium of power above a peoples' right to sovereignty. Such was the case when America supported the Provisional Government in Russia, gave succor to Masaryk's revolutionary movement, and recognized the Republic of China. Thus, with Crane and Masaryk's support, Wilson did his best to resist the intervention project in Siberia designed to "halt" Bolshevism before accepting, half-heartedly and with some misgivings, a limited expedition to help the Czechoslovakian troops in Russia. Similarly, Wilson hesitated for a long time and often stood alone against the other Allied leaders before grudgingly ratifying the French mandate in Syria, knowing all the while that the King-Crane Commission's preliminary report, a reflection of the wills of the local population, advised against such a decision. Later, Wilson had to concede once more, this time to Japan's demands in Versailles. He did this very much against his own instinct to support China's claims, which he considered to be in full agreement with the Fourteen Points that he so cherished. Nevertheless, he fought valiantly and vigorously in favor of China's right to sovereignty, standing up to the adepts of the old diplomacy and to all of their secret maneuvers and imperialist interests.

As far as this secret diplomacy is concerned, one need look no further than Crane to find a shining example of a man who strove, all throughout his involvement with Wilsonianism, to build direct, nonimperialistic relations with various reformist, nationalist, and sometimes revolutionary regimes. As he had once written to Wilson in 1917 about America's relations with revolutionary Russia and China, "We ought to do everything in our power to develop and to establish on firm foundations these two peoples and hold strongly to the principles of direct relations with them."[33] In short, Crane believed that the United States had to distance itself from the motives and diplomatic tendencies of the other powers and build its own network of friendlier and more egalitarian international relations with the regimes that sought to achieve national sovereignty and democracy.

Crane believed that these new "direct" relations, which stood in opposition to imperialist interference and diplomacy, would emerge from a current of cooperation and generosity rooted in Anglo-Protestant values and in the social gospel, a founding block of progressivism in the United States. This new diplomacy, which he named "altruistic politics" before beginning his term in China, fit into a Christian and Protestant view of humanitarian engagement in the world and of Christianity's overall commitment to this task. In this regard, Crane's interest in foreign religions and particularly his sympathy toward Islam in no way prevented him from staunchly pursuing the objectives of Christian proselytism. This was often demonstrated by the comments made throughout his career, particularly during the Root Mission and the King-Crane Commission and on the subject of the work carried out for the YMCA by his friend John R. Mott. It was precisely this philanthropic element in

Crane's work that resonated so strongly with Wilson and ensured their good relationship until the president's death. Crane was part of Wilson's circle as an activist, a reformer, and a militant who worked hard to unite the partisans and the progressives and to carry out the president's programs. Yet his presence in Wilson's entourage also constitutes proof of the president's own philanthropic and missionary ideals, as well as those of his administration.

Notes

1. *Crane Papers*, "CRC to JCB," August 20, 1921; "CRC to JCB," August 28, 1921.
2. *Crane Papers*, "CRC to Cornelia S. Crane," February 26, 1922.
3. As Crane was traveling across Syria in 1922, rumors spread that he was sentenced to twenty years in prison by the French for "inciting to upheaval." Diplomats immediately denied the story. *Oberlin College Archives*, "Newspaper clipping about Charles Crane in Syria" Digital Collection, May 25, 1922 (On-line).
4. *Crane Papers*, "CRC to Eliot," September 29, 1922.
5. *Crane Papers*, "CRC to C. H. Dodge," November 26, 1920.
6. *PWW*, "C. H. Dodge to C. T. Grayson," Vol. 67, February 14, 1921. In an editorial note, Link writes that "We have not been able to identify this individual, but he was almost certainly Charles R. Crane," thus hinting at the part Crane might have played. Link also assumes that Wilson had no knowledge of the donation, as these same friends had also previously procured a car for the president, and upon discovering the provenance of the present, he had promptly thanked his benefactors. Gene Smith, in *When the Cheering Stopped: the Last Years of Woodrow Wilson* (1964), suggests that Bernard Baruch also purchased the plot of land adjacent to Wilson's new house to give the couple more privacy, but provides no sources to confirm this. See p. 174. Interestingly, Edith B. Wilson wrote Crane a letter several weeks after moving into the new home and underlined the word "privacy" in her description of the house, ("The house is airy and home-like and we are filled with the comforting sense of "home" and privacy which is, to me, enchanting"), which might be a reference to the empty plot of land adjacent to the house and could suggest Crane's involvement in its purchase. See *Crane Papers*, "E. B. Wilson to CRC," March 31, 1921.
7. *Crane Papers*, "CRC to C. H. Dodge," November 26, 1920.
8. Crane did not, however, mention the version written by House and titled *What Really Happened at Paris: The Story of the Peace Conference, 1918–1919, by American Delegates* (1921). House had also fallen into disgrace after the debacle in Versailles and had an even harsher view of Wilson than Lansing. Like Lansing, he was striving to regain his good standing in the eyes of the public.
9. *PWW*, "Diary of R. S. Baker," Vol. 67, March 22, 1921, 238.
10. *Crane Papers*, "CRC to JOC," December 27, 1922.
11. *Crane Papers*, "W. E. Dodd to CRC," July 2, August 14, 1922; "D. M. Brodie to R. R. Gailey," September 24, 1923. In this letter, Brodie confirmed that Crane had indeed come

up with the idea of publishing Wilson's texts abroad and that his initiative led Baker and Dodd to begin their collaborative work of archiving Wilson's documents for posterity.

12. *Crane Papers*, "CRC to WW," January 12, 1923. Nothing proves, however, that Wilson received this message as it does not feature in the *Wilson Papers*. Curiously, at the end of his letter, Crane expressed the hope of seeing Wilson again the following March "if God wills it" ("In sh'allah!").
13. *Crane Papers*, "Memorandum Regarding the Suppression and the Publication in 1922 of the King-Crane Report on Mandates in Turkey," August 28, 1940. The rumor that Brandeis convinced Wilson to ignore the report because of its anti-Zionist conclusions (mentioned in Chapter 5) does not feature in Brodie's analysis. In fact, Wilson's extreme exhaustion, his physical and mental inaptitude and the state of quarantine imposed on him by Edith around the time the report was sent to him makes Brodie's theory much likelier than Bruce Murphy's (cited in Chapter 5).
14. *Crane Papers*, "WW to CRC," July 6, 1922.
15. *Crane Papers*, "CRC to Eliot," November 7, 1920.
16. *Crane Papers*, "CRC to N. Hapgood," December 10, 1920.
17. *Crane Papers*, "CRC to Mildred N. Page," January 13, 1923.
18. Arthur S. Link, "What Happened to the Progressive Movement in the 1920s?," *American Historical Review*, 64, 4 (1959): 833–51. Also see Henry F. May, *The End of American Innocence*, 393–8; Hofstadter, *The Age of Reform*, 282–301. More recent literature on the subject, however, reconsiders the idea that the reaction of the Progressives to the war and to the 1920s constituted an "unfortunate interregnum" (May) or an "intermission" (Hofstadter) in what was otherwise a century of reforms.
19. Let us note, for instance, that his remarks about the Jews (particularly Zionists) became increasingly caustic in the 1920s: with some sarcasm, he took to calling them the "chosen people" or "our chosen friends." He also extended his approval to Hitler's regime from 1933 until his death in 1939, a puzzling inclination which could be the subject of a separate study. Furthermore, Crane's views on French policy in Syria radicalized, especially as of 1922, and he became very critical of King Faisal's rebellious gestures against France's presence in mandated Syria. Even where domestic policy was concerned, Crane reacted to Bolshevism in Russia by adopting a harsh stance toward the socialists. This earned him several reprimands from his sister, who considered herself a socialist and was very disappointed in her brother's attitude toward the repression in the United States.
20. *Crane Papers*, "CRC to JOC," February 7, 1924.
21. *Crane Papers*, "J. R. Bolling to CRC," February 3 and 4, 1924.
22. *Crane Papers*, "CRC to Wickham Stead (Foreign Editor, *London Times*)," November 1, 1922. Though this comment was made in 1922, two years before Wilson's death, Crane was referring to the defeat of the Democratic Party during the 1920 presidential election and to the political void which he felt had appeared after the war.
23. *Crane Papers*, "Memoirs," 341.
24. An account of this event can be found in the archives of John O. Crane, who was accompanying his father. It is cited in David Hapgood, *Charles R. Crane. The Man Who Bet on People*, 80–3, 197–202.

25. Crane in fact expressed this sentiment directly to Wilson: "I have always felt that Andrew Furuseth had one of the finest brains in the world [...] entirely unspoiled by education—that is, conventional education." *Crane Papers*, "CRC to WW," December 25, 1917.
26. *Crane Papers*, "CRC to JOC," February, 1931.
27. Hapgood, *Charles R. Crane. The Man Who Bet on People*, 89–96.
28. *Crane Papers*, "Memoirs," 347.
29. For more information on the role Crane played as a mediator in this territorial conflict, see *Crane Papers*, "Arbitration Agreement Between Ibn Saud and the Imam of the Yemen—1931–1934 (by George Antonius)," 1–2.
30. *Crane Papers*, "CRC to Wickham Stead (Foreign Editor, *London Times*)," November 1, 1922.
31. Christopher Lasch, *The American Liberals and the Russian Revolution*, viii–xix, 45–6.
32. Richard Hofstadter, *The Age of Reform*, 144.
33. *Crane Papers*, "CRC to WW," March 28, 1917.

Bibliography

Archives

Charles Richard Crane Papers, 1869–1967. Rare Books & Manuscript Library, University of Columbia.

Published Primary Sources

Baker, Ray S. and William E. Dodd, ed. *The Public Papers of Woodrow Wilson*. New York: Harper, 1925–26.

Baker, Ray S. *Woodrow Wilson: Life and Letters*. Garden City, NY: Doubleday, 1927–39.

Baruch, Bernard M. *Baruch*. New York: H. Holt, 1957–1960.

Daniels, Josephus. *The Wilson Era*. Chapel Hill: University of North Carolina Press, 1946.

House, Edward M and Charles Seymour. *What Really Happened at Paris: The Story of the Peace Conference, 1918–1919, by American Delegates*. New York: Scribner's, 1921.

Houston, David F. *Eight Years with Wilson's Cabinet, 1913–1920*. Garden City, NY: Doubleday, 1926.

Lansing, Robert. *The Peace Negotiations: A Personal Narrative*. Boston, MA: Houghton Mifflin, 1921.

Link, Arthur S., ed. *Papers of Woodrow Wilson*. Princeton, NJ: Princeton University Press, 1966–92.

Seymour, Charles, ed. *The Intimate Papers of Colonel House Arranged as a Narrative*. London: Ernest Benn, 1926–28.

Tumulty, Joseph P. *Woodrow Wilson as I Know Him*. Garden City: Doubleday, 1921.
U.S. State Department. *Papers Relating to the Foreign Relations of the United States*.

Bibliographic Guides

Buckingham, Peter H. *Woodrow Wilson: A Bibliography of His Times and Presidency*. Wilmington, DE: Scholarly Resources, 1990.
Beisner, Robert L. and Hanson Kurt W., ed. *American Foreign Relations since 1600. A Guide to the Literature*. Santa Barbara, CA: ABC-CLIO, 2003.
Bellot, Hugh Hale. *American History and American Historians: A Review of Recent Contributions to the Interpretation of the History of the United States*. Norman: University of Oklahoma Press, 1952.
Parish, Peter J., ed. *Reader's Guide to American History*. Chicago: Fitzroy Publishers, 1997.

Encyclopedias

Balmer, Randall Herbert. *Encyclopedia of Evangelicalism*. Louisville, KY: John Knox Press, 2002.

Monographies

Aaron, Daniel. *Men of Good Hope. A Story of American Progressives*. New York: Oxford University Press, 1961.
Ambrosius, Lloyd E. *Woodrow Wilson and the American Diplomatic Tradition: The Treaty Fight in Perspective*. Cambridge: Cambridge University Press, 1987.
———. *Wilsonian Statecraft: Theory and Practice of Liberal Internationalism during World War I*. Lanham, MD: SR Books, 1991.
———. *Wilsonianism: Woodrow Wilson and His Legacy in American Foreign Relations*. New York: Palgrave Macmillan, 2002.
Baker, Ray S. *Woodrow Wilson and World Settlement*. Garden City, NY: Doubleday, 1922.
Bell, Sidney. *Righteous Conquest. Woodrow Wilson and the Evolution of the New Diplomacy*. Port Washington, NY: Kennikat Press, 1972.
Blum, John M. *Woodrow Wilson and the Politics of Morality*. Boston: Little, Brown & Co., 1956.
Calhoun, Frederick S. *Uses of Force and Wilsonian Foreign Policy*. Kent, OH: Kent State University Press, 1993.
Clements, Kendrick A. *The Presidency of Woodrow Wilson*. Lawrence, KA: University Press of Kansas, 1992.
Cohen, Warren I. *Empire Without Tears: America's Foreign Relations, 1921–1933*. New York: Knopf, 1987.
Cooper, John M. *The Vanity of Power. American Isolationism and the First World War, 1914–1917*. Westport, CT: Greenwood Publishing Corp., 1969.
———. *The Warrior and the Priest*. Cambridge: Harvard University Press, 1983.

———. *Woodrow Wilson*. New York: Alfred A. Knopf, 2009.
Duroselle, Jean-Baptiste. *Histoire diplomatique de 1919 à nos jours*, 11th ed. Paris: Éditions Dalloz, 1993.
Ekirch, Arthur A. *Progressivism in America: A Study of the Era from Theodore Roosevelt to Woodrow Wilson*. New York: New Viewpoints, 1974.
Ferrell, Robert H. *Woodrow Wilson and World War I, 1917–1921*. New York: Harper & Row, 1985.
Gardner, Lloyd C. *Safe for Democracy. The Anglo-American Response to Revolution, 1913–1923*. New York: Oxford University Press. 1984.
Hansen, Jonathan M. *The Lost Promise of Patriotism. Debating American Identity, 1890–1920*. Chicago: University of Chicago Press, 2003.
Hapgood, David. *Charles R. Crane. The Man Who Bet on People*. New York: ICWA, 2000.
Hofstadter, Richard. *The Age of Reform. From Bryan to FDR*. New York: Vintage Books, 1955.
Iriye, Akira. *From Nationalism to Internationalism. U.S. Foreign Policy to 1914*. London: Routledge, 2002.
Israel, Jerry. *Progressivism and the Open Door. America and China, 1905–1921*. Pittsburgh: University of Pittsburgh Press, 1971.
Kaplan, Robert D. *The Arabists. The Romance of an American Elite*. New York: The Free Press, 1993.
Kennan, George F. *American Diplomacy, 1900–1950*. New York: New American Library, 1954.
Kennedy, David M. *Over Here. The First World War and American Society*. New York: Oxford University Press, 1980.
Kloppenberg, James T. *Uncertain Victory. Social Democracy and Progressivism in European and American Thought, 1870–1920*. Oxford: Oxford University Press, 1986.
Knock, Thomas J. *To End all Wars. Woodrow Wilson and the Quest for a New World Order*. New York: Oxford University Press, 1992.
LaFeber, Walter. *The New Empire. An Interpretation of American Expansion, 1860–1898*. Ithaca, NY: Cornell University Press, 1963.
Lasch, Christopher. *The American Liberals and the Russian Revolution*. New York: McGraw, 1962.
Levin, Norman G. *Woodrow Wilson and World Politics: America's Response to War and Revolution*. New York: Oxford University Press, 1968.
Link, Arthur S. *Wilson*. Princeton, NJ: Princeton University Press, 1947.
———. *Woodrow Wilson and the Progressive Era, 1910–1917*. New York: Harper & Brothers, 1954.
———. *Wilson the Diplomatist. A Look at His Major Foreign Policies*. Baltimore: Johns Hopkins Press, 1957.
———. *Woodrow Wilson. Revolution, War, and Peace*. Arlington Heights, IL: Harlan Davidson, 1979.
Lippmann, Walter. *U.S Foreign Policy, Shield of the Republic*. Boston: Little & Brown, 1943.
Manela, Erez. *The Wilsonian Moment: Self-Determination and the International Origins of Anticolonial Nationalism, 1917–1920*. New York: Oxford University Press, 2007.

May, Ernest. *Imperial Democracy. The Emergence of America as a Great Power*. New York: Harper & Row, 1973.

May, Henry F. *The End of American Innocence. The First Years of Our Own Times, 1912–1917*. New York: Oxford University Press, 1959.

Mayer, Arno. *Politics and Diplomacy of Peacemaking: Containment and Counterrevolution at Versailles, 1918–1919*. New York: Knopf, 1967.

McCartney, Paul T. *Power and Progress: American National Identity, the War of 1898, and the Rise of American Imperialism*. Baton Rouge: Louisiana University Press, 2006.

McGerr, Michael. *A Fierce Discontent. The Rise and Fall of the Progressive Movement in America, 1870–1920*. Oxford: Oxford University Press, 2003.

McLoughlin, William G. *Revivals, Awakenings, and Reform. An Essay on Religion and Social Change in America, 1607–1977*. Chicago: The Chicago University Press, 1978.

Noble, David W. *The Paradox of Progressive Thought*. Minneapolis: University of Minnesota Press, 1958.

———. *The Progressive Mind, 1890–1917*. Minneapolis: Burgess, 1981.

Nordholdt, Jan W. S. *Woodrow Wilson: A Life for World Peace*. Berkeley: University of California Press, 1991.

Notter, Harley. *The Origins of the Foreign Policy of Woodrow Wilson*. New York: Russell & Russell, 1965.

O'Neill, William L. *The Progressive Years. America Comes of Age*. New York: Dodd, Mead and Company, 1975.

Osgood, Robert E. *Ideals and Self-Interests in America's Foreign Relations. The Great Transformation of the Twentieth Century*. Chicago: University of Chicago, 1964 [c.1953].

Saul, Norman E. *The Life and Times of Charles R. Crane, 1858–1939. American Businessman, Philanthropist, and a Founder of Russian Studies in America*. Lanham, MD: Lexington Books, 2013.

Smith, Gene. *When the Cheering Stopped: The Last Years of Woodrow Wilson*. New York: Morrow, 1964.

Smith, Neil. *American Empire: Roosevelt's Geographer and the Prelude to Globalization*. Berkeley: University of California Press, 2003.

Steel, Ronald. *Walter Lippmann and the American Century*. Boston: Little, Brown & Co. 1980.

Thorsen, Niels A. *The Political Thought of Woodrow Wilson, 1875–1910*. Princeton, NJ: Princeton University Press, 1988.

Trachtenberg, Alan. *The Incorporation of America. Culture and Society in the Gilded Age*. New York: Hill & Wang, 1982.

Trask, David F. *Victory without Peace. American Foreign Relations in the Twentieth Century*. Huntington, New York: Robert E. Krieger Publishing Company, 1975.

Van Alstyne, Richard W. *The Rising American Empire*. Oxford: Oxford University Press, 1960.

Weinstein, Edwin A. *Woodrow Wilson: A Medical and Psychological Biography*. Princeton, NJ: Princeton University Press, 1981.

Wiebe, Robert H. *Businessmen and Reform. A Study of the Progressive Movement*. Cambridge: CUP, 1989 [c.1962].

———. *The Search for Order, 1877–1920*. London: Macmillan, 1967.

Williams, William A. *The Tragedy of American Diplomacy*. New York: Dell Publishing, 1972 [c.1959].
———. *Some Presidents: Wilson to Nixon*. New York: Vintage Books, 1972.

Theses

Bocage, Leo J. "The Public Career of Charles R. Crane." Ph.D. diss., Fordham University, 1962.
Sulzbach, Jacob John, Jr. "Charles R. Crane, Woodrow Wilson, and Progressive Reform: 1909–1921." Ph.D. diss., Texas A&M University, 1994.

Journal Articles

Clements, Kendrick A. "The Papers of Woodrow Wilson and the Interpretation of the Wilson Era." *The History Teacher*, 27, 4, 1994, 475–489.
Leuchtenburg, William E. "Progressivism and Imperialism: The Progressive Movement and American Foreign Policy, 1898–1916." *The Mississippi Valley Historical Review*, 39, 3, 1952, 483–504.
Link, Arthur S. "The Higher Realism of Woodrow Wilson." *Journal of Presbyterian History*, 41, 1, 1963, 1–13.
———. "What Happened to the Progressive Movement in the 1920s?" *The American Historical Review*, 64, 4, 1959, 833–851.
Malkasian, Mark. "The disintegration of the Armenian Cause in the United States, 1918–1927." *International Journal of Middle East Studies*, 16, 3, 1984, 349–365.
McCormick, Richard L. "The Discovery That Business Corrupts Politics: A Reappraisal of the Origins of Progressivism." *The American Historical Review*, 86, 2, 1981, 247–274.
Osgood, Robert E. "Woodrow Wilson, Collective Security, and the Lessons of History." *Confluence*, 5, 1957, 341–354.
Pomerance, Michla. "The United States and Self-determination: Perspectives on the Wilsonian Conception." *The American Journal of International Law*, 70, 1, 1976, 1–27.
Rodgers, Daniel T. "In search of Progressivism." *Reviews in American History*, 10, 4, 1982, 113–132.
Saito, Natsu T. "Crossing the Border: The Interdependence of Foreign Policy and Racial Justice in the United States." *Yale Human Rights and Development Law Journal*, 1, 1998, 53–84.
Seltzer, Alan L. "Woodrow Wilson as Corporate-Liberal: Toward a Reconsideration of Left Revisionist Historiography." *The Western Political Quarterly*, 30, 2, 1977, 183–212.

Collective Works

Allerfeldt, Kristofer, ed. *The Progressive Era in the USA: 1890–1921*. Burlington, VT: Ashgate, 2007.
Braeman, John, ed. *Wilson*. Englewood Cliffs, NJ: Prentice-Hall, 1972.
Haines, G. K. and J. S. Walker, ed. *American Foreign Relations. A Historiographical Review*. Westport, CT: Greenwood Press, 1981.

BIBLIOGRAPHY

Archives

American Board of Commissioners for Foreign Mission Papers. Houghton Library, Harvard University.

Charles Richard Crane Papers, 1869–1967. Rare Books & Manuscript Library, University of Columbia.

James Ford Rhodes Papers. Massachusetts Historical Society.

Oberlin College Archives. King-Crane Commission Digital Collection: www.oberlin.edu/library/digital/king-crane/

Published Primary Sources

Baker, John E. *Report of the China Famine Relief. American Red Cross. October 1920–September 1921*. Cornell University Library, 1921.

Baker, Ray S. and William E. Dodd, ed. *The Public Papers of Woodrow Wilson*. New York: Harper, 1925–26.

Baker, Ray S. *Woodrow Wilson: Life and Letters*. Garden City, NY: Doubleday, 1927–39.

Barton, James L. *Story of Near East Relief*. New York: Macmillan, 1930.

Baruch, Bernard M. *Baruch*. New York: H. Holt, 1957–1960.

Bryce, James and Arnold J. Toynbee. *Le livre bleu du Gouvernement britannique concernant le traitement des Arméniens de l'Empire ottoman, 1915–1916*. Paris: Payot, 1987 [c.1916].

Burnett, Philip M. *Reparation at the Paris Peace Conference, from the Standpoint of the American Delegation*. New York: Octagon Books, 1965 [c.1940].

Capek, Karel. *Entretiens avec Masaryk*. Paris: Éditions de l'aube, 1991 [c.1936].

Crane, Richard T. *The Autobiography of Richard Teller Crane*. Chicago, 1927.

Croly, Herbert. *The Promise of American Life*. New York: Capricorn Books, 1964 [c.1909].

Daniels, Josephus. *The Wilson Era*. Chapel Hill: University of North Carolina Press, 1946.

Edib, Halide. *Memoirs of Halide Edib*. New York: The Century, 1926.

———. *The Turkish Ordeal. Being the Further Memoirs of Halide Edib*. New York: The Century, 1928.

Harper, Samuel N. *The Russia I Believe In: The Memoirs of Samuel N. Harper*. Chicago: University of Chicago Press, 1945.

Hart, Albert B. *The War in Europe. Its Causes and results*. New York: D. Appleton, 1914.

House, Edward M and Charles Seymour. *What Really Happened at Paris: The Story of the Peace Conference, 1918–1919, by American Delegates*. New York: Scribner's, 1921.

Houston, David F. *Eight Years with Wilson's Cabinet, 1913–1920*. Garden City, NY: Doubleday, 1926.

Krooss, Herman E., ed. *A Documentary History of Banking and Currency in the United States*. New York: Chelsea Pub., 1969.

La Follette, Robert Marion. *La Follette's Autobiography*. Madison: University of Wisconsin Press, 1968 [c.1912].

Lansing, Robert. *The Peace Negotiations: A Personal Narrative*. Boston, MA: Houghton Mifflin,1921.

Laufer, Berthold. *Sino-Iranica. Chinese Contributions to the History of Civilization in Ancient Iran*. Field Museum of Chicago, 1919.

Link, Arthur S., ed. *Papers of Woodrow Wilson*. Princeton, NJ: Princeton University Press, 1966–92.

Mantoux, Paul. *Les délibérations du Conseil des Quatre, 24 mars-28 juin 1919. Notes de l'officier-Interprète Paul Mantoux*. Paris: Ed. CNRS, 1955.

Masaryk, Tomas G. *The New Europe: the Slav Standpoint*. Lewisburg: Bucknell University Press, 1972 [c.1918].

Morgenthau, Henry. *Ambassador Morgenthau's Story*. Detroit: Wayne State University Press, 2003 [c.1918].

Mucha, Jiri. *Alphonse Maria Mucha. His Life and Art*. New York: Rozzoli, 1989.

Pinchot, Amos. *The History of the Progressive Party, 1912–1916*. New York: New York University Press, 1958.

Powell, John B. My *Twenty-Five Years in China*. New York: Macmillan, 1945.

Seton-Watson, R. W. *Masaryk in England*. Cambridge: Cambridge University Press, 1943.

Seymour, Charles, ed. *The Intimate Papers of Colonel House Arranged as a Narrative*. London: Ernest Benn, 1926–28.

Steffens, Lincoln. *The Shame of the Cities*. New York: Sagamore Press, 1957 [c.1904].

———. *The Autobiography of Lincoln Steffens*. New York: Harcourt, Brace & Co., 1931.

Sun Yat-sen, *Souvenirs d'un révolutionnaire chinois*. Paris: Éditions d'aujourd'hui, 1983 [c.1920].
Tarbell, Ida M. *The History of the Standard Oil Company*. New York: Harper & Row, 1966 [c.1904].
Taylor, Graham. *Chicago Commons through Forty Years*. Chicago: Chicago Commons Association, 1936.
Tumulty, Joseph P. *Woodrow Wilson as I Know Him*. Garden City: Doubleday, 1921.
U.S. State Department. *Papers Relating to the Foreign Relations of the United States*.

Bibliographic Guides

Buckingham, Peter H. *Woodrow Wilson: A Bibliography of His Times and Presidency*. Wilmington, DE: Scholarly Resources, 1990.
Beisner, Robert L. and Hanson Kurt W., ed. *American Foreign Relations since 1600. A Guide to the Literature*. Santa Barbara, CA: ABC-CLIO, 2003.
Bellot, Hugh Hale. *American History and American Historians: A Review of Recent Contributions to the Interpretation of the History of the United States*. Norman: University of Oklahoma Press, 1952.
Parish, Peter J., ed. *Reader's Guide to American History*. Chicago: Fitzroy Publishers, 1997.

Encyclopedias

Balmer, Randall Herbert. *Encyclopedia of Evangelicalism*. Louisville, KY: John Knox Press, 2002.
Shelton, Dinah L., ed. *Encyclopedia of Genocide and Crimes against Humanity*. Detroit: Macmillan Reference USA, 2004.

Monographies

Aaron, Daniel. *Men of Good Hope. A Story of American Progressives*. New York: Oxford University Press, 1961.
Ambrosius, Lloyd E. *Woodrow Wilson and the American Diplomatic Tradition: the Treaty Fight in Perspective*. Cambridge: Cambridge University Press, 1987.
———. *Wilsonian Statecraft: Theory and Practice of Liberal Internationalism during World War I*. Lanham, MD: SR Books, 1991.
———. *Wilsonianism: Woodrow Wilson and His Legacy in American Foreign Relations*. New York: Palgrave Macmillan, 2002.
Akçam, Taner. *From Empire to Republic. Turkish Nationalism and the Armenian Genocide*. London: Zed Books, 2004.
Balakian, Peter. *The Burning Tigris: The Armenian Genocide and America's Response*. New York: Harper Collins, 2003.
Bailey, Thomas A. *Woodrow Wilson and the Lost Peace*. New York: Macmillan, 1944.
———. *Woodrow Wilson and the Great Betrayal*. Chicago: Quadrangle Books, 1945.

Bainville, Jacques. *Les conséquences politiques de la paix*. Paris: Éditions de l'Arsenal, 1995 [c.1919].

Baker, Ray S. *Woodrow Wilson and World Settlement*. Garden City, NY: Doubleday, 1922.

Balmer, Martin. *The Chicago School of Sociology. Institutionalization, Diversity, and the Rise of Sociological Research*. Chicago: University of Chicago Press, 1984.

Bell, Sidney. *Righteous Conquest. Woodrow Wilson and the Evolution of the New Diplomacy*. Port Washington, NY: Kennikat Press, 1972.

Berlin, William S. *On the Edge of Politics. The Roots of Jewish Political Thought in America*. Westport, CT: Greenwood Press, 1978.

Blum, John M. *Woodrow Wilson and the Politics of Morality*. Boston: Little, Brown & Co., 1956.

———. *The Republican Roosevelt*. Cambridge: Harvard University Press, 1954.

Bouchard, Carl. *Le citoyen et l'ordre mondial. Le rêve d'une paix durable au lendemain de la Grande Guerre*. Paris: Éditions A. Pedone, 2008.

Bradley, John F. N. *Czech Nationalism in the Nineteenth Century*. New York: Columbia University Press, 1984.

Bu, Liping. *Making the World Like Us: Education, Cultural Expansion, and the American Century*. Westport, CT: Praeger, 2003.

Buenker, John D. *Urban Liberalism and Progressive Reform*. New York: Scribner's Sons, 1973.

———. *The Income Tax and the Progressive Era*. New York: Garland, 1985.

Burns, James M. *The Workshop of Democracy. From the Emancipation Proclamation to the Era of the New Deal*. New York: Vintage Book, 1985.

Calhoun, Frederick S. *Uses of Force and Wilsonian Foreign Policy*. Kent, OH: Kent State University Press, 1993.

Čapek, Thomas. *The Čechs (Bohemians) in America*. New York: Arno Press, 1969 [c.1920].

Chamberlain, John. *Farewell to Reform. The Rise, Life and Decay of the Progressive Mind in America*. Chicago: Quadrangle, 1965 [c.1932].

Chambers II, John W. *The Tyranny of Change. America in the Progressive Era, 1900–1917*. New York: St-Martin's Press, 1980.

Chernow, Ron. *Titan: The Life and Time of John D. Rockefeller, Sr*. New York: Random House, 1998.

Chessman, G. W. *Theodore Roosevelt and the Politics of Power*. Boston: Little, Brown & Co., 1969.

Childs, Marquis and James Reston, ed. *Walter Lippmann and His Times*. Freeport, NY: Books For Libraries Press, 1968 [c.1959].

Chow Tse-tsung. *The May Fourth Movement: Intellectual Revolution in Modern China*. Cambridge: Harvard University Press, 1960.

Clements, Kendrick A. *William Jennings Bryan, Missionary Isolationist*. Knoxville, TE: University of Tennessee Press, 1982.

———. *The Presidency of Woodrow Wilson*. Lawrence, KA: University Press of Kansas, 1992.

Clifford, A. J. *The Independence of the Federal Reserve System*. Philadelphia: University of Pennsylvania Press, 1965.

Cohen, Warren I. *America's Response to China. An Interpretative History of Sino-American Relations*. New York: Wiley, 1971.

———. *Empire Without Tears: America's Foreign Relations, 1921–1933*. New York: Knopf, 1987.

Cooper, John M. *The Vanity of Power. American Isolationism and the First World War, 1914–1917*. Westport, CT: Greenwood Publishing Corp., 1969.

———. *The Warrior and the Priest*. Cambridge: Harvard University Press, 1983.

———. *Woodrow Wilson*. New York: Alfred A. Knopf, 2009.

Craft, Stephen G. *V. K. Wellington Koo and the Emergence of Modern China*. Lexington: University of Kentucky Press, 2004.

Cranston, Alan. *The Killing of the Peace*. New York: The Viking Press, 1945.

Crunden, Robert M. *Ministers of Reform. The Progressives' Achievement in American Civilization, 1889–1920*. Chicago: University of Illinois Press, 1982.

Curti, Merle E. *The Roots of American Loyalty*. New York: Columbia University Press, 1946.

———. *American Philanthropy Abroad*. New Brunswick, NJ: Rutgers University Press, 1963.

Davis, Donald E., and Eugene P. Trani. *The First Cold War. The Legacy of Woodrow Wilson in U.S.-Soviet Relations*. Columbia: University of Missouri Press, 2002.

Denovo, John. *American Interests and Politics in the Middle East: 1900–1939*. Minneapolis: The University of Minnesota Press, 1963.

Diamond, William. *The Economic Thought of Woodrow Wilson*. Baltimore: The Johns Hopkins Press, 1943.

Diggins, John Patrick. *The Promise of Pragmatism: Modernism and the Crisis of Knowledge and Authority*. Chicago: University of Chicago Press, 1994.

Diner, Steven J. *A City and Its Universities: Public Policies in Chicago, 1892–1919*. 1980.

Dorreboom, Iris. *The Challenge of Our Time: Woodrow Wilson, Herbert Croly, Randolph Bourne and the Making of Modern America*. Atlanta, GA: Rodopi, 1991.

Duroselle, Jean-Baptiste. *Histoire diplomatique de 1919 à nos jours*, 11th ed. Paris: Éditions Dalloz, 1993.

Eckes, Alfred E. *Opening America's Market. U.S. Foreign Trade Policy Since 1776*. Chapel Hill: University of North Carolina Press, 1995.

Ekirch, Arthur A. *Progressivism in America: A Study of the Era from Theodore Roosevelt to Woodrow Wilson*. New York: New Viewpoints, 1974.

Evans, Lawrence. *United States Policy and the Partition of Turkey, 1914–1924*. Baltimore: The Johns Hopkins University Press, 1965.

Fairbank, John K. *The United States and China*. Cambridge: Harvard University Press, 1979.

———. *The Cambridge History of China. Vol. 12, Republican China, 1912–1949*. Cambridge: Cambridge University Press, 1983.

Feingold, Henry L. *Zion in America*. New York: Twayne Publishers Inc., 1974.

Ferrell, Robert H. *Woodrow Wilson and World War I, 1917–1921*. New York: Harper & Row, 1985.

Figes, Orlando *A People's Tragedy. The Russian Revolution, 1891–1924*. New York, Penguin Books, 1996.

Forcey, Charles. *The Crossroads of Liberalism. Croly, Weyl, Lippmann and the Progressive Era, 1900–1925*. Oxford: Oxford University Press, 1961.

Freud, Sigmund and William C. Bullitt. *Le Président Thomas Woodrow Wilson*. Paris: Albin Michel, 1967 [c.1939].

Fromkin, David. *A Peace to End All Peace. Creating the Modern Middle East, 1914–1922*. New York: Holt, 1989.

Gardner, Lloyd C. *Safe for Democracy. The Anglo-American Response to Revolution, 1913–1923*. New York: Oxford University Press. 1984.

Gerson, Louis L. *Woodrow Wilson and the Rebirth of Poland 1914–1920. A Study in the Influence on American Policy of Minority Groups of Foreign Origin*. Hamden, CT: Archon Books, 1972 [c.1953].

Gidney, James. B. *A Mandate for Armenia*. Kent, OH: Kent State University Press, 1967.

Girault, René. *Diplomatie européenne. Nations et impérialisme, 1871–1914*. Paris: Armand Colin, 1995.

Goldstein, Judith. *Ideas, Interests, and American Trade Policy*. Ithaca, NY: Cornell University Press, 1993.

Gould, Lewis L. *The Progressive Era*. Syracuse, NY: Syracuse University Press, 1974.

———. *Four Hats in the Ring. The 1912 Election and the Birth of Modern American Politics*. Lawrence, KA: University Press of Kansas, 2008.

Grabill, Joseph L. *Protestant Diplomacy in the Near East. Missionary Influence on American Policy, 1810–1927*. Minneapolis: University of Minnesota Press, 1971.

Hansen, Jonathan M. *The Lost Promise of Patriotism. Debating American Identity, 1890–1920*. Chicago: University of Chicago Press, 2003.

Hapgood, David. *Charles R. Crane. The Man Who Bet on People*. New York: ICWA, 2000.

Harbaugh, William H. *The Life and Times of Theodore Roosevelt*. London: Oxford University Press, 1975 [c.1961].

Harr, John E and Peter J. Johnson. 1991. *The Rockefeller Conscience. An American Family in Public and in Private*. New York: Macmillan.

Hays, Samuel P. *American Political History as Social Analysis*. Knoxville: University of Tennessee Press, 1980.

Hermet, Guy. *Histoire des nations et du nationalisme en Europe*. Paris: Seuil, 1996.

Hofstadter, Richard. *Social Darwinism in American Thought*. Boston: Beacon Press, 1992 [c.1944].

———. *The American Political Tradition and the Men Who Made It*. New York: Vintage Books, 1989 [c.1948].

———. *The Age of Reform. From Bryan to FDR*. New York: Vintage Books, 1955.

———. *Anti-Intellectualism in American Life*. New York: Vintage Books, 1963.

———. *The Paranoid Style in American Politics*. New York: Alfred A. Knopf, 1965.

Holmes, James R. *Theodore Roosevelt and World Order. Police Power in International Relations*. Washington: Potomac Books, 2006.

Hopkins, Charles H. *John R. Mott, 1865–1955: A Biography*. Grand Rapids: Eerdmans, 1979.

Howard, Harry. *The King-Crane Commission. An American Inquiry in the Middle-East*. Beyrouth: Kayats, 1963.

Iriye, Akira. *From Nationalism to Internationalism. U.S. Foreign Policy to 1914*. London: Routledge, 2002.
Israel, Jerry. *Progressivism and the Open Door. America and China, 1905–1921*. Pittsburgh: University of Pittsburgh Press, 1971.
Kaplan, Robert D. *The Arabists. The Romance of an American Elite*. New York: The Free Press, 1993.
Keegan, John. *The First World War*. New York: Random House, 1998.
Kennan, George F. *American Diplomacy, 1900–1950*. New York: New American Library, 1954.
———. *The Soviet-American Relations, 1917–1920*. Princeton, NJ: Princeton University Press, 1956.
Kennedy, David M. *Over Here. The First World War and American Society*. New York: Oxford University Press, 1980.
Keynes, John Maynard. *Les conséquences économiques de la Paix*. Paris: Nouvelle Revue Française, 1920.
King, Wunsz. *China at the Paris Peace Conference in 1919*. New York: St-John's University Press, 1961.
Kitsikis, Dimitri. *Le rôle des experts à la Conférence de la Paix de 1919. Gestation d'une technocratie en politique internationale*. Ottawa: Éditions de l'Université d'Ottawa, 1972.
Kloppenberg, James T. *Uncertain Victory. Social Democracy and Progressivism in European and American Thought, 1870–1920*. Oxford: Oxford University Press, 1986.
Knock, Thomas J. *To End all Wars. Woodrow Wilson and the Quest for a New World Order*. New York: Oxford University Press, 1992.
Kolko, Gabriel. *The triumph of Conservatism: a Reinterpretation of American History, 1900–1916*. New York: Free Press, 1963.
LaFeber, Walter. *The New Empire. An Interpretation of American Expansion, 1860–1898*. Ithaca, NY: Cornell University Press, 1963.
Lake, David A. *Power, Protection, and Free Trade. International Sources of U.S. Commercial Strategy, 1887–1939*. Ithaca, NY: Cornell University Press, 1988.
Lasch, Christopher. *The American Liberals and the Russian Revolution*. New York: McGraw, 1962.
———. *The New Radicalism in America. The Intellectual as a Social Type*. New York: Knopf, 1965.
Laserson, Max M. *The American Impact in Russia, 1784–1917*. New York: Collier, 1950.
Latham, Earl. *John D. Rockefeller. Robber Baron or Industrial Statesman?* Boston: Heath & Co., 1949.
Leuchtenburg, William E. *The Perils of Prosperity, 1914–1932*. Chicago: University of Chicago Press, 1993 [c.1958].
Levin, Norman G. *Woodrow Wilson and World Politics: America's Response to War and Revolution*. New York: Oxford University Press, 1968.
Lewis, Bernard. *The Emergence of Modern Turkey*. London: Oxford University Press, 1961.
Lindberg, Richard C. *The Gambler King of Clark Street: Michael C. McDonald and the Rise of Chicago's Democratic Machine*. Carbondale: Southern Illinois University Press, 2009.
Link, Arthur S. *Wilson*. Princeton, NJ: Princeton University Press, 1947.

———.*Woodrow Wilson and the Progressive Era, 1910–1917*. New York: Harper & Brothers, 1954.

———. *Wilson the Diplomatist. A Look at His Major Foreign Policies*. Baltimore, Johns Hopkins Press, 1957.

———.*Woodrow Wilson. Revolution, War, and Peace*. Arlington Heights, IL: Harlan Davidson, 1979.

Lippmann, Walter. *U.S Foreign Policy, Shield of the Republic*. Boston: Little & Brown, 1943.

Livermore, Seward W. *Woodrow Wilson and the War Congress 1916–1918*. New York: Octagon Books, 1968 [c. 1957].

Livingstone, James. *Origins of the Federal Reserve System. Money, Class, and Corporate Capitalism, 1890–1913*. Cornell University Press, 1986.

Lundberg, Ferdinand. *The Rockefeller Syndrome*. Secaucus, NJ: Lyle Stuart Inc., 1975.

Mamatey, Victor S. *The United States and East Central Europe, 1914–1918. A Study in Wilsonian Diplomacy and Propaganda*. Princeton, NJ: Princeton University Press, 1957.

Manela, Erez. *The Wilsonian Moment: Self-Determination and the International Origins of Anticolonial Nationalism, 1917–1920*. New York, Oxford University Press, 2007.

Mason, Alpheus T. *Brandeis: A Free Man's Life*. New York: Viking Press, 1946.

Maxwell, Robert S. *La Follette and the Rise of the Progressives in Wisconsin*. New York: Russell & Russell, 1973 [c.1956].

May, Ernest. *The World War and American Isolation, 1914–1917*. Cambridge: Harvard University Press, 1966 [c.1959].

———. *Imperial Democracy. The Emergence of America as a Great Power*. New York: Harper & Row, 1973.

May, Henry F. *The End of American Innocence. The First Years of Our Own Times, 1912–1917*. New York: Oxford University Press, 1959.

Mayer, Arno. *Politics and Diplomacy of Peacemaking: Containment and Counterrevolution at Versailles, 1918–1919*. New York: Knopf, 1967.

McCormick, Richard L. *The Party Period and Public Policy. American Politics from the Age of Jackson to the Progressive Era*. New York: Oxford University Press, 1986.

McCartney, Paul T. *Power and Progress: American National Identity, the War of 1898, and the Rise of American Imperialism*. Baton Rouge: Louisiana University Press, 2006.

McGerr, Michael. *A Fierce Discontent. The Rise and Fall of the Progressive Movement in America, 1870–1920*. Oxford: Oxford University Press, 2003.

McLoughlin, William G. *Revivals, Awakenings, and Reform. An Essay on Religion and Social Change in America, 1607–1977*. Chicago: The Chicago University Press, 1978.

Michel, Bernard. *Nations et nationalismes en Europe centrale, XIXe-XXe siècle*. Paris: Aubier, 1995.

Mowry, George E. *The Era of Theodore Roosevelt, 1900–1912*. New York: Harper, 1958.

Murphy, Bruce. *The Brandeis/Frankfurter Connection. The Secret Political Activities of Two Supreme Court Justices*. New York: Oxford University Press, 1982.

Muukkonen, Martti. *Ecumenism of the Laity. Continuity and Change in the Mission View of the World's Alliance of YMCA, 1855–1955*. Joensuu: University of Joensuu Publications in Theology, 2002.

Nevins, Allan. *John D. Rockefeller: The Heroic Age of American Enterprise*. New York: C. Scribner's Sons, 1941.

Noble, David W. *The Paradox of Progressive Thought*. Minneapolis: University of Minnesota Press, 1958.

———. *The Progressive Mind, 1890–1917*. Minneapolis: Burgess, 1981.

Nordholdt, Jan W. S. *Woodrow Wilson: A Life for World Peace*. Berkeley: University of California Press, 1991.

Notter, Harley. *The Origins of the Foreign Policy of Woodrow Wilson*. New York: Russell & Russell, 1965.

O'Neill, William L. *The Progressive Years. America Comes of Age*. New York: Dodd, Mead and Company, 1975.

Osgood, Robert E. *Ideals and Self-Interests in America's Foreign Relations. The Great Transformation of the Twentieth Century*. Chicago: University of Chicago, 1964 [c.1953].

Payaslian, Simon. *United States Policy toward the Armenian Question and the Armenian Genocide*. New York: Palgrave, 2005.

Pérennès, Roger. *La Palestine et la Décadence de l'Empire Ottoman, 1820–1920*. Nantes: Ouest Éditions & Université Permanente de Nantes, 1999.

Peterson, Merrill D. *Starving Armenians. America and the Armenian Genocide, 1915–1930 and After*. Charlottesville: University of Virginia Press, 2004.

Platt, Stephen R. *Autumn in the Heavenly Kingdom. China, the West, and the Epic Story of the Taiping Civil War*. New York, Vintage Books, 2012.

Preston, Diana. *The Boxer Rebellion. China's War on Foreigners, 1900*. London: Robinson, 1999.

Quirk, Robert E. *An Affair of Honor. Woodrow Wilson and the Occupation of Veracruz*. New York: McGraw-Hill, 1964.

Ratner, Sidney. *The Tariff in American History*. New York: Nostrand Co., 1972.

Saul, Norman E. *The Life and Times of Charles R. Crane, 1858–1939. American Businessman, Philanthropist, and a Founder of Russian Studies in America*. Lanham, MD: Lexington Books, 2013.

Schaller, Michael. *The United States and China in the Twentieth Century*. New York: Oxford University Press, 1979.

Schneirov, Richard. *Labor and Urban Politics. Class Conflict and the Origins of Modern Liberalism in Chicago, 1864–97*. Chicago: University of Illinois Press, 1998.

Sklar, Martin J. *The Corporate Reconstruction of American Capitalism, 1890–1916: The Market, the Law, and Politics*. Cambridge: Cambridge University Press, 1988.

Smith, Gene. *When the Cheering Stopped: The Last Years of Woodrow Wilson*. New York: Morrow, 1964.

Smith, Neil. *American Empire: Roosevelt's Geographer and the Prelude to Globalization*. Berkeley: University of California Press, 2003.

Soutou, Georges-Henri. *L'or et le sang. Les buts de guerre économiques de la Première Guerre mondiale*. Paris: Fayard, 1989.

Steel, Ronald. *Walter Lippmann and the American Century*. Boston: Little, Brown & Co. 1980.

Stettner, Edward A. *Shaping Modern Liberalism. Herbert Croly and Progressive Thought*. Lawrence, KA: University Press of Kansas, 1993.

Storr, Richard J. *Harper's University: The Beginnings*. Chicago: University of Chicago Press, 1966.

Thelen, David P. *The New Citizenship. Origins of Progressivism in Wisconsin, 1885–1900*. Columbia: University of Missouri Press, 1972.

———. *Robert M. La Follette and the Insurgent Spirit*. Boston: Little Brown & Co., 1976.

Thomas, William H. Jr. *Unsafe for Democracy. World War I and the U.S. Justice Department's Covert Campaign to Suppress Dissent*. Madison: University of Wisconsin Press, 2008.

Thorsen, Niels A. *The Political Thought of Woodrow Wilson, 1875–1910*. Princeton, NJ: Princeton University Press, 1988.

Trachtenberg, Alan. *The Incorporation of America. Culture & Society in the Gilded Age*. New York: Hill & Wang, 1982.

Trask, David F. *Victory without Peace. American Foreign Relations in the Twentieth Century*. Huntington, New York: Robert E. Krieger Publishing Company, 1975.

Trocmé, Hélène. *Chicago, 1890–1930. Audaces et débordements*. Paris: Éditions Autrement, 2001.

Unterberger, Betty M. *The United States, Revolutionary Russia, and the Rise of Czechoslovakia*. Texas A&M University Press, 2000.

Urofksy, Melvin I. *Louis D. Brandeis and the Progressive Tradition*. Boston: Little, Brown & Co., 1981.

Van Alstyne, Richard W. *The Rising American Empire*. Oxford: Oxford University Press, 1960.

Walworth, Arthur. *Wilson and His Peacemakers. American Diplomacy at the Paris Peace Conference, 1919*. New York: Norton, 1986.

Wegener, Charles. *Liberal Education and the Modern University*. Chicago: University of Chicago Press, 1978.

Weinstein, Edwin A. *Woodrow Wilson: a Medical and Psychological Biography*. Princeton, NJ: Princeton University Press, 1981.

Weinstein, James. *The Corporate Ideal in the Liberal State, 1900–1918*. Boston: Beacon Press, 1969.

Well, Donald R. *The Federal Reserve System. A History*. Jefferson, NC: McFarland & Co., 2004.

White, Morton G. *Social Thought in America. The Revolt Against Formalism*. Boston: Beacon Press, 1976 [c.1949].

Wiebe, Robert H. *Businessmen and Reform. A Study of the Progressive Movement*. Cambridge: Cambridge University Press, 1989 [c.1962].

———. *The Search for Order, 1877–1920*. London: Macmillan, 1967.

Williams, William A. *The Tragedy of American Diplomacy*. New York: Dell Publishing, 1972 [c.1959].

———. *Some Presidents: Wilson to Nixon*. New York: Vintage Books, 1972.

Wright, Quincy. *Mandates Under the League of Nations*. New York: Greenwood Press, 1968 [c.1930].

Zorgbibe, Charles. *Wilson. Un Croisé à la Maison-Blanche*. Paris: Presses de Sciences Po, 1998.

Theses and Memoirs

Bocage, Leo J. "The Public Career of Charles R. Crane." Ph.D. diss., Fordham University, 1962.

Daley, Anna. "Alphonse Mucha in Gilded Age America, 1904–1921." M.A. diss., Parsons New School for Design, 2007.

Miller, Joan S. "The Politics of Municipal Reform in Chicago during the Progressive Era." M.A. diss., Roosevelt University, 1966.

Moranian, Suzanne E. "The American Missionary and the Armenian Question, 1915–1927." Ph.D. diss., University of Wisconsin, 1994.

Neuman, William L. "Why Reform Fails: the Rise and Fall of Antimonopoly Reform in the United States, 1875–1975." Ph.D. diss., University of Wisconsin, 1982.

Sulzbach, Jacob John, Jr. "Charles R. Crane, Woodrow Wilson, and Progressive Reform: 1909–1921." Ph.D. diss., Texas A&M University, 1994.

Journal Articles

Ahonen, Risto. "John R. Mott as an Ecumenical Leader. What Was Mott's Vision?" *The Finnish Evangelical Lutheran Mission*, 2010, 1–5.

Anghie, Antony. "Cultural Differences in International Law: The League of Nations and Two Visions of Nation-State." *International Center for Comparative Law and Politics Review*, 5, 2002, 4–13.

Beloff, Max. "Self-Determination Reconsidered," In *Confluence*, 5, 1956, 195–203.

Bloxham, Donald. "Three Imperialisms and a Turkish Nationalism: International Stresses, Imperial Disintegration and the Armenian Genocide" *Patterns of Prejudice*, 36, 4, 2002, 37–58.

Blumenthal, Henry. "Woodrow Wilson and the Race Question." *The Journal of Negro History*, 48, 1, 1963, 1–21.

Brecher, F. W. "Charles R. Crane's Crusade for the Arabs, 1919–1939." *Middle Eastern Studies*, 24, 1, 1988, 42–55.

Clements, Kendrick A. "The Papers of Woodrow Wilson and the Interpretation of the Wilson Era." *The History Teacher*, 27, 4, 1994, 475–489.

Curti, Merle E. "Woodrow Wilson's Concept of Human Nature." *Midwest Journal of Political Science*, 1, 1, 1957, 1–19.

Diggins, John P. "Republicanism and Progressivism." *American Quarterly*, 37, 4, 1985, 572–598.

———. "From Pragmatism to Natural Law: Walter Lippmann's Quest for the Foundations of Legitimacy." *Political Theory*, 19, 4, 1991, 519–538.

Fuller, Pierre. "North China Famine Revisited: Unsung Native Relief in the Warlord Era, 1920–1921." *Modern Asian Studies*, 2012, 1–31.

Grabill, Joseph L. "Cleveland H. Dodge, Woodrow Wilson, and the Near East." *Journal of Presbyterian History*, 48, 1970, 249–264.

Hollinger, David A. "Science and Anarchy: Walter Lippmann's Drift and Mastery." *American Quarterly*, 29, 5, 1977, 463–475.

Hunt, Michael H. "1898: The Onset of America's Troubled Asian Century." *OAH Magazine of History*, 12, 3 (Spring, 1998): 30–36.

Leblanc, Lawrence J. "United States Foreign Policies toward Genocide and Crimes against Humanity." *Encyclopedia of Genocide and Crimes against Humanity*, Vol. 2. New York: Macmillan Reference USA, 2004, 1107–1116.

Lebow, Richard N. "Woodrow Wilson and the Balfour Declaration." *The Journal of Modern History*, 40, 4, 1968, 501–523.

Leuchtenburg, William E. "Progressivism and Imperialism: The Progressive Movement and American Foreign Policy, 1898–1916." *The Mississippi Valley Historical Review*, 39, 3, 1952, 483–504.

Link, Arthur S. "The Higher Realism of Woodrow Wilson." *Journal of Presbyterian History*, 41, 1, 1963, 1–13.

———. "What Happened to the Progressive Movement in the 1920s?" *The American Historical Review*, 64, 4, 1959, 833–851.

———. "That Cobb Interview." *The Journal of American History*, 72, 1, 1985, 7–17.

Malkasian, Mark. "The disintegration of the Armenian Cause in the United States, 1918–1927." *International Journal of Middle East Studies*, 16, 3, 1984, 349–365.

McCormick, Richard L. "The Discovery That Business Corrupts Politics: A Reappraisal of the Origins of Progressivism." *The American Historical Review*, 86, 2, 1981, 247–274.

Morris, Stuart. "The Wisconsin Idea and Business Progressivism." *Journal of American Studies*, 4, 1, 1970, 39–60.

Muzzey, David S. "Colonel House's Story." *Political Science Quarterly*, 44, 1, 1929, 79–86.

Nichols, David K. "The Promise of Progressivism: Herbert Croly and the Progressive Rejection of Individual Rights." *Publius*, 17, 2, 1987, 27–39.

Noble, Charles. "Wilson's Choice: The Political Origins of the Modern American State." *Comparative Politics*, 17, 3, 1985, 313–336.

Noble, David W. "The *New Republic* and the Idea of Progress, 1914–1920." *The Mississippi Valley Historical Review*, 38, 3, 1951, 387–402.

O'Leary, Kevin C. "Herbert Croly and Progressive Democracy," *Polity*, 24, 6, 1994, 533–552.

Osgood, Robert E. "Woodrow Wilson, Collective Security, and the Lessons of History." *Confluence*, 5, 1957, 341–354.

Parry, Albert. "Charles R. Crane, Friend of Russia." *Russian Review*, 6, 2, 1947, 20–36.

Pomerance, Michla. "Methods of Self-determination and the Argument of Primitiveness." *Canadian Yearbook of International Law*, 12, 1974, 38–66.

———. "The United States and Self-determination: Perspectives on the Wilsonian Conception." *The American Journal of International Law*, 70, 1, 1976, 1–27.

Rodgers, Daniel T. "In search of Progressivism." *Reviews in American History*, 10, 4, 1982, 113–132.

Saito, Natsu T. "Crossing the Border: The Interdependence of Foreign Policy and Racial Justice in the United States." *Yale Human Rights and Development Law Journal*, 1, 1998, 53–84.

Seltzer, Alan L. "Woodrow Wilson as Corporate-Liberal: Toward a Reconsideration of Left Revisionist Historiography." *The Western Political Quarterly*, 30, 2, 1977, 183–212.

Smith, Daniel M. "National interest and American intervention, 1917: A Historiographical Appraisal." *The Journal of American History*, 52, 1, 1965, 5–24.

Taussig, F. W. "The Tariff Act of 1913." *The Quarterly Journal of Economics*, 28, 1, 1913, 1–30.

Turner, Henry A. "Woodrow Wilson and Public Opinion." *The Public Opinion Quarterly*, 21, 4, 1957–58, 505–520.

Unterberger, Betty. "The Arrest of Alice Masaryk." *Slavic Review*, 33, 1, 1974, 91–106.

Van Alstyne, Richard W. "Woodrow Wilson and the Idea of Nation-State." *International Affairs*, 37, 1961, 293–308.

Walker, Larry. "Woodrow Wilson, Progressive Reform and Public Administration." *Political Science Quarterly*, 104, 3, 1989, 509–525.

Wish, Harvey. "Altgeld and the Progressive Tradition." *The American Historical Review*, 46, 4, 1941, 813–831.

Wolgemuth, Kathleen L. "Woodrow Wilson and Federal Segregation." *The Journal of Negro History*, 44, 2, 1959, 158–173.

Collective Works

Allerfeldt, Kristofer, ed. *The Progressive Era in the USA: 1890–1921*. Burlington, VT: Ashgate, 2007.

Braeman, John, ed. *Wilson*. Englewood Cliffs, NJ: Prentice-Hall, 1972.

Carlier, C. and Georges-Henri Soutou, dir. *1918–1925, comment faire la paix?* Paris: Ed. Economica, 2001.

Castellan, Georges, dir. *Histoire de la Bulgarie des origines à nos jours*. Paris: Horvath, 1977.

Haines, G. K. and J. S. Walker, ed. *American Foreign Relations. A Historiographical Review*. Westport, CT: Greenwood Press, 1981.

Nash, Stephen E. and Gary M. Feinman, ed. *Curators, Collections, and Contexts: Anthropology at the Field Museum, 1893–2002*. Chicago: Fieldiana Anthropology, 2003.

Temperley, H. W. V, ed. *A History of the Peace Conference of Paris*. London: Oxford University Press, 1969 [c.1920].

Winter, Jay, dir. *America and the Armenian Genocide of 1915*. Cambridge: Cambridge University Press, 2003.

INDEX

A

B

C

D

E

F

G

J

K

L

M

N

O

P

R

S

T

U

V

W

X

Y

Z

Washington College

Studies in Religion, Politics, and Culture

Joseph Prud'homme
General Editor

Washington College Studies in Religion, Politics, and Culture explores the role of religious belief in political and cultural life, both in the United States and across the world. Special emphasis is placed on theoretical, historical, and legal assessments of the relationship of religion to public life, the meaning and practice of citizenship, and cultural development. Empirical work is also welcome.

For additional information about this series or for the submission of manuscripts, please contact:

Dr. Joseph Prud'homme
Director, Institute for Religion, Politics, and Culture
Washington College
300 Washington Avenue
Chestertown, MD 21620
E-mail: jprudhomme2@washcoll.edu

To order other books in this series, please contact our Customer Service Department:

(800) 770-LANG (within the U.S.)
(212) 647-7706 (outside the U.S.)
(212) 647-7707 FAX

Or browse online by series at www.peterlang.com

www.ingramcontent.com/pod-product-compliance
Ingram Content Group UK Ltd.
Pitfield, Milton Keynes, MK11 3LW, UK
UKHW021826130926
8597IPUK00003B/6

9 781433 137372